INTRODUCTION TO
INTERNATIONAL POLITICS

INTRODUCTION TO
INTERNATIONAL POLITICS
A Theoretical Overview

WILLIAM D. COPLIN

Syracuse University

MARKHAM PUBLISHING COMPANY / Chicago

MARKHAM POLITICAL SCIENCE SERIES
Aaron Wildavsky, Editor

Axelrod, *Conflict of Interest: A Theory of Divergent Goals with Applications to Politics*

Barber, *Citizen Politics: An Introduction to Political Behavior*

Barber, ed., *Readings in Citizen Politics: Studies of Political Behavior*

Cnudde and Neubauer, eds., *Empirical Democratic Theory*

Coplin, *Introduction to International Politics: A Theoretical Overview*

Coplin, ed., *Simulation in the Study of Politics*

Coplin and Kegley, eds., *A Multi-method Introduction to International Politics: Observation, Explanation, and Prescription*

Dolbeare and Dolbeare, *American Ideologies: The Competing Political Beliefs of the 1970s*

Dvorin, ed., *The Senate's War Powers*

Greenstein, *Personality and Politics: Problems of Evidence, Inference, and Conceptualization*

Greenstein and Lerner, eds., *A Source Book for the Study of Personality and Politics*

Lane, *Political Thinking and Consciousness: The Private Life of the Political Mind*

Lyden and Miller, eds., *Planning-Programming-Budgeting: A Systems Approach to Management*

McDonald, *Party Systems and Elections in Latin America*

Mitchell, *Public Choice in America: An Introduction to American Government*

Payne, *The American Threat: The Fear of War As an Instrument of Foreign Policy*

Ranney, ed., *Political Science and Public Policy*

Ross and Mitchell, eds., *Introductory Readings in American Government: A Public Choice Perspective*

Russett, ed., *Economic Theories of International Politics*

Sharkansky, *Public Administration: Policy-Making in Government Agencies*

Sharkansky, ed., *Policy Analysis in Political Science*

Strickland, Wade and Johnston, *A Primer of Political Analysis*

Copyright © 1971 by Markham Publishing Company
Second Printing March 1971
All Rights Reserved
Printed in the U.S.A.
Library of Congress Catalog Number: 72–136616
Standard Book Number: 8410–3033–2

To Debbie and Laura

Acknowledgments

This book is a product of a long and arduous process ranging over almost four years, involving the advice of a large number of scholars and employing the reaction and suggestions of over 1,000 students. By far the latter input has been the most important. The first draft was developed and tested at Wayne State University in the Spring and Fall of 1967. The fourth draft of the book was printed in a pre-publication edition thanks to the foresight and intelligence of Markham Publishing Company. It was tested under classroom conditions at Syracuse University by the author, at Ohio State University by James Harf, and at Michigan State University by Edward Azar. Professors Harf and Azar studied the reactions of the students and made suggestions on how the manuscript should be revised. It was these suggestions that led to the final draft of the manuscript. Hence, the format and style of, as well as the substantive ideas of, the book have been thoroughly shaped by student reaction to the book.

I would like to acknowledge all of the individuals who have read and commented on some aspect of the book even though in many cases I failed to heed their advice. They include Max Mark, David S. Blake, John Burke, Arthur Johnston, Larry Taylor, Stephen Richardson, Michael R. Leavitt, Richard Strachan, Richard Caddy, J. David Singer, Hayward R. Alker, Jr., Raymond Hopkins, Russell J. Leng, Gene E. Rainey, John Sullivan, Charles A. McClelland, Robert Axelrod, Walter H. Corson, Joseph S. Nye, Bernard C. Cohen, Kenneth N. Waltz, Lloyd Jensen, Edward Azar, James Harf, Michael K. O'Leary, Patrick McGowan, Robert D. McClure, Dana Young, Stephen Mills, Russ Osmonds, J. Martin Rochester, and Charles W. Kegley, Jr.

To John Applegath and Markham Publishing Company for having

the kind of faith necessary to make the commitment to my approach that the publication of this book symbolized.

To the Markham editorial staff, and particularly Eleanor McConnell, I am particularly grateful for providing extensive advice and assistance.

To Danielle Kellogg, June Dumas, and Nancy Detweiler, particular thanks for the typing assistance and to Dana Young for aiding in the administrative details necessary to get a book of this size into final shape.

Finally, to my wife Merry for helping me to raise to maturity this, our third "child."

Contents

Introduction

This book represents a radical departure from existing texts in the field. In writing an introduction to international politics, I have had to deal with a number of substantive and pedagogical issues. My decisions on these issues are reflected in both the substance and style of this book.

A central issue lies in the traditional distinction of theory from fact. Authors of existing texts, while asserting the importance of theory, have nonetheless felt compelled to inundate their texts with vast amounts of historical information. Unfortunately, this overwhelming historical coverage has tended to obscure the theory and deprive the student of rigorous development of concepts and theories. Because authors of international politics textbooks have allowed their use of history to become less a matter of illustrating concepts or propositions and more a case of trying to prove their validity, the student is shown a highly selective view of history. Therefore, existing texts in the field provide the student with neither clearly developed concepts and propositions nor a balanced historical perspective.

In an effort to circumvent these problems, I have taken three steps. First is positive affirmation of the importance of clearly developed concepts and propositions. The student is encouraged to make his own judgment as to the utility of these concepts and validity of the propositions.

Second, no historical background is provided. History is used to illustrate, not to validate, the propositions. Historical examples are drawn from the most well known and highly visible events.

Finally, a Summary Outline at the end of each chapter lists the basic assumptions in the chapter and provides an opportunity for students to develop conceptual ability. The Summary Outline not only serves as a brief review of the chapter, it also focuses on the theoretical structure of the chapter.

To navigate such a course involves certain risks. Some students may decide the text lacks substance because it fails to give sufficient coverage to a particular historical event or a specific approach. Moreover, many of the concepts and propositions can be attacked for ambiguity, lapses in logical consistency, or failure to explain certain historical events. These weaknesses might be considered substantial if the book were viewed as a general treatise on international politics.

But the book is not a panacea to remedy the many weaknesses in the field of international politics. When operating from a position of weakness, a text that reflects the field is bound to have certain basic weaknesses. To cover up the deficiencies with extended historical discussions or esoteric arguments would create a false sense of security in a field that is in a state of flux. Hence, a certain lack of substance is appropriate for introducing the student to a field where vital tools are critical awareness and the attitude of aggressively challenging accepted uses of concepts and theories.

This text, then, constitutes a concise overview of essential concepts and propositions that are now or may be employed in the study of international politics. The instructor always has the option of employing supplementary materials to provide more detailed coverage of a particular approach or field. One such supplement is a book of readings by the author and Charles W. Kegley, Jr., *A Multi-method Introduction to International Politics* (Chicago: Markham, 1971). Its structure is similar to this book and it illustrates various approaches to the study of specific concepts and propositions in the field.[1] With or without supplements, however, the highly compact treatment of essential concepts and assumptions is the primary feature of this book.

A second issue affecting the nature of this book is the balance between methodology and substance. Contemporary international politics texts usually are short on discussion of methods and long on substance even though the author's original intent may have been just the opposite. It is generally agreed that the student should learn not only *about* international politics but also *how to study* international politics. The primary difficulty is that discussions of how to study something usually become both dull and difficult to follow. Too often the author's commitment to a particular approach prevents balanced discussion of current approaches.

Instead of exposing the student to methodology through sustained exhortation, I have attempted to teach it by example, and explicit discussion of methodological issues is replaced by methodological points made in the bibliographical essays for each chapter. These essays are designed not only to provide basic bibliography in each subarea of the field, but also to point out some strengths and weaknesses of the existing approaches in the international politics literature.

In addition, many chapters are designed to illustrate certain approaches. For example, Chapter 2 on foreign policy decision makers describes the decision-making approach and tells how interdisciplinary knowledge and analogies may be used to infer the characteristics of foreign policy decision making. Chapter 3 indicates how a set of classifications may be employed in developing comparative generalizations about the role of domestic politics in the foreign policy-making process. Chapter 4 attempts to hypothesize how economic and military tools might be used if no other factors were operating (an abstract model). Chapter 5 examines concepts and propositions about the determinants of foreign policy from the point of view of logical consistency and historical meaning. Problems of identifying environmental pressures that affect states who deal with each other are discussed in Chapter 7, while Chapters 11 and 12 develop the concept of political systems in analyzing international politics. Although the problems that confront the advanced student when testing propositions with empirical data are not systematically examined, those relating to the formulation of concepts and assumptions are. The intended effect of this approach to method is to acquaint the student with methodological issues in the context of the subject matter. In learning about international politics he may also learn how to formulate and evaluate concepts, propositions, and theories —the building blocks of knowledge.

A third issue in writing a textbook in this field is whether or not to use existing concepts. Most authors continue to utilize such time-honored concepts as national interest, power, and balance of power despite their awareness of the shortcomings of these concepts. Often writers will criticize concepts such as these but continue to use them, thus becoming guilty of the shortcomings they criticize in others.

Although I have used as many of the traditional concepts as feasible, I chose to avoid those that are more venerable than useful. The concepts of national power and national interest in particular are not used in the text, although they are discussed in terms of their traditional use. Rather than speak of national power, I have identified economic and military constraints and tools in the making of foreign policy. To explain how states interact—the dynamics of power—I have developed a set of concepts based on bargaining models of international behavior. Instead of using the term national interest, I have focused on intellectual, social, and organizational factors affecting the formation of national goals. The role of competing interpretations of the national interest are analyzed in terms of the positions taken by domestic political groups on issue areas. Hopefully, I have been able to avoid the use of these two terms while still being able to explain those aspects of international politics in which these terms are often employed.

At the same time, I have tried to relate the field of international politics to the mainstream of concepts currently in use by American political scientists. The fields of organizational behavior, bargaining and game theory, political culture, and socialization contain a number of valuable concepts that can be beneficial to students. Although the study of international politics has some peculiar limitations, it can still profit from the conceptual development and tested propositions that are part of the general political science literature.

A fourth issue is the role of footnotes and bibliography. Footnotes generally have two distinct purposes: first, to indicate literature supporting the author's position and second, to locate additional information on the subject. In this text, the footnotes fulfill only the first purpose—they indicate positions similar to mine on historical interpretations. Relevant bibliography for each chapter is viewed more systematically in the bibliographical essays.

A fifth issue generally confronting textbook writers is the difficulty in bridging the gap between foreign policy and international politics. Most texts thoroughly mix the two by interlacing discussions of international politics with discussions of foreign policy making. As a result, the discussion of the latter is poorly developed, lacking the systematic and comparative bases necessary for understanding the field.

I have emphasized the behavior of states and, to a lesser extent, intergovernmental organizations, by introducing (in Chapters 2 to 6) the determinants of behavior for actors in the international political system, but also by developing early a set of categories for comparative study of the actors. An explicit attempt is made to provide necessary groundwork for comparative study of the foreign policy-making process by viewing the actors, then interaction among actors, and finally the patterns of interactions that taken together constitute the international political system. This unorthodox organization was chosen because I have learned that it is easiest to discuss international politics at the introductory level by starting with a "part" that is closest to the student—the foreign policy of his state —and then to construct a "whole" from the parts.

A sixth and final question is that of specific subject matter covered. Most contemporary textbooks emphasize war-peace issues and slight all others, unless the author has specialized in a particular nonrelated area. Their great fault lies in their failure to provide an integrated picture of the variety of activities that affect the field. As a result, factors that ultimately might have an impact on war-peace issues are ignored or underemphasized because their influence is not yet clearly understood. In contrast, I have attempted to give proper weight to the broad range of factors affecting international politics and not just to such topics as the balance of power or the cold war. I have attempted to show the complex interdependencies that exist among states, including how those interdependencies are affected by domestic conditions within states. Intergovernmental organizations are treated both comparatively, as actors, and functionally, as a setting for the interactions among states. International law and economics are not discussed as a separate subject but are viewed as part of the environment for interactions among states. In short, I have obscured the distinction between international *politics* and international *relations* because contemporary events are making the traditional distinction meaningless.

In the final analysis, however, the positions taken on these six issues are only important if they establish the proper relationship between instructor and student. It is not enough for the instructor merely to agree with the positions taken on the issues. Nor is it sufficient for the student to find the book easy to use or enlightening. The book will have been successful only if it provides the common theoretical ground on which the instructor and student can learn to explore each other's ideas about international politics regardless of whether the concepts and propositions in the book are accepted, rejected or, hopefully, reserved for further study.

1

Problems in the Study of International Politics

It is perhaps a mistake to begin a textbook with an admission that professional scholars of international politics who have been working so hard for so long continue to be faced with many basic problems in the study of international politics. After all, a textbook is supposed to supply knowledge as a mother supplies milk or a Bible supplies faith. If there are weaknesses in the discipline, they are supposed to be at the frontiers of postdoctoral, or, at the very least, graduate research, not at the very foundations of the discipline. "Problems in the study of international politics" might conceivably be the title for an epilogue, but certainly not for an introductory chapter.

However, the admission that problems exist is a necessary beginning for the study of a subject that has fascinated but also confounded men since Thucydides. International politics textbooks cannot offer knowledge neatly packaged in generally accepted concepts or clearly organized around a set of logically consistent and empirically tested generalizations. The best that can be done is to offer some basic approaches, concepts, and generalizations, now in use by some scholars, that might be helpful in understanding international politics.

Even before that, however, we must examine the problems that confront a student in this field. We will do this by (1) examining the problems faced by anyone attempting to gain knowledge about anything and (2) discussing the particular difficulties facing the student of international politics.

BASIC PROBLEMS IN ACQUISITION OF KNOWLEDGE

Many people consider acquisition of knowledge to be merely a mechanical process of accumulating and reproducing information (at the propitious moment, of course, particularly for the college student). To these people, study means memorization and the mind is compared to a photocopy machine. Although the photocopy approach is employed in many stages of education and is no doubt essential to the study of certain areas of any subject, the idea that one learns *merely* by accumulating information leaves much to be desired.

The reason for the limited scope of this approach is that the human mind learns things—and people express what they learn—through words and, in some very special cases, nonverbal symbols like numbers. Since various meanings can be attributed to these words and symbols one is never sure that he is learning the knowledge that others think is represented in the words he has memorized. The process of studying a subject cannot be a simple matter of copying and reproducing information because of the nature of the human mind. It is a very poor copy machine if standards of exact duplication are held to be essential.

Unlike the photocopy machine, the human mind needs to *organize* information in order to learn. Information that does not appear to be arranged in a pattern will be more difficult to remember than the same amount of information organized according to an explicit scheme. We are not just referring to the physical process of organizing information (for example, arranging it on paper) but also to the intellectual process of relating information to a set of categories. The categories may be based on distinctions the scholar has derived from his experience or based on his likes and dislikes. The human mind learns by classifying and arranging information into meaningful patterns, no matter what is the source of that meaningfulness.

Types of Analysis

In organizing information, the student performs what we will call *analysis.* Although it is difficult to provide a satisfactory definition of "analysis," for purposes of discussion we can define it as the process of applying some organizing framework to the information one receives. It involves many intellectual activities including application of inductive and deductive logic, awareness of one's uses of terms, and application of criteria for making judgments. When one analyzes, he organizes information to suit his goals. For purposes of discussion, we might identify four types of analysis relating to four goals one might pursue in studying a subject.

The most common type is *descriptive analysis,* the purpose of which is to describe what exists or has existed. The meaning we attach to the verb "describe" is very important. In descriptive analysis, we can describe in the sense of providing a photocopy of a given event or in the sense of explaining what has happened.

Although some writers like to distinguish between description and explanation by saying that the former is concerned with *what* has happened and the latter is concerned with *why* it has happened, the distinction is difficult to make in practice. As noted above, the human being is not well suited for providing exact representations through words; no matter how hard he tries his descriptions tend to become explanations. Hence, we have lumped together concern for both the "what" and the "why" under descriptive analysis.

The process of descriptive analysis covers a large variety of techniques and styles. The analyst may use intuition or more systematic methods to develop ideas. He may build a description by making a set of interconnected deductions from one or two pieces of information, or he may take an enormous amount of information and try to make some useful generalizations. The actual presentation of the descriptive analysis may take the form of purely verbal statements, an explanation based on some statistics, or a combination of the two. It is probably the most frequently used type of analysis among students of any subject because it serves as a basis for the other three types. Most of the analysis presented in this book will be descriptive or will discuss how better descriptive analysis can be achieved in the study of international politics.

The second type, *predictive analysis,* is closely related to the first since its goal is to describe what will exist in the future. The sources of one's predictions are usually found in one's descriptive analysis. Past experience —whether it is the history of the real world or data from laboratory experiments—constitutes the basis for predictions about future happenings. Often, descriptive and predictive analyses are made simultaneously. Sometimes, predictions are provided in order to illustrate or test the validity of the descriptive analysis. Prediction is frequently one of our prime objectives in the study of a subject as well as a test for ourselves or others of how well we understand the subject.

A third type is *normative analysis.* It consists of making an explicit or implicit judgment of what is viewed to exist or will exist on the basis of our values. It is the application of our values—whether they be viewed as personal preferences or a consequence of some moral order—to our view of reality. Normative analysis is also based on some type of descriptive analysis. One's likes and dislikes are always formed in response to what one assumes his world to be.[1] However, this form should be clearly distin-

---

[1] The reverse is also true but to a lesser degree; that is, one's values often shape the way one describes his environment. As discussed in the following pages, one of the

guished from both descriptive and predictive analysis because the information used for normative analysis is ultimately organized according to one's values; notions of goodness and badness become a central aspect of the intellectual processes involved.

A final type is *prescriptive analysis*. This form is a mixture of normative and predictive analysis because it makes suggestions about what actions should be taken to realize a set of values. Like the other forms, prescriptive analysis is usually based on what one assumes to exist since this assumption will influence one's choice of goals and strategies. The prescriptive analyst has a picture of how he wishes the world were and a plan of how to make it that way.

Prescriptive analysis can take a variety of forms. First, it can be used as an illustrative device to indicate more clearly the conclusions reached in one or all of the other three types of analysis. For example, some writers make policy suggestions merely to indicate implications of certain goals given their descriptions of existing conditions. Second, prescriptive analysis can involve a specific policy suggestion directed at a specific actor. For example, suggestions are often made to the President on how to stop the spread of nuclear weapons. Finally, prescriptive analysis can be performed at a very general level without specifying when, where, or by whom the prescribed policy should be followed. The suggestion that mankind should become more peaceful, for example, is extremely general and yet still prescriptive.

The four types of analysis have different purposes in terms of what the author is attempting to communicate to the reader. In descriptive analysis, the author attempts to make the reader understand the past and present; in predictive analysis his goal is to help the reader anticipate the future. The purpose of normative analysis is to convince the reader that certain conditions are good or bad either by getting him to accept the author's value positions or by showing how certain situations threaten or support values held by the reader. Finally, the prescriptive analyst is trying to indicate how to achieve certain goals. Clearly, the purpose of the four types of analysis are different.

However, in spite of differences between the four types, there should be a logical relationship among them. Descriptive analysis ought[2] to pro-

---

prime difficulties that have faced men who attempt to acquire knowledge has been their difficulty in separating what exists from what they would like to exist. Nevertheless, one can still make the distinction between analysis which has a descriptive purpose and that which has the purpose of expressing the writer's values.

[2] The reader should have noted that the type of analysis presented at this point represents a shift from descriptive to prescriptive. Previously, we were describing some general attributes of the acquisition of knowledge. In this paragraph, we have begun

FIGURE 1

Interaction Between the Four Kinds of Analysis

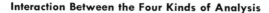
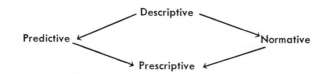

vide a basis for the other three types of analysis. One should not attempt to predict, make normative judgments, or prescribe until one has attempted to understand reality as fully as possible. In addition, prescriptive analysis is a product of predictive and normative analysis. In Figure 1, the arrows indicate ways the four types of analysis should influence each other. The major point of the illustration is that one should understand reality *before* he attempts to predict the future, make value judgments, or prescribe actions.

Although we have shown the relationships that *should* exist between the four types of analysis, students sometimes allow other relationships to develop. For example, the following passage contains descriptive, predictive, normative, and prescriptive implications so thoroughly mixed that one cannot help but assume that the writer has allowed his "likings" to color his view of what exists or is possible.

> The revival of diplomacy requires the elimination of the factors, or at least of some of their consequences, responsible for the decline of the traditional diplomatic practices. Priority in this respect belongs to the depreciation of diplomacy and its corollary: diplomacy by parliamentary procedure. . . . Diplomacy, however morally unattractive its business may seem to many, is nothing but a symptom of the struggle for power among sovereign nations, which try to maintain orderly and peaceful relations among themselves.[3]

The author's remarks in this passage constitute an argument for the return to "traditional diplomatic practices." In making this argument, he is providing descriptive analysis by maintaining that traditional diplomacy has been replaced with "diplomacy by parliamentary procedure." His normative implication, although never explicit, is that the decline of traditional diplomacy is bad; this is implied by the prescriptive plea that it must be

to *prescribe* the ways in which the four types of analysis ought to be related to each other.

[3] Hans J. Morgenthau, *Politics Among Nations,* 3d ed. (New York: Knopf, 1961), p. 552.

revived. An additional predictive implication is that struggle for power will cause the return to traditional diplomacy. Hence, the author has made a series of statements that include elements of all four types of analysis but has failed to distinguish clearly among the four. Even more important, the reader begins to suspect that the writer cherishes traditional diplomacy for its own sake and wishes (prescribes) that it would return by implying that its resurgence is inevitable (prediction) because power politics is inevitable.

It is very often difficult to be clear about the types of analysis one is performing. The very act of selecting a subject involves the application of one's values to the task. Although writers claim they are describing something, often their implicit evaluations are based on their likes and dislikes. The most dangerous byproduct of the inherent tendency to be unclear about the types of analysis being performed is that the writer may allow his likes and dislikes to color the way in which he describes or predicts. A classic illustration of the confusion between description and evaluation is this statement made by Norman Angell in 1914: "Military power is irrelevant to the promotion of the aims, moral and material, (of states)."[4] Angell was actually arguing that the use of force is an ineffective tool of statecraft although he realized better than many that the leaders of states and public opinion did not share his view. Because policy makers have not shared his view on the ineffectiveness of the use of force, military power has been anything but irrelevant to the foreign policies of states. Hoping to convince policy makers that war *should* be irrelevant, however, Angell often took poetic license by saying that it *is* irrelevant. The result of his mixing normative analysis with description was to promote a misunderstanding of the realistic basis for his position. Therefore, it aids neither the author nor the reader to mix evaluation and description because it hinders the clear statement and thorough understanding of the writer's position—a device permissible for pamphleteers and debaters but not for serious scholars.

If one is primarily interested in descriptive analysis, as it is assumed the beginning student of any subject is, it is crucial for him to distinguish clearly among description, prediction, normative analysis, and prescription. Failure to do so can only lead him to shape his views of the world to fit his own preferences and to make dogmatic interpretations that prevent him from adequately examining contrary interpretations. This is not to say that the student should not attempt to predict, to be normative, or to suggest

---

[4] Norman Angell, *Arms and Industry: A Study of the Foundations of International Polity* (New York: Putnam, 1914), p. xv.

future courses of action, but only that when he is doing so he should be clear about what he is doing. Because his predictive, normative, and prescriptive analysis will only be as good as his grasp of what exists, however, he must build a firm basis in descriptive analysis before proceeding to the other levels.

Scientific Method As An Approach to Knowledge

The history of the acquisition of knowledge in many fields is found in the scholar's struggle to overcome tendencies to confuse likes and dislikes (value judgments) with views of what exists. The most important development in that struggle is the evolution of an approach to the acquisition of knowledge which has come to be known as the scientific method. Science is a set of procedures for building knowledge about what exists so that men not only are more knowledgable but also are better able to predict, make normative judgments, and prescribe. Because science as an approach to study has been so successful and because it consists of a series of steps which can contribute to more effective analysis (even if one does not believe it is completely applicable to a given field of study), we will now discuss its basic components.

The goal of science is to provide a basis for building *shared knowledge*. This goal implies two related but distinct processes. The first is contained in the word "shared" and is sometimes referred to by the technical term "intersubjective transmissible." Knowledge is intersubjective transmissible if scholars can communicate information that enables them to understand and build on each other's work. Given the propensity of men to bias information they acquire and transmit, this is no easy task. The building of a basis for shared knowledge presupposes that one scientist's conclusions and studies will be understood by other scientists in the way the original scientist intended them to be understood. The second process revolves around the question of what is knowledge, and concerns how one assesses the accuracy of his ideas. Statements which are considered to be valid may be called knowledge.

One should never underestimate the importance of a common language to development of a scientific field. The key to the effectiveness of any branch of science is the existence of shared terms—specialized language through which professional students communicate. Although this specialized language, or jargon, is sometimes overused, it is frequently necessary. Coining new words may add to precision in communicating scientific information. The history of every science may be viewed in terms of the development of specialized language that includes not only precisely defined terms but also systems of measurement[5] to define conditions. In a sense, the scientific approach to study has developed ways of minimizing loss and bias of information that normally exists and hinders the attempt to study any field.

Development of a common language may be viewed in part as a process of evolving shared concepts. A *concept* is a word or group of words used to describe something precisely so that others in the field will know what is being said. Concepts are effective if they enable scholars to understand each other and aid them in describing the subject under study.

Concepts should receive similar interpretations from all students in a field. One test of this ability is whether or not concepts can be transformed into *variables* through *operational definitions;* that is, definitions couched in precise and explicit language so that different scholars using the same definitions are able to collect similar data on the same sample of phenomena. A variable is said to be reliable when the definition is precise and explicit enough to generate the same (or relatively similar) data through the hands of different scholars. Although all concepts might not be successfully transformed into variables, one test of their usefulness is whether or not they permit operational definitions that yield variables producing reliability in data collection.

For example, one might have a concept of a militaristic foreign policy and might construct a variable whose operational definition is the number of man-hours of military activity for any given state. Such an operationally defined variable would probably be acceptable in terms of reliability because similar answers would be found by various collectors of data.[6] The procedure for developing variables is extremely important, for it allows scientists to minimize errors that might result from different interpretations of concepts. Whether a given concept aids students in describing what they are studying is distinct from the question of whether or not the concept yields variables or facilitates communication. The mere fact that a concept is similarly interpreted by many scholars cannot alone justify its use. It is very difficult to determine the degree to which a concept describes reality, especially at the initial stages of a study when concept formation is so important. Only after the study has been completed can one assess the usefulness of the initial concept; even then, the judgment might have to be tentative. Ultimately, the question of whether or not a particular concept

[5] "Systems of measurement" may be viewed as nothing more than elaborate concepts (through operational definitions) which allow the scholar to determine when, where, or how certain concepts are applicable in describing phenomena.

[6] Even this operational definition might not produce reliable data if there were no sources indicating the length of wars fought by a state and the number of men fighting. However, one may assume that the variable is defined with sufficient precision.

contributes to knowledge depends on how that concept can be related to other concepts and on how much meaning it has for scholars in the field.

A number of techniques exist for constructing concepts that describe what they are supposed to describe. The practice of developing variables through operational definitions and checking the reliability of data collections using those variables is based in part on the viewpoint that if scientists attach the same meaning to the concept, then it describes what it is supposed to be describing. In addition, statistical techniques can be used to discover clusters of phenomena that can be subsumed under a single concept. For example, general characteristics of underdeveloped states can be discovered through statistical analysis by examining what characteristics —such as low gross national product—certain states share. In spite of the use of operational definitions and statistical analyses, however, the descriptive usefulness of many concepts cannot be ascertained until they have been employed in many studies.

Related to the development of concepts in contributing to a shared language is the explicit identification of relationships among concepts. As we will see in the following discussion, various terms are given to a statement in which two or more concepts are related to each other. When the statement represents an untested idea, it is usually called a proposition. If the proposition is stated in a testable form, it is called a hypothesis. Sets of propositions and/or hypotheses that are logically related to each other are called theories. We will briefly discuss propositions and theories in the context of the development of a shared language.

A proposition is a statement relating two or more concepts. For example, the statement "as temperature rises, gas expands" includes two concepts—temperature and gas—and a relationship between them—proportional increase. This particular proposition contains concepts for which scales of measurement already exist so that the relationship between the two concepts can be clearly described. Such a situation is not frequently found in many fields of study, particularly international politics. However, even though one might not always be able to relate concepts to each other in the form of a scaled relationship between variables, he can focus a great deal of intellectual power on the acquisition of knowledge by attempting to state his ideas clearly in the form of precise propositions; that is, relationships between two or more concepts.

Because the number of propositions one could make in any field of study is infinite, it is also necessary to attempt to develop a set of propositions that are related to each other. Such a set of logically related propositions, usually termed a theory, brings organization and the capacity to accumulate knowledge to a field or subfield of a discipline. Theories allow scholars to tie together propositions they have developed at different levels of generality. For example, consider the following three propositions, which are related to each other logically, but are at three different levels of generality:

1. Men are ambitious.
2. Men in politics will choose a course of action designed to increase their influence.
3. A Congressman will vote in roll call in a manner approved by the majority of his constituents.

In this example, the proposition about human nature leads to *one* of many more specific assertions possible about what men will do in politics, which in turn leads to *one* of many possible statements about what men will do in a particular political role. Together the three statements represent a theory of human behavior that is applied to politics but might be applied to other fields as well. In addition, any one of the three propositions may be viewed as the basis for a theory because each suggests a whole set of related propositions. Theories, then, are groups of propositions that can be applied to a class of phenomena and that aid scholars in organizing and accumulating their ideas.

Let's turn from a discussion of the nature of concepts and theory and the necessity of clarity and precision in their use to the question of determining the accuracy of our propositions. Not that clarity and precision are closely related to the search for truth. Arthur Stinchcombe, a distinguished sociologist, notes:

> Other investigators can easily show that I am wrong if I am sufficiently precise. They will have much more difficulty showing by investigation what, precisely I mean if I am vague. I hope not to be forced to weasel out with, "But I didn't really mean that." . . . (one) should prefer to be wrong rather than misunderstood.[7]

No matter how one chooses to assess the accuracy of a particular proposition, then, an absolute prerequisite is clarity and precision.

But clarity and precision alone do not solve the problem of determining the accuracy of a particular proposition. Even if the reader is not familiar with philosophical arguments about the nature of truth, he must know from his own experience how difficult it is to determine the accuracy of a given idea. In fact, one should not consider it necessary to determine the accuracy or truth of a particular proposition or theory in an absolute sense; rather, he should seek to increase his (and other scholars') confidence in the accuracy of a particular proposition or theory.

[7] Arthur L. Stinchcombe, *Constructing Social Theories* (New York: Harcourt, Brace & World, 1968), p. 6.

One procedure for judging this accuracy is to transform a proposition such as "as temperature rises, gas expands" into a hypothesis. A *hypothesis* is a restatement of a proposition so that tests of validity can be performed. Our example, for instance, might be stated in the following form: Given all other factors (pressure, for example) as constant, if the temperature of any gas rises, the volume of the gas will expand proportionally. The hypothesis, then, is a special form for testing a proposition in which—given the proper measuring instruments and the ability to control necessary conditions—the criteria exist for disproving the hypothesis. If the test does not disprove the hypothesis, our confidence will increase in the accuracy of the proposition from which it was derived.

The procedure outlined above is very demanding. One must correctly deduce the hypothesis from the proposition. He must be able to operationally define the variables suggested by the concepts in the proposition, collect the relevant data, and measure the behavior of the variables. He must also be able to exercise experimental controls so that confounding conditions do not lead to an unwarranted disconfirmation of the hypothesis. Then he faces the problem of interpreting the results in terms of the theory from which the proposition was drawn and weighing different experiments that are designed to assess the accuracy of the same proposition or theory but yield contradictory results. To use such procedures, a field of study must have shared concepts and at least minimal agreement about general theories.

Because these testing procedures are so demanding, it is necessary to develop less rigorous methods of assessing the accuracy of propositions and theories. Although scholars in a field of knowledge—including political science—may use scientific procedures to test hypotheses in certain areas where well developed concepts and theories exist, in other areas tests of *face validity* might be more appropriate. The term suggests intuitive tests of the accuracy of propositions—that is, "does the proposition or model seem to be correct in the light of available data?" We may not be able to increase our confidence in a particular proposition or theory as much as we would by transforming the propositions into measurable variables and performing a test of derived hypotheses. We can, however, discuss whether or not our intuitive grasp of relevant phenomena combined with our awareness of studies in related fields and buttressed by all available reliable data gives us a basis for increasing our confidence in its accuracy. If we are as explicit as possible about the propositions and theories being tested and are circumspect in interpreting our findings by carefully pointing out necessary qualifications, then the process of assessing face validity of ideas can be crucial in developing a field of knowledge. If our ultimate goal is to place less reliance on intuitive assessments of accuracy of ideas, and more reliance on systematic testing of hypotheses, a crucial path to that goal is the use of the notion of face validity to discriminate *tentatively* between true and false propositions, and therefore to suggest the most fruitful lines for further research.

In discussing the problems one faces in acquiring knowledge, we have introduced a number of terms and tasks that summarize the scientific approach. Figure 2 illustrates and relates those activities. One should think of the flow indicated by the arrow as a set of highly interrelated processes characteristic of the scientific approach. The more cycles or iterations a particular set of concepts or theories goes through, the more confidence we have in the clarity and validity of those concepts and theories. In this way, the scientific approach calls for a cumulative set of activities through which shared knowledge can be generated.

PROBLEMS SPECIFIC TO INTERNATIONAL POLITICS

Now, let's apply some of these general points about acquisition of knowledge to the study of international politics. Although our primary focus will be on the scientific approach, the discussion will raise issues faced by all students of international politics, including those not committed to the scientific approach. Our discussion will be divided into (1) difficulties in

FIGURE 2

Terms and Tasks in the Scientific Approach to Knowledge

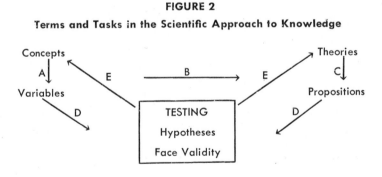

TASKS

A Concepts are transformed into variables via operational definitions to make reliable data collection possible

B Two or more concepts are related to each other to become a theory

C Propositions are logically deduced from general theories

D Testing is carried out through (1) hypotheses-testing in which propositions and/or theories are transformed into if-then statements in such a manner so that they allow for falsification through experimental tests; and/or (2) face-validity testing in which intuitive assessments of a proposition are made using available but unsystematic evidence

E Revision of concepts and theories as a result of performing the other tasks.

developing concepts and theories and (2) difficulties in testing theories and derived propositions. The first has to do with the sharing (or intersubjective transmissibility) of the knowledge; the second, the validity of the theories.

Difficulties in Developing Concepts and Theories

One basic reason for the difficulties confronting the student of politics is that what he writes and says can be used in the political arena itself. Many writers on politics have been participants in the political process, and the pursuit of knowledge has often been secondary, serving as an instrument to achieve political ends. Traditionally, the line between the political analyst and the political pamphleteer has been very thin. Moreover, even if the political analyst were willing to abstain from influencing politics, his writings have often become a factor despite his intentions. For the past, present, and future, the student of politics and the actor in politics have had and will continue to have a very complex and intimate relationship.

The implications of this relationship for the development of concepts and theories in international politics are clear. Although concepts like sovereignty, national interest, and power as well as theories like the balance of power or the effect of geography on the behavior of states may have been developed by scholars trying to describe aspects of international politics, they have been used by politicians and foreign policy leaders in both their speeches and their thinking. The result of this shared usage has been lack of precision in the development of concepts and theories. Employed by political leaders to justify the policies of their states, these concepts and theories have taken on so many meanings that building shared knowledge around them is impossible.

The difficulty is basically a result of the confusion of the four types of analysis discussed earlier. Scholars may develop a descriptive concept, but because they or their readers are so involved in the political arena, they often employ that concept for predictive, normative, or prescriptive analysis. A classic illustration is the concept of "power vacuum," frequently employed in the discussion of international politics. The term is used to describe a particular geographical area in which governmental control over political forces is weak. However, the term itself implies certain predictions, normative evaluations, and prescriptions; namely, (1) the power vacuum will be filled, (2) it would be bad if it were filled by a hostile state, and (3) therefore, it ought to be stabilized (which means filled by your state or a friendly state). Hence, a concept that is basically descriptive takes on a variety of meanings and inhibits the development of clear propositions and theories.

Another well-known example of the confusion of concepts and theories is the term "balance of power." Ernst Haas and others have shown how different scholars and statesmen have used the concept to mean different things.[8] Some have argued that balance of power operates more or less automatically to promote stability in relations among states, which might be viewed as a general theory. Others have advocated that a particular country—usually their own—follow a policy designed to maintain the balance of power. With little agreement among scholars as to the precise meaning of the term, it is not surprising that little progress has been made in determining the factors that contribute to international stability.

The infusion of politics into scholarship and confusion of the various types of analysis is only one of the reasons why development of concepts and theories in international politics is so difficult. An equally serious problem is inherent in the nature of the subject matter itself. The pattern of behavior we identify as international politics is a product of a large number of factors that interact in an extremely complex fashion.

International politics involves the entire world, not simply in the relationship among states but also in conditions occurring *within* states that have an effect on the relations *among* states. As a result, the student of international politics must be able to analyze the impact of all types of related activities. He must understand economics to appreciate the role of domestic and international economic systems in political activities. He must consider social factors to appreciate the role of culture and social processes in world politics. He must be aware of psychological forces in order to assess the role of attitudes and other psychological processes in foreign policy actions. Finally, he must be aware of the role of technology and its interrelation with psychological, economic, and sociological phenomena in order to understand the factors structuring international politics. Given the immense complexity that characterizes international politics, it is difficult to determine which factors are affecting what types of activities.

Complexity poses a serious problem for those interested in developing concepts and theories for this field. Overwhelmed by the complexity, some scholars simply attempt a journalistic description of the reality of international politics. Although they may claim they are interested in developing concepts and theories, these writers are usually more concerned with describing a particular foreign policy or international event. The concept or theory then becomes a veneer covering a piece of detailed description. The "cold war," the "superpowers," the "policy of containment," or the "balance of terror" might serve as concepts or theories in a particular description, but the author's primary purpose will be to describe a particular event

[8] Ernst B. Haas, "The Balance of Power: Prescription, Concept or Propaganda?" *World Politics,* 5 (1953), 442–77.

or process. As a result of their overconcern with giving a complete picture of a small part of international political reality, these writers tend to ignore the problems inherent in developing concepts and theories.

In contrast, some scholars react to the complexity of the field by developing fragmented and excessively abstract concepts and theories. In such a complex field it is natural that different scholars have different orientations. Evidence of this difficulty is found in the "level-of-analysis" problem discussed by J. David Singer.[9] Some scholars focus on foreign policy decision making while others concentrate on the international system even though the two levels are closely interrelated. The result is that the scholars concerned with one level often fail to be aware of work done at the other level, despite clear evidence that foreign policy behavior and conditions in the international system are highly interdependent. Other types of fragmentation include overemphasis on "pet" concepts and theories that apply only to a portion of international politics but are used to explain the entire field. For example, the concept of power and the theory that all states seek to maximize power might be useful in analyzing the behavior of two hostile states bordering each other but most definitely would not pertain to activities in the World Health Organization. Yet numerous writers have argued that the concept of power can be used to organize the entire study of international politics.

Thus, the complexity of the field of international politics produces opposite tendencies, both of which inhibit the development of concepts and theories. The tendency to be too concrete and to ignore the need to generalize is just as detrimental as the tendency to develop excessively simplified explanations to fit particular concepts or theories. A balance is necessary between concepts and theories that are too narrowly defined and applied and those that are too broadly defined and applied, even though the complexity of the subject matter tends to push scholars to either extreme.

Difficulties in Testing Theories and Derived Propositions

The complexity of international politics also makes testing the theories difficult. Theories that involve a large number of interacting variables are not easily reduced to testable propositions. Forced to construct multicausal theories of international politics, the scholar is limited in formally testing the accuracy of his ideas.

For example, if we developed a theory stating that foreign policy behavior is a product of the personalities of the people making decisions,

---

[9] J. David Singer, "The Level-of-Analysis Problem in International Relations," in *The International System: Theoretical Essays,* ed. Klaus Knorr and Sidney Verba (Princeton, N.J.: Princeton University Press, 1967), pp. 77–93.

political pressures brought upon these people, economic and military capabilities of the state, and the international situation in which the state finds
itself, how could we go about testing the theory? The personality of the
decision makers may be the most important factor in some decisions but
the least important in others, while domestic politics may play a paramount
role preceding elections and be quite incidental during other periods.
Although the situation is not hopeless, the student of international politics
is faced with enormous difficulties in testing his theories, given the multicausal nature of most international political phenomena.

The second limitation on the testing of theories is the shortage of
relevant data. Emphasis should be placed on the term *relevant*. Despite the
richness of relevant data in some fields such as voting behavior, the
political scientist is data-poor when it comes to getting the information
necessary to determine why and how political actors have acted in certain
situations. The data he can easily acquire is often not directly relevant to
the kinds of questions he is asking (for example, survey data tells little
about the foreign policy-making process). Data that is directly relevant is
frequently very expensive to acquire in terms of time or money or both (for
example, a systematic survey of public statements). Finally, some data is
simply unavailable (for example, the President's thoughts during a crisis).

The primary reason for lack of data is that the most relevant data for
the study of politics is often the information most sensitive to use by
political actors. Information which could be instructive in analyzing the
behavior of a political actor can also be very explosive if made public.
Political scientists have done a great deal to develop sources of data from
what is made public (census data, public documents, and the like). Even
so, some kinds of information are not readily available because of the
conscious decision by political actors to make them unavailable. Unfortunately, it is this kind of information that would allow for testing the types
of hypotheses crucial to the understanding of many areas of politics.

If anything, the problem is even more acute for the student of
international politics than for students in other areas of politics. Foreign
policy makers are committed at least as strongly as domestic policy makers
to the idea that details on how decisions are made should be kept secret. In
addition, one often has difficulty in ascertaining what foreign policy action
has occurred if it involves complex international negotiations and strategic
plans. Even historical perspective does not eliminate different interpretations of intentions and strategies. Unlike a policy decision on domestic
matters, where the decision is frequently expressed in a formal law or
official pronouncement, the foreign policy decision is frequently hidden
because the policy maker can only try to influence rather than command
the behavior of other actors. Moreover, most governments have developed
bureaucratic systems to ensure that the materials that would be helpful in

the study of international politics do not reach the scholar until a long period of time has elapsed. While the purpose of the system is not to inhibit the scholar, the governmental policy of secrecy on matters of foreign policy actions is severely limiting. It should also be remembered in this context that many studies in the field of international politics demand data from more than one country. This means the student is faced not only with a limitation imposed by his own government but also with limitations imposed by foreign governments, not to mention difficulties created by different languages and cultures.

It would not be an exaggeration to say that the international politics scholar is isolated from many materials he would find useful in his studies. He can neither go to the data as easily as the archaeologist can in the field nor bring the data to him as readily as the chemist can in his laboratory. Although other scientists (especially but not exclusively social scientists) share the problem, his position is often more difficult because frequently the data he wants to find are those that others do not want him to find. He may develop laboratory experiments using human participants as the social psychologists have, but as the complexity of the phenomena and the scope of the questions he asks increase, the experiments become more difficult to design and execute.

Given all of these conditions, what sources of data does the international politics scholar have? First, he may examine written documents produced by governmental action or the action of other actors involved in a particular event (such as Democratic party platform statements on foreign policy). Second, he may examine the public and private statements and writings of those involved in foreign policy decision making. Third, he may look at the publications of organs whose business it is to record activities relating to foreign affairs. These organs range from the hundreds of newspapers operating throughout the world to organizations like the United Nations that seek to monitor the activities of states. Finally, he may turn to experts whose detailed knowledge of specific events or processes is respected enough to allow him to have confidence in their views of the events.

Each of these sources contains certain biasing factors that make the international politics scholar's dependence on them unfortunate even though necessary. The first source is closest to the foreign policy activities of a state because it represents firsthand information. However, public documents represent statements of momentary significance that have import only in terms of other related events. Moreover, certain foreign policy actions are not documented at all—such as activities of the United States Central Intelligence Agency in the 1950's. The second and third sources also produce biased pictures of reality. The public and private statements of people involved in international events are made after the event and often are formulated so that the individuals producing the statements appear to have been correct. Institutionalized reporting by newspapers or the statistical bureaus of governmental and international organizations are also subject to extensive biasing by the individuals making the initial report as well as through the alteration of the information as it passes up the organizational hierarchy. Finally, the expert whose view of a particular event or process might be used in general study is also subject to human errors like loss of memory or wishful thinking.

The student of international politics, then, faces difficulties at two levels: developing concepts and theories as well as testing them. The tendency of men to confuse description and prediction with normative judgment and prescription is compounded by the tendency of the student of international politics to play politics himself. In addition, the immense complexity of factors determining international politics makes the development and testing of ideas very difficult. Finally, the shortage of data limits the student when testing the reality of theories he develops.

Although we have discussed these difficulties as if our main aim were to create a science of international politics, most of them also plague those who analyze international politics outside the scientific framework. The concern for the difficulty in developing concepts and theories is a major theme in political theory—both classical and modern. The difficulties in acquiring relevant data confront the nonscientific student of international politics as well. Even if we were to give up the hope of a science of international politics we would still confront essentially the same difficulties as the scientific student of international politics does; we would now be able, however, to lapse into normative statements and prescription more easily to cover up our lack of shared knowledge.

THE PLAN OF THE BOOK

Given the lack of shared concepts and tested theories in the field of international politics, it would be dishonest to say: "Learn what is in this book and you will know about international politics." One could not write a textbook at this point in the history of the discipline if he were to include only what scholars in the field agree is knowledge about international politics. Instead, this book attempts to introduce a set of concepts, propositions, and theories that should enlarge the student's understanding of international politics and may ultimately contribute to shared knowledge in the field. At the very least, the book seeks to provide *by example* an approach to analyzing contemporary international politics.

To accomplish these aims, the following format has been employed. First, the eleven chapters following this one cover the entire field of international politics by introducing a small number of concepts along with a compact set of propositions designed to provide basic ideas on the crucial aspects of international politics. Presentation of these concepts and propositions has been kept as simple as possible, introducing historical examples for illustration only. For the most part, propositions appearing throughout the book are not tested according to the scientific procedures outlined in this chapter. Although the author assumes the propositions have some face validity, he has not devoted the major part of the text to proving their accuracy because adequate testing cannot take place in a textbook. The reader is encouraged to challenge the concepts and propositions appearing throughout the book, and the eleven chapters should be viewed as tentative statements about the reality of international politics. They are subject to evaluation by the reader himself according to criteria set forth in describing the basis of shared knowledge.

In addition to the normal presentation, each chapter contains a summary outline. Each chapter is summarized in statements, definitions, and propositions. Statements that are propositions are italicized in these outlines. Hence, the outlines may be used by the reader not only to improve his grasp of the material or to refresh his memory of earlier chapters, but also to develop his ability to think in terms of concepts and propositions.

Finally, to acquaint the student with some major literature that already exists in the relevant fields, a bibliographical essay is also provided for each chapter. The purpose of these essays will not be merely to aid the student in writing a term paper but, more important, to give him an idea of how others have studied each subject. In addition, it should serve to remind him that a great deal of scholarly effort has already been expended in the study of international politics and that before he expends any more he should learn of the successes and failures of those who have gone before him. Organic growth of a discipline around a series of shared concepts and theories can occur only if students—beginning as well as advanced—are aware of the works of others.

It might be useful at this point to discuss the general organization of the book. As noted earlier, some scholars tend to distinguish sharply between foreign policy and international politics, and moreover to emphasize one aspect rather than the other. In order to provide as balanced a picture of both aspects as possible, we have divided the remaining chapters into three parts: (1) the actors, (2) interactions among actors, and (3) the international political system.

Part One will examine the processes within states and intergovernmental organizations[10] that lead to international activities. Chapters 2 to 4

[10] The term "intergovernmental organization" will be used throughout this text to refer to what the laymen usually call "international organizations." We will explain why we use the more technical term in Chapter 6.

will discuss determinants of the foreign policies of states, including the behavior of foreign policy decision makers, the impact of domestic political pressures on their behavior, and the role of economic and military conditions in shaping foreign policy. Chapter 5 will attempt to relate patterns of foreign policy behavior to the determinants as a way of analyzing foreign policy. We will close this section by discussing the policy making process within various types of intergovernmental organizations such as United Nations and European Economic Community.

Part Two will deal with official interactions among states and intergovernmental organizations. Chapter 7, the first chapter in this section, will examine the social, economic, technological, and legal conditions which serve as a setting for international interactions. Our discussion of the interactions *per se* will be divided as follows: Chapter 8, routine official interactions among states; Chapter 9, collective problem solving among states; and Chapter 10, competitive bargaining among states. Although these three types of interactions overlap in some aspects, it is still useful to make these distinctions when discussing the way states deal with each other.

Part Three will deal with international politics as a system of politics and will be divided into two chapters. Chapter 11 will present a historical overview of factors that have contributed to maintenance of the international political system, particularly in the face of threats of widespread warfare and empire building. Chapter 12 will look at major trends in the international political system, attempting to provide some general predictions of the future based on the descriptive analysis presented in this book.

The student should keep the outline of the book in mind. Because international politics is complex, a great deal of interdependency exists among the various aspects the book will discuss. Therefore, an awareness of the order in which various subjects will arise is crucial for understanding the entire field. It is suggested that the student briefly skim the outline at the end of the chapter he has already read as review before reading a new chapter. Also, two chapters should serve as a review of preceding chapters: Chapter 5 reviews Chapters 2, 3, and 4 by presenting a general framework for foreign policy analysis; Chapter 12 reviews the entire book by looking at broad trends in the international political system.

The substantive approach of the book, then, is to move from the simple to the more complex by starting with the nature of the actor in international politics, moving to the patterns of interactions among actors and concluding with the international political system. The methodological approach is to provide a set of concepts and theories that illustrate an approach to the study of international politics. Written in the hope that a clear awareness of limitations of the field will not discourage the beginning student, the book is designed to challenge those interested in improving the concepts and theories now employed in understanding contemporary international politics.

SUMMARY OUTLINE

I. The process of acquiring knowledge requires more than the simple collection and reproduction of information.
   A. People do not learn only by collecting and reproducing information.
   B. *In acquiring knowledge, people add something to the information they get.*[11]
      1. *People organize information by applying criteria based on their prior experience or values.*
      2. Analysis may be defined as the process of organizing information to achieve any or all of the following purposes: (1) description, (2) prediction, (3) normative judgment, or (4) prescription.
      3. Description should serve as a basis for the other three types of analysis.
      4. *The tendency of men to be unclear about the type of analysis they are performing leads to poor description which in turn undermines all types of analysis.*
II. Science is a set of procedures for building shared knowledge about what exists so that men are not only more knowledgable but are also better able to predict, normatively evaluate, and prescribe.
   A. *Science seeks to provide a basis for more precise communication among students than usually exists at the journalistic or narrative levels.*
      1. *Science demands clarity and precision in the use of concepts and theories.*
      2. Operational definitions of the components of propositions are necessary if there is to be reliability in the collection of data necessary to test the propositions.
   B. Science provides methods for building confidence in one's theories.
III. A number of difficulties exist in the development of concepts and theories in the field of international politics.
   A. *The frequent and intense interaction between the international*

---

[11] Propositions are indicated by italics in this and succeeding outlines.

       politics scholar and the political actor increases the lack of pre-cision and clarity in the use of concepts and theories.

  B. *The complexity and broad scope of international politics pro-duces two opposite but inhibiting tendencies in the development of concepts and theories.*

      1. *Some scholars tend to focus exclusively on particular poli-cies or events without adequate concern for developing generalizations.*

      2. *Other scholars tend to develop excessively abstract expla-nations without recognizing the multicausal nature of inter-national politics.*

IV. A number of difficulties exist in the testing of theories and derived propositions.

  A. *The multicausal nature of most international political phe-nomena make testing theories a difficult task.*

  B. *The lack of adequate data limits the extent to which theories can be systematically tested with empirical data.*

BIBLIOGRAPHICAL ESSAY

A bibliographical essay after each chapter will present the most important relevant works, containing a variety of viewpoints. Although these essays will of necessity omit many relevant citations, they should provide the student with a general feel for the literature in a particular area. Designed to be used with this book's bibliography, they will also provide initiative to use bibliographies in cited works. For general bibliographical help in the field (other than book reviews appearing in various periodicals) the stu-dent is advised to study the annotated bibliography in *The Universal Reference System: International Affairs* (Volume I, 1965).

    The general philosophical assumptions underlying the pursuit of knowledge can be found in a number of works. General discussions of the history and philosophy of science, with particular relevance if not reference to the social sciences, are found in Bronowski (53), Nagel (291), and Kuhn (236). An overview of achievements of the behavioral sciences may be acquired from Berelson and Steiner, (34). The nature and importance of the idea of reliability is examined in Cohen and Nagel (80), Brecht (45), Kerlinger (221), and Kaplan in (231). Processes for constructing concepts are examined in Cohen and Nagel (80), Hempel (166), Nagel (291), and Kaplan's essay in (231). The question of testing for validity, again with particular reference to the social sciences, is examined in Cohen and Nagel (80), Nagel (291), Kaplan (231), and Kerlinger (221).

Works in the field of international politics that address themselves to scope and method are both numerous and diverse. Writers who are concerned with both descriptive and prescriptive analysis include Carr (67), Herz (169), Tucker (407), and Morgenthau (285). The last has a more substantial impact on the study of international politics following World War II than any other writer. These authorities are by no means uncritical of each other, and in fact have engaged in numerous disputes involving both substantive and methodological assumption, particularly during the early 1950's. Works directed more explicitly at the development of descriptive analysis—although not totally devoid of the other types of analysis despite their claims—are Wright (427), Singer in (231), Brody in (389), Sprout and Sprout (393), Alker (8), Kaplan (206), Aron (16), and Deutsch (102). Again, there is wide variation in this group, particularly around the question of how scientific the study of international politics can or should be. In addition, articles reviewing descriptive analysis include Hoffmann (178) and Snyder in (383). Seven books of essays may be consulted for a cross section of existing approaches in international politics— Hoffmann (178), Rosenau (348), Kriesberg (235), Singer in (231), Knorr and Rosenau (230), and Coplin and Kegley (85). Traditional concepts and assumptions in the field are explored in Russell (354) and Thompson (404). In addition, a number of scholars have employed simulation models as an approach for developing concepts and assumptions in the study of international politics. Defined as an "operating model," simulation is useful in developing concepts and seeking interrelationships of concepts. See Coplin in (362) for a discussion of uses and application of simulation models. Where to find data for the study of international politics is partially answered by Zawodny (435) in terms of documentary and standard data sources, and data on national characteristics can be found in Russett et al. (361), and Banks and Textor (24). How to use different types of data to measure aspects of international politics is discussed in Mueller (287). Kelman's essays in (215) present ways in which social psychological data may be helpful to the student of international politics. Finally, the Singer essays in (231), indicate what types of empirical data may be utilized in the study of international politics.

In addition, the student might want to consult available literature on political science methodology, since many of these problems also face the international politics scholar. Ultimately, however, the best way to understand and resolve methodological problems is to participate in research directly. Without practical experience in conducting research, abstract methodological points may not appear worthy of serious discussion.

Part One

THE ACTORS

When we think of international politics we frequently think first of Adolf Hitler's attempt to dominate Europe, the threat of nuclear war, or the United Nations. Although all three are well publicized, they represent three different levels of international politics. Hitler's attempt to control Europe has to do with the way a particular state behaved; that is, with the behavior of *actors* in international politics. The threat of nuclear war refers to the *interaction* between two or more states because it involves fears about each other's behavior. The United Nations, an institution that exists among states, may be viewed as a manifestation of an *international political system*. This threefold distinction among levels has been employed as the organizational structure of the book. Part One will deal with the actors; Part Two will examine interactions among actors, and Part Three will describe the international political system.

Although we have employed this threefold distinction to organize the book, the distinctions among the three levels are not totally clear. Hitler's Germany behaved in relation toward other states and toward the international political system as a whole. Similarly, the threat of nuclear war involves the foreign policy actions of particular states as well as conditions within the international political system. Finally, the United Nations may be viewed as the product of foreign policies of separate states and interactions among states. Hence, the parts of the book describe three overlapping aspects of international politics.

Although the components do overlap, none of the three alone would provide a sufficiently broad base to describe international politics. Faced with the necessity of looking at actors, interactions, and the international political system, we have found it necessary sometimes to include certain relevant aspects of one level in the part of the book describing a different level. Similarly, our decision to start the discussion by looking at the actor

first is also somewhat arbitrary. Many books reverse the order. Nevertheless, as long as the reader keeps in mind the high degree of interdependence
between actors, interactions, and the system, he should be able to follow
the discussion.

In Part One, we will be examining two very different actors—the state
or nation[1] and the intergovernmental organization. Because the state is
much more important than the intergovernmental organization as an actor
in contemporary international politics, we will devote four of the five
chapters in this part to the state.

These four chapters will be organized according to a specific theoretical framework, based on the assumption that politics is produced by people
—even though those people might be occupying extraordinary political
roles. Our primary interest will be in those people who occupy foreign
policy decision making roles; that is, who have the official responsibility or
actual influence to make decisions involving their states in world affairs.
To be interested in why states behave as they do in the international arena,
we have to be interested in why their leaders make the decisions they
make.

However, it would be a mistake to think that foreign policy decision
makers act in a vacuum. On the contrary, any given foreign policy act may
be viewed as the result of three broad categories of considerations affecting
the foreign policy decision maker. First is domestic politics within the
foreign policy decision maker's state. Second is the economic and military
capability. And third is international context, that is, the particular position
in which his state finds itself specifically in relation to the other states in the
system. Figure 3 illustrates how the factors we have just mentioned interact
to produce foreign policy actions.

Based on this framework, the next four chapters will describe the
factors that produce foreign policy actions. Chapter 2 will study the foreign
policy decision maker by looking at the types of decisions he makes and the
behavior he exhibits in reaching those decisions. Chapter 3 will discuss the
role of domestic politics by focusing on the relationship between the foreign
policy decision maker and those in his domestic political environment who
influence him. Chapter 4 will describe the role of economic and military
conditions in the formation of foreign policy. Chapter 5 will attempt to
synthesize previous chapters by examining patterns of foreign policy behavior as they are determined by domestic politics, economic-military
conditions, foreign policy decision makers, and the international context.

Chapter 6 will briefly discuss intergovernmental organizations as ac-

---

[1] The terms "state," "nation," and "country" are frequently used synonomously.
Throughout the book, we will use the term "state."

FIGURE 3

How Four Determinants Affect International Foreign Policy Actions

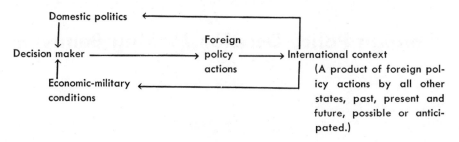

International context (A product of foreign policy actions by all other states, past, present and future, possible or anticipated.)

tors in international politics. Although their role is modest at this period in time, intergovernmental organizations should be examined as actors because they do represent a locus of relatively independent activity in the contemporary world. To the extent possible, we will attempt to analyze the behavior of intergovernmental organizations in the same framework we used to discuss the behavior of states.

2

Foreign Policy Decision Making Behavior

Foreign policy decision makers are human beings confronted with certain situations, responsible to other human beings, pressured by a variety of conditions, and forced to make decisions. Hence, we will look at the nature of foreign policy as it affects the types of decision problems facing the decision maker, the intellectual difficulties generated by the particular nature of foreign policy decisions, the psychological factors that operate in the making of foreign policy decisions, and finally, the organizational context in which the foreign policy decision maker operates.

THE NATURE OF FOREIGN POLICY

It is very difficult to describe the nature of foreign policy because as Roger Hilsman, a political scientist as well as a former State Department official, has said:

> Very often policy is the sum of a congeries of separate or only vaguely related actions. On other occasions, it is an uneasy, even internally inconsistent compromise among competing goals or an incompatible mixture of alternative means for achieving a single goal. . . . A government does not decide to inaugurate the nuclear age, but only to try to build an atomic bomb before its enemy does. . . . Rather than through grand decisions on grand alternatives, policy changes seem to come through a series of slight modifications of existing policies emerging slowly and halt-ingly by small and usually tentative steps, a process of trial and error in which policy zigs and zags, reverses itself, and then moves forward in a series of incremental steps.[1]

[1] Roger Hilsman, *To Move a Nation: The Politics of Foreign Policy in the Administration of John F. Kennedy* (Garden City, N.Y.: Doubleday, 1967), p. 5.

In describing the nature of foreign policy, we will discuss three types of foreign policy decisions: (1) general foreign policy decisions, (2) administrative decisions, and (3) crisis decisions.

General foreign policy consists of a series of decisions expressed through policy statements as well as direct actions. The American policy of "containment" after World War II, for example, included both broad policy statements, such as Presidential Addresses, and specific actions such as the Marshall Plan. The target of foreign policy can be the entire international environment, as in the containment policy; a specific group of states, as in the Monroe doctrine; or one state, as in the American policy of military and economic cooperation with Canada. Frequently, but not always, the general policies themselves are mutually supporting so that they form a hierarchy of relatively consistent decisions.

Often it is difficult to ascertain the nature of a general policy in the field of foreign policy. Unlike domestic policy decisions, which take the form of legislative programs or the allocation of financial resources, many foreign policy decisions involve only public statements and perhaps contingency planning. Frequently, the policy statements do not reveal the true nature of the policy but constitute a ploy in interactions among states. For example, the policy statements made by President Eisenhower and Secretary of State John Foster Dulles calling for "liberation of eastern Europe" was not indicative of any American decision to take direct military action against the Soviet position in eastern Europe even though they made implications to that effect. Sometimes there appears to be no internal consistency between specific decisions even if the leaders themselves attempt to argue that a consistent policy has been in operation. Soviet policy towards the United Arab Republic, for example, has vacillated during the 1950's and 1960's between the encouragement of Egyptian expansion and attempts to counter that expansion. Hence, although it is useful to discuss the general foreign policy of a state, it is frequently difficult to be sure that one has properly identified it.

The second type of foreign policy decision is administrative. It is taken by members of the governmental bureaucracy charged with the conduct of the nation's foreign affairs. The foreign office (called the Department of State in the United States) is the primary bureaucratic organization, but other agencies of the government such as the military, the intelligence agency, and commerce often are involved in administrative decisions affecting foreign policy.[2] Administrative decisions, in addition to being made by lower-level governmental officials, are usually bounded by

[2] See Chapter 8 for a more thorough discussion of the activities of the foreign policy bureaucracy.

space, scope, and time; that is, they are taken in regard to a specific foreign country on a particular problem and for a definite period of time. The admission of foreign students to the United States from a specific country for a particular year, for example, is an administrative decision made at a relatively lower level in the State Department bureaucracy.

The nature of the relationship as well as the distinction between general policy and administrative policy is illustrated in American policy toward Berlin and West Germany in the late 1940's and early 1950's. The general policy of the United States was "containment," this meant that the Soviet Union was to be prevented from expanding its control into West Germany and Berlin. Given this general policy, a number of important detailed decisions had to be made, particularly concerning procedures for determining the flow of people and goods across the borders that separated West Germany and Berlin from the rest of eastern Europe. Because an important part of the containment strategy was to communicate to the Soviet Union the resolute intentions of the United States, even the smallest American decision could have a far-reaching impact. Hence, questions arising out of the many incidents on the borders had to be handled by lower-level military and foreign policy officials to insure that firmness but not aggressiveness was communicated to the Soviet Union. Although bounded in space, time, and level of detail, the hundreds of actions by lower-level American officials played an important role in America's general foreign policy toward that troubled area of the world.

Ostensibly, administrative decisions are determined by the general foreign policy of the state. Political leaders are supposed to decide the general policy of state A toward state B, and the members of the bureaucracy are supposed to implement that decision in particular circumstances. In American foreign policy toward Berlin and West Germany during the late 1940's, it appears that the general foreign policy for the most part did control the administrative decisions. However, it is frequently the case that just the opposite occurs; lower-level bureaucrats take actions that shape the general foreign policy. For example, Bernard Fall points out that French bureaucrats and military men on location played an important role in shaping French foreign policy toward Indochina in the late 1940's.[3] Despite modern communications, geographical distance often allows the ambassador and his staff a substantial degree of autonomy in making administrative decisions. Even within the home office, lower-level officials have considerable autonomy given their specialized knowledge and the enormous awareness of detail necessary to make foreign policy decisions.[4]

[3] Bernard B. Fall, *The Two Viet-Nams: A Political and Military Analysis* 2d ed. (New York: Praeger, 1967), pp. 60–130.
[4] See Chapter 3 for more discussion of this topic.

The third type of foreign policy decision—crisis decision—combines the other two levels. On the one hand, the crisis decision has a large impact on the general foreign policy of a state. It can reaffirm existing policy as United States' behavior in successive Berlin crises has (1948–61), or it can indicate a shift in foreign policy as the 1950 United States decision to intervene on behalf of South Korea did with respect to American policy in Asia. On the other hand, the crisis decision is directed at a specific situation in spite of its worldwide significance. It is bounded geographically because it does not directly involve universal or even regional activities. It is also usually limited to a few states as direct participants although in modern times a large number of states tend to become involved in relatively minor incidents. Finally, it is usually limited to actions in the present, although the actions usually have long-range consequences.

Crisis decisions occur in all types of activities, but they are particularly important in the field of foreign policy. Because basic relationships among states depend upon the way they bargain with each other rather than the way common institutions regulate their behavior, crisis is common to foreign policy decision making, whether it is created intentionally by one party or is an unintended effect. A crisis is often necessary to convince an opponent that its bargaining position is unreasonable. Given its importance in the general foreign policies of states and given the frequency with which it occurs, crisis decision making must be understood in order to understand foreign policy decision making.

A foreign policy crisis may be defined as a condition in which at least one state feels that a situation represents a turning point in its relationship with one or more states in the system. In addition, there is usually a sense of urgency about the situation; that is, recognition of the need for a decision of some kind within a short period of time. Even if a decision to act is not forthcoming, a crisis situation creates a condition which stimulates foreign policy decision makers to weigh various alternatives. Usually, an element of surprise is part of foreign policy crisis. The surprise might not be in the nature of the situation itself—for example, leaders in most countries have assumed ever since 1948 that crises will occur between Egypt and Israel—but rather in the exact timing of the crisis. Finally, one or both parties usually feel that crucial objectives are severely threatened by a crisis situation.

Because crises create conditions for relatively specific decisions that have general foreign policy consequences, they also usually involve both high- and low-level officials. In the Cuban missile crisis, for example, lower-level intelligence officials were the first to learn of the Soviet Union's actions in placing missiles in Cuba. The information was passed to high-level officials but the speed and precision with which the intelligence officers transmitted the information was an important part of the way the crisis was handled by President Kennedy and his advisors. In addition, the sense of importance and urgency that usually accompanies crisis decision making often leads the high-level officials to form an *ad hoc* or working group to deal with the situation. In the Cuban missile crisis, for example, President Kennedy formed a group consisting of "highly respected Foreign Service officers as well as political appointees, retired statesmen as well as personal presidential assistants."[5]

Foreign policy decision making, then, is a mixture of general policy, administrative, and crisis decision making. General foreign policy positions are a product of actions taken by low-level administrative officials as part of their daily routine just as they are a product of decisions made during a time of crisis. At the same time, general foreign policy serves as a guide for administrative officials on routine matters and for crisis decision makers in their hour of need. Administrative decisions can also serve as a gateway to a crisis decision—either stopping a crisis before it starts or creating conditions that make a crisis more likely. Finally, given the peculiar nature of international relations, crisis decisions often change the entire course of a general foreign policy—as the decision to intervene in Korea did for the United States—as well as shape the administrative procedures that will be employed—as the Berlin Blockade in 1948 did for United States occupation forces in West Germany. Keeping the nature of these three types of foreign policy decisions in mind, we now turn to a discussion of the intellectual, psychological, and organizational factors that shape the behavior of the foreign policy decision maker.

THE FOREIGN POLICY DECISION MAKER AS A RATIONAL PROBLEM SOLVER

To explore the intellectual processes necessary to successfully deal with foreign policy decision problems, we will employ in this section an ideal model; that is, a set of propositions that pinpoints certain attributes of a situation but ignores others. A classic example of an ideal model is the one used by Adam Smith in his study of economics. Smith as well as some modern economists assumed that men are motivated only by the desire for wealth and that they would always make the decision most likely to increase their wealth. Referred to as "economic man," this model has aided students of economics not only in describing economically motivated be-

---

[5] Theodore C. Sorensen, *Decision-Making in the White House* (New York: Columbia University Press, 1963), p. 65.

havior but also in understanding at what points the assumptions of economic man are not realistic.

In this section, we are going to use the model of man as a rational problem solver to explore the intellectual processes involved in foreign policy decision making. Like the model of economic man, the view that man is a rational problem solver is ideal because it assumes that the foreign policy decision maker—subject neither to his own psychological characteristics nor to pressures coming from his role in his organization or society —can reach decisions merely by performing the necessary intellectual tasks. As we will see in later parts of this chapter and in the next chapter, such an assumption bears little resemblance to reality. Nevertheless, by employing this model we will be able to assess some of the intellectual—as distinct from psychological or organizational—problems confronting the foreign policy decision maker as if he were free from his own biases and social pressures.

Decision Making as an Intellectual Task

Before examining the model, it is necessary to discuss the general attributes of rational decision making. We will do this by identifying four ideal steps in making a decision and by illustrating those four steps through a decision problem with which the reader should be thoroughly familiar—a college student choosing a course.

Early in the decision making process a rational problem solving student must *define the situation;* in this case, he must acquire adequate information on course offerings. The college catalog might do for a start, but he will want to know more than just the time, place, and name of the instructor (even assuming the catalog's reliability). Thus, to define the situation adequately, the rational problem solving student will tap many sources of information.

Either before, during, or immediately after he has acquired the necessary information, the rational problem solving college student will need to *select his goals.* Perhaps the student wants to fulfill requirements for a degree to broaden his intellectual perspective or to prepare himself for a post college career. It is important for him to select the goals early in the decision making process because they can help him determine what information is most relevant. With goals established, he can quickly narrow down the universe of information (in this case, on what courses to gather information).

At some point, our student should start thinking about the relationship of his goals to the courses being offered (definition of the situation.) The *search for alternatives* is the process of exploring the various ways in which the selected goals may be achieved; that is, examining the *means* necessary to achieve the *ends* or goals desired. Often the goals themselves might be the means to another goal as, for example, the goal of an "A" in a course is usually viewed as part of the means to acquiring a good job while a good job is often viewed as the means to enjoying a good life.

The search for alternatives, then, is the process of looking for ways of solving problems; that is, of examining various courses of action in terms of achieving goals. Assume, for example, that the student's primary goal is to complete the requirements for a degree, and an investigation of the catalog reveals ten courses that would satisfy his requirements. Such a determination would allow him to focus his information gathering on ten courses rather than the hundreds offered by the university.

After the rational problem solving student has sufficiently explored all possible alternatives, he is ready for the final stage in the decision-making process—*choosing an alternative.* Sometimes the process of choosing an alternative is not necessary because only one alternative exists. If our hypothetical student had enough goals and each were hierarchically arranged so that only one course would satisfy all the goals, it would not be necessary to choose an alternative. The difficult task would be to find one satisfactory alternative. Many times, however, the search turns up a number of alternatives none of which is clearly superior to the others. When this occurs, the rational problem solving student might choose at random from equally attractive alternatives.

These four tasks constitute the intellectual processes we normally call rational problem solving. They are designed to maximize the chances of making the right decisions because they place a premium on gathering and assessing relevant information. As an ideal model of rational problem solving, the four processes are based on a number of assumptions: (1) the decision maker is aware that he is making a decision rather than acting out of habit or necessity; (2) he is conscious of the goals that motivate him; (3) the goals are not conflicting but instead can be hierarchically arranged; (4) he explores all alternatives suggested by application of his goals to the defined situation; and (5) he is conscious of the need to accumulate as much information as possible not only about the field but also about his own ambitions in that field.

Foreign Policy Decision Making as an Intellectual Task

Assuming that any given foreign policy decision maker were a rational problem solver following the ideal intellectual tasks outlined above, the question is: What is inherent in the nature of foreign policy decision problems that would make it difficult for him to perform the four tasks? The contrast between the rational problem solver as a normal college student choosing a course and the rational problem solver as a foreign policy decision maker is striking. We will briefly discuss the intellectual problems foreign policy decision makers encounter.

The first difficulty a rational problem solving foreign policy decision maker would face is in defining the situation. Foreign policy decision problems involve an immensely complex set of factors because the international environment is a product of interaction of a large variety of psychological, social, economic, political, technological, and geographical factors. Any given foreign policy decision problem demands knowledge about relationships among states and estimates about how other states will react to particular situations. The foreign policy decision maker may employ experts to collect pertinent information but information alone does not solve the problem. Putting the information together in order to intelligently estimate the future course of events is even more difficult than acquiring the information in the first place. Given the difficulties he faces in properly understanding the international environment, the foreign policy decision maker—even though he be a rational problem solver—is confronted with extensive uncertainty in defining the situation.

The selection of foreign policy goals is also difficult for the foreign policy decision maker. The basic value that underlies the goals of most foreign policy decision makers is the continued survival of the nation. But this value does not represent a very concrete goal in international affairs, particularly in the contemporary world. Some leaders have justified wars of expansion on the basis of national security, as Japan did in the 1930's; others have justified policies of isolation, as the United States did in the same period. Still other leaders have tried to promote international peace and security through the development of international organizations in the name of national security.

National security is an amorphous basis for national goals because the security of a state depends upon the capabilities and intentions of other states in relation to its own capabilities and intentions. Hence, intermediate goals designed to promote national security can be extremely varied depending upon the decision maker's information about international conditions. For example, since World War II, the United States' conception of conditions necessary to strengthen its national security have been cohesion in the western bloc, diversity in the Soviet bloc, and protection of neutral states from Communist influence. However, one could argue that these goals are meaningful only if the Soviet Union is viewed as the prime threat to United States security. Perhaps a more cohesive Soviet bloc would better counter Communist Chinese plans if we were to assume that Red China is the primary threat.

National security goals are also difficult to work with because they provide no clear criteria for degrees of success. If failure is measured by the destruction and control of a nation by another nation, success in maintaining national security can only be measured in avoiding these alternatives. However, it is difficult to measure degrees of success because so much depends on the intentions of other states. For example, was the United States more secure after the Cuban missile crisis than it was before? The answer to the question could be that the United States was more secure because it had convinced the Soviet Union of its willingness to risk nuclear war if it perceived a threatening condition in the international system. Conversely, one could say the United States was less secure because the Soviet Union had been so thoroughly embarrassed by the crisis it would react more violently in the next encounter.

Success is also difficult to achieve in nonsecurity areas of foreign policy. Questions of economic interest or national honor occupy the attention of foreign policy decision makers, but the goals associated with these questions are set in complex situations where outcomes are difficult to evaluate. Economic concessions on paper do not always produce what is intended because radically changing economic and political conditions can quickly alter benefits and costs. Actions affecting national honor such as the proper treatment of visiting dignitaries frequently result in unintended effects through unforeseen events that even the most meticulous planning cannot prevent.

Foreign policy goals are difficult to achieve not only because there are few clear criteria for measuring success but also because the goals themselves often conflict. Economic needs often clash with military security needs. For example, the American economy might gain extensively from trade with Communist China, but the American goal of keeping China militarily weak conflicts with such economic goals. Even goals based on the general aim of national security often conflict with each other. In fighting an extensive war in South Vietnam on the premise that it is necessary for American security, for example, the United States has had to reduce military commitments in other areas.

Given the limitations on the decision maker's ability to know about conditions in the international environment as well as the amorphousness and often conflicting nature of foreign policy goals, the search for policy alternatives takes place under less than ideal circumstances. Lack of information about the environment combines with the unstructured nature of policy goals to create almost an unlimited number of potential policy alternatives. Moreover, because many decisions are made under crisis conditions, the foreign policy decision makers have neither the time nor the inclination to make an exhaustive search of the innumerable policy alternatives that might exist for any given decision problem.

Finally, the foreign policy decision maker is faced with the task of choosing an alternative. The college student chooses a course from a small number of alternatives examined on the basis of a few goals and the relatively clear information in the course catalog. The foreign policy decision maker, on the other hand, faces a large number of alternatives that cannot be thoroughly assessed. Whereas the college student knows the few areas in which his information might be poor (for example, the grapevine), the foreign policy decision maker has to worry about incorrect information and prediction in many areas. The way events work themselves out in the international environment, it is often difficult to estimate the consequences of any policy even if information is available.[6]

From the above discussion, it should be apparent that even if the foreign policy decision maker were the rational problem solver carefully going through the various intellectual tasks in reaching a decision, he would encounter many difficulties. Inability to define international conditions in sufficiently manageable terms coupled with generally amorphous foreign policy goals make the tasks of searching for alternatives and choosing alternatives formidable, to say the least. Inherent in the very relationship between the state and its international environment, then, are problems that make the intellectual tasks of decision making difficult to perform even if the decision maker acted as pictured in the rational problem solving model.

PSYCHOLOGICAL FACTORS IN FOREIGN POLICY DECISION MAKING

However, decision makers are not intellectual machines performing the four tasks of rational problem solving. On the contrary, they are individuals subject to psychological factors that influence all human behavior. In this section, we will discuss the impact of psychological factors on foreign policy decision making. Although the foreign policy decision makers in the real world are not rational problem solvers, we will continue to use the four tasks of rational decision making as a framework for analysis.

Defining the Situation

Some social scientists have developed the concept of image to discuss the role of psychological variables and personal experiences in the way people define their environment. An image is produced by interaction of attitudes,

---

[6] As we saw in Chapter 1, more than information is necessary to make adequate predictions. Theories are also necessary, so that the political decision maker is often given information which provides little help in adequately defining international conditions because he does not possess the theoretical framework to fit the pieces of information together correctly.

values, and assumptions the individual has developed in dealing with his environment. Although psychologists are just beginning to learn about the nature of the processes that produce images, they do know that past experiences, current attitudes, and value commitments, not to mention personality development, influence the way individuals look at their world. Because these factors differ for each individual, different individuals perceive their environment differently.

One attribute of images that greatly affects how an individual defines his environment and ultimately how he will behave can be viewed as part of a continuum between what may be called "open" and "closed" images. An open image is flexible, that is, it adjusts to new information so that the individual is given a picture as up to date and close to reality as possible. In contrast, a closed image is one that does not adjust to new information. The possessor of a closed image tends to be out of date because new conditions have not been adequately recognized.

Images can never be completely open or closed. On the one hand, a completely open image would presuppose continuous awareness of change, something which would be so time consuming that the possessor would be able to do nothing but update his images. On the other hand, even the most static view would be susceptible to some alteration if the change in the environment were clear enough. Hence, we are really discussing a *relative* concept when we talk about closed or open images.

Given the complexity and uncertainty of information about the international environment, decision makers develop relatively closed images of international conditions. People tend to want security in their images since if their views of the world were under constant flux, they would not be able to act. This is particularly true in the field of foreign affairs. Simplifying assumptions become dogma in many cases; given the high stakes usually involved, the foreign policy decision maker cannot always afford the insecurity that would result from reevaluating existing images. Because the foreign policy decision maker depends upon his images to orient his behavior, a change in his images can have broad policy consequences.

The importance of images in foreign policy and the difficulties surrounding conflicting images is illustrated in the following quotation from Geoffrey Taylor of the *Manchester Guardian Weekly* concerning United States foreign policy in Vietnam during the mid-1960's:

> Vietnam is usually discussed from the point of view either that Americans are intruding in a war of liberation, a civil war which the Vietnamese should be left to settle, or that the North Vietnamese are aggressors determined to overthrow the established Government of the country they are invading and with which the United States is allied. It is simple to argue from either

point of view because the facts will admit equally well of both interpretations. Which view one adopts may well depend on one's general political outlook on quite unrelated matters.

Either view sustains a logical policy. For those who see the war as an intrusion the answer is for the Americans to withdraw. For those who see it as an invasion the answer is to beat the invaders so that other potential invaders will learn their lesson.[7]

Images of the international environment thus play a large role in foreign policies. They provide one of the basic rationales for any given foreign policy. As in the case of United States policy towards Vietnam, uncertainty over images can lead to confusion and debate over foreign policy. For this reason, foreign policy decision makers often cling to their initial images even after those images become incorrect or irrelevant—not only because they find it difficult to convince themselves their images might have been wrong but also because they have often made their images public in order to defend their policies. Once they present an official definition of a given situation, foreign policy decision makers have an investment they are often not willing to lose. Contrary information becomes a threat not only in terms of the integrity and security of his own images but also in terms of building political support for himself and his policies. While it is not unusual for the foreign policy decision maker to have two images of a particular situation—one for his own use and one for public consumption —there appears to be a tendency for the public image to dominate particularly over a long period of time.

While conditions contributing to relatively closed images in foreign policy are substantial, certain factors produce some pressure toward openness. Events in the international environment can be so dramatic that even dogmatically held views are altered. For example, decision makers in Great Britain during the 1930's were almost as contemptuous and fearful of Stalin's Russia as they were of Hitler's Germany, which in part accounts for their failure to ally with the Soviet Union even after it became clear that Germany was a more dangerous enemy. However, once Germany attacked Russia, British leaders altered some of their views toward the Soviet Union enough at least to allow for a military alliance.

The key to whether or not a particular international event or series of events will change a decision maker's image is related to the clearness of "signals" or "cues" inherent in the event. Prior to World War II, it appears the cues were not clear enough to convince British leaders that a different assessment of the Soviet Union's role in world affairs was necessary. Only the Nazi attack on the Soviet Union appears to have been sufficiently clear.

[7] Geoffrey Taylor, "What Attitude to the 5 per cent Movements?" *Manchester Guardian Weekly,* January 25, 1968, p. 5.

However, even relatively clear cues can be missed, as Wohlstetter asserts in a study of American foreign policy prior to the Japanese attack on Pearl Harbor. The study reveals that information sufficient to predict the attack had reached various organizations in Washington but that the decision makers failed to evaluate the signals properly.[8]

A concept often employed in discussing the impact of changes in the environment on the decision maker's image is the *signal-to-noise ratio.* Adapted from communication sciences, the concept implies that although certain events that might occur in the environment ought to alert the decision makers to a particular situation (signal), other random events may obscure the meaningful ones (noise). In the Pearl Harbor case, the indications of an impending attack were lost among the steady stream of information about Japanese actions that did not indicate attack. Given the enormous number of factors in the international situation, of which the foreign policy decision maker must be aware, noise is frequently substantial. This in turn means that signals must be extremely clear to maintain a sufficiently high signal-to-noise ratio.

In addition to the impact of events in the international environment, foreign policy images are also sometimes altered through the give and take of debate within the policy process itself. Whether the debates occur privately or publicly, the decision maker is forced to at least "explain" new conditions as they occur. Even if he attempts to explain them in terms of traditional images, his image of the situation may be somewhat altered. Although debate sometimes forces the decision maker to cling to his images even more desperately than he normally would, it also frequently leads him, either directly or indirectly, to alter his views.

It might be useful at this point to indicate the impact of the three types of foreign policy decisions—general, administrative, and crisis—on the relative closeness of images. Both general and administrative policy demand some coherence and stability in the interpretation of the international environment. Hence, an official definition of the situation must be provided that does not change from day to day. The American viewpoint that a Soviet-led Communist bloc is attempting to "take over" the world has served as a relatively closed image for American foreign policy at both the administrative and general level for a number of years. Even as it has become apparent that there is no solid Communist bloc of nations—particularly with the Soviet-Chinese split—the image continues to be maintained by many American decision makers.

Crisis decision making, an essential part of foreign policy decision

---

[8] Roberta Wohlstetter, *Pearl Harbor: Warning and Decision* (Stanford, Calif.: Stanford University Press, 1962).

making, also contributes to a relatively closed image. Lack of information, shortage of time, and a high value attached to the situation are characteristics of crises; they create conditions in which leaders seek to rely on traditional attitudes and assumptions. For example, President Truman referred to the failure to stop Hitler in the 1930's as the prime reason for his decision to fight in Korea in 1950. Given the enormity of the stakes involved and the shortness of time available for a decision, it is natural that Truman's memory of the 1930's would color his image of the 1950's. In times of crisis, one is forced to rely on images he has developed in the past because he lacks time and the detached atmosphere necessary to question basic assumptions about the international environment.

In addition to pressures that are a part of foreign policy decision making and that contribute to relatively closed images, the personality of a decision maker also influences the way he defines a situation. Psychologists have studied how such factors as tolerance for ambiguity and intelligence shape the way individuals view their world. In foreign policy decision making, certain personality conditions appear to affect an individual's images of the international environment. For example, Professor Ole R. Holsti has found that the personality of John Foster Dulles, the American Secretary of State during the Eisenhower Administration, affected his views of the Soviet Union. Claiming that Dulles' personality led him to value high consistency within elements of his attitudes and to discredit information that conflicted with his preexisting views, Holsti argues that Dulles would reject for one reason or another any "information that might challenge the inherent-bad-faith model of the Soviet Union" that he held.[9] Because such factors as high self-esteem affect the willingness of individuals to accept conflicting evidence, according to Holsti, Dulles maintained a set of relatively closed images particularly in regard to the Soviet Union.

One question that students of foreign policy decision making should be concerned with is the degree to which these relatively closed images are typical of most foreign policy decision making. We can assume that certain personality attributes such as high self-esteem, a willingness to clearly define the situation, and a tendency to make independent judgments are more often found in individuals who populate foreign policy decision making roles than in the general population. At the same time, however, it does not appear that the personality of foreign policy decision makers must necessarily lead to images as closed as some argue Dulles maintained.[10]

[9] Ole R. Holsti, "Cognitive Dynamics and Images of the Enemy," *Journal of International Affairs,* 21 (1967), 23–24.

[10] Although there appears to be general agreement that John Foster Dulles maintained a series of closed images, particularly when it came to the Soviet Union,

Selecting Goals

In the view of decision making as a rational intellectual process, goals are defined as explicitly and hierarchically as the environment will allow. Even though the international environment makes clear-cut statement and hierarchical arrangement of goals extremely difficult, the rational foreign policy decision maker would attempt to do so to the best of his ability. However, such a view does not correspond to the way human beings actually behave in foreign policy decision making situations.

An individual placed in the role of foreign policy decision maker is acting with the same motivations that got him to that role in the first place. In its crudest terms, this means the foreign policy decision maker will tend to assume that what is good for him is good for his country. A study by John Raser found that experts on various countries felt that political leaders exhibit what psychologists call "the need for power" and the "need for achievement" more intensely than other individuals in the society.[11]

Hence, we might conclude that prime motivations in foreign policy behavior of political leaders as well as their bureaucratic subordinates are the desires to stay in office and to increase the power of their office. Evidence of this is manifest in the decision maker's commitment to the physical security of his nation—loss of which would almost automatically mean loss of office—and in the desire to avoid any substantial foreign policy reversal.

Furthermore, national security as a foreign policy goal is convenient to the personal ambitions of political leaders. More power to deal with international problems usually means more power to insure political support at home. This is as true for decision makers in politically stable states who are able to have bigger budgets, and therefore the capability to fill more political promises, as it is for the decision makers in the unstable states who are able to increase their troops to maintain internal order.

The tendency of a political leader to maintain and improve political position within his own state, then, has clear consequences for definition of foreign policy goals. The need for power and achievement among foreign policy decision makers has doubtless contributed to the emphasis on threats

---

most of the studies are based primarily on his public statements. Because it is always possible (but not very likely given the consistency of his positions and evidence from other sources) that Dulles maintained a closed image for public consumption only, inferences concerning the degree to which he was unable to change his mind should be kept to a minimum. The fact that he was able to cooperate with the Soviet Union in the 1956 Suez crisis indicates that his images were not entirely closed.

[11] John R. Raser, "Personal Characteristics of Political Decision-Makers: A Literature Review," *Peace Research Society (International) Papers,* Vol. 5 (1966), pp. 161–82.

to the national security frequently made by leaders in all countries. The constant debate over the "true" national interest, which political leaders have with their domestic political opponents, is in part attributable to the self-serving nature of foreign policy goals to the existing political authorities.

One should not interpret the above discussion as a moral condemnation of foreign policy leaders. On the contrary, individuals in every walk of life seek to increase their wealth and position. When acting in behalf of a group—be it a corporation or a bowling league—actions often appear and are self-serving. Given the psychological needs of individuals, it appears only natural that foreign policy decision makers will act as representatives of their group—the state—in a manner which serves their own interests.

The key to "good" decision making is not whether the political leader is truly unselfish but whether or not he is able to keep his ambition within certain limits. Can he at a critical point say to himself that he can no longer take actions which will help him politically but harm the public interest? Some argue that President Lyndon Johnson in March 1968 showed this balance when he announced that he would not seek a second term as President. There is reason to believe that a more selfish type of action would have been feasible. He might have precipitated a worldwide crisis which would have drawn his party and country around him. Whether or not this interpretation of Johnson's behavior is correct, the point remains that the key factor in the foreign policy decision maker's choice of goals is not his altruism but his willingness to maintain certain limits on his ambition.

Searching for Alternatives

The rational version of the decision-making process assumes that individuals search for the alternative that would best achieve their goal. Given the psychological processes that affect the way in which individuals define their environment and select goals, the search for alternatives is usually neither systematic nor exhaustive. Instead of maximizing their search for alternatives, individuals usually "satisfice."

"Satisficing" is a term first developed by Herbert Simon to characterize the behavior of decision makers in administrative organizations.[12] It applies particularly to behavior of foreign policy decision makers. The term can be illustrated by the following example: Assume that an individual wants to buy a three-bedroom house for no more than $20,000 and begins

---

[12] Herbert A. Simon, *Administrative Behavior,* 2d ed. (New York: Free Press, 1957).

looking at houses for sale according to the numbered sequence. Assume there are five possibilities: (1) a two-bedroom house for $20,000; (2) a three-bedroom house for $40,000; (3) a three-bedroom house for $20,000; (4) a two-bedroom house for $18,000; and (5) a three-bedroom house for $17,500. If he looks at the houses in the sequence according to the numbers and is following a "satisficing" policy, he will have bought house number three; he would not have continued to explore all possibilities and would have missed house number five. Satisficing is searching for alternatives until the minimal satisfactory alternative is discovered.

One should not assume that maximizing alternatives is always the best route in making decisions. Often, it costs time and money to explore all alternatives, and it is possible that the cost would be greater than the benefit one could expect. One does not shop—which is really a form of maximizing—to see which store sells chewing gum cheaper, unless of course he is going to buy a great deal of gum or his financial resources are extremely limited while his time is unlimited. Moreover, because one can never expect to acquire complete information, the desire to learn about all alternatives is usually impossible to fulfill.

Nevertheless, the impact of psychological factors on the search for alternatives is substantial. The attention span of individuals is limited, and the number of factors they can remember and think about simultaneously rarely matches the complexity of the problems they have to solve. Furthermore, failure to define the goals they are pursuing tends to limit their ability for seeing competing alternatives, and the cognitive processes surrounding their interpretations of the environment sometimes result in failure to see conditions that would suggest different alternatives. For all of these reasons, the assumption that individuals as decision makers seek to maximize their information on various alternatives can only be considered an ideal which rarely explains human behavior.

Given the conditions under which foreign policy decisions are usually formulated, the concept of satisficing best describes the search for foreign policy alternatives. On the one hand, the complexity of the decision problems facing the foreign policy decision maker, combined with the lack of clear direction for the pursuit of his policy, creates an unlimited number of potential alternatives for any situation. Lack of structure characterizes both his goal orientation and his images because of the variety of problems and alternatives facing him. On the other hand, because of this lack of structure, the foreign policy decision maker tends to cling to past formulae in his search for alternatives. Although he could potentially explore a vast number of significantly different alternatives, he usually narrows down his search.

One primary method by which foreign policy decision makers narrow down alternatives is to look to the past. Following previous policy has a number of virtues for him. First, it removes part of his own responsibility for making decisions, placing it on his predecessors' shoulders. Second, it introduces a starting point in what would otherwise be a very fluid situation. Finally, it constitutes a partial testing of policy because the consequences of past decisions can be at least partially evaluated.

Even when previous policies are rejected, the effect is not always to open up the search for alternatives. A classic example in contemporary American foreign policy is the continued reference to the "mistakes of Munich." American policy decisions in both Korea and Vietnam have been based partially on lessons learned from the British and French attempts to appease Hitler in 1938. The strong emotional reaction to the failure of the Munich strategy, which appears to have been a major factor in the thinking of American foreign policy decision makers in both the 1930's and 1960's, has placed policy alternatives that hint of appeasement beyond serious consideration, even though it is sometimes difficult to maintain historical analogy between the 1930's and the 1960's.

In addition to the factors already mentioned that impede the search for alternatives, another consideration influences the foreign policy decision maker. He does not usually have the luxury of spending a great deal of time searching for alternatives. The crisis nature of many foreign policy decisions as well as the normal crush of day-to-day considerations results in a shortage of time and resources necessary to acquire information on various alternatives. In addition, the high stress under which foreign policy decision makers operate tends to create an emotional atmosphere incongenial to the cool assessment of a large number of alternatives. Furthermore, the need for secrecy limits the number of alternatives that can be investigated because knowledge of alternatives under consideration might give a bargaining advantage to another state.

Choosing Alternatives

Given the intellectual difficulties and the psychological processes surrounding foreign policy decision makers in their definitions of the situation, selection of goals, and search for alternatives, the choosing of alternatives does not follow the pattern outlined in the idealized model of decision making. The lack of clear-cut information complicates the task of estimating the consequences of actions. The amorphous nature of national security goals provide equally amorphous guidelines for weighing various alternatives. In short, the foreign policy decision maker has difficulty in determining the consequence of a particular action as well as determining the value of that consequence even if it were to occur.

Added to these difficulties is the general nature of foreign policy decision making, that there is more to lose than to gain in any given situation. As Dean Rusk has said, when asked if he was going to solve the Berlin crisis, "No, I'm not quite that vain. But I do want to go down in history as one of the Secretaries of State who succeeded in passing the Berlin crisis on to his successor!"[13] The statement "politics is the art of the feasible" also clearly expresses the commonly held notion that it is the decision maker's job to achieve both physical and political survival rather than to construct a new world. For this reason, we can assume that for the foreign policy decision maker the characteristic pattern of choosing alternatives is to take risks that involve low negative consequences and a high probability of success. Like horserace betting, such choices also produce low gains.

Risk taking in foreign policy decision making, then, usually involves choosing an alternative the failure of which will not have dire consequences. As a result, foreign policy decision making is at best incremental; which means that changes in foreign policy occur slowly and in small steps. The big gamble is uncommon because the fear of loss is usually greater than the expectation of gain.

It would be a mistake, however, to assume that the big gamble never occurs. Superficial knowledge of history indicates that although moderation appears to be the rule, instances of high-risk policies have occurred. The foreign policies of Napoleon and Hitler, for example, are classic examples. Sometimes high risks cannot be avoided, as in most crisis situations. In the 1962 Cuban missile crisis, for example, President Kennedy did not necessarily seek to take great risks but he felt that he had no other choice, given the Soviet decision to send missiles to Cuba. Although not characteristic of the large majority of foreign policy decisions, then, high risks are sometimes taken in foreign policy actions.

Personality factors often play a role in risk-taking behavior. An illustration is found in the behavior of Woodrow Wilson, as analyzed by Alexander and Juliette George.[14] The Georges found that Wilson's personality characteristics affected his decision to force the Versailles Treaty and the League of Nations Covenant through the Senate without revision. Let us say that Wilson had two alternatives with respect to ratification of the Treaty and Covenant: (1) accepting moderate revision and increasing the chance of getting Senate approval (lowering the risk but also, according to

---

[13] Quoted in Hilsman, *To Move a Nation,* p. 41.

[14] Alexander L. George and Juliette L. George, *Woodrow Wilson and Colonel House* (New York: Dover Publications, 1956).

his viewpoint, the utility), and (2) forcing the unrevised documents through the Senate (high risk with what Wilson considered higher utility). According to the Georges, Wilson chose the second alternative not because he was an idealist and believed in playing long odds (many argue that the revised version would not have been much different from the unrevised one anyway) but because he was driven by a feeling to prove himself. They write:

> He could brook no interference. *His* will must prevail, if he wished it to. He bristled at the slightest challenge to his authority. Such a characteristic might well have represented a rebellion against the domination of his father, whose authority he had never dared openly challenge.[15]

This discussion of Wilson is included merely for illustration. Many interpretations of Wilson's behavior have been expressed, some arguing that he was a thorough idealist, always taking long risks, while others argue that he was actually a realist, taking what he considered to be very few risks. As in the case of Dulles, the example of Wilson raises certain questions for the student of foreign policy behavior. How typical is Wilson's behavior of that of foreign policy decision makers? And how does one identify the risk-taking patterns exhibited by a particular decision maker? Even in such a well-studied case as Woodrow Wilson's, controversy still exists over the degree of risk taking in his decision patterns.

Even more important than methodological and substantive points about the relationship between risk-taking behavior and personality is the question of the psychological health of foreign policy decision makers. Forced to work long hours under extraordinary stress, these individuals are not immune to physical and mental breakdown. In a study of the role of psychological factors in foreign policy behavior, Joseph H. De Rivera argues that personality difficulties are often found in high governmental circles. In addition to Wilson, he discusses Joseph Stalin and James Forrestal, the first American Secretary of Defense, both of whom exhibited a variety of psychological abnormalities. De Rivera deplores the fact that

> . . . when we remember that strokes, doses of tranquilizers, and many other medicinal drugs have psychological side effects, we may well be puzzled by the fact that less provision is made for detecting and helping psychological problems in public officials than in private industrial managers.[16]

[15] *Woodrow Wilson*, p. 11.
[16] Joseph H. De Rivera, *The Psychological Dimension of Foreign Policy* (Columbus, Ohio: Charles E. Merrill, 1968), p. 206.

Psychological factors, therefore, should not only be of interest to us in explaining foreign policy hehavior; they should also be viewed as vital to the future of mankind.

ORGANIZATIONAL FACTORS IN FOREIGN POLICY DECISION MAKING

To understand foreign policy decision-making behavior, not only is it important to examine the intellectual problems facing the foreign policy decision maker and the psychological factors affecting him, but it is also important to understand the impact of the organizational setting in which he works. The foreign policy decision maker operates within a set of organized roles. He might be President, Premier, or the head of the foreign office (Secretary of State in the United States), or he might be an advisor to one of the top decision makers. It is also possible that he occupies a lesser position somewhere in the foreign policy bureaucracy. In any case, he is affected by the general organizational structure in which he works; that is, by the flow of communications and the social interaction within the organization.

In this section, we will examine the general characteristics of decision making in large-scale organizations as well as the particular impact of organizational factors on the foreign policy decision maker. Again, we will organize our discussion around the four tasks of decision making to assess the impact of large-scale organizations on both general and foreign policy decision making.

One might assume that the view of decision making as a rational intellectual process can be more closely approximated in large-scale organizations such as the foreign policy bureaucracy. Theoretically, the vast support of an organized set of people should multiply the eyes and ears and increase the intellectual powers of the decision maker so that he can better evaluate conditions and goals in order to reach the "proper" decisions. On the contrary, our study of decision making in the foreign policy bureaucracy will reveal a number of conditions that make rational decision making as difficult as it is for the individual acting alone. The difficulties, however, are of a different kind and magnitude.

Defining the Situation

One of the prime functions of any foreign policy bureaucracy is to supply decision makers with information about the international environment. The image the foreign policy decision maker has of that environment is to a large extent formed and maintained by information supplied by intelligence-gathering operations of the bureaucracy. Whether the intelligence is produced by the foreign office, the military service, or a general intelligence service such as the U.S. Central Intelligence Agency, it plays a large role in the decision makers' view of the world.

Many factors that characterize the development of images about the environment in most large-scale organizations also operate in foreign policy bureaucracies. Viewpoints and even information that conflict with previous images are often ignored or forgotten because the intelligence services want to remain "relevant" to the decision makers. Even more frequently, the vast amount of information supplied is rarely digested by the upper-level decision makers. In fact, the foreign policy bureaucracy may be viewed as a large set of filters through which information about the international environment is "refined" for the decision maker's use, and the refining process is often one of shaping the incoming information to fit the user's preexisting images. A classic example of the tendency to cling to past images is the U.S. State Department's use of the phrase "Sino-Soviet bloc" long after the Soviet Union and Communist China ceased to cooperate militarily. Arthur M. Schlesinger, Jr., an advisor to President Kennedy, notes that State Department officials continued to use the phrase two years after there was clear evidence that relations between the two states were highly hostile.[17]

In times of crisis, the role of the bureaucracy in filtering information is particularly crucial. De Rivera reports that prior to North Korea's attack on South Korea, a cable from the American Ambassador in South Korea warned of the buildup of North Korean forces along the 38th parallel. The cable was ignored because it was viewed by the Assistant Secretary for Far Eastern Affairs as a supporting argument for the Ambassador's previously stated contention that the South Korean army should be fortified through American aid.[18] This incident reveals the enormous effect organizational structure can have on defining the situation; the Assistant Secretary and his staff acted as a filter by assuming that the information did not imply a serious threat of North Korean attack and by failing to pass the information with the proper emphasis up to higher-level decision makers.

Realizing the tendency for the bureaucracy to present a biased view of the world, foreign policy decision makers often seek to tap outside sources. University experts, local newspapers, and even personal friends are frequently employed as alternative sources of information. However, these sources are also likely to be working under certain biases, although not the same ones as the bureaucracy. Moreover, in crisis situations, the regular

---

[17] Arthur M. Schlesinger, Jr., *A Thousand Days: John F. Kennedy in the White House* (Boston: Houghton Mifflin, 1965), p. 415.

[18] De Rivera, *Psychological Dimension of Foreign Policy,* p. 19.

bureaucratic channels for gathering information must be relied upon, particularly at the precrisis and early crisis stages.

Selecting Goals

Selection of foreign policy goals is not usually considered to be the legitimate function of the foreign policy bureaucracy. In both domestic and autocratic states, political leaders theoretically representing the will of the society are the agents who articulate foreign policy goals. Nevertheless, because the foreign policy bureaucracy needs these goals to organize its activities, it plays some role in their selection.

We can assume that the process of selecting goals in a foreign policy bureaucracy is similar to that in any large-scale organization. Goals help to build consensus within the bureaucracy by giving a general direction to administrative personnel; as a result, goals are usually broadly defined and relatively stable over a long period.

The "Containment of Communism" is an example of the broadly defined and enduring nature of foreign policy goals. Although articulated in the late 1940's, Containment represented more of a general predisposition toward the Soviet Union than a foreign policy. For example, it was not clear prior to 1950 that the United States would consider it necessary to defend South Korea from North Korea in order to contain Communism. Because of its general character, Containment has been a primary goal of American foreign policy ever since the late 1940's without precluding a wide variety of American foreign policy activities. Like any large-scale organization, then, foreign policy bureaucracies often employ highly general but long-standing formal goals.

While the formal statement of foreign policy goals remains the same from year to year, however, the actual goals which appear to be organizing the behavior of the foreign policy bureaucracy are frequently left undefined. On the one hand, this provides a certain degree of necessary flexibility so that administrative officials can handle matters as they arise. On the other hand, it produces a plurality of activities which on the whole often appear inconsistent. American foreign policy toward Latin America, for example, appears to contain conflicting components: it combines support for conservative forces within the Latin American republics with economic developmental aid often aimed at increasing the wealth of the poorer classes.

Although a certain amount of pluralism exists in all large-scale organizations, it has a more pervasive effect in the foreign policy bureaucracy. Unlike business organizations, which ultimately measure their success by the objective standard of profits foreign policy bureaucracies cannot easily tell when and where they succeed. Hence, individual initiative is apt to go unnoticed and unrewarded because other members of the bureaucracy or those to whom the bureaucracy is responsible will have different standards or implicit goals with which to judge the innovative action. Whether this will result in more or less innovative behavior—more because the plurality of interpretations of goals and the chances that different interpretations will go unnoticed; less because there is no reward for innovative behavior and the fear of pursuing an incorrect goal is great—probably depends upon the individuals and societies involved.

Searching for Alternatives

The search for alternatives in the foreign policy bureaucracy is limited by factors that operate in almost all large-scale bureaucracies. Large-scale organizations are usually departmentalized along some functional line, which means that new conditions must be defined and dealt with by units designed to cope with old conditions. Furthermore, the units in the organization often guard their existing functional competences while attempting to acquire new ones. Bureaucratic imperialism is a product of the drive by leaders of a particular department to increase their departmental budget.

Generally speaking, the overall effect of these tendencies is to make large-scale organizations more "satisficing" than "maximizing" in their search for alternatives. Although most modern large-scale organizations—whether governmental or business—realize the importance of planning, which in effect is a systematic search for alternatives, the overwhelming majority of resources go into the execution of specific activities. Long-range planning is often performed by one department that still must compete with other departments in the organization for funds and for the attention of the top decision maker. Hence, the vast resources necessary to explore a wide variety of alternatives are rarely available. Moreover, as decision problems increase in complexity, the range of alternatives is usually radically narrowed down at the outset. Consequently, alternatives are eliminated before the problem has received adequate study. Hence, radical alternatives stand less chance of surviving the initial narrowing-down stage.

The search for alternatives in foreign policy bureaucracies takes place under conditions similar to those operating in most large-scale organizations. Groups within the bureaucracy become champions of certain policies; this makes even the inevitable questioning that results from a general search for alternatives highly suspect. Members of the bureaucracy stake their career on certain policies; this makes them unwilling to consider radical alternatives.

A classic illustration of the refusal of a foreign policy bureaucracy to seriously consider a broad set of alternatives is American foreign policy towards Communist China between 1952 and 1968. Following a policy of isolating Communist China as much as possible from other states, members of the American foreign policy bureaucracy have been particularly steadfast on this issue. We can assume that a large share of this refusal to explore radical alternatives is a product of the failure of American foreign policy in China in the 1940's and the resulting attack by Senator Joseph McCarthy on the State Department. Unwilling to risk opening old wounds, members of the American foreign policy bureaucracy have maintained steady pressure on foreign policy decision makers to continue the same policy towards Communist China.

Given the high vulnerability to attacks based on past policy failures, foreign policy bureaucracies tend to subscribe to the following statement of an American career diplomat:

> . . . there were few or no new ideas, bold or otherwise, that would solidly produce the dramatic changes then sought . . . bold ideas and actions were personally dangerous and could lead to congressional investigations and public disgrace.[19]

This attitude toward innovation—the exploring of new and radically different alternatives—might be viewed as the healthy skepticism of experienced public servants, but it may also be viewed as part of the conservative influence foreign policy bureaucracies exert on the search for foreign policy alternatives.

Choosing Alternatives

Foreign policy bureaucracies usually choose alternatives that do not break radically from the past and that do not involve high risk. Members of this bureaucracy enjoy greater longevity in their positions than most high-level decision makers. This longevity creates tension between foreign policy decision makers who might wish to introduce a radically different policy and members of the permanent bureaucracy who see such breaks with the past as at least a threat to their positions, if not an implied criticism of performance. This is particularly true in foreign policy bureaucracies where the attitude persists that nonmembers of the bureaucracy do not understand the "real" problem. John Davies, a career diplomat for the United States, expressed the attitude of many members of the bureaucracy when he said that outside foreign policy decision makers often exhibit "crusading activism touched with naiveté."[20]

While the foreign policy bureaucracy might not openly fight a foreign policy decision maker seeking to introduce a revolutionary policy, it can

---

[19] Quoted in Schlesinger, *A Thousand Days,* p. 431.
[20] *A Thousand Days,* p. 431.

greatly affect the course of that policy in its subsequent actions. Because the bureaucracy implements the general policy decisions through a series of administrative decisions in specific cases, it can slowly alter the policy to suit its views. The reason for this is not merely a product of recalcitrance among the members of the foreign policy bureaucracy. It also results from the relative autonomy enjoyed by administrative officials within that bureaucracy, particularly in the overseas missions. Separated by time, space, and an entirely different cultural-political milieu from their home office, the ambassador and his staff have to apply general policy directives developed in the home office to specific situations which the original framers of the policy guidelines probably never anticipated. Hence, even if administrative officials in the foreign policy bureaucracy were finally committed to the policies made at the top, significant slippage would occur. When they are not in agreement, even greater divergence from the high-level decisions takes place.

In addition to dealing with an organization that tends to resist new policy alternatives, the foreign policy decision maker frequently confronts conflicting opinion on policy choices from within the bureaucracy itself. American foreign policy toward China may again be used as an example of this point. As Haas and Whiting point out,

> . . . the Departments of State and Defense, after 1949, differed sharply in their evaluations of the military and political power of the exiled Kuomintang regime on Formosa, and on the importance to American strategy of Syngman Rhee's South Korean government. Defense wished to withdraw from Korea and support Formosa; State argued for—and obtained—commitment in Korea in 1950 and a momentary reduction of aid to Chiang.[21]

Differences of opinion—not only between the State Department and the Department of Defense but also within the two departments played a large role in post-World War II American foreign policy towards China.

The product resulting from such conflicts within the bureaucracy also often contributes in the long run to the choice of conservative foreign policy alternatives. Realizing that differences of opinions exist, foreign policy decision makers find it difficult to plan radical alternatives. Their desire to appease factions within the bureaucracy frequently leads to compromise on foreign policy choices. Hence, even when unsettled on a particular issue, foreign policy bureaucracies tend to contribute to conservative choices. Innovation, if it occurs at all, usually occurs in a series of small or incremental steps. Together with the intellectual difficulties inherent in the tasks of foreign policy decision making and the psychological

---

[21] Ernst Haas and Allen S. Whiting, *Dynamics of International Relations* (New York: McGraw-Hill, 1956), p. 269.

factors which we can assume operate on the decision maker, the dynamics of organizational behavior contribute to moderate foreign policies. Although these pressures can be and have been overcome, particularly by extraordinary leadership, incrementalism rather than revolution remains the characteristic pattern of most foreign policy decision making.

We have implied that the foreign policy decision maker is a prisoner of his own bureaucracy and that the bureaucracy will generally lead him to accept moderate images, goals and policy alternatives. In most cases, this is probably true, although the variation for different states under different circumstances is great. However, like the decision maker in any large-scale organization, it is possible for the foreign policy decision maker to escape the prison set up by his bureaucracy. He can bring in new appointees whom he hopes will reshape the bureaucracy rather than being reshaped by it. He can reorganize the existing machinery to create more dynamic units. Or, he might set up an alternative bureaucracy, as some think President Kennedy did when he created a White House Staff that handled much of the foreign policy decision making early in the 1960's. Finally, he can inaugurate policies that have enough vitality and appeal to engender support from within the bureaucracy even if the bureaucracy itself would not have originated the policies.

An even greater chance for change, particularly in terms of circumventing the bureaucracy's moderating effect, is provided by the role crises play in foreign policy decision making. As pointed out earlier, it appears that most foreign policy crises are not handled through normal channels in the bureaucracy but rather through an *ad hoc* group of trusted advisors. Both the decision to intervene in Korea[22] and the Cuban missile crisis were handled in such a manner.[23] A crisis decision can be more radical than would otherwise be possible, because the foreign policy decision maker is able to confront the bureaucracy with a *fait accompli*.

SUMMARY

This picture of foreign policy decision making contrasts sharply with the view of rational decision making as purely an intellectual problem-solving process. The foreign policy decision maker cannot pursue the tasks of making decisions as if he were a professor of international politics gather-

[22] See Glenn D. Paige, *The Korean Decision: June 24–30 1950* (New York: Free Press, 1968), pp. 281–87.

[23] See Ole R. Holsti, Richard A. Brody, and Robert C. North, "Measuring Affect and Action in International Reaction Models: Empirical Materials from the 1962 Cuban Missile Crisis," *Peace Research Society (International) Papers,* Vol. 2 (1965), pp. 170–90.

TABLE 1

Limitations of the Rational Model in Describing Foreign Policy Problem Solving

	Intellectual Difficulties	Psychological Limitations	Organizational Limitations
Definition of the situation	Inability to gather and analyze information about the international environment	Relatively closed images prevents adjusting to new conditions	Organizations filter information which contributes to static view of environment
Selecting goals	Lack of explicit criteria for measuring success	Personal motivations color national goals	Amorphous goals which provide little direction and remain static
Searching for alternatives	Limitations on seriously exploring all alternatives	Attachment to traditional alternatives to provide structure to fluid situation	Departmentalization of bureaucracy and the press of daily business makes extensive search impossible
Choosing alternatives	Difficult to assess correct payoff utilities and estimate proper probabilities	Commitment to a course of action as a result of personal needs	Competing bureaucratic units necessitate compromise decisions on the part of the decision maker

ing data on international conditions and a professor of logic applying a set of ordered preferences. He cannot afford the luxury of exploring every available policy alternative, and he does not possess the capability of correctly estimating the probability of success of different policy choices. He differs from the rational problem-solving decision maker—if such a one could possibly exist—because he is a human being operating within a set of organizational roles and attempting to affect an emotion-laden but nevertheless ambiguous environment.

Table 1 shows the limitations of the rational problem-solving model in explaining foreign policy decision-making behavior by listing the major intellectual, psychological, and organizational limitations on the successful performance of the four ideal tasks around which we have organized the chapter.

Our general conclusion is that the overall impact of these limitations is to make foreign policy decision making more moderate than it would be if it were done by a rational problem solver. That is, foreign policy decision makers tend to avoid new interpretations of the environment, to select and act upon traditional goals, to limit the search for alternatives to a small number of moderate ones, and finally to take risks which involve low costs if they prove unsuccessful. Although we have emphasized that certain personality features and leadership styles vis-à-vis the organization might result in a foreign policy decision maker who makes radically different interpretations of the environment, selects revolutionary goals, explores hitherto unheard-of alternatives, and takes big risks, such a decision maker would be an exception rather than the rule.

SUMMARY OUTLINE

I. Foreign policy decision making is an important focus for the study of international politics and can be viewed in terms of an intellectual process, a psychological process, and an organizational process.

II. Foreign policy consists of a number of activities and can be classified into three types: general policy, administrative decisions, and crisis decisions.

    A. General foreign policy consists of a series of decisions, often only indirectly related to each other.

    B. Foreign policy decisions on the administrative level are made by low-level officials regarding specific conditions bounded by scope, time, and space.

    C. Crisis foreign policy decisions usually involve specific conditions with long-range consequences in which the participants feel a sense of urgency, threat, time constraint, and surprise.

    D.   The three types of foreign policy decisions are interdependent.

III.   Foreign policy decision making can be examined in terms of a rational problem-solving model to assess specific intellectual difficulties inherent in making foreign policy.

    A.   The rational problem-solving model prescribes the four related steps of defining the situation, selecting goals, searching for alternatives, and choosing alternatives.

    B.   *Defining the situation existing in the international environment is difficult because the large amount of complexity and necessary information leads to uncertainty.*

    C.   *Foreign policy goals are generally amorphous, which makes the ranking of goals and the definition of criteria of success almost impossible.*

    D.   *The uncertainty over the international environment and the amorphousness of foreign policy goals tend to create unlimited foreign policy alternatives, which can only be partially assessed.*

    E.   *Choosing a foreign policy alternative takes place under conditions of uncertainity about the environment as well as goals.*

IV.   Psychological factors that operate on all foreign policy decision makers make the rational problem-solver model unrealistic.

    A.   Images are a crucial part of foreign policy decision making.

    B.   *Foreign policy images about the international environment tend to be closed not only because of the general psychological factors, which breed closed images, but also because (1) there are political costs to altering foreign policy images; (2) lack of information concerning the international environment breeds insecurity, and hence a tendency to be inflexible; and (3) crisis conditions do not allow for flexibility in defining conditions.*

    C.   *Under conditions where the signal-to-noise ratio is high, international events can alter decision makers' images of the international environment.*

    D.   *Personality characteristics such as intelligence, self-esteem, and tolerance for ambiguity affect the images foreign policy decision makers have of the international environment.*

    E.   *Foreign policy decision makers have high need for power and achievement: this has the effect of focusing their attention on national security concerns and reinforcing their desire to avoid clear policy reversals.*

    F.   *Foreign policy decision makers follow a satisficing pattern in*

*searching for policy alternatives, and depend heavily on their
sense of history to narrow down alternatives.*

   G. *Foreign policy decision makers usually opt for low-risk alternatives.*

   H. *Foreign policy decision makers under strong and often abnormal
personality pressure often pursue high-risk policy alternatives.*

V. Organizational factors play a large role in foreign policy decision
making.

   A. *The foreign policy bureaucracy acts as a filter by supplying information that confirms existing images about the international
environment.*

   B. *The foreign policy bureaucracy tends to develop highly general
and static foreign policy goals.*

   C. *The foreign policy bureaucracy tends to avoid exploring a wide
range of foreign policy alternatives, particularly if a current
policy is a reaction to prior foreign policy failure.*

   D. *The foreign policy bureaucracy tends to pressure for choices of
low-risk foreign policy alternatives not only at the formulation
stage but also in the execution stage through low-level administrative decisions.*

   E. *Foreign policy change, if it occurs at all, tends to occur incrementally rather than through major policy reversals.*

   F. *Foreign policy decision makers can overcome the moderating
pressure of the bureaucracy through reorganization, the introduction of new personnel, dependence upon other institutions
or groups, and gaining the bureaucracy's support through new
programs or during crisis.*

BIBLIOGRAPHICAL ESSAY

Analysis of foreign policy is undertaken at one time or another by almost
every scholar in the field of international politics. Textbooks are written on
the foreign policy of a particular state and articles are produced on
particular aspects of foreign policy. In spite of the extensive writings, until
recently little concern has been given to explicit development of concepts
and proposition. The primary reason for this is many writers on foreign
policy fail to separate the four types of analysis we discussed in Chapter 1.
They make the implicit assumption that foreign policy decision making *is*
or *should be* rational problem solving rather than a product of interaction
of psychological and organizational forces with domestic and international
environments. They try to reconstruct the foreign policies of a state by

examining its view of the environment; its goals, values, and objectives; and its choice of strategies through an intuitive survey of the foreign policy statements and actions of the state. See, for example, Reitzel, Kaplan, and Coblenz (331) and Kissinger (224). Instead of dwelling on the supporting evidence, their interpretations of the state's foreign policy, scholars frequently follow another course of analysis. They examine the logical consistency of the policies and decide whether or not the images they have attributed to the foreign policy decision maker correspond to their own images of the international environment. Although this type of analysis is legitimate, it fails to acknowledge the difficulties one faces in trying to perform descriptive analysis of the foreign politics of states; as a result, the literature is poor in concepts that might yield operational definitions and propositions for testing.

Another type of analysis assumes foreign policy decision making is an ideal problem solving activity. This is found in policy analysis in other areas of political science. However, starting with Simon (376), continuing through the debate between Banfield (23) and Simon (377), the work of Cyert and March (90), as well as Lindblom (249) and Braybrooke and Lindblom (44), writers have examined the relationship between two views of decision making—as a rationalized problem-solving activity and as a product of interaction among social, psychological, and environmental factors in the general study of policy formation. Most of these authors are summarized in a group of readings by Alexis and Wilson (4). Particular attention has been paid to the contrast between what Braybrooke and Lindblom (44) called the synoptic (maximizing) approaches pictured in the traditional writings and the disjointed incrementalism (satisficing) approaches that actually take place. This change of focus is relevant for foreign policy study because most analysis in the field continues to assume that foreign policy decision making *is* or *should be* rationalistic maximizing, rather than the behavior it usually is (and, given the conditions, usually has to be).

Building on insights of Simon and others on decision making in general, Snyder, Bruck, and Sapin (389) in their 1954 essay, "Decision-Making as an Approach to the Study of International Politics" attempted to provide a framework that would allow for better descriptive analysis of foreign policy decision making. McClosky's criticism of that essay also appears in the 1962 Snyder-Bruck-Sapin volume (389). Condensed and refined later in a much briefer essay by Robinson and Snyder, in the Kelman collection (215), the framework is essentially a checklist of factors that must be taken into consideration when analyzing foreign policy decision making. Although the framework has been explicitly applied only to the U.S. decision to intervene in Korea—Snyder and Paige in (389) and

Paige (308)—it has been generally recognized as a valuable contribution to the study of foreign policy decision making. Except for the possibility that an essay on a foreign policy approach by Brody, in the Harvey work (161) and Rosenau in Farrell (124) might serve as a general framework sometime in the future (see also Chapter 5), most other attempts to develop a general approach to the study of foreign policy have not been developed beyond the original work. Examples are Modelski (282), Haas and Whiting (149), Frankel (128), and Gross (142). However, if nothing else, the impact of Simon as well as Snyder, Bruck, and Sapin has been to suggest looking at psychological and organizational factors in foreign policy decision making—even though attempts to do so are rare.

Building on the literature of general decision making, social scientists not only from political science but from psychology as well have attempted to examine psychological and organizational factors in foreign policy decision making. Among those who have attempted to provide a framework, particularly for the role of psychology in foreign policy making, are Kelman in (215), Verba in (231), and Stagner (394). Two recent books on foreign policy are particularly important in this respect. In one, De Rivera (97), a psychologist, makes an explicit attempt to apply organizational and psychological concepts and assumptions to case materials on foreign policy decisions. The other is written by two experts on the Soviet Union, Triska and Finley (406) who examine both the organizational environment and the psychological predispositions of foreign policy decision makers in the Soviet Union. Many writers examine foreign policy in the framework of psychological concepts. Verba in (231) offers an excellent study of elements of rationality and nonrationality in foreign policy decision making. The role of elite and foreign policy decision maker attitudes and personality are examined by Haas and Whiting (149), Singer (380), Lindholm (250), Jensen (192), Raser (330), Galtung in Rosenau (347), and George (138). Additional studies are Holsti (180) and Boulding (41) on images in foreign policy; D'Amato (92) on personality categories; George and George (139), White in (215) and Holsti (180) on personality analysis; and Jervis (196) on the concept of misperception. Finally Argyris (14) has combined psychological concepts with techniques he developed for business organizations and applied them to the role of organizational environment in the U.S. State Department while Allison (10) has used bureaucratic and other models in analyzing the Cuban missile crisis.

Despite the beginnings of a crossdisciplinary literature on foreign policy decision making and the conceptual work of Snyder, Bruck, and Sapin, studies of foreign policy decision making remain primarily traditional description thoroughly mixed with prescriptions. With a few exceptions, the study of the definition of the international environment is examined under the rubric of intelligence gathering or images. For the former, see Hilsman (172), Kent (220) and Sapin (363), pp. 287–328; for the latter, the entire issue of *Journal of International Affairs,* Vol. 21 (1967), No. 1. Exceptions are Pruitt in (215), who uses the concept of definition of the situation, and Wohlstetter (425) who employs the concept of information signals from the environment to study United States policy prior to Pearl Harbor. Foreign policy goals and values have been examined almost exclusively in the framework of doctrinal implications, as in Osgood (303). Studies of foreign policy bureaucracies, particularly for the United States and Great Britain, are available. See especially the Wriston article in (319), Elder (116), Hammond (155), Bishop (35), and Sapin (363). Crisis foreign policy is examined by a number of writers with methodological and theoretical perspectives running from the Snyder-Bruck-Sapin view in (308) to the more traditional case analysis in Buchan (57) and Cleveland (75). For an analysis of the consideration of alternatives and the patterns of choice-making in foreign policy making—one exception is Triska and Finley (406)—one has to examine materials written in relation to particular historical events as, for example, Sorensen (390) for the Cuban missile crisis; but these works usually do not provide an analysis of the patterns of alternative search and choice in foreign policy decision making. Finally, the role of foreign policy leadership is examined in McLelland's work in (174), Bowie in (319), and Sapin (363).

3

Domestic Politics and the Making of Foreign Policy

George F. Kennan, an American diplomat, historian, and foreign policy analyst, describes in his *Memoirs* one of the first lessons he learned about American foreign policy:

> . . . the tendency to make statements and take actions with regard not to their affect on the international scene to which they are ostensibly addressed, but rather to their effect on those echelons of American opinion, congressional opinion first and foremost, to which the respective statesmen are anxious to appeal. The question, in these circumstances, became not: how effective is what I am doing in terms of the impact it makes on our world environment? but rather: how do I look, in the mirror of domestic American opinion, as I do it? Do I look shrewd, determined, defiantly patriotic, imbued with the necessary vigilance before the wiles of foreign governments? If so, this is what I do, even though it may prove meaningless, or even counterproductive, when applied to the realities of the external situation.[1]

Notwithstanding the hyperbole of Kennan's remarks and the implication that American foreign policy makers are particularly subject to such criticisms, this lesson is one that every student of international politics should learn well. One key to understanding any state's foreign policy is understanding of the impact of domestic politics on the formulation of foreign policy.

In this chapter, we are faced for the first time with the need to develop a set of concepts to deal with a wide range of political conditions. Unlike

---

[1] George F. Kennan, *Memoirs: 1925–1950* (Boston: Little, Brown, 1967), p. 53.

our discussion of foreign policy decision-making behavior, which assumed that the way individuals act in decision-making roles is constant for different states,[2] our examination of the role of domestic politics in foreign policy making will assume that substantial crossnational variety does exist. Our discussion of the impact of domestic politics on foreign policy making must, therefore, permit crossnational or comparative generalizations; that is, to allow for a meaningful discussion of the various patterns in the more than one hundred and forty states in the contemporary world.[3]

To say that we must approach the study of the role of domestic politics in foreign policy making from a crossnational viewpoint, however, is not to say that we cannot employ a single set of concepts or conceptual framework. In fact, because political conditions in different states vary, it is necessary to employ one set of concepts. By applying the same concepts to different phenomena, we can build a classification scheme that will provide us with an overview of similarities and differences in the relationship of domestic politics to foreign policy making.

The conceptual framework for this chapter focuses on the relationship between foreign policy decision makers and those domestic political actors who attempt to influence their foreign-policy behavior. We will call these political actors "policy influencers"; the relationship between them and the foreign policy decision makers we will call the "policy-influence system." By viewing the role of domestic politics in foreign policy making as the interaction between decision makers and policy influencers, we hope to provide a sufficiently broad and meaningful framework to permit crossnational generalizations that will explain both similarities and differences in the domestic political processes that produce foreign policy.

Several words of warning to the reader are in order. First, it will become apparent that while the distinction between the policy influencers and the decision makers is useful for purposes of discussion, it sometimes is difficult to make in practice. Often the same individuals—particularly in foreign policy bureaucracy—play both policy-influencing and decision-

---

[2] Although this assumption is never explicit in Chapter 2, the reader should be aware it clearly underlies the theoretical structure of the chapter. There is some reason to believe that the cultural differences throughout the world affect the decision-making styles of people; however, evidence to the contrary and supportive of the assumption underlying Chapter 2 can also be found. At any rate, the more pertinent question would be *how much* of an impact cultural differences have on foreign policy decision making. We have assumed the impact is not sufficient to make the discussion of a foreign policy decision maker for all nations useful.

[3] We use the term crossnational and comparative interchangeably in this context because we are comparing the foreign policies of different nations. However, in general political science, it is not necessary that comparative studies be only crossnational, since different political units or actors within the same society may be examined.

making roles. Second, the existing literature on the role of domestic politics in foreign policy making does not frequently attempt to make crossnational generalizations. Most of it focuses on a particular state or a particular foreign policy issue, and does not contain the conceptual framework necessary to develop comparative generalizations on the role of domestic politics in foreign policy making.[4] Consequently, the categories developed in this chapter should be viewed as a rudimentary attempt to develop the *kind* of conceptual framework necessary for crossnational research. Finally, because the material covered is broad and previous scholarly work is scarce, the chapter is most concerned with clearly developing a set of categories to aid the student in evaluating the role of domestic politics in foreign policy making. The propositions that appear throughout the chapter should be viewed as speculative suggestions about how the various categories may be related and how a conceptual framework may be employed to make crossnational generalizations.

Given these considerations, the best way for the reader to approach this chapter is to view it as a "pre-theory." Developed by James N. Rosenau, the term "pre-theory" refers to a tentative set of categories or concepts formulated with preliminary relationships; that is, a beginning point from which more useful concepts and theories can be formulated.[5] Although it would be better to present the beginning student with more firmly constructed concepts and propositions—tested by constant usage and empirical data—the development of this particular aspect of international relations literature does not permit such a treatment. With this in mind, the reader should be able to learn not only about the relationship between domestic politics and foreign policy making in different states but also about the way such a relationship can be studied on a comparative basis.

We will begin the chapter with a discussion of the concept of the policy-influence system—both its analytical features and its historical development. The focus will then shift to policy influencers with emphasis on different types of policy influencers and the manner in which they operate in different political systems. The remainder of the chapter will be primarily concerned with two processes in the policy-influence system: (1) how policy influencers develop images of the international environment, and (2) how they interact with decision makers in certain foreign policy issue areas.

---

[4] The bibliographical essay that refers to this chapter explores existing studies on the role of domestic politics in foreign policy making.

[5] James N. Rosenau, "Pre-Theories and Theories of Foreign Policy," in *Approaches to Comparative and International Politics,* ed. R. Barry Farrell (Evanston, Ill.: Northwestern University Press, 1966), pp. 27–93.

THE NATURE OF THE POLICY-INFLUENCE SYSTEM

The policy-influence system of any state may be viewed as a set of reciprocal and highly complex relationships between the decision makers and their policy influencers. On the one hand, the decision maker needs policy influencers because they are a source of support for his regime.[6] In both democratic and autocratic states, the leaders depend to a large extent on the willingness of the members of society to provide support. Whether this support takes the form of the loyalty of the army, the financial backing of businessmen, the electoral support of the people, or the willingness of the people not to take up arms against their government, it is vital to the decision maker because it makes his stay in office more certain and provides him with the resources to carry out his policies.

On the other hand, the policy influencers—whether foreign or domestic—make demands upon the decision maker. The demands may be for better roads, in the case of domestic policy, or "respect from other nations," in the case of foreign policy. If these demands are not satisfied in one way or another, partial or total withdrawal of support is likely. The demands are expressed in democracies by vote; in autocratic states, by other, nonpublic means. If demands go unsatisfied and increase in number and intensity, support from influencers is less easy to obtain. Of course, the decision maker does not always have to respond positively to demands. He may reject them and convince the influencers that the demands need not be filled. Decision makers, however, ultimately reach a limit on the extent to which they can ignore these demands. Hence, while demands and supports are not always balanced, policy makers must satisfy at least minimal demands.

We have made the assumption that some interaction between decision makers and influencers exists in every state. This assumption should not be taken to mean that all nations are democratic or that all leaders follow their people's desires. On the contrary, leaders often respond to the demands of their supporters with propaganda rather than with policies. Rather, the above assumption means that in every state some people and groups are capable of withholding or supplying support; decision makers deal with them in some way.

We might point out that the more democratic the state, the greater the number of people to whom the leaders tend to listen. Because democracy

---

[6] The concepts of demands and supports are used by a number of writers who have developed general schemes of political systems. See, for example, David Easton, *A Systems Analysis of Political Life* (New York: John Wiley, 1965), pp. 37–247.

means, among other things, elections, anybody who votes has some capacity to command the attention of the decision maker even though in many cases the capacity is small. In autocratic states, the policy influencers are limited to a few very powerful individuals who control important organizations such as the army. Although every leader has some policy influencers with whom to be concerned, there is a large variation in the number and types of policy influencer, depending on the nature and size of the political system.

A BRIEF HISTORICAL OVERVIEW

The nature of the interaction between official decision makers of a state and its policy influencers has changed radically as the state has developed as a form of political organization. Because the European state has served as a historical antecedent for states of the contemporary world, a brief overview of the evolution of its policy-influence systems might be instructive for understanding the role of contemporary policy-influence systems.

One can trace the development of the system back to the feudal period when the king represented the official decision maker and the nobility were his prime policy influencers. However, during the feudal period the king was so weak and the nobility so strong that we might just as easily consider the king one of the policy influencers. Decisions were made on the basis of consensus among nobles and king. It was not unusual for nobility owing nominal allegiance to one king to join forces with that king's enemies. In this period,

> Loyalty was to individuals or to families, not to the state. . . . And even this personal loyalty was not wholly reliable; it was tested afresh every time there was a request for service or a demand for obedience. Political power more and more entered the domain of private law; it was a personal possession which could be transmitted by marriage or divided among heirs. Being personal, political power was difficult to exercise at a distance or through agents. Hence, there was a constant tendency for local representatives of the king to become independent rulers, a tendency aggravated by the low level of economic activity, which made each district almost self-sufficient.[7]

Hence, we might characterize the feudal period as *policy-influence dominant;* it was a period when the relationship between decision maker and policy influencers was dominated by the latter.

---

[7] Joseph R. Strayer, "The Historical Experience of Nation Building in Europe," in Karl W. Deutsch and William J. Foltz, eds., *Nation-Building* (New York: Atherton, 1966), pp. 18–19.

The state developed into the supreme political organizational form in Europe as the king and a small number of supporting leaders were able to control the nobility. Instead of being one policy influencer among a number of powerful leaders, the king became the supreme leader. He was able to maintain the upper hand in dealing with factions within his society. With most of the people widely dispersed because they were farming the land, only the landed aristocracy and the commercial classes had substantial ability to provide supports or make demands. Because the aristocracy had long since given up or been forced by technological developments to relinquish their function of providing military services, they could provide only the same thing as the commercial classes in support of the monarch— money. With both classes vying to win the king's favors with their support, neither had the option of threatening to withdraw support—the other could always fill the void.

In addition to the opportunity to play off one group of policy influencers against another, the king also became identified with his state as a symbol of national honor and prestige. As the common citizen became more aware of the world around him and more important militarily and economically in the welfare of the state, he became a more important source of support. National honor and prestige could cut across class lines, which meant that the king could benefit most because he was the "living extension of his nation." Not only was he able to check the nobility's power with the aid of the commercial classes; he was able to engender more broadly based support, particularly in times of national crisis. Although his ability to do this was extremely limited when compared to late nineteenth and twentieth century nationalistic figures, he was able to acquire some support from the forces of national identity even as early as the sixteenth century.

For these reasons, the post feudal policy-influence system was *decision-maker dominant*. It is difficult to pinpoint the exact historical period for this dominance because it occurred at different times for different states. The "age of absolutism," as it is sometimes called by historians, extended for some states as far back as the fifteenth century and continues for a few even today. However, the period between the sixteenth and the nineteenth centuries are the years that can be most readily characterized as decision-maker dominant.

Thereafter, events took place that greatly altered the supremacy of the decision maker over the policy influencers. Occurring in the technological as well as the socioeconomic-political realms, these events combined to create what may be termed the *pluralization of the policy-making process*. By this we mean the relative strength decision makers enjoyed in making foreign policy diminished because the number and importance of policy-influencer groups increased.

By the twentieth century, the leaders of states found that a large number of groups were needed for support and, hence, could make demands upon them in their formulation and execution of policy. The Wars of the French Revolution had stimulated the use of large conscript armies which in turn meant a large number of officers to lead and a supporting bureaucracy to administer the army. The industrial revolution had created the need for a large working force which in turn meant that the general populace was now beginning to concentrate in urban areas rather than be dispersed over the countryside. In addition, the industrial revolution enhanced the power of the commercial class and stimulated the growth of government bureaucracy to facilitate the integration of the diverse activities necessary to keep an industrial society functioning. Occurring simultaneously with these developments was the growth in ideas of popular government. The citizen's role in government was expanded in theory if not always in practice. Even autocratic rulers began to recognize the necessity of appearing to listen to a large number of people when making policy, and, as history would have it, appearances often become reality.

Support in the form of taxes, loans, loyalty, and intrasociety cooperation was necessary for maintenance of governmental leadership as well as stability of society. Leaders of states recognized that a mass army could maintain internal order as well as fight international wars. By the same token, that army could rise up against its own regime if part of its leadership became dissatisfied. Whether in a democracy or not, it was necessary for the entire populace to cooperate to ensure smooth functioning in the industrial society. Labor and management had to cooperate not only with leadership, but also with each other. Initially, the "cooperation" was necessarily a result of mutual satisfaction and agreement, but almost every industrial nation learned by experience that a balance among diverse interests within the society must be reached if the fabric of society were to be maintained. Starting in the nineteenth century and continuing today, all of these developments led to an enormous increase in the power of policy influencers in providing and withholding support for the decision maker.

The demands of policy influencers have also increased in scope and intensity. These demands have led to the development of political parties, which serve *inter alia* as devices for channeling demands from the general population to official decision makers of the state. Revolutionary parties have also developed in states where some portion of the population has felt that its demands could never be adequately handled without a change in regime. An almost infinite variety of issues arises out of the demands, although a number of themes are basic. In the domestic area these themes include equality of economic opportunity and of treatment under law as well as economic prosperity for the nation as a whole. In the foreign policy area they include national security and world peace. As we shall see the foreign policy demands can be much more specific than those listed above, including policies toward specific states and towards specific problems.

The increase in the number of policy-influencer demands and the ability of the policy influencers to provide support, however, has not meant the return to the policy-influencer-dominant system of the early postfeudal period. There are more powerful and more numerous policy influencers in most states today, but the decision maker has also increased his ability to deal with them. Modern governmental structures have, in most cases, been able to preserve substantial autonomy for the decision maker. Part of the reason for this is the realization among the policy influencers themselves that a certain amount of autonomy must be allowed the decision maker if he is to have any chance of dealing with the problems with which they want him to deal.

The policy-influence systems of today can best be characterized as *pluralized*. The pluralized policy-influence system is one in which both policy influencers and decision makers have increased power if only because there are more people to deal with and more activities to coordinate. It is a system where the decision maker has many tools to build a consensus for his policies among the policy influencers, and the policy influencers have the channels necessary to make their wishes heard by the decision makers. It is shaped by the same revolutions in economics, military, social organization, and ideas of popular government that have left their impact on all aspects of modern life.

THE STRUCTURE OF CONTEMPORARY POLICY-INFLUENCE SYSTEMS

In analyzing the structure of policy-influence systems and the role of those systems in the foreign policy-making process, we will introduce two sets of concepts. These concepts will provide the basic framework to analyze the role of domestic politics in the foreign policy actions of states.

The first set of concepts is based on the distinction between open and closed political systems. R. Barry Farrell writes:

> The term "open political system" will be used as synonymous with constitutional democracy. Among its characteristics are competitive regular electoral contests, legalised two- or multi-party organizations aimed at offering alternative governmental leadership, a high degree of toleration for autonomous groups in politics, and an acceptance of constitutional restraints on governmental power. Closed systems [can be characterized by the following six features]: an official ideology, a single mass party consisting of a relatively small percentage of the total population,

a system of terroristic police control, near complete party control of all means of effective mass communication, similar control of all means of armed combat, and a central control and direction of the entire economy typically including most associations and group activities.[8]

The open-closed distinction should be viewed as a continuum upon which any given state could be placed even though our discussion will be phrased in terms of open and closed systems as if any state were clearly either one or the other.

The second set of concepts comprises four categories of policy influencers, similar to four types identified by Gabriel Almond: political elites, which include elected officials and party members; administrative or bureaucratic elites; interest elites; and communications elites.[9] We will discuss the role of domestic politics in foreign policy making by distinguishing among our four types of policy influencers—(1) partisan, (2) bureaucratic, (3) interest, and (4) mass influencers. Because we distinguish between influencers and decision makers, our partisan influencer category will not contain elected officials as Almond's does except as they simultaneously play a role within their party. The concepts of bureaucratic and interest influencer are similar to Almond's categories of administrative and interest elites. We have substituted mass influencer for Almond's communications elite to emphasize the importance of what Cohen calls the "climate of opinion" within the society.[10]

We will discuss how the role of each type of policy influencer varies in open and closed political systems. Our purpose will be to provide the reader with a general overview of the relationship between domestic politics and foreign policy making by focusing on the similarities and differences in the behavior and impact of policy influencers in the foreign policies of these two political systems.

Bureaucratic Influencers

One type of policy influencer that exists in all modern states is the *bureaucratic influencer.* Given the complex functions performed by governments, large-scale organizations have developed as part of the executive branch.

---

[8] R. Barry Farrell, "Foreign Policies of Open and Closed Political Societies," in *Approaches to Comparative and International Politics,* ed. Farrell (Evanston, Ill.: Northwestern University Press, 1966), p. 168.

[9] Gabriel A. Almond, *The American People and Foreign Policy* (New York: Praeger, Inc., 1962), pp. 139–40.

[10] Bernard C. Cohen, *The Political Process and Foreign Policy: The Making of the Japanese Peace Settlement* (Princeton, N.J.: Princeton University Press, 1957), pp. 29–62.

These organizations are usually constructed along functional lines of economic policies, foreign policies, or welfare policies, although the various bureaucratic structures often overlap. We use the term "bureaucratic influencers" to designate various individuals and organizations within the executive branch of the government that aid the decision maker in making and executing policies. Often, formal organizational charts of the governments do not designate all bureaucratic influencers, since actual operating "units" might be only a segment of the formal governmental department or might cut across a number of formal departments. (The importance of organization factors in foreign policy decision making is discussed in Chapter 2.)

Because members of any bureaucracy are also sometimes part of the group that makes the decisions, it is difficult to draw a definite line separating those members of the bureaucracy who are policy influencers and those who are decision makers. This, of course, is one factor that makes bureaucratic groups so influential in the policy-making process. They have direct access to the decision maker because he depends on them for essential information in making policy and for aid in executing policies. Given the extensive services bureaucratic groups provide for decision makers, their impact on final policies is substantial.

Conversely, because bureaucratic groups exist to aid the decision maker, their ability to influence policy is limited. In most cases, bureaucratic influencers cannot openly oppose existing policies except through specific channels created to handle such opposition. If a bureaucratic influencer disagrees with existing policy and finds formal channels ineffective, its opposition must be covert. Members of the group may try to influence members of the decision-making group on a personal basis or through more powerful policy influencers. For example, information is often leaked to the press by bureaucratic officials in the hope of arousing some political opposition to prevent an unwarranted decision.[11] Officials may also alter the policy at the administrative level by applying directives in a way different than intended by decision makers. Because they do not usually challenge a decision once it has been made, bureaucratic groups can operate most effectively in areas where policy has yet to be formulated and least effectively in areas where long-standing policy is clearly defined. Only in the rarest circumstances and usually in situations of governmental instability do bureaucratic influencers openly oppose decisions taken by the official decision makers. Under more stable conditions, they shape policy covertly through administrative decisions and intelligence functions.

[11] Roger Hilsman, *To Move a Nation* (Garden City, N.Y.: Doubleday, 1967), pp. 7–8.

The role of bureaucratic influencers in the foreign policy-making process does not differ sharply for open and closed political systems. In both types, bureaucratic groups operate most often behind the scenes by providing information for decisions and serving as instruments through which decisions are implemented. Influence in the decision-making process is determined by the degree to which bureaucratic groups have the confidence of the top leaders. Hence, the popular support important in open political systems plays little or no role in the way bureaucratic groups attempt to influence policy.

Partisan Influencers

The second type of policy influencer is comprised of political parties. We shall call them *partisan influencers*. These influencers exist to translate societal demands into political demands, that is, demands on decision makers regarding governmental policies. They seek to influence policy both by pressuring those in power and supplying personnel for decision-making roles. Partisan influencers may be viewed as a two-way information and influence channel between official decision makers and members of society. Focusing much of their interest on shaping domestic policy, they also attempt to influence foreign policy, particularly when these policies have critical domestic ramifications.

In closed political systems, partisan influencers exist either as outlawed political groups or as part of a one-party system. Most stable autocracies have a one-party system although in some cases no "legitimate" party exists at all. Where single parties do exist, as in the Communist states, the party usually contains a number of factions having different interests and ideological commitments. However, because party unity is considered a sacred norm in the one-party state, intraparty factionalization is usually kept secret. Debate over issues takes place within the party itself, but intraparty dissent is expressed only before a final decision is reached and then rarely in public. Because debate is not public and party norms prohibit opposition voting, partisan influencers are in a position somewhat similar to bureaucratic groups. They can greatly influence policy before it is formalized, but once the decision maker has begun to implement a given policy, partisan opposition is limited because it implies a general withdrawal of support for the regime. Nevertheless, in attempting to maintain this support, the foreign policy decision maker often attempts to follow policies which will build rather than destroy consensus within the party.

In closed systems, "illegitimate" or revolutionary partisans are usually weak, if they exist at all. Frequently, as in the case of the anti-Castro forces in the United States directed toward Cuba, and the Nationalist Chinese in Formosa directed toward Mainland China, the revolutionary partisan influencers exist outside the geographical confines of the state. In both examples, the United States protects these partisan influences from the ruling governments. Other revolutionary partisans exist within the state, as for example the National Liberation Front (the political arm of the Viet Cong) in South Vietnam. In either case, the revolutionary partisans shape foreign policy in an indirect way, if only because the foreign policy decision makers know that they must lessen the appeal of these influencers to others in the system.

In open political systems, there are a number of partisan influencers. They might work together in two parties or might find it better to create a large number of parties. In both the two-party and the multiparty open system, however, a large number of viewpoints are usually expressed on each issue even within a particular party. If party discipline is weak, the variety of views will be expressed openly, and votes in legislative bodies might be taken without consideration for party lines. This is the case in the United States where there is sometimes more agreement between members of the Democratic and Republican parties than there is agreement within the parties themselves. If the party discipline is strong, as in Great Britain for example, the disparity of viewpoints might result in open intraparty debate but rarely in voting against party-approved policies.

The ability of partisan influencers in open systems to shape foreign policy is limited. In studying the role of Congress in U.S. foreign policy, James Robinson has concluded that Congress rarely takes the initiative but rather serves to legitimate or, in some exceptional cases, veto policy actions taken or proposed by the executive. Based on 22 foreign policy actions between the 1930's and 1961, Robinson's study found only three that were formally initiated by the Congress; none of these were major decisions such as Lend-Lease, development of the atomic bomb, NATO, the Korean decision or the Bay of Pigs invasion.[12] From our knowledge of other stable democracies, we would have to conclude that the United States' example is the rule rather than the exception. Partisan influencers in most stable democracies play the limited role of approving or rejecting foreign policy actions initiated by the foreign policy decision maker, although they may play a long-run role in changing basic attitudes of the general populace through public debate.

There are a number of reasons for the limited role played by partisan

[12] James A. Robinson, *Congress and Foreign Policy-Making* (Homewood, Ill.: Dorsey, 1967), pp. 23–71.

influencers in the foreign policy of stable democracies. Foremost is the tendency of partisan influencers to be more concerned with domestic than international politics. In addition, the executives frequently use the criterion of national security to limit foreign policy debate and opposition. Partisan influencers are often put in the difficult position of deciding whether to avail themselves of classified material and then to refrain from criticizing for fear of causing a "security leak," or to remain ignorant of existing documents so that they can criticize without being accused of violating secrecy. Furthermore, the complexity of foreign policy issues often demands the kind of expertise that busy legislators are not able to acquire. For these reasons, the partisan influencer not only refrains from making foreign policy initiatives but also rarely attempts to veto or withold legitimacy from the policies of the foreign policy decision-maker.

At the same time, however, it would be a mistake to assume that the partisan influencers in stable democracies are merely a rubber stamp. Because he needs their support to maintain the regime, the decision maker usually seeks to gain their consent for most policy decisions. Moreover, certain foreign policy areas, such as immigration and foreign aid in the United States, often receive intense partisan scrutiny. Because such areas are not usually associated with matters of national security, the partisan influencers feel more secure in posing serious opposition. Even in national security matters, prolonged dissatisfaction with foreign policy can produce a revolt among some partisan influencers, as for example, in the case of the partisan opposition to United States policy in Vietnam during the middle 1960's in both parties.

Interest Influencers

A third type of policy influencer, the *interest influencer,* consists of a group of individuals tied together by a common set of interests that are not broad enough to constitute the basis for partisan activity but nonetheless necessitate mobilization of resources to gain support among other policy influencers and decision makers. Many of the interests are economic because individuals are often motivated to collective action by mutual economic interests. Noneconomic interests can also serve as a basis for collective action, particularly if there are ethnic or geographic ties among the individuals. The nature and tactics of interest influencers vary for the two types of political systems.

In closed systems, interest influencers have to operate behind the scenes, particularly in one-party states. In the one-party state, the interest influencers cannot pursue their objectives too openly since the implicit rules of the political system permit no divergent interests. However, divergent interests sometimes cut across organizational lines. For example, industrial managers in the Soviet Union belong to various bureaucratic groups but nonetheless pursue some interests in common even though they conflict with interests of other members of the bureaucracy. In closed systems where there is no one-party structure, or when the structure is very weak, as in Spain, interest influencers may have more public positions. For example, the Catholic Church plays a large role in Spanish politics even though it cannot be classified as a political party.

In open systems, interest influencers play a larger role. There are usually a large number of organizations and informal groups representing various economic and noneconomic interests. Because these groups sometimes have substantial financial resources, they are able to influence voters and partisan influencers. In the United States, for example, the Zionist organization has played a large role in influencing American policy towards Israel, primarily by financing some partisan leaders and having some crucial voting strength of its own.[13] In open systems, there is a tendency for organizations to develop around a particular policy issue. Because the right of protest is usually accepted as part of the rules of the democratic political system, individuals who object to certain policies readily find others who agree with them so they can organize to exert pressure on other policy influencers and decision makers. Interest influencers use a number of techniques in attempting to build support for their interest. They may launch a letter-writing campaign directed not only at the decision makers but also at partisan and bureaucratic influencers. Or, they may promise financial support or threaten to withdraw such support. Occasionally, they may finance a publicity campaign to build support among the people generally which in turn will bring pressure on decision makers and partisan influencers.

Although interest influencers do play a role in the foreign policy-making process of open systems, it should not be assumed that they dictate the foreign policies of states. On the contrary, as Bauer, Pool, and Dexter indicate in their study of business and public policy, business interests and lobbyists in America are often "restrained in exerting pressure or woefully ignorant of where pressure could be profitably exerted."[14] However, these interest influencers are still important factors in the foreign policy-making

[13] See Ernst Haas and Allen Whiting, *Dynamics of International Politics* (New York: McGraw-Hill, 1956), pp. 283–84.

[14] Raymond A. Bauer, Ithiel de Sola Pool, and Lewis A. Dexter, *American Business and Public Policy* (New York: Atherton, 1963), p. 484. See also pp. 396–401.

process because they affect the complexities of the domestic political process. They may not *determine* foreign policy, but they certainly play a role in the calculations of foreign policy decision makers.

Mass Influencers

The final type of policy influencer is public opinion or the *mass influencer.* We are referring here to the climate of opinion shared by a population that decision makers consider in making foreign policy. As we shall see, the impact of the attitudes of mass influencers on foreign policy decision makers varies greatly according to type of political system.

In closed systems, attitudes of people are greatly influenced by the decision makers themselves. Using modern mass communications media (newspapers, radio, and television), as well as the pro-regime party itself, decision makers in states like the Soviet Union attempt to build a favorable climate of opinion for their foreign policies. However, one should not conclude that mass approval of policies is automatic. Decision makers might so thoroughly cultivate a climate of opinion at one point in time so that it becomes impossible for them to reverse policy decisions later on. Furthermore, certain deeply felt attitudes, such as resentment towards another state or the desire for peace, operate as limitations on the extent to which mass opinion can be manipulated. Nevertheless, because the mass media is usually controlled from above, and freedom of expression is usually limited by censorship, decision makers in closed systems manipulate their mass influencers to a greater extent than their counterparts in other types of systems.

In open systems, the climate of opinion is freer from direct manipulation by the decision makers—although not as free as one might expect given the principles of free speech and press so much a part of democratic states. People in a democracy receive information from a number of sources. The press as well as radio and television newsmen provide enormous quantities of information. Although decision makers sometimes attempt to "manage" news by holding back certain information, the vast resources of the mass communications establishment precludes the type of control leaders of closed systems are able to exercise. Just as important a role is played in forming the climate of opinion by what Katz and Lazarsfeld have identified as the two-step flow of communication.[15] They have demonstrated that formation of attitudes throughout the population does not result merely from communication of information through the mass

---

[15] Elihu Katz and Paul Lazarsfeld, *Personal Influence* (New York: Free Press, 1955).

media. Rather, an intervening set of community leaders or influentials usually is responsible for developing broadly based ideas. Because autonomy occurs in the formation of mass opinion, not only by the private resources of mass media, but also as a result of the role played by community leaders in discussing issues, the primary constraints on mass influencers are a product of attitudes the mass influencers themselves hold.

Mass influencers are important to decision makers in open systems because of their role in elections. Decision makers formulate policies with an eye toward their effect on public opinion and the next election. Public opinion polls, although not always believed, represent a constant source of information on decision makers' status vis-à-vis the public. This information becomes particularly pertinent as elections draw closer because it provides significant evidence for predicting the outcome of elections.

To say that decision makers are aware of public opinion in open systems, however, is not to say that they are controlled by it or the mass influencers which shape it. As has been indicated by the variety of public moods toward the Soviet Union since 1939 (from distrust in 1939, to trust in the early and middle 1940's, to extreme distrust and fear in the 1950's, to moderate distrust in the 1960's), public opinion can readily be molded not only by international events but also by political leaders. Decision makers know they have a good chance of manipulating public opinion to support their policies. Although the public gets an enormous amount of information, it rarely digests the information and usually tends to adopt simplistic positions on broad issues. Finally, even if the public were well aware of the facts and had given substantial thought to foreign policy issues, it still would not have the capacity to provide clear direction for the foreign policy decision maker given the specialized and complex nature of most foreign policy decisions.

Public opinion serves as a tool of decision makers and other policy influencers as much as if not more than it does as a force directing foreign policy decision makers. These officials often use public opinion to rationalize foreign policy actions, rather than to shape policy. For example, American foreign policy decision makers have argued throughout the late 1950's and 1960's that the public will not permit more friendly relations with China when in fact members of the foreign policy bureaucracy and certain partisan and interest influencers have been the main opponents to improved Sino-American relations.[16] In the United States it is frequently reactions from Congressmen rather than from the general public that is seen as public opinion by foreign policy decision makers.

[16] For a discussion of the role of partisan, interest, and mass influencers in American foreign policy towards China see A. T. Steele, *The American People and China* (New York: McGraw-Hill, 1966).

If the mass influencers play a major role in foreign policies of open systems, probably most important are those broadcasters and journalists who provide the "news" for foreign policy decision makers. For example, Glenn D. Paige, in his exhaustive study of the American decision to intervene in Korea, reports that on June 26, 1950—the day many of the major decisions regarding American intervention were made—President Truman read morning newspapers that made statements concerning our need to meet the North Korean invasion with firmness.[17] Although it is impossible to assess whether the newspaper statements merely confirmed Truman's view or played an active role in shaping them, they did serve as part of his "world" on the day of decision. Hence, while the public does not dictate foreign policy, the mass influencers play a substantial role because they "create" the perceptual world of the decision maker.

PROCESSES IN CONTEMPORARY POLICY-INFLUENCE SYSTEMS

The preceding discussion of policy influencers in open and closed political systems has provided a partial explanation of the role of domestic politics in the foreign policy-making process. In order to complete the picture, we must investigate the processes that affect the ways in which policy influencers interact with foreign policy decision makers. We will do this by looking at (1) the source and nature of policy influencers' images of international affairs and (2) the types of issues around which influencers and decision makers interact.

The Images of Policy Influencers

In Chapter 2 we discussed the role of images in the behavior of foreign policy decision makers. We pointed out that images constitute the way people view the world and that they serve to orient decision makers in dealing with their environment. We can apply the same concept to policy influencers because in a sense they are also decision makers dealing with their environment. Their images of the international environment play a decisive role in the way they attempt to shape the behavior of foreign policy decision makers. As we will see, different types of policy influencers in different political systems view the international environment differently.

Bureaucratic and interest influencers in open and closed systems both maintain images that are limited in scope. Because bureaucratic groups have specialized functions in the governmental structure, their views are

---

[17] Glenn D. Paige, *The Korean Decision: June 24–30, 1950* (New York: Free Press, 1968), p. 145.

circumscribed by daily activities. Events surrounding their activities are filtered through a set of highly specialized and technical images that tend to be closed. For example, manufacturers as interest influencers have images of the world revolving around the degree to which their products in the domestic market will be protected from foreign competition and the degree to which foreign markets can be opened up for their products. Totally involved in pursuing a narrow goal in relation to the international environment, most bureaucratic and interest influencers maintain images with enormous detail about a small part of the international environment while their images of the remainder of the international environment are shaped by their particular interests and responsibilities.

To illustrate the fragmented and specialized nature of the images possessed by bureaucratic groups and interest influencers, we might look at the impact of the short Israeli-Arab War during late spring of 1967 on bureaucratic and interest influencers in the United States. American military leaders tended to view the conflict in terms of the position of their armed forces in the Middle East, while members of the State Department were concerned primarily with following a policy that would not anger the Arab states and would leave Israel intact. The Department of Commerce was concerned about the impact of the whole crisis on world trade. Interest influencers who had a stake in the oil industry watched to see the impact of the war and its aftermath on Middle Eastern oil production and distribution while pro-Israeli and pro-Arab influencers (the former being much more influential than the latter) watched American reaction to see which side benefited. Because these bureaucratic and interest influencers were concerned primarily with specific aspects of the crisis rather than the general impact, events were viewed and interpreted differently by each.

Partisan influencers tend to have broader images of international affairs than most bureaucratic and interest influencers if only because their function is to aggregate the interest of mass and interest influencers. However, images of partisan influencers vary for open and closed political systems.

In the former, partisan influencers tend to view the international environment in terms of their position vis-à-vis the regime. Partisan influencers that are in power—that is, are represented by official decision makers—usually look for justification of the existing policy, while out-of-power influencers seek to discredit it. With different purposes, partisan influencers on opposite sides of the political fence will interpret events to confirm their political positions. For example, in the 1930's and 1940's, members of the Conservative party in Britain usually saw the British Empire as vital to British interests; Labor saw Empire as a burden with few direct payoffs.

When party discipline is weak, as in the United States, the view of the international environment will not be determined by party membership as much as by political beliefs of the partisan influencer. For example, debates in the Senate over United States policy in Vietnam during the 1960's illustrate that opinion does not divide strictly along party lines. Hence, in open systems partisan influencers maintain broad but different views of the international environment.

In closed political systems, partisan influencers also maintain broad views of the international environment, but usually with less variety. The ruling party in closed systems is provided with an official view from the foreign policy decision makers. Although members of the ruling party may develop images that differ from the official view, they cannot voice their differences unless they are prepared to undermine party authority. Unable to engage in open questioning of existing viewpoints, members of the ruling party are less likely to develop radically different broad interpretations of the international environment among themselves and in relation to official decision makers.

Mass influencers also appear to maintain a particular predisposition to formation of images about international affairs. Because both the public and those who try to influence the public have secondary interests in world affairs, they do not give sufficient time to formulating views—given the complexity of phenomena that comprise international affairs. A pronounced tendency results to pass on and store information that is simplistic. Many writers have argued that the public possesses a black-and-white view of world politics, and part of this tendency is a result of the limited time and interest put into learning about international affairs.[18] Moreover, those trying to influence the public—whether in democracies or autocracies— employ pat phrases and simplistic language to insure rapid communication. Although the mass influencers do possess a broad picture of international affairs (at least when compared to interest influencers), their views lack the knowledge of detail and nuances that would make them sophisticated and involved observers.

In studying the images of policy influencers, we should also be interested in comparing their images to those of decision makers. Because decision makers are placed in the position of formulating and executing policies, they also have a particular set of images about the world. These images are both broadly based and detailed, although they are not as broadly based as some of the more sophisticated mass influencers nor as detailed as some of the bureaucratic groups or interest influencers. However, decision makers are in the position of building a consensus not only to

[18] For examples, see Gabriel A. Almond, *American People and Foreign Policy*, pp. 54–68 and Walter Lippmann, *Essays in the Public Philosophy* (Boston: Little, Brown, 1955), pp. 16–27.

satisfy the various policy influencers but also to develop an action orientation toward foreign policy.

In addition to this difference in orientations, decision makers also differ from policy influencers in their sources of information. Information is received second- or third-hand by all influencers except the specific bureaucratic group involved. And one of the hands through which information usually passes is the decision maker's. This means that partisan, interest, and mass influencers are dependent, to some extent, on decision makers themselves for information. Certain interest influencers might be able to get some firsthand information through the investment of sufficient time and money, but they still often depend upon willingness of decision makers to release the information. Bureaucratic groups often supply information to the decision maker, but because their methods of gathering information are fragmented, they receive less of it than the decision maker ultimately does.

This difference in information sources can have a major impact on foreign policy processes. Given the changing conditions that characterize international relations, if information were the only variable, decision makers would be much more adaptable to changing circumstances than most of their policy influencers. The process of learning about new situations takes time so policy influencers tend to respond to changing conditions more slowly than decision makers. Of course, as we saw in the previous chapter, decision makers themselves are subject to certain conditions that hinder their ability to adjust their images to changing situations. This means they might change more slowly than some influencers but less slowly than others.

The important point is that images possessed by decision makers and policy influencers are not subject to the same social and psychological processes nor to the same information sources. This results in a substantial time differential in learning about new conditions in the international environment. Therefore, we can assume that policy influencers and decision makers usually have different images about the nature of international affairs—given both their different perspectives and this time differential. To further complicate matters, decision makers and policy influencers are often consciously and unconsciously trying to shape each other's views of the world.

Issue Areas for Policy Influencers

The concept of "issue area" has been used by a number of political scientists in various fields. Borrowing from the work of Robert Dahl and others in the field of community politics, Rosenau has employed the concept to examine the foreign policy process.[19] In the following analysis of the types of issue areas that most concern policy influencers, we will focus on four categories: (1) national security, (2) economic interests, (3) specific issue areas involving ideological or historical interests, and (4) procedural questions—how foreign policy objectives are sought. In examining these issue areas, we will be particularly concerned with two factors: degrees of importance attached by various influencers to a particular issue area, and whether the influencers approach the issue area with an orientation that is national (What is good for the country?) or particularist (What is good for the particular influencer?).

National security is a highly important issue area for most policy influencers in most states. Except for revolutionary partisans, policy influencers of all types are vitally concerned with preservation of the state. In open systems, this concern is so great that opposing partisan influencers— even revolutionaries—are often willing to cooperate on national security matters if they feel that a foreign state threatens security.

At the same time, and almost by definition, the national security issue area represents a nationalist rather than a particularist focus for the policy influencers. Except for those who for one reason or another favor some form of partition, policy influencers conceive their national security interests to be shared by the entire community. This does not assume that policy influencers maintain the same images concerning national security or even agree on how best to ensure national security, but it does assume that when they think about national security they are concerned with the interests of the state as a whole rather than their own particular interests.

However, the great emphasis on national security by most policy influencers does not mean agreement on specific policies. In the modern world, all states are vulnerable to some other state or states; national security cannot be defined solely in terms of military superiority. Being strong is more than being able to wage a successful war. As we will see when discussing bargaining among states (see Chapter 10), strength depends on all events and conditions related to establishing an appearance of strength and courage that might convince potential enemies to refrain from attacking. Given the relativity of the conditions surrounding maintenance of national security, it is easy for conflicting opinions to develop on whether or not a given policy enhances national security. Policy influencers tend to have different views of the world, and therefore they disagree on specific policies designed to promote national security.

[19] James N. Rosenau, "Foreign Policy as an Issue-Area," in James N. Rosenau, ed., *Domestic Sources of Foreign Policy* (New York: Free Press, 1967), pp. 11–51.

Because the decision maker and most policy influencers are committed to the pursuit of national security, the decision maker is usually able to manipulate the issue area to his advantage. He can claim superior information on existing conditions when confronted by criticism for policy influencers. Under certain conditions, he can quell dissent by implying that disagreement on policy itself will weaken the chances of the state for maintaining its security. For example, in the mid-1960's American officials tried to limit debate in the United States over its Vietnamese policy on the grounds that debate encourages the enemy to assume American unwillingness to pursue the war.

If the national security issue area presents a tool that can be used by decision makers in quelling dissent among policy influencers toward government policy, it also constitutes a source of great vulnerability if a sufficient number of important policy influencers feel the decision makers are failing to promote national security. This point is illustrated by the way John F. Kennedy was able to use the "missile gap" in his campaign in 1960. By suggesting that America lagged behind the Soviet Union in missile development, Kennedy capitalized on the powerful impact the issue area of national security can have on the American voter. Although national security is difficult to define and is often used by decision makers in building a consensus or quelling dissent, it can also serve as source of powerful opposition once the faith of the policy influencers has been shaken. Foreign policy decision makers are potentially vulnerable to charges of failing to maintain national security, and most policy influencers view the national security issue area (naturalistically) as highly important. Nonetheless, foreign policy decision makers can usually follow an autonomous foreign policy in this area. Exceptions occur when events in the international environment create changes in attitudes among policy influencers. Perhaps they lose confidence in the foreign policy of decision makers as, for example, the British people's reaction to the takeover of Czechoslovakia in 1938. Because such clear-cut events rarely occur, the official justification of national security policy is usually sufficient to maintain support.

A second issue area for policy influencers is the foreign economic relations of their state. Here, the distinction between nationalist and particularist approaches is extremely important. Conflict often emerges between influencers who advocate economic policies such as free trade for the good of the economy as a whole and those who advocate policies such as protective tariffs to benefit themselves. Although both sets of influencers couch their arguments in nationalistic terms as United States watchmakers did when they argued that they must be protected from foreign competition to maintain skilled labor that might be needed in wartime, one can still apply the distinction.

In open systems, bureaucratic and mass influencers are the clearest advocates of foreign economic policies to benefit the nation as a whole. Partisan influencers sometimes act on the basis of a nationalist orientation but just as often do not. The interest influencers most clearly opt for policies that benefit themselves rather than the nation as a whole. This applies to labor unions who seek to preserve their jobs through protectionist legislation as well as to industrial managers who want to protect their markets. One of the important factors in the dynamics of policy-influencer pressure on foreign economic policies, however, is that those groups with nationalist orientations are not as vitally concerned as those with particularist orientations. Hence, interest and partisan influencers actively support foreign economic policies with a particularist orientation because it means their own economic gain. Bureaucratic, mass, and other partisan influencers who act on a nationalist basis do not actively support their positions on foreign economic policy because their outlook involves long-run rather than short-run interests. As a result, if foreign policy decision makers were merely to act according to the amount of pressure applied to them, they would probably follow protectionist foreign policies.

In closed systems, policy influencers ostensibly follow nationalist foreign economic policies. Bureaucratic influencers, as servants of the nation; the party as the political will of the state; and mass influencers all theoretically pressure for nationalistic policies. However, interest influencers, operating behind the scenes and through both the bureaucracy and the party, often mobilize support for particular economic interests. In fact, because economies are under greater political control in most stable autocracies than they are in other types of systems, we can assume that particularist economic pressures become substantial. In the area of foreign trade, specific industries might pressure for a bigger overseas market or a greater return on economic investment.

In both types of systems, then, stronger pressure is applied by policy influencers whose orientations to foreign economic policies are particularist rather than nationalist. Those with nationalist orientations do not usually attach as much importance to foreign economic policy as particularists. As a result, the foreign policy decision maker must serve the particularist interests if they want support for their foreign economic policy.

The third category of issue area involves those nonsecurity and noneconomic interests that involve particular conditions in the international environment. A result of historical experience or ideological predisposition, these issues include disputes over territory and particular policies of friendship or hostility toward another state. The distinction between particularist and nationalist orientation is important because, as we will see in the list below, some issues are a result of a general feeling throughout most policy influencers and some involve only a particular set of them. Here are some obvious examples:

1. *Israeli-Arab animosity.* Policy influencers on both sides have expressed almost unanimous mistrust of each other. (National.)

2. *Korean policy towards Japan.* Many policy influencers in Korea have favored hostile policies toward Japan because of the long history of Japanese dominance in Korea. (National.)

3. *American policy towards eastern European states like Poland.* Certain interest influencers in the United States have expressed support for a more active policy towards eastern Europe because they are refugees from that area. (Particularist.)

4. *British foreign policy towards the excolonies.* Policy influencers in each of the four categories (bureaucratic, partisan, interest, and mass), because of historical ties, have emotional and economic attachments toward excolonial areas that lead them to pressure foreign policy decision makers in Britain. (Particularist.)

In almost every state, part or all of the population has certain attitudes toward other nations or to specific international conditions involving other nations that result in pressures on decision makers to follow a specific foreign policy. These issues are often emotion laden because they are based on past experience and supporting attitudes. Years of suspicion merely breed heightened animosity, and it is very difficult to create conditions that result in basic changes in orientation. Hence, decision makers are forced to deal with basic policy influencers' predispositions.

A final issue area involves the way foreign policy objectives are pursued rather than the nature of the specific objectives. Demands for a more peaceful or a more aggressive foreign policy, for example, are demands not that certain policy objectives be sought but that certain means be employed. The debate in the United States over policy towards Vietnam, for example, has been as much a debate over the proper means as over the proper goals. Similarly, the desire to have one's nation treated with "respect" or "honor" implies an emphasis on the manner in which the state is treated, not necessarily on the final outcome.

Procedural issues are particularly salient for mass influencers. The reason for this is that arguments over the proper way of conducting a foreign policy can be made at a higher level of generality and therefore demand less knowledge of detail on the part of the listener. The statement that more force is needed to solve a particular situation or that a particular state is acting aggressively can be used through mass media to build support. For this reason, partisan influencers—particularly in open systems —often build their foreign policy arguments around procedural issues in their attempt to gain popular votes. Conversely, the emphasis on procedural issues is not as great in closed systems because the mass influencers play a very small role in pressuring foreign policy decision makers, although as opposition within the Soviet Union to the occupation of Czechoslovakia in 1968 would indicate, procedural criticisms do occur in closed political systems.

SUMMARY

In an attempt to pull together the concepts and propositions employed in this chapter in describing the role of domestic politics in the foreign policy-making process, we will follow a strategy frequently employed by scholars of international politics—the construction of an illustrative model. In this case the model will be used to synthesize a complex set of ideas about domestic politics and foreign policy using a small number of abstract concepts.

Assume that the relationship between domestic politics and foreign policy making can be represented in Figure 4. In this model, the international environment acts as a stimulus to both the foreign policy decision makers and the policy influencers. Given the differences introduced as a consequence of the types of images maintained by the two actors in the process, however, the stimulus will be viewed differently not only by the foreign policy decision makers and the policy influencers but also among different policy influencers themselves. Having different images of the international environment and playing different roles within the domestic political system, the two actors will take different positions on various issues. They will attempt to influence each other through issue area interaction, and the results of that interaction will be the foreign policy of the state.

FIGURE 4

The Foreign Policy-Making Process

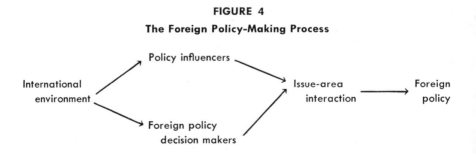

The relative importance of policy influencers in shaping behavior of the foreign policy decision maker depends upon the type of political system and the type of issue area. Table 2 is based on our discussion of the role of policy influencers in various issue areas and is provided for purposes of discussion and synthesis. Each box represents a particular issue area in an open or closed political system. Policy influencers in four categories are listed in order of their importance in shaping foreign policy actions of the state.

The table illustrates a basic difference between open and closed systems involving the role of mass influencers. In the open system, mass influencers are listed as the weakest element only in the issue area of foreign economic policy. In the other three areas, they rank second or third in importance. This contrasts with the closed system where mass influencers rank fourth in each case. Moreover, because elections and the politics surrounding them permeate so much of the political life of open systems, interest and partisan influencers generally play a more important role in open than in closed systems. In short, the structural differences of open and

TABLE 2

Importance* of Foreign Policy Influencers According to Type of Political System and Issue Area

Issue Area	Open System	Closed System
National security	1. Partisan 2. Mass 3. Bureaucratic 4. Interest	1. Partisan 2. Bureaucratic 3. Interest 4. Mass
Economic policy	1. Interest 2. Partisan 3. Bureaucratic 4. Mass	1. Bureaucratic 2. Partisan 3. Interest 4. Mass
Ideological-historical specific	1. Interest 2. Partisan 3. Mass 4. Bureaucratic	1. Partisan 2. Interest 3. Bureaucratic 4. Mass
Procedural	1. Partisan 2. Mass 3. Bureaucratic 4. Interest	1. Partisan 2. Bureaucratic 3. Interest 4. Mass

* Most important = 1; least important = 4.

closed political systems greatly affect the issue area interaction between decision makers and influencers that is at the heart of the relationship between domestic politics and foreign policy.

One point about this discussion should be kept clearly in mind. The argument is *not* that the public controls foreign policy in open political systems while it has no control over foreign policy in closed political systems. Rather, it is the type of influence wielded that is substantially different for the two systems. In the open system, the public or crucial portions of it may be mobilized by interest and partisan influencers to affect the political life of a partisan influencer (for example, Congressmen from a heavily Jewish district) or the foreign policy decision maker himself (for example, Lyndon Johnson's reversals in the 1968 presidential primaries). In the closed system, foreign policy decision makers need not fear partisan or interest influencers appealing to the public. Hence, the difference between open and closed political systems resides in the strategies and relative importance of the four types of policy influencers, rather than in the degree of responsiveness of leaders to the people directly.

SUMMARY OUTLINE

I. Domestic politics has a great impact on the foreign policy of any state.

II. The policy-influence system of any state consists of the relationship between foreign policy decision makers and policy influencers, because the latter provide support for and make demands upon the former.

 A. *In the early postfeudal period, the relationship was dominated by the policy influencers.*

 B. *In the classical state system, the relationship was dominated by the decision makers.*

 C. *In the contemporary period, the relationship is pluralized with increased interaction and influence between decision makers and policy influencers.*

III. A twofold distinction (open and closed) on the type of political system can be used in examining the effect of policy influencers on the foreign policy decision maker.

 A. *Bureaucratic influencers usually influence the foreign policy decision maker by providing him with information at the formulation stage and administrative aid at the execution stage.*

 B. *Bureaucratic influencers rarely openly oppose an existing policy although they might seek to change it through low-level administrative decisions.*

C. *In a closed system the partisan influencers, if they exist and are not revolutionary, have the ability sometimes with and sometimes without the agreement of bureaucratic influencers to determine the continuance of the decision maker's stay in office.*

D. *Revolutionary partisans in closed systems do not have much leverage on the foreign policy decision maker.*

E. *In an open system, partisan influencers supply a major portion of the support for a regime given the importance of elections.*

F. *In an open system, the ability of partisan influencers to pressure the foreign policy decision maker is limited by the fact that the executive usually takes the initiative and the demands of security and secrecy often limit opposition.*

G. *In a closed system, interest influencers operate through the partisan and bureaucratic influencers on a covert basis which makes their role in pressuring foreign policy decision makers secondary.*

H. *In an open system, the role of interest influencer is large because some interest influencers have financial resources or popular appeal to affect the ability of partisan influencers and decision makers to win elections.*

 I. *In a closed system, the climate of opinion has some impact although it is substantially shaped by the decision maker and the partisan influencers.*

J. *In an open system, mass influencers are able to obtain information that often provides a basis for disagreement with the foreign policy decision maker although the latter has usually been successful in the past in shaping public opinion.*

IV. Images play a large role in the behavior of policy influencers.

A. *Both bureaucratic and interest influencers tend to have a specialized view of the international environment with great detail in their area of interest and a very thin perspective in other areas.*

B. *Partisan influencers tend to have broader images but they are more varied in open than closed systems.*

C. *Mass influencers have broad images of the international environment but lack detailed knowledge.*

D. *Foreign policy decision makers tend to have different images of the international environment than policy influencers not only because their perspectives are different but also because they receive and are attuned to more information than most but not all policy influencers.*

V. Policy-influencer pressure on foreign policy decision makers can be analyzed in terms of four issue areas.

   A. *National security as an issue area concerns all four types of policy influencers, but in spite of their interest little clear pressure (in one particular direction) is exerted.*

   B. Foreign economic policies are pressured in different ways by different policy influencers.

      1. *Particularist economic orientations are pursued with high intensity by interest influencers in all systems.*

      2. *Nationalist economic orientations are pursued, but only with moderate intensity, in all types of systems by bureaucratic, mass, and, to a lesser degree, partisan influencers.*

   C. *Issues which involve neither national security nor economics directly but are based on historical or ideological conditions play a large role in the activities of policy influencers, both at the national and particularist levels.*

   D. *Issues concerning foreign policy means rather than objectives frequently become the focus for mass and partisan influencers.*

VI. *The difference between open and closed political systems lies in the strategies and relative importance of the four types of policy influencers rather than in the degree of responsiveness of the leaders to the people directly.*

BIBLIOGRAPHICAL ESSAY

The literature on the role of domestic politics in the making of foreign policy is weak. Some interesting studies focus on particular countries: Kogan (232) for Italy, Deutsch and Edinger (105) for West Germany, and Almond (11) for the United States. Some deal with a particular policy, as Bauer, Pool, and Dexter (29), an event, as Cohen (78) and Dawson (96), or an institution, as Robinson (341). Attempts to develop general rules that would apply across several countries require monographs like Frankel's (128) or collections of essays that treat each nation separately, as Macridis (267). Some writers attempt to construct typologies or general frameworks. In the latter category, Haas and Whiting (149), Snyder in (389), Kissinger (224), Farrell in (124), Rosenau in (347), Hammond (156), and Deutsch (98) attempt to provide a framework. A book of essays edited by Rosenau (347), has the interesting title *Domestic Sources of Foreign Policy* but focuses primarily on American domestic sources of foreign policy.

Of the literature concerning the role of bureaucratic politics in foreign and domestic policy making, most of that which does not focus solely on the United States examines the military. Interesting theoretical value can be found in the works of Huntington (187) and Edinger (113). Studies of the role of the military might allow for some crossnational comparisons. Studies of the following countries are available: France, Furniss (133); Latin America, Johnson (198); and the United States, Hammond (156) and Huntington (187). Only a few works refer to nonmilitary bureaucratic influencers—Hammond (156), for example—although one might be able to generalize from works on comparative administration (such as Riggs (337).

The role of partisan influencers in the making of foreign policy is studied almost solely by students of democratic politics. Except for a few, most studies are concerned with democratic states. Exceptions are Slusser in (201); and Triska and Finley (406), dealing with the impact of party on Soviet foreign policy. Studies on the role of partisan influencers in the formulation of United States foreign policy focus on institutions, as Dahl (91) and Robinson (341), political parties, as Westerfield (418) and Crabb (88); elections, as Waltz (413) and Miller in (347); and legislative voting blocs, as O'Leary (300); and Rieselbach (336). Two studies on the role of partisan influencers in British foreign policy are Meehan (275), and Epstein (118).

The literature on the role of interest influencers in foreign policy is also focused on American politics. Examples are Pool, Keller, and Bauer (315); Adler and Bobrow (2); Fuchs (131); Cohen (78); Bauer, Pool, and Dexter (29); and Milbrath in (347). Some help might be found in such general works on comparative politics as Ehrmann (115) and Macridis (267).

The study of the role of mass influencers (public opinion and opinion makers) in foreign policy has a number of distinct focal points. Significant empirical data are available on attitudes held by a representative sampling of the population. See Buchanan and Cantril (58), Klingberg (228), Hero (168), and Steele (395). On the development of public opinion, see Rosenau's article in (347). Lippmann (251) represents an early but very perceptive study on public opinion. An examination of the role of mass media in the formation of public opinion can be found in Davison (93), Hero (168), Cohen, (79), and the article by Cohen in (347). Important theoretical questions concerning the relationships between public opinion and foreign policy making are examined by Deutsch (98), Fagen (122), and Mueller (287). A study by Deutsch and Merritt in Kelman (215), examines how public images change as a result of events in the international environment. Deutsch (102) also developed a more formal model of the role of images and various elites in the foreign policy-making process.

The body of literature on the role of elites in foreign policy is growing. These studies cut across categories employed in this chapter. Nevertheless, they could aid the student in his general study of domestic politics and foreign policy. For a discussion of the concept of elite, see Marvick's article in (270) and Lasswell's in (270). Soviet elites are examined in Djilas (109) and Angell, Dunham, and Singer (13). German and French elites are examined in Deutsch et al. (106). Finally, Rosenau in (347) has done an empirical study on elites in the United States.

4

Economic and Military Factors in Foreign Policy Making: Dimensions and Tools

As if his domestic environment weren't complicated enough by the existence of demanding and competing policy influencers, the foreign policy decision maker also must consider economic and military strengths and weaknesses of his state when making foreign policy. He must balance his commitments with his capabilities by recognizing the constraints imposed upon him by his and others' economic and military conditions. In this chapter, we will examine the role of economic and military factors in the making of foreign policy. After looking at the historical evolution and interdependencies of economic and military conditions as well as the dimensions of economic and military capability, we will discuss economic and military factors as tools for the pursuit of foreign policy objectives.

HISTORICAL DEVELOPMENT OF ECONOMIC AND MILITARY CONDITIONS

When the troubador sang of gallant Arthur plunging into mortal combat with his sword Excalibur, he never mentioned the blacksmith who toiled thanklessly to forge the steel that became the sword. Nor is the modern general in the field often linked with the broker on Wall Street or the steel magnate in Pittsburgh, but the fact is that throughout history military strategies and goals have been closely associated with economic development and financial practices. Innovations in one sector have often served as a catalyst for innovations in the other. The conquest of Africa by European states in the nineteenth century was expedited by such technological developments as the invention of food canning and the discovery of tropical medicines. The highspeed American freeways that lace the United States today are replicas of the German *Autobahnen* built by Hitler to transport war material. When discussing foreign policy, therefore, it is essential to consider and explore the interaction between military and economic factors.

In past ages, the relationship between the economic and military sectors was equally apparent, if less intricate. The feudal system that prevailed throughout Europe from the ninth to the sixteenth century was based on "a combination between agriculture and military service."[1] The feudal peasant, or serf, did not own the land he cultivated and did not retain the fruits of his labor. Rather, the land was owned by a lord who extracted heavy taxes in kind, or fealty, from the peasant. However, in exchange for the taxes, the lord was obliged to protect the peasant on his land. Although their interests were not always compatible, lord and peasant had struck a deal: security for food.

Given the technological, social, and economic conditions of the period, this was a reasonable arrangement. In the medieval era, the almost prohibitive cost of outfitting a warrior limited the number of combatants. It has been calculated that several years' income of a whole village was necessary to cover the costs of equipping one knight. And nothing could oppose a knight clad in armor on an armored charger—until the introduction of the crossbow and gunpowder—which meant that the peasant was of little use as a soldier.[2] Given the agrarian base of the economy and the technological conditions that made it necessary for a large number of peasants to farm the land, the division of feudal society into an elite warrior class and a peasant class was an understandable outcome.

The feudal system itself was eroded by a changing pattern of relationships between the military and economic sectors. The agrarian economy of the late middle ages stood in contrast to the developing urban economy of commerce. Cities—with their money economy, larger and more diversified resources, and higher technology—developed a class of merchants to challenge the landed aristocracy in terms of wealth and power. Mercenary armies were financed by the merchants and equipped with new weapons, such as muskets, cannons, and rapid-firing bows.[3] The introduction of

---

[1] Robert L. Heilbroner, *The Making of Economic Society* (Englewood Cliffs, N.J.: Prentice-Hall, 1962), p. 33. Also, see pp. 18–72 for a general discussion of the evolution of economic and military conditions in medieval and postmedieval Europe.

[2] Stanislaw Andrejewski, *Military Organization and Society* (London: Routledge and Kegan Paul, 1954), p. 58.

[3] Alfred Vagts, *History of Militarism* (New York: Norton, 1937), p. 40.

gunpowder rendered obsolete both the knight and his self-protected feudal estate. A new system, based on capital and defended with the products and profits of capital, evolved from the old system, based on land and barter.

The territorial state characteristic of the classical international political system arose as a result of innovations in both the military and economic sectors. "The gunpowder revolution," writes John H. Herz, "caused a real revolution in the superstructure of economic, social, and political relationships because of its impact on the units of protection and security. . . . The large area state came finally to occupy the place that the castle or fortified town had previously held as the unit of impenetrability."[4] The new states were built "by the new revenues bigger business operations could generously provide."[5] And in a letter to his monarch, a German merchant wrote, "Remember that you could not have obtained your crown without my help."[6]

Acquiring and accumulating gold became the prime occupations of kings in the postmedieval period. The pursuit of gold had repercussions on both the economic and military sectors. Trade itself became more important as its proceeds—gold bullion—enriched monarchs, and as the objects of trade provided a higher and more diversified standard of living for the fortunate classes. Gold symbolized power and procured stronger armies. In the early sixteenth century, using gold carried off from colonies, the king of Spain equipped an army with Dutch weapons. The lesson—if a nation wanted power, it needed gold—was not lost on other nations. Early thrusts of colonial expansion were motivated primarily by the desire to acquire gold. Even the English settlers in Virginia were instructed to concentrate on mining in the hope of discovering deposits of gold ore.

As the military capability of a state came to be a function of its wealth, monarchs began to exercise extensive control over trade and business. They created tariffs, fathered new industries, passed restrictive laws, financed overseas expeditions, and established commercial companies such as the famous Dutch East India Company. The aim of the monarchs was to secure a favorable balance of trade, (that is, an excess of exports over imports) in order to produce a favorable flow of gold bullion into the country. This strategy became known as the policy of *mercantilism* and it structured a great deal of foreign policy from the Peace of Westphalia (1648) to the Congress of Vienna (1815).

Like the feudal period, the mercantile era was characterized by inter-

---

[4] John H. Herz, "Rise and Demise of the Territorial State," *World Politics,* 9 (1957), 476.

[5] Robert L. Reynolds, *Europe Emerges* (Madison: University of Wisconsin Press, 1961), p. 409.

[6] Vagts, *History of Militarism,* p. 45.

dependence of the military and economic sectors. But the relationship between the two sectors had become less direct and more complex. As one author has noted:

> A king could back up the power of trading companies by his fleets and armies which could win wars to obtain monopolies or privileges for the trading companies, who in turn paid the king with their profits what it cost to build such armies and fleets.[7]

The economic function of colonies in the mercantile era was to provide gold as well as other primary products that could readily be converted into bullion. But the relationship between the military and economic sectors did not remain static. As the industrial revolution gained momentum in the Netherlands, England, and elsewhere, gold itself—which had earlier replaced land as the primary object of value in the economic-military system—came to be less important than capital equipment and skilled laborers. New technological developments, such as the use of steam to move heavy machinery, the factory organization of industry, improvements in refining iron, and more sophisticated agricultural techniques, permitted large-scale, even more efficient production and yielded healthy profits. Countries which failed to divert gold resources into industrial development began to decline in power and wealth. While capital generated more capital in the Netherlands and Great Britain, in countries such as Spain the gold entering the country at Cadiz and Seville was drained by the merchants of the Netherlands and Italy.

Acquisition of gold became secondary when it became obvious that a better standard of living could be attained and military capability improved through industrialization of the economy. Industrialism revolutionized both the military and social order. The industrialized economy depended upon the close cooperation of various groups within the society. The lower classes became even more important to the well-being of the society than they had been in the feudal period. They provided labor to run the industrial machinery and soldiers to protect the industrial state.

It is no mere coincidence that the industrialized economy, the mass army, and the growth of a potentially influential working class occurred within the same period. Before the industrial age, the opinion of members of the lower classes had been of minor importance if only because of geographical dispersion. As the industrial economy and the mass army supported by it grew, the influence of the lower class increased, not only because its members were now less dispersed geographically but also

[7] Reynolds, *Europe Emerges,* p. 10.

because their cooperation was essential for the economic health of the society—and for serving in the army. The technological revolution also helped to produce a revolution in population growth, the impact of which was greatest in the lower classes. Their greater numbers, their geographical concentration, their increasing skills and education, and their essential role in industry and the army led the lower classes to assume an important political influence in the nineteenth and twentieth centuries.

If the industrialized economy produced the mass army as well as the seeds of social revolution, it also ultimately produced the capacity for mass destruction. World Wars I and II demonstrated that the industrial machine built by modern man can also be converted into a vehicle of its own destruction. The lesson led to a different formula in the relationship between the economic and military sectors. As land in the feudal period and gold in the mercantile period served as the nexus for connection of the two sectors, industrial development has come to occupy the central position in the twentieth century.

In spite of its destructive capacity, industrial development is a catalyst to both economic well-being and military strength. Although some states enjoy economic prosperity because they have extensive natural resources (Kuwait, for example), most of the wealthy states in the world (those with the highest standards of living) are highly industrialized. At the same time, the modern army is so costly and so dependent on sophisticated equipment produced by industrial techniques, those states that are most industrialized are generally those with the most military strength. The relationship between industrial development and military capability might be changing as production of nuclear weapons becomes cheaper and as some wealthy states may decide not to develop military strength. Nevertheless, it appears that for the immediate future industrial development will continue to be the key to military capability. For the contemporary world, then, industrial development appears to serve as the essential link between the economic and military sectors of the states.

In this brief historical overview, we have seen the degree to which the economic and military sectors of a state are interrelated. In addition, we have seen that the interrelationship has been dynamic; that is, altering and growing more complex in response to changing technological and social conditions. As the economic basis of states has evolved from agriculture, to gold, to industrial production; the military strength of nations has been based in turn on an aristocratic warrior class depending on the toil of peasants for food and materials; on the purchasing power of gold; and finally on the military capability that can be manufactured by an industrial society.

DIMENSIONS OF ECONOMIC CAPABILITY

As students of foreign policy, we should be aware that economic capability of a state plays an important role in that state's foreign policy. Later in this chapter we will examine that role by looking at economic capability as a tool of foreign policy. Our purpose in this section is to describe what makes states economically strong or weak in general. Although we should remember that strength is a relative term (that is, strong to perform what task), a number of criteria can help us to assess the general economic strengths and weaknesses of a particular state. In this section, we will consider: (1) capacity to produce goods and services, and (2) relative independence from international trade and finance.

Capacity to Produce Goods and Services

Assessment of a state's economic capacity should include analyses of the wealth of the country, the degree to which that wealth satisfies the needs of the society, and the growth patterns of the economy. We are interested, therefore, in the absolute amount of goods and services produced; the relative amount (that is, relative to the demands made upon the economy); and the prospects for economic growth.

Economists have developed the concept of gross national product (GNP) to measure the value of all goods and services produced by a nation in any year. Since GNP figures can be converted to a single currency standard, it is possible to use them to compare the wealth of one state with the wealth of another although the difference in currency values poses some problem.

While GNP provides a general indication of a state's overall wealth, it should not be used to infer the capacity of the nation to satisfy economic wants of the people. A more useful economic indicator of relative wealth is GNP per capita (wealth divided by the number of people in the state). This indicator gives a better idea of whether or not the absolute amount of goods and services produced by the economy meets the demands of the people. For example, the Chinese Peoples' Republic ranked fifth in total GNP for all countries of the world in 1957, but on GNP per capita it ranked 101.[8] We can interpret the two rankings to mean that the overall wealth of China was very great but wealth measured in terms of economic needs of the people was extremely small. Although the per capita figure

[8] Bruce M. Russett et al., *World Handbook of Political and Social Indicators* (New Haven, Conn.: Yale University Press, 1964), pp. 152–57.

provides only a rough indicator of relative wealth, it is useful in studying economic capacities of states.

The scatter diagram (Figure 5) roughly indicates the general distribution of economic capacity (absolute and per capita) for 1955. Note that GNP totals for states like China and India were relatively high, but that per capita figures for those countries fell below $150 a year. Note also that very few of the 82 countries enjoyed a per capita GNP greater than $600 and that the majority fell below $300. A similar diagram computed for 1968 would include fifty more nations, most of which would fall below the $150 GNP per capita line.

In addition to the absolute and relative capacities to produce quantities of goods and services, the types of goods and services produced should be considered. Given different geographical, historical, and cultural backgrounds, states tend to have different capacities to produce different types of goods and services. These differences in capacity are vital in foreign affairs because consumers usually want a wide variety of goods that can only be attained through foreign trade.

States with poorly developed economies produce the most limited variety of goods and services, usually limited to agricultural products and raw materials. The chief characteristics of agricultural and raw material products—except for a few like oil and gold, which have long been in high demand throughout the world—is that their prices fluctuate greatly in the short run and would tend downward in the long run if not for intervention in the market mechanism via international commodity agreements. Therefore, in addition to having a shortage of wealth, poorly developed economies tend to produce a small number of items that cannot satisfy their own people and are not always in demand internationally.

The economically underdeveloped states are not the only ones, however, that fail to produce all goods and services their populations require. A number of highly developed states, such as the United Kingdom, do not produce enough agricultural products and raw materials to satisfy the needs of their populations. Nevertheless, the economically developed states usually find a more stable international market for their goods and services because they involve a wide variety of manufactured goods.

Currently, only a very few states are *potentially* self-sufficient; that is, seem to have the capacity to maintain similar standards of living within the country without depending upon foreign trade. We have underscored the term "potentially" however, because even the United States and the Soviet Union, the two states now most capable of becoming economically self-sufficient, are still dependent upon international trade for current standards of living. Although the two superpowers could produce within their borders

FIGURE 5

Population, GNP and GNP per Capita for Eighty-two Nations in 1955

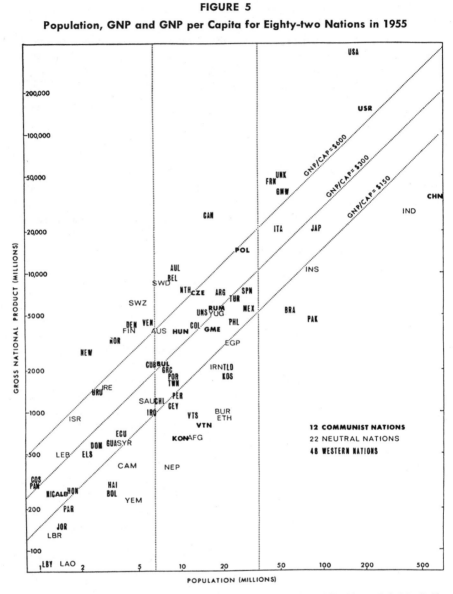

Reprinted from Jack Sawyer, "Dimensions of Nations: Size, Wealth, and Politics," *The American Journal of Sociology* 73, No. 2 (September 1967): 158. Copyright 1967 by University of Chicago Press.

almost everything they require, their economies are so structured that a policy of complete self-sufficiency would produce a lower standard of living for a substantial period of time.

A final dimension of economic capacity is particularly important in terms of foreign policy: the economic growth potential of the state. Students of economic development usually make a clear distinction among states that are economically developed, states that show signs of sustained economic growth, and states that have yet to begin the long road to economic development. Table 3 illustrates W. W. Rostow's notion of the stages of economic growth, as adapted by the authors of the *World Handbook of Political and Social Indicators*.[9] The first category includes economically stagnant societies whose prospects for growth are extremely slight. The second category includes other economically stagnant societies that might soon be able to turn the corner to economic development. The

Key to Abbreviations in Figure 5

AFG	Afghanistan	GMW	Germany (West)	PAK	Pakistan
ALB	Albania	GRC	Greece	PAN	Panama
ARG	Argentina	GUA	Guatemala	PAR	Paraguay
AUL	Australia	HAI	Haiti	PER	Peru
AUS	Austria	HON	Honduras	PHL	Philippines
BEL	Belgium	HUN	Hungary	POL	Poland
BOL	Bolivia	IND	India	POR	Portugal
BRA	Brazil	INS	Indonesia	RUM	Rumania
BUL	Bulgaria	IRE	Ireland	SAU	Saudi Arabia
BUR	Burma	IRN	Iran	SPN	Spain
CAM	Cambodia	IRQ	Iraq	SWD	Sweden
CAN	Canada	ISR	Israel	SWZ	Switzerland
CEY	Ceylon	ITA	Italy	SYR	Syria
CHL	Chile	JAP	Japan	TWN	Taiwan
CHN	China (Mainland)	JOR	Jordan	TLD	Thailand
COL	Colombia	KON	Korea (North)	TUR	Turkey
COS	Costa Rica	KOS	Korea (South)	UNK	United Kingdom
CUB	Cuba	LAO	Laos	UNS	Union S. Africa
CZE	Czechoslovakia	LEB	Lebanon	URU	Uruguay
DEN	Denmark	LBR	Liberia	USA	United States
DOM	Dominican Rep.	LBY	Libya	USR	USSR
ECU	Ecuador	MEX	Mexico	VTN	Vietnam (North)
EGP	Egypt	MON	Mongolia	VTS	Vietnam (South)
ELS	El Salvador	NEP	Nepal	VNZ	Venezuela
ETH	Ethiopia	NTH	Netherlands	YEM	Yemen
FIN	Finland	NEW	New Zealand	YUG	Yugoslavia
FRN	France	NIC	Nicaragua		
GME	Germany (East)	NOR	Norway		

[9] Russett et al., *World Handbook*, pp. 293–303. The table is based on a more elaborate one in the *World Handbook of Political and Social Indicators* which shows how a number of social, economic and political variables relate to the five stages discerned by the authors.

TABLE 3
Stages of Economic and Political Development

Traditional Primitive Societies

Nepal	Afghanistan	Laos
Togo	Ethiopia	Burma
Angola	Libya	Sudan
Tanganyika	Uganda	

Traditional Civilizations

Mozambique	Pakistan	China (Mainland)
India	South Vietnam	Nigeria
Kenya	Madagascar	Congo (Leopold.)
Thailand	Bolivia	Cambodia
Liberia	Sarawak	Haiti

Transitional Societies

Iran	Paraguay	Ceylon
Jordan	Indonesia	Rhodesia and
Egypt	Morocco	Nyasaland
Surinam	South Korea	Iraq
Nicaragua	Taiwan	Saudi Arabia
Ghana	Syria	Tunisia
Albania	Algeria	Peru
Ecuador	Guatemala	Honduras
Barbados	El Salvador	Philippines
Turkey	Portugal	Mauritius
British Guiana	Dominican Republic	

Industrial Revolution Societies

Mexico	Colombia	Yugoslavia
Hong Kong	Brazil	Spain
Japan	Jamaica	Panama
Greece	Malaya	Costa Rica
Romania	Lebanon	Bulgaria
Malta	Chile	South Africa
Singapore	Trinidad and	Cyprus
Poland	Tobago	Uruguay
Argentina	Hungary	Italy
Ireland	Puerto Rico	Iceland
East Germany	Soviet Union	Venezuela
Austria	Czechoslovakia	Israel
Finland		

High Mass Consumption Societies

Netherlands	West Germany	France
Denmark	Norway	United Kingdom
Belgium	New Zealand	Australia
Sweden	Luxembourg	Switzerland
Canada	United States	

Source: Bruce M. Russett, et al., *World Handbook of Political and Social Indicators* (New Haven, Conn.: Yale University Press, 1964), pp. 294–98.

third comprises states with developing economies where growth appears probable—but only in the distant future. The fourth category comprises those that are clearly developing economically and where sustained growth appears highly probable. Fifth are the states that are already well developed economically.

The table indicates a large majority of states today are in stages of economic growth that involve the greatest amount of social and economic change. Leaving behind them the social, economic, and political life of the stagnant agricultural economy, these developing states are attempting to reach the level of economic development enjoyed by only a few states in the world today. As we will see, the striving for economic development characteristic of many of the states today clearly affects their foreign policies.

Thus, when we discuss the economic capacity of a country we are concerned not only with its total capacity to produce, but also with that capacity when compared to the capacity of other states and with the state's ability to satisfy the economic demands of its people quantitatively (wealth per capita) and qualitatively (kinds of products). A final dimension worth knowing, if only because foreign policy always involves expectation of future conditions, is the state's prospects for economic growth.

Dependence on International Trade and Finance

In one way or another, every state in the contemporary world is affected by international trade and finance. The relationship between the state and elements of the international economy is often viewed in terms of *balance of payments*. All foreign transactions, including foreign purchases and sales, overseas investments, military expenditures in other countries, and other expenditures and receipts, comprise the balance of payments. *"Balance"* refers to the net difference between certain debits (payments) and certain credits (receipts), and indicates whether a nation is having difficulty meeting its international obligations and is forced to draw on reserves; or whether wealth coming into the country puts the nation in a favorable position. One should clearly distinguish between balance of payments and balance of trade. The latter plays a large, but far from conclusive, role in the former. For example, the United States in the early 1960's had a very favorable balance of trade (more exports than imports) but an unfavorable balance of payments, resulting primarily from foreign aid overseas, private investment, and military expenditures. Factors affecting the balance of payments for the United States in 1964 are shown in Table 4. Despite trade advantage of more than six billion dollars, the United States still had a balance of payments deficit for the year of more than three billion dollars.

TABLE 4
United States Balance of Payments, 1964
(In billions)

Payments		Receipts	
Imports	$18.6	Exports	$25.2
Transportation and tourism	5.6	Transportation and tourism	5.3
New investments abroad	6.4	Foreign investments	5.2
U.S. foreign aid	2.8	Military sales and other	1.4
Military expenditures	2.8	Increase in foreign assets	0.6
Remittances	0.8		
Other	2.3		
TOTAL	$39.3	TOTAL	$37.7

Source: Adapted from Maxwell S. Stewart, *The Balance of Payments Crisis,* Public Affairs Pamphlet No. 378 (New York: Public Affairs Committee, 1965), p. 5.

So trade is only one aspect of the balance of payments picture for most countries.

States may be classified according to their problems in avoiding an unfavorable balance of payments. The first group is those nations that have no difficulty maintaining a favorable balance. These states produce enough to pay for their imports and for other financial outlays their governments or citizens might make. These states fall into two types: those that demand little from outside their country so they do not need to sell a great deal overseas to maintain a favorable balance, and those that spend a great deal but also sell a great deal.

The second group of nations has chronic difficulty in selling enough to pay for imports. It includes states with underdeveloped economies that produce only primary products. Sale of these primary products is rarely enough to pay for imports consumed by the underdeveloped state and to provide capital needed for economic development. Given their chronic balance-of-payment difficulty and general lack of capital, states with under-developed economies depend on foreign sources of capital for economic development. Before World War II, development investments were supplied by western nations that controlled these underdeveloped areas under colonial systems. Unfortunately from the standpoint of the colonies' economic development, the western nations frequently invested in industries that had the highest payoff for the lowest investment. Hence, they invested in industries like mining and agriculture which provided little industrial capability. After the war, these colonies became independent but remained economically underdeveloped. Usually, the new nations have barely enough to satisfy basic needs and cannot invest in new industries. Hence, they have become dependent on foreign sources of capital.

Foreign investment can be private or public. The former tends to follow the colonial pattern of minimum capital outlay for maximum profit. Therefore the schools, roads, dams, and so forth that form the economic structure of any developed economy cannot be privately financed because they involve immense capital investment with little (if any) immediate or short-term profit. Public foreign investment can be long-term low-interest loans or direct aid from either international institutions or states. Foreign aid from states is often thought by decision makers and policy influencers in the recipient state to carry limitations that restrict freedom of action in their economic, military, or political realms. In terms of economic development goals, aid from international institutions seems to be preferable, although the resources of these institutions are limited. For these reasons, one cannot be optimistic in assessing the prospects for economic development in states with underdeveloped economies. This also means that chronic balance-of-payment difficulties will remain for these states for the foreseeable future.

The third group of states comprises those with balance-of-payment difficulties due to their demand for certain products—usually primary products—that they cannot pay for with exports. Great Britain is the classic example. Although Great Britain could have a favorable balance of payments because she does produce enough exports to cover essential imports, her present standard of living could not be maintained on that basis. Many developed economies suffer from the same problem. Given the high standard of living demanded by their people, some industrialized states cannot cover overseas expenditures with income from exports. However, unlike the states with underdeveloped economies, they are not as eager to amass capital because they already have the economic structure they need for economic development.

The fourth group of states are confronted with balance-of-payment difficulties as a consequence of involvement in overseas enterprises. These enterprises run the gamut from foreign aid and military expenditures to private business investment. This is the difficulty facing the United States. Although the exports have exceeded imports in recent times, its balance-of-payment difficulties are due to heavy private foreign investment, foreign aid, and military commitments.

Therefore, while we can distinguish between states with favorable balance of payments and those with unfavorable balance, the latter may result from a number of causes, ranging from inability to produce exportable products that command large revenues, to high demands for imports that cannot be paid for by exports, to extensive overseas involvement in private investment and/or public activities. It is difficult to predict which states will have favorable or unfavorable balance of payments purely from internal economic considerations because factors determining the balance shift from year to year. For example, France had fewer difficulties in this area in the early and middle 1960's than in the 1950's or the late 1960's. International market conditions and political decisions such as the stationing of troops in foreign lands or extending foreign aid can have an impact on a state's balance of payments. Finally, the decision makers can take steps to correct balance-of-payment difficulties as, for example, the President of the United States did in 1967 and 1968 to curb overseas expenditures by private citizens.

DIMENSIONS OF MILITARY CAPABILITY

We will look at three aspects of military strengths and weaknesses in the contemporary world. The first is the relative capacity of states to employ military force at three different levels: nuclear, conventional, and subversive. The second aspect is the degree to which states depend upon foreign sources for military equipment. Finally, we will examine how internal instability affects a state's military capability. Each of these three aspects is important in assessing overall military capability.

Capacity to Use Military Force

The job of assessing capacity to use military force is difficult if we are interested in predicting the outcome of a specific military conflict. It is less difficult, however, to make a general assessment by determining the crucial criteria of military strength. At the outset, we might note three such criteria: (1) number of men, (2) degree of training, and (3) nature of the military equipment.

One might quarrel with the distinction between being well trained and being well equipped, since one might assume a nation that can acquire sophisticated military equipment can also acquire (or has already acquired) the skilled labor and trained men necessary to employ and maintain the equipment. However, because it is possible for underdeveloped states to acquire advanced military equipment from the developed states, it is also possible for those acquiring the equipment to lack sufficiently skilled and trained men to handle the equipment. The Arab-Israeli war of 1967 illustrates the role of training in modern warfare, in that the numerically superior and well-equipped but poorly skilled and trained Arab forces were defeated by a smaller but better trained Israeli army. It should be emphasized that training is not merely a matter of technical skill in handling the machines of warfare but also is a matter of developing the capacity of men to fight well and to make the correct decisions under battle conditions. We assume here that what has been traditionally called the "morale" of the armed services is directly related to the degree to which the men have been properly trained.

In terms of equipment, a crucial difference exists between nations with nuclear force and those without. Given the vast destructive power of nuclear weapons and the inability of states to defend against efficient nuclear attack, possession of such weapons is viewed as a tremendous military asset. There is no question that states having both nuclear weapons and effective delivery systems possess military strength of a different order of magnitude than nations that do not. Moreover, nuclear capability with the necessary delivery systems can make a relatively small armed force capable of extensive destruction.

If nuclear weapons have made the number of men less important and the quality of equipment and training more important, guerrilla warfare has also changed the relative importance of number of men, training, and equipment. Techniques of guerrilla warfare—terrorism, small-scale interchanges with the opposing army, and sabotage—do not demand a large number of troops or sophisticated equipment. Guerrilla warfare does require, however, specially trained troops who have a strong commitment to the war's purpose as well as the support of the indigenous population. With these conditions, the guerrilla army is practically invulnerable to complete destruction. The United States has learned this in the Vietnam War; the Germans, in dealing with popular underground movements in Europe. Without the support of the local population and the dedication and experience of the soldiers, however, guerrilla activities are usually doomed, as Che Guevara discovered when he attempted to lead a guerrilla movement in Bolivia in the middle 1960's but failed to find support in the Bolivian countryside. We can conclude that guerrilla warfare gives capability to the state without large armies and sophisticated military equipment only if the guerrilla army is attempting to harm foreign troops or to overturn an unpopular regime.

Military strength, then, is related to number of men, quality of equipment, and degree of training. In special types of warfare, such as nuclear and guerrilla, the number of men is less important than training and type of equipment. Thus capacity to fight cannot always be measured by counting troops or equipment alone. History is full of examples where superior numbers have not resulted in victory, and modern times do not appear to be any different in this respect. Manpower, however, is still important, particularly, in extended, conventional wars. Hence, it must continue to be one of the primary elements in determining a nation's capacity to use military force.

In discussing the use of military force we should distinguish between two relatively distinct capacities. One is the capacity to destroy; the other is mobility of troops. It is not necessarily true that all states that have large capacities to cause damage through military force also have the ability to strike anywhere with great speed. For example, the Chinese Peoples' Republic has an army that is capable of great destruction but is unable to strike very far beyond its own border.

It is also important to mention the impact of two societal conditions on the military strength of the nation. The first is GNP, which indicates general resources available for building and maintaining military strength. States with high GNP might not be militarily strong at a given time because they have chosen to spend most of their resources on consumer rather than military goods, but in general the higher the GNP the higher the capacity to create military strength, particularly over a long period of time. A second condition is the society's willingness to support military effort to increase military strength. A classic study of the economies of national defense indicates it takes both GNP and willingness to make sacrifices to yield resources to national defense.[10] The dual conditions of (1) economic strength and (2) commitment of the general population (particularly the policy influencers) to deflect economic resources to develop military strength, constitute a prime requirement for the development of military capability.

Degree of Dependence on Foreign Sources

In addition to assessing military capacity, it is important to be aware of whether the sources of the capability are domestic or foreign. The more a state depends on foreign states for the strength of its armies, the more vulnerable that state is to outside constraints on the use of force. Since all economies of the world are involved to some extent in trade and since many of the goods traded are related to defense industries, all states are somewhat dependent upon foreign states for military strength, particularly if stockpiles are depleted. A clear distinction can be made, however, between dependence on foreign states for (1) primary products and logistical support and (2) finished military products.

The United States and the Soviet Union are the two prime suppliers of military equipment. Other major suppliers along with the weapons they

---

[10] Charles J. Hitch and Roland N. McKean, *The Economics of Defense in the Nuclear Age* (New York: Atheneum, 1965), p. 34.

TABLE 5

Major Arms Suppliers to the Third World, 1969–70

Supplier	Weapons Supplied
United States	
Soviet Union	
Britain	Most types of major weapons
France	
West Germany	Aircraft and tanks, small arms
China	Aircraft, tanks, small arms
Italy	Aircraft, tanks warships
Canada	Aircraft
Netherlands	Small arms, aircraft
Switzerland	Small arms
Czechoslovakia	Aircraft, small arms
Israel	Small arms

Source: Geoffrey Kemp, "Arms Traffic and Third World Conflicts," *International Conciliation* 577 (March, 1970), 18.

supply are indicated in Table 5. These nations sell (and sometimes give) military equipment and weapons to states lacking the industrial foundations to manufacture their own. The supplier acquires some measure of control over the purchasing state. For example, in the India-Pakistani conflict over Kashmir in 1965 both sides had received large amounts of American arms; withholding of spare parts by the United States and other suppliers, including the Soviet Union, helped to contain the fighting. A state's dependence upon foreign suppliers of military equipment extends beyond mere acquisition of the equipment. It involves acquisition of spare parts for peacetime and wartime maintenance as well as use of foreign advisors to employ the military equipment correctly. In a number of ways, then, states that supply military equipment can exert influence over the states that receive it.

States having ability to produce their own military equipment are not completely independent of others. Besides the dependence that might grow out of an alliance commitment, these states depend on others for raw materials and logistical support through the use of territory. States with global interests are more dependent upon others for logistical support than those with narrow interests. Hence, Sweden depends on other states for some raw materials necessary for military production while the United States depends on other states for both raw materials and use of their territory for logistical support.

Examination of contemporary military capability will indicate that very few states are not dependent upon foreign suppliers for finished military equipment. Only Communist China, France, Sweden, the United Kingdom, the United States, and the Soviet Union enjoy relative independence. The emphasis should be on *relative* since even these states depend on other states for strategic primary products. Moreover, France and the United Kingdom still use some American military equipment while Communist China has suffered immensely from the Soviet Union's withdrawal of military support. Nevertheless, these six are much stronger militarily than other states because they do not depend substantially on foreign military equipment.

Dependence on foreign states is different for the two superpowers. The Soviet Union depends upon eastern European states primarily for logistical support; the United States depends upon states scattered around the globe for use of territory to maintain military bases and supply lines. Table 6 indicates locations of American and Soviet overseas troops in 1967–68. As we will see, the difference in the patterns of dependence of foreign states for logistical support has an impact on the military strength of the two states.

Internal Instability and Military Capability

Although ostensibly the primary purpose of military force is to protect the state from foreign attack and to be employed in wars as foreign policy decision makers deem necessary, a very important role of military troops is the capacity to prevent domestic social and political unrest from overthrowing the existing governmental regime or from causing extensive dam-

TABLE 6
Location of Soviet and U.S. Troops, 1967–68

Country	Approximate Numbers	Geographical Region
Soviet Union	253,500	Eastern Europe
	3,000	Cuba
United States	352,000	Europe and Mediterranean
	23,000	Caribbean
	550,000	Southeast Asia
	217,000	Far East
	400,000	Elsewhere (on route, Canada, Iceland, etc.)

Source: *The Military Balance 1967–1968* (London: Institute for Strategic Studies, 1968), pp. 5–9, and "Where 1.5 Million Americans are Fighting—Or Standing Guard," *U.S. News and World Report* (Jan. 1968), 20–21.

age. Other internal roles for the military include use of troops in times of natural disaster, but suppression of domestic violence is the primary internal use. In countries where regimes are faced with massive and frequent instability, use of military forces often becomes the only means by which the regime can stay in power. Even if the regime is not threatened, as in the case of the riots in American cities in the middle and late 1960's, troops are often necessary to restore control to local authorities.

In order to adequately estimate the capacity of a state to employ military force in its foreign policy, it is important to determine the degree to which its military capacity is "tied down" by the threat of internal instability. Armed forces available for foreign policy objectives will be reduced to fill the ranks designated to promote internal order. In addition, states depending on military force for internal control cannot rely upon support from their citizens in case of foreign attack. Of course, there is always the possibility that foreign attack will generate internal support, but this is a gamble, at best, under such circumstances.

ECONOMIC AND MILITARY FACTORS AS TOOLS OF FOREIGN POLICY

A complete picture of the tools of foreign policy should include examination of the complex factors surrounding *who* uses *what* tools in *what* ways against *whom* to achieve *which* objectives. To present such a discussion right now, however, would force us to examine patterns of interactions rather than of foreign policy making—something which we are not prepared to do within the approach and structure of this book. Nevertheless, it is necessary to study in what ways the dimensions of economic and military capability we have just discussed are related to foreign policy. We will do this by examining the *potential* roles of economic and military capability in foreign policy and by ignoring all factors other than economic and military capability that might affect the way two states interact. Since the only purpose of the discussion is to show the way in which economic and military capability might affect foreign policy if no other factors were involved, the discussion will ignore the various roles of domestic politics, third parties such as the United Nations or alliances, mutual perceptions, and the specific nature of foreign policy objectives. In later chapters we will present a more complete picture of all the tools of foreign policy.[11]

[11] Chapters 8, 9, and 10 employ a general bargaining framework to discuss the various ways in which states attempt to influence each other. In these chapters, the role of economic and military tools is examined in the proper perspective with other foreign policy tools.

Our previous discussion of dimensions of economic and military capability suggests a threefold typology of states that will help to present our analysis of the role of economic and military factors as tools of foreign policy. We can distinguish between the cluster of economic and military factors associated with the *underdeveloped* states, and the cluster associated with the *developed* states. The *superpowers,* which right now are the United States and Soviet Union, constitute a special kind of developed state. Economic and military conditions of an underdeveloped state are usually (1) low GNP per capita, with a specialization in raw materials and agricultural products; (2) an economy depending upon foreign states for manufactured products, capital, and markets; (3) balance-of-payment difficulties due to a lack of exports to cover consumer and investment demands; and (4) a poorly trained conventional army dependent upon foreign support, the primary purpose of which is to preserve internal stability. In contrast, the developed state is characterized by (1) relatively high GNP per capita; (2) industries with a more varied productive capacity and some specialization in manufactured products; (3) a well-trained conventional army that plays an extensive foreign policy role although it may also be employed to maintain internal stability; and (4) a major involvement in world trade. The two superpowers share the above economic and military capabilities with the developed states, but they also have an extensive nuclear arsenal as well as the capacity to deliver nuclear weapons anywhere on the globe plus extensive economic and military involvement in a number of areas beyond their borders. Concerning distribution of the three types throughout the world, underdeveloped states comprise the majority including the nations of Africa with the exception of South Africa; the nations of the Middle East with the exception of Israel; and the nations of Asia, except Japan and Central and South American nations. The developed states, for the most part, are in Europe and North America.

The threefold distinction will help to organize our discussion of the role of economic and military capability as tools of foreign policy. We will look at what the various combinations of pairs of the three types of states can do to harm and help each other economically and militarily. Hence, we will discuss possible military and economic actions between (1) two underdeveloped states, (2) two developed states, (3) one underdeveloped and one developed state, (4) the Soviet Union and the United States, and (5) the Soviet Union and the United States toward a developed state. Drawing upon our previous discussion of dimensions of economic and military capability, our presentation should aid the reader in understanding how the dimensions of military and economic capability shape foreign policy.

Two Underdeveloped States

The first and most important fact to remember when assessing the role of economic and military capability in the foreign policy of one underdeveloped state directed toward another is that, unless they are closely situated geographically, two underdeveloped states can neither seriously harm nor significantly assist one another either economically or militarily. The characteristic absence of well-equipped troops implies lack of mobility; they cannot reach each other. Economically, underdeveloped states are not good trading partners because they usually produce few exportable items.

If the underdeveloped states are territorially adjacent or at least within a few hundred miles of each other, economic and military tools can be useful but only to a very limited extent. Because the costs of long-term, full-scale warfare are so great, particularly in relation to the limited stockpiles available to underdeveloped states, military hostilities between underdeveloped states tend to be limited to sporadic border incidents and subversive activities. The subversive activities might consist of paramilitary subversive forces sent to infiltrate, incite insurrection, terrorize, and promote political instability; or they might be in the form of quasi-guerrilla forays sent to destroy vital communication links or supply depots and to engage in selective combat with the enemy. In any case, use of military force demands only limited logistical support. For the same reason, only limited military cooperation is feasible if both states are faced with what they perceive to be a mutual enemy, but the possibility of extensive coordination is precluded by the poorly trained nature of the troops, backward transportation systems that hinder troop mobility, and a similar dependence of both states on one or more developed nations for weapons and equipment.

In the economic sector, two adjacent underdeveloped states can do little for or against one another unless geographical position gives an advantage to one side; for example, when neighbors control access to the high seas for landlocked states like Upper Volta in Africa or Nepal in Asia. Otherwise underdeveloped states cannot use economic weapons like boycotts because they do not depend as much on trade from each other as they do on trade from developed states. Similarly, economic conditions provide few occasions for cooperative foreign policy among underdeveloped states, although bilateral and multilateral economic cooperation appears to hold some promise at least in creating a common front for dealing with the developed states.

In the final analysis, the poor economic and military conditions of underdeveloped states seriously limit the variety and effectiveness of actions they can initiate against, or with, one another. The underdeveloped state that takes a hostile action usually risks more damage to its own economic and military capabilities than it can hope to gain. This does not mean that underdeveloped states do not take such actions, but that the tools for such actions are not likely to produce much success.

Two Developed States

Unlike the underdeveloped states, whose ability to employ economic and military tools is inherently limited by the weakness of their economic-military systems, the developed states can and do have significant impact on each other's policies, welfare, and military capability. Although distance can be an important constraint, the developed states are not essentially geographically limited. Highly sophisticated logistical systems permit rapid transport of troops and equipment over moderately long distances. Given the speed and efficiency with which an attack can be carried out, and given the concentration of wealth and productive capability in large and centralized urban manufacturing areas, mass devastation of an opponent's resources becomes an available alternative. However, the option is easily reciprocated, so the material, short-range gains of an attack might be lost as a result of counter-attack. At the same time, given the extensive economic integration among many developed nations of the world, destruction of economic capability of one developed state by another can be self-defeating. Severe economic dislocations in one state can have an equally severe impact on another. Thus at the close of World War II the allies realized the necessity of putting postwar Germany back on its economic feet, not only because the Soviet threat was growing but also because the German economy affected other European economies.

Both militarily and economically, developed states are potentially more interdependent than underdeveloped ones. Sophisticated weaponry and highly efficient transportation systems permit close military coordination and effective division of military labor in alliance networks such as the North Atlantic Treaty Organization. Economically, developed states tend to increase their trading and financial relationships yearly. Specialization in the manufacture of diverse products makes trade essential to their standard of living. As a result, acts of hostility as well as cooperation in the economic realm have an important impact on relations between developed nations.

Given the ability of developed states to harm each other as well as their capacity to help each other, economic and military tools have been increasingly employed for cooperation rather than conflict since the end of

World War II. Developed states find economic cooperation more advantageous and warfare more costly than underdeveloped states. Rising standards of living and economic stability depend to some extent on international commerce and to even a greater extent on the avoidance of large-scale war. Although ideological and historical animosities may lessen the chances of economic and military cooperation among certain sets of developed states, the economic and military vulnerability of developed states to each other has significantly lessened the chance of large-scale warfare among them since World War II.

Underdeveloped versus Developed States

A crucial factor in the relations of underdeveloped to developed states is mobility of the latter, which provides a strategic advantage. Military conflicts between the two invariably take place within the underdeveloped country. The technology and economic capability of a developed nation permits mass production and maintenance of a large and complex logistical system. Thus, the developed nation possesses the mobility necessary to bring swift and perhaps decisive damage to the underdeveloped state, while at the same time remaining relatively immune to a reciprocal attack. A developed nation can bring pressure to bear on a less developed one by threatening to cut off the supply of arms; by threatening to develop substitutes for, or find other markets for the underdeveloped state's products; by refusing to make good on investment promises; or by physically boycotting or blockading the underdeveloped state. At the same time, the developed nation has the capability to assist the underdeveloped ones by providing vital weapons, capital and manufactured products, and technological assistance, as well as aid in the area of military security and internal political stability.

One should not conclude, however, that an underdeveloped state is completely defenseless in relations with developed states. First, the products it supplies to the developed state may be the lifeblood of that state's economy. For example, intermittent oil boycotts by Middle East states have significantly affected the economy of the United Kingdom by severely limiting the supply of oil. Second, private investments by citizens of the developed states create a degree of vulnerability for the developed state because of the threat of nationalization. That means the underdeveloped states that receive the investment can take over the business of a potentially powerful policy influencer from the developed state. While nationalization may be very costly in some respects to the underdeveloped state, it will also have a major effect on the willingness of the developed state to employ economic and military tools. Third, developed nations may need underdeveloped ones as allies for logistical reasons. Military as well as nonmilitary transportation may be facilitated or hindered by strategically placed underdeveloped states. This is particularly true if the state controls a vital seaway such as in Panama or Suez or borders an area where the developed state has vital military interests. Finally, the underdeveloped state need not be a passive victim of military attack and occupation. Over the past two decades, guerrilla tactics employed by members of the underdeveloped states have often humbled much more powerful occupying states.

Nevertheless, the developed states enjoy certain advantages. Prior to World War II, these advantages were manifested in *colonialism*. The developed states were able to exercise substantial control over underdeveloped areas as a result of superior economic and military capability. Although most of the underdeveloped nations today have destroyed colonial relationships by threat or use of military force, an economic-military basis remains for manipulation of the underdeveloped states by the developed states.

Neocolonialism, a term often used to describe current relationships between developed and underdeveloped states, rests to a large extent on the developed states' economic and military superiority. The unfavorable balance-of-payment situation confronting most underdeveloped states makes them dependent on preferential treatment and on private as well as public capital from the developed states. In addition, many citizens from developed states own and operate businesses in underdeveloped states, the profits from which they take out of the country. In the military realm, the assistance underdeveloped states receive makes them vulnerable, particularly during wartime. Furthermore, military advisors, sent to the underdeveloped country to assist in technical military matters, often exert general political pressure, as, for example, French advisors in African states.

What we have said about the relationship between developed and underdeveloped states also applies to the relationship between either of the two superpowers and the underdeveloped states. Both the United States and the Soviet Union have contributed economic and military assistance to underdeveloped states, and both have tended to treat the recipients as areas for competition between themselves. When comparing relative strengths of each superpower toward these states, one basic difference is important. While the United States clearly has more economic potential for manipulating the economies of the underdeveloped states because of the volume of her trade and investment, the Soviet Union enjoys the advantage of not having its private citizens involved in business ventures in the underdeveloped states. In spite of these differences, however, both superpowers employ economic and military superiority in dealing with these nations.

The Soviet Union and the United States

Economic and military tools available to the Soviet Union and the United States create conditions in which the superpowers can both harm and help each other to a great extent. Given the advanced technological stages enjoyed by both states, geography does not greatly alter the potential economic and military capability of either vis-à-vis the other.

In the military area, the potential for harm is so great the military sector tends to contribute to cooperation in the sense that both states tacitly coordinate their behavior to avoid direct military confrontation. Like other developed states, the two superpowers are highly vulnerable to attack from each other. Although both are trying to develop greater defenses against nuclear attack, their prospects do not appear promising. While tacit cooperation between them extends to avoiding direct military confrontation, it does not extend to an attempt either to avoid indirect confrontation (through allies) or to create opposing formal military alliance systems.

In the economic area, both states could be extensive trading partners just as most developed states in the world are potentially good trading partners. However, except for some small-scale trading, the Soviet Union and the United States are independent of each other in the economic realm. The primary reason for this lies in their mutual distrust as well as the absence of a large U.S. market for Soviet goods. Although there are some signs that Soviet-American trade might increase, we can expect that increase to be extremely gradual within the foreseeable future.

Concerning economic and military tools available to the two superpowers, there is little advantage for either side. It is true that the United States has a substantial edge in both nuclear weapons and economic development, but given the strength of the Soviet Union, this edge can provide little conclusive support to United States decision makers in a face-to-face encounter. Probably the most important difference is that the United States has been able to build up a set of allies surrounding the Soviet Union while the Soviet Union has not been able to acquire allies surrounding the United States. Even Cuba has not been a valuable military ally because of the unwillingness of both Cuba and the Soviet Union to build a Soviet military base in Cuba (particularly since the 1962 missile crisis). Notwithstanding some absolute superiority enjoyed by the United States, direct interaction between the superpowers is stalemated because both have sufficiently extensive economic and military capability to harm. To assume that this stalemate is inevitable would be a mistake, since changing technological or economic factors could cause a radical shift in the economic and/or military conditions within either or both states. Neither state is invulnerable to economic disintegration (depression, crop failures, and the like) or immune to the effect of a technological break-through (antimissile systems). Moreover, there is an important discrepancy between *actual* and *perceived* economic and military conditions; this can result in unpredictable behavior. Although we can expect that economic and military conditions will continue to contribute to a stalemate between the superpowers, we must realize that a stalemate is not inevitable.

The Two Superpowers and the Developed States

The United States and the Soviet Union have a great advantage over the other developed nations through nuclear weapons and advanced delivery systems. In effect, the two superpowers can destroy any developed nation without fearing extensive damage from retaliation. Even France, Great Britain, and Red China—the other states currently possessing nuclear capability—could not extensively destroy either of the superpowers. This means the developed states have approached the Soviet Union and the United States in a defensive manner. In the 1950's they either made an alliance commitment to one of them (NATO, Warsaw Pact) or maintained a clearly neutral position. Concomitantly, the Soviet Union and the United States have viewed the developed states as potential allies. In the period since 1960, however, a tendency has been growing for many of the allies to move away from the close ties that characterized the 1950's. In some cases, such as France in NATO, this has not yet resulted in the complete end of military coordination; in other cases, such as Red China with the Soviet Union, it has. Although many states in both NATO and the Warsaw Pact express policies of political independence from the bloc, they continue to cooperate militarily.

The United States has an economic advantage over the Soviet Union when dealing with other developed states. The United States has become very powerful in international economic matters, even more than it was during the interwar period. Initially, this power resulted from conditions following World War II when the United States was the only developed state with an undamaged economic system. Through the Marshall Plan, the United States exercised a great deal of economic control over the developed states of Europe. In addition, the U.S. monetary policy has made the dollar a medium of international exchange. Although this policy places unusual demands on the American economic system, it also has given the nation the most powerful voice in international economic matters, at least until now. Finally, immense overseas investment by American businessmen has led to extensive influence in the economic systems of developed states. In recent years, some of the developed states—most notably France—have attempted to limit economic influence by limiting American investments and building up strong currencies as substitutes to the dollar. However, the United States continues to have extensive influence over the economic systems of other states.

In contrast, the Soviet Union has not been able to wield similar economic influence. Only in eastern Europe, where its military superiority has helped it, has the Soviet Union been able to influence the economic systems of developed states. Its currency does not have the international financial stature that the American dollar enjoys, and it does not have extensive capital investments overseas. Consequently, except in eastern Europe the Soviet Union receives little support from her economic system in dealing with other developed states.

Thus, the Soviet Union and the United States have potentially great military superiority over the developed nations. Both superpowers have exercised their superiority, although differently. The United States has developed an alliance policy tying the military security of some of the developed states to its own security while the Soviet Union has used a similar alliance policy, and also has threatened and sometimes used military force to keep allies in line. In the economic realm, the United States enjoys more support than the Soviet Union in dealing with the developed states. In fact, some economic development within the Soviet Union appears dependent upon cooperation with the developed states in both eastern and western Europe, so that to some extent it is the Soviet Union that "needs" the other developed states. Although the extensive wealth of the United States will continue to provide an advantage for American decision makers in dealing with the developed states in the near future, it appears that some states are attempting to limit this source of American influence.

SUMMARY

In the last section, we have attempted to illustrate the potential role of economic and military tools in the foreign policies of states. The presentation has been partial in the sense that it has looked at the potential operation of economic and military tools as if they operated in a vacuum. As a result, it has purposely neglected considerations of policy not directly involving military and economic capability. It has ignored historical and ideological attitudes, the role of policy influencers, and the effect of third parties, as well as the role of perception on the part of foreign policy decision makers in evaluating each other's capabilities.

Even with this partial treatment, however, it should be apparent that one cannot discuss economic and military capability merely by looking at quantities. States that lack superiority in some economic and military areas often have counterbalancing capabilities in other areas. In the contemporary world, economic interdependencies work both ways so that while one state might receive greater benefits from an economic relationship than another state, both would suffer if that relationship were broken. This makes economic strength a limited tool for the foreign policy maker. At the same time, military capability has changed so that although the militarily strong can damage the militarily weak more extensively than the other way around, the weak can harm the strong sufficiently to make the strong less willing to use force. This is particularly true in cases where the strong attempt to establish military controls over an area that has the capacity to carry on guerrilla resistance. If nothing else, the above discussion should indicate that economic and military conditions have a complex impact on formulation and execution of foreign policy and that superiority in military capacity to destroy and in economic capacity to produce wealth do not automatically provide foreign policy decision makers with the tools to achieve their objectives.

The above presentation carries implications for the concept of "power," which is frequently employed in textbooks as well as in journalistic accounts of international politics.[12] Although writers in the field frequently hedge their definitions of power to account for many noneconomic and military factors, they nevertheless uniformly use the concept to denote the *general* ability of one state to force another state to perform a particular act. The emphasis is on "general" because writers and even actors often assume that, because of an ordering of states in the world, the more powerful can get the less powerful to do what the more powerful want in all or most cases. Our discussion of economic and military capability reveals, however, that economically and militarily strong states enjoy no clear-cut and automatic advantage in dealing with the economically and militarily weak. Although the strong can more easily punish or help the weak, they are not invulnerable to the other's actions. More important, the option of subjugating or capturing the territory of the target state is rarely an acceptable alternative because even the weakest military power is capable of waging a costly guerrilla war.

That there is no such easy ordering of states is vividly illustrated by difficulties the two superpowers have had even in their own backyards. The United States' inability to manipulate Cuba after Castro came to power and the Soviet Union's difficulties in many eastern European states show that the ability of the strong to control the weak is highly limited. For this reason, then, it is necessary to look at economic and military factors as

---

[12] See, for example, Hans J. Morgenthau, *Politics Among Nations* 3d ed. (New York: Knopf, 1960), pp. 101–67, and A. F. K. Organski, *World Politics,* 2d ed. (New York: Knopf, 1968), pp. 101–222.

highly complex tools in the interactions among states. (See Chapter 10.) Although it is important to evaluate the economic and military capabilities of states in examining their foreign policies, one should not make the simplified assumption that the strong always dominate the weak.

SUMMARY OUTLINE

I.   Historically, economic and military factors have been highly inter-related in shaping the foreign policies of states.
  A. *In the feudal and early postfeudal period, the agricultural economy produced an upper class that was free to provide military force.*
  B. *In the classical period, gold was a source of both wealth and military capability.*
  C. *In the modern period, industrialization has changed the basis of both wealth and military capability from gold to economic development.*

II. . Two economic dimensions are relevant to foreign policy making: the productive capacity of the economy and the economy's dependence on international trade and finance.
  A. *Few states have highly developed economies (high GNP per capita, capital-intensive industries) but many have underdeveloped economies (low GNP per capita, labor-intensive industries).*
  B. *Many states have balance-of-payment difficulties. They stem from a variety of sources, including poor capacity to produce goods and services valued internationally, high standard of living dependent upon imports without sufficient exports to pay for imports, and overseas involvements of both a private (investment) and public (war, foreign aid) nature that result in a new outflow of capital.*

III. *The military strength of a nation depends not only on the number of men, degree of training, and equipment of the armed forces; it also depends upon degree of foreign support and the role of the armed forces in maintaining internal stability.*
  A. *Large numbers of men are more important in fighting conventional wars than in fighting nuclear or guerrilla wars.*
  B. *Equipment and training are most important for the use of nuclear capability.*
  C. *Success in guerrilla warfare depends upon dedication and experience of the men as well as popular support.*

D. *Both sufficient productive capability and support of policy influencers within a country are necessary to maintain substantial nuclear and/or conventional capacity.*

E. *Few countries have military capability that is not heavily dependent on foreign trade or aid in military equipment.*

F. *Military capability tied down at home by the threat of violence cannot be used for foreign wars although it probably can be used for defense of the homeland if it is attacked by another state.*

IV. Economic and military conditions of a state provide foreign policy tools.

A. *Unless they are closely situated geographically, underdeveloped states cannot substantially harm or help each other in either the economic or military realm.*

B. *If they are closely situated geographically, underdeveloped states can only harm each other to a limited extent because of poor military capability, and help each other to a limited extent because of similar economies.*

C. *Developed states have military capability to attack the underdeveloped state's homeland while underdeveloped states do not have capacity to attack the developed state's homeland.*

D. *Developed states have capacity to manipulate the economy of the underdeveloped state.*

E. *Underdeveloped states have substantial capacity to defend their homeland using guerrilla tactics even against developed states.*

F. *Underdeveloped states can harm the developed state economically by nationalizing property of the developed state's nationals.*

G. *Although the United States has a much stronger economy than the Soviet Union, the latter is less vulnerable than the former in dealing with underdeveloped states.*

H. *Because the two superpowers have capacity to destroy each other militarily, they tend to cooperate in minimizing the chances of a direct military confrontation.*

I. *Developed states have approached the two superpowers in a defensive manner either by claiming neutrality or by forcing an alliance with one side.*

J. *The United States has a definite economic advantage over the Soviet Union in dealing with developed states because of its position in the world monetary structure.*

V. Economic and military superiority does not automatically provide foreign policy decision makers with generally powerful tools in achieving foreign policy objectives.

BIBLIOGRAPHICAL ESSAY

A great deal of source material exists on what might be called the dimensions of economic and military conditions within states. Information on economic variables may be obtained from the *United Nations Statistical Yearbooks* and the *Statesmans Yearbooks* as well as from Russett et al. (361) and Banks and Textor (24). Information on military capability can be acquired from *The Military Balance*, published yearly in London by the Institute for Strategic Studies. Studies on the dynamics of economic conditions abound, including these that suggest relevance to foreign policy: Rostow (350), Pentony (310), Millikan and Blackmer (280), Hagen (153), Heilbroner (164), Deutsch (99), Horowitz (182), and Galbraith (134). A few works dealing with international trade that might be easily read by political science students are: Deutsch and Eckstein (103) and (104), Kindleberger (222), Neumark (292), Pryor (322), and Mac-Bean (257). Literature that might provide an understanding of the history and dynamics of military factors is also abundant. The following should be considered basic reading: Knorr (229), Kissinger (224), Kahn (202), Fuller (132), and Wright et al. (429).

Although there is substantial material, both empirical and analytical, examining the dimensions of economic and military capability, the literature attempting to relate that capability to foreign policy is extremely weak. The most common attempt in the literature employs the concept of power as discussed at the end of the chapter. Textbook writers usually discuss economic and military capability under the topic, "national power." For example, Organski (302) lists geography, natural resources, population, economic development, political development, and national morale. Clearly, the list mixes economic and military factors with noneconomic and nonmilitary ones, justifying the assumption that national power is more than the capacity to fight a war. However, discussions such as this one do not systematically describe the relationships between economic and military capabilites and other capabilities; the implication remains that the ability to wage war is power. In Chapter 4, we have not adequately developed the relationship either, but we have clearly distinguished economic and military capability on the one hand and the general ability to influence states (usually implied in the concept of national power) on the other hand. The primary point is that the notion of general powerfulness that usually underlies discussions of national power can no longer explain how or why states influence each other. The same confusion is also introduced by others such as Ash (17) and Jones in (348) in use of the term national power.

Other attempts in the field more explicitly approach the problem of the relationship between economic and military capability and foreign policy. Among them are the empirical works of Rummel (34), Russett et al. (361), and Sawyer (37), which employ various methods of correlation statistics to search for relationships between economic, military, and some foreign policy variables. In addition, more traditional attempts are made to relate economic and military factors to foreign policy. Aside from studies on colonialism by Emerson (117) and Easton (112), the relationship between economics of foreign policy has been discussed in Beard (30), Hitch and McKean (176), and Russett (357). The impact of military capability on domestic politics and indirectly on foreign policy is examined in Schilling et al. (370), Snyder (389), and Baldwin (21). Hirschman (175) and Milen (278) have examined the role of foreign trade in political relationships among states. Foreign aid as a tool of foreign policy is seen from various viewpoints in Goldwin (140), and in the military area, Stambuck in (40) discusses the general role of overseas forces in contemporary international politics; Wolf (427) looks at economic and military factors operating in guerrilla warfare; and Kemp (217) traces the flow of military equipment to the third world.

The major portion of the literature dealing with economic and military factors as tools of foreign policy is examined in the bibliographical essay following Chapter 10. The books and articles discussed above should provide sufficient supplementary material on the dimensions of economic and military factors, particularly as they relate to tools of foreign policy.

5

Descriptive Analysis of Foreign Policy: Patterns and Determinants

In the preceding three chapters, we have discussed three relatively distinct components of the foreign policy-making process. Although we have attempted to show the points at which the foreign policy decision maker, domestic politics, and economic and military capabilities affect each other, the emphasis has been on separate components. We now face the task of combining these factors and others in a more integrated framework.

In this chapter, we will present a basic framework for descriptively analyzing foreign policy.[1] Partially built on the three components discussed in earlier chapters, our framework will approach foreign policy from a more integrated viewpoint by searching for patterns of foreign policy behavior and determinants of those patterns. We have adopted an explicitly *causal* framework by assuming that we can discover what causes (determinants) produce what effects (patterns of behavior) even though we are aware of the long-standing philosophical debate over whether or not one can ever know causes.[2] Despite the philosophical debate, scholars generally

[1] See Chapter 1 for a discussion of descriptive and other types of analysis. Although the framework presented in this chapter might be useful in predictive analysis also, the primary aim is to describe or explain foreign policy.

[2] The nature of the debate, as well as the underlying position for the presentation in this chapter, is described in Hubert M. Blalock, *Causal Inference in Non-Experimental Research* (Chapel Hill, N.C.: University of North Carolina Press, 1964). Also, James N. Rosenau, "Comparative Foreign Policy: Fad, Fantasy, or Field," *International Studies Quarterly,* 12 (1968), 296–330, emphasizes the importance of thinking in terms of determinants. For two radically different treatments of the problems of examining international politics in a multicausal framework, see Hayward R. Alker, Jr., "The Long Road to International Relations Theory: Problems of Statistical Nonadditivity," *World Politics,* 18 (1966), 623–56; and Feliks Gross, *Foreign Policy Analysis* (New York: Philosophical Library, 1954), pp. 22–38.

think in terms of cause and effect, particularly in the early stages of a research problem. As long as we remain aware of the philosophical and intellectual dangers of considering problems in terms of cause and effect, we believe that we can usefully employ a causal framework in descriptively analyzing foreign policy.

By approaching this analysis in terms of cause and effect, we have specified certain intellectual tasks. First, we must be able to describe the nature of foreign policies, something we have done only at a very rudimentary level previously. In this chapter, we will examine various ways of classifying foreign policy behavior. Once we have classified the effects we will be ready to look for the causes. With our previous discussion of three components of foreign policy making as a starting point, we will look at four determinants. Finally, because we are creating a multicausal rather than a monocausal explanation of foreign policy behavior, we will attempt to describe relative interaction among the four determinants to produce patterns of behavior.

In reading this chapter, the student should be aware of the exploratory nature of the framework. Like the concepts and propositions that have been presented so far, those examined in this chapter should be viewed as the *kinds of but not necessarily the exact* concepts and propositions that could be useful in descriptively analyzing foreign policy. In examining ways of classifying this behavior, the nature of its determinants and the relationship between them and patterns of behavior, this chapter should provide an overall approach to descriptive analysis of foreign policy. As we will illustrate, the framework can be useful in studying specific foreign policy actions as well as comparing the ways states behave generally.

CLASSIFYING FOREIGN POLICY ACTIVITIES

One major difficulty facing the student of foreign policy is classifying activities that represent a state's foreign policy. Unlike domestic policy, foreign policy is not usually represented in laws authoritatively promulgated by the institutions of the society. Rather, the student of foreign policy must learn to infer the characteristics of a state's foreign policy from the speeches of its leaders, from the laws it makes directed at its own citizens with foreign policy ramifications, from the treaties it signs, from the actions it takes in international organizations, and from the things it says and does to other states in the system. Sometimes, the foreign policy of one state towards another is expressed in one document or one act, but more frequently it is represented by a series of acts over a period of time. In short, to classify a state's foreign policy, the student must piece together a lot of data that is sometimes difficult to collect and frequently hard to analyze.

An important recent development in the study of international politics has been the attempt to collect reliable data on foreign policy output (that is, what states do to each other). One major source has been voting patterns in the United Nations. Alker and Russett, in their study of voting in the United Nations General Assembly, have been able to identify voting groupings that provide evidence of certain foreign policy patterns.[3] Major newspapers are another source of data; events reported have been classified according to some particular scheme. Tanter and Rummel, for example, have ascertained the number and types of hostile acts directed by one state against another for a number of years.[4] A content analysis of messages among states prior to the outbreak of World War I by North and others has also provided indications of levels of hostility among states.[5] Although this data has been used to answer a different theoretical question (conflict interaction among states), it remains an important source of material for our purposes.

Even with these newer techniques, classifying the foreign policies of states continues to be difficult. First, foreign policies tend to change over time without clear-cut indications. Like most political decision making, foreign policy decision making is done incrementally. This means that many small decisions that might individually escape the student could be combined to signify substantial alterations in the course of a state's foreign policy. Second, a state's foreign policy is often a conglomeration of a number of foreign policies. States not only treat different states differently; they often treat the same state differently. For example, a striking characteristic of contemporary Soviet-American relations has been the complex mixture of hostile and friendly actions towards each other during the same period. Examples are the Berlin crises and the Nuclear Test Ban Treaty.

---

[3] Hayward R. Alker, Jr., and Bruce M. Russett, *World Politics in the General Assembly* (New Haven, Conn.: Yale University Press, 1965). Russett argues in another book, *International Regions and the International System: A Study in Political Ecology* (Chicago: Rand McNally, 1967), pp. 59–80, that U.N. voting can be used to identify political attitudes of states.

[4] Rudolph J. Rummel, "The Relationship between National Attributes and Foreign Conflict Behavior," in J. David Singer, ed., *Quantitative International Politics: Insights and Evidence* (New York: Free Press, 1968), pp. 187–215, and Raymond Tanter, "Dimensions of Conflict Behavior Within and Between Nations, 1958–60," *Journal of Conflict Resolution,* 10 (1966), 283–97.

[5] See Robert C. North, Ole R. Holsti, M. George Zaninovich, and Dina A. Zinnes, *Content Analysis: A Handbook with Applications for the Study of International Crisis* (Evanston, Ill.: Northwestern University Press, 1963).

Foreign policy has been called a set of "separate or only vaguely related actions,"[6] and so attempts to find general patterns are extremely difficult.

Therefore, to classify foreign policy activities, one must deal with a number of problems. What data will he use to study the foreign policies of a state? What level should he study—specific policies on specific issues to specific states or the general policy towards the entire international system? How does one piece together the elements that make up a foreign policy in order to generalize about a given state? These questions are difficult to answer because we face a very complex set of phenomena with limited, albeit increasing, sources of data.

However, although a number of factors complicate this task, other factors make such classification both possible and desirable: possible, because states share common sets of internal characteristics and are confronted with similar types of international problems; desirable, because it is impossible to provide useful descriptive analyses of foreign policy behavior without developing and interrelating categories of behavior. In our attempt to classify patterns of foreign policy, we will examine two traditional classification schemes that developed prior to World War II, two classifications currently used, and three suggested classifications that could aid the student of contemporary foreign policy.

Two Traditional Classifications

Two classifications that developed in the nineteenth century and have continued into the twentieth are (1) the *great power/small power* dichotomy and (2) the distinction between *status quo* and *revisionist* states. These distinctions have been used by writers as well as decision makers in analyzing the behavior of states. However, in spite of their long tradition, the distinctions are not as valuable today as they once were.

The great power/small power distinction. Although international law and the rhetoric of statesmen maintain that all states are equal, decision makers as well as international relations analysts have traditionally distinguished the great from the small power. The distinction is not merely based on territorial or geographical size. Many great powers have had a relatively small territory and population (Great Britain, for example). Rather, the distinction relates more to the scope of a state's international interests and its relationships with other states. States concerned primarily with their immediately adjacent neighbors or with those states posing a direct military threat have been classified as small powers. Those whose

[6] Roger Hilsman, *To Move a Nation* (Garden City, N.Y.: Doubleday, 1967), p. 5.

concerns range far beyond their borders and who are major actors in alliance systems have been classified as great powers.

The distinguishing feature, then, is a state's economic and military capability as well as the scope and nature of its interests. Although it has not always been true that interest expands as capability expands (for example, the United States between the two world wars) or that interest contracts as capability contracts, for example, Spain after the sixteenth century), the distinction between great power and small power based on capability and scope was made frequently for good reason.

The traditional relationship between great and small was character-ized by a number of features. The great powers often treated the small as stakes in the competition among themselves. Except for a few states like Switzerland that were able to establish a neutral position, most small powers have sought the protection of one great power against another. In the eighteenth century, for example, most small German states sought the protection of either France or Austria, and in the period before World War II, small European states like Czechoslovakia and Yugoslavia attempted to get France to guarantee their existence. Wars were often fought on the territory of the small power—hence, the fruit of war was often control over the small powers. One distinction between great power and small power is whether or not the state is capable of maintaining its own security or has to depend on the support of another.

Prior to World Wars I and II the great/small dichotomy made sense. Since the classical state system was centered in Europe, it was easy to distinguish those states who were merely interested in preserving the integ-rity of their borders from those who sought empire and dominance. Be-cause so many small states dotted the map of Europe, it was necessary to separate the competitors from those who served only as stakes in the competition.

In the contemporary period the distinction is not as useful. With over 120 actors covering the globe, few states have interests in every area of the world. But many states do have interests beyond their immediate borders. Modern technology has rendered obsolete the concept of the state whose interests are limited to within its borders; economic and military conditions tie the world closely together. In addition, small states no longer serve as pawns for the great powers, at least insofar as they are concerned with national survival. Small nations are aware of the limitations on use of military power to occupy foreign states, so they no longer need depend on some great power to guarantee survival. Moreover, the category of great power seems to be less meaningful now because two types of great powers are appearing—those with extensive nuclear capability and those with little or none. In terms of capabilities and scope of interest, the United States and the Soviet Union cannot be placed in the same great-power category as France, Great Britain, or Red China.

For these reasons the distinction seems to be less useful in classifying foreign policy today than it was in the past. On the other hand, the relationship between them is less clearly defined than it once was.[7] Great powers no longer are willing or able to treat a small power as merely a territorial stake in their own conflict. On the other hand, the great powers must now be classified as super or nonsuper power, and the classification of small power covers a wide variety of foreign policies of differing scopes.

Status quo versus revisionist. Analysts and statesmen have also traditionally tried to classify states according to their attitudes toward existing international conditions. States seeking to preserve existing conditions were classified as *status quo* powers, while those attempting to change conditions were classified as *revisionist* powers. In the interwar period, for example, France was viewed as a status quo power while Germany was viewed as revisionist because the former tried to maintain the terms of the Versaille Peace Treaty while the latter (after 1933) tried to change it.

The distinction is somewhat similar to the conservative-liberal distinction found throughout the discussion of politics, in which inherent tension is presumed to exist between status quo and revisionist factions since their objectives are in direct conflict. Unlike the liberals and conservatives, however, status quo and revisionist states cannot resolve their differences by gaining political control of the government because there is no world government. Hence, revisionists seek to overthrow and replace existing territorial arrangements while the status quo states seek to protect them.

Prior to World War II, this distinction between status quo and revisionist was useful because of the importance of territory and territorial stakes in competition among states. Because possession of territory was an important factor in a state's economic well-being and military security, a primary foreign policy goal was to maintain or increase territorial holdings. Hence, status quo and revisionist classifications pertained to the question of maintenance or alteration of territorial boundaries. The peace settlement ending major wars often created the conditions for renewed conflict: states that had lost territory became revisionist; those that had gained became defenders of the new status quo.

Today, however, the status quo or revisionist distinction does not seem to be as meaningful as it once was. Territorial control has become a less important objective for most states. No longer needing open control of

<hr>

[7] For a discussion of a way of classifying states, and an attempt to develop a classification scheme using operational definitions, see J. David Singer and Melvin Small, "The Composition and Status Ordering of the International System, 1815–1940," *World Politics,* 18 (1966), 236–82.

small states around them, the great powers are able indirectly to support friendly regimes among the small states they deem most important to their security. The Soviet Union, for example, does not find it necessary to subjugate the eastern European states in order to maintain the kind of security arrangements it wishes. Hence, although many contemporary states seek to influence and even control what other states do, they do not seem to be driven by the desire to put their flags over new territory. Territorial goals remain in the numerous border disputes throughout the globe, but distribution of territory no longer appears to be in question, particularly where the major powers are concerned. Therefore, the status quo/revisionist distinction, which is based mainly on attitudes toward the existing territorial distribution, no longer provides an adequate scheme for classifying foreign policies.

Two Contemporary Classifications

In the period following World War II, two new classification schemes have emerged. They are the east-west-neutral classification and the distinction between "rich" and "poor" nations. We will look at the background of these classifications and their usefulness in analyzing foreign policies of states.

East-west-neutral. In recent years many analysts and statesmen have divided the world into three sectors. Basic to the rationale for threefold division is the assumption that the world is dominated by the Soviet-American or, as it is sometimes called, Communist-Free World split. The third world consists of those states who take neither side. Unfortunately, this classification scheme is based on historical conditions that appear to have already changed sufficiently to make the classification questionable.

The assumption behind this division is based on bloc membership. A member of the Soviet bloc, it was assumed, is hostile to members of the American bloc, friendly to members of its own bloc, and conciliatory to members of the third bloc (hoping to win them over to its own bloc). It was also assumed that members of the neutral bloc hold enough in common so that their foreign policies followed common patterns. The same was said to apply for members of the American bloc. However, events since 1960 have changed conditions. Members of the American and Soviet blocs are often as antagonistic to members of their own blocs as they are to members of other blocs. One need only cite the tension between Greece and Turkey (members of the American bloc), Communist China and the Soviet Union, and France and the United States as examples. In addition, certain neutrals support one bloc or the other more strongly than some of the bloc members. For example, in 1967 the United Arab Republic appeared to be a "better" political ally to the Soviet Union than Communist China, Albania, or even Rumania.

However, even though it appears to be a gross oversimplification in the light of alliance patterns and disagreements among states, the threefold division continues to be important in the United Nations. In their study of voting in the United Nations General Assembly, Alker and Russett note that the trend between 1947 and 1961 is to greater, not less, voting behavior that can be explained by the east-west division.[8] Although the distinction is not as meaningful as it once was outside the United Nations (for example the growth of Soviet-French friendship and Soviet-Rumanian hostility), it still has some relevance in describing participation in the United Nations.

Rich and Poor. During the 1960's, the distinction between the rich and the poor has become current. This distinction is sometimes referred to as the split between the north and the south or the haves and the have-nots. Building on an analogy from domestic politics interpreted through Marxian eyes, writers have felt that the inherent tension between those who have wealth and those who do not is also manifested in international relations. The distinction is somewhat similar to the distinction between status quo and revisionist, although the emphasis is not on territorial goals but on economic goals. Implicit in the distinction is that conflicting interests separate the two groups of states.

The distinction between rich and poor has a number of implications for contemporary international politics. First, it places the United States and the Soviet Union on the same side and, therefore, somewhat contradicts the east-west-neutral distinction discussed above. Second, the rich-poor distinction has racial overtones since the only nonwhite nation that falls into the rich category is Japan. Just as race and economics are interwoven into many political issues in the United States, race and economics are also part of political relations among states. Finally, the distinction between rich and poor shifts the emphasis from territorial distribution, as in the status quo/revisionist dichotomy, to economic wealth and security.

Because poor nations greatly outnumber rich ones, the distinction appears most pertinent in the analysis of global intergovernmental organizations. In particular, Alker and Russett point out that north-south issues account for a large number of votes in the United Nations General Assembly although the number declined somewhat in the period between 1947 and 1961.[9] In many international meetings and conferences, the rich nations and the poor are involved in continuous confrontations. For exam-

---

[8] Alker and Russett, *World Politics in the General Assembly,* p. 135.
[9] Alker and Russett, *World Politics in the General Assembly,* p. 135.

ple, the United Nations Committee for Trade and Development was established at the instigation of the poor nations to get trading and other economic concessions from the rich nations. In another example, Robert Friedheim found the rich and poor distinction explained voting behavior and other activities in the Geneva Conference on the High Seas (a Conference which drafted a general set of rules governing activities on the seas).[10]

If one compares the relationship between the rich and the poor in a domestic society like the United States and relations among rich and poor states, one finds a striking difference. In a domestic society, the poor have some power, because of their large numbers, in demanding concessions from the rich. This is true whether the poor people threaten to vote against those not granting concessions or threaten to take what they want violently. In contrast, in spite of the larger number of poor nations in the world, there is little that they can do to harm the rich states given current technological conditions. Intergovernmental organizations provide them with their only source of capability to threaten the rich states because of the usual one nation—one vote rule, but they must be careful not to force the rich states to withdraw from the organization. While the poor states remain more numerous they remain relatively incapable of forcing the rich to make significant concessions.

For this reason, the distinction between the rich and the poor states does not have the same consequence that it has had in the domestic political systems of many states. Unlike the poor in domestic society, poor states as a group do not have the capability to seriously threaten the rich. This does not mean they cannot acquire concessions from certain rich states as a result of playing one state off against another, but it does mean that the class conflict that has been so much a part of political activities within states will remain more or less peripheral in relationships among states.

Three Suggested Classifications

In an attempt to contribute some classification schemes more appropriate to contemporary international conditions than the traditional distinctions between great and small and between status quo and revisionist, we have developed three schemes. The first observes the scope of a state's foreign policy by distinguishing regional from supraregional states. The second applies to the approach or style of one state towards another by distinguishing between interventionist and noninterventionist foreign policies.

---

[10] Robert L. Friedheim, "The 'Satisfied' and 'Dissatisfied' States Negotiate International Law: A Case Study," *World Politics,* 18 (1965), 20–42.

The third attempts to characterize foreign policies along a continuum of hostility and friendship.

Regional versus supraregional states. This typology is a revision of the classical distinction between great and small powers. It takes into account the universalization of the international system—that is, the existence of a system of states throughout the world. It recognizes the increased scope of the foreign policy of all states as well as the growing importance of regional ties in international relations. Although all states have some universal interests—if only because all but a few are members of the United Nations—it is still possible to make a distinction between those states whose interests and activities are centered primarily on their own region and those whose interests and activities extend beyond their own regions.

The regional foreign policy actor is primarily concerned with states within its region—although it might be forced to deal with supraregional actors from other regions. The regional actor might have some conflict with its immediate neighbors and might compete and cooperate with other regional actors in regional and global international institutions. Its basic activities, however, involve states within its regions. When it does interact with other states, those states are supraregional actors. In cases where the regions overlap, such as North Africa and the Middle East, a regional actor may deal with regional actors in other regions, but it always interacts with other regional actors that are nearby.

It is difficult to identify "regions" in the contemporary world because they include different states in different times and contexts. If we assume that the western hemisphere is a region, for example, we are forced to recognize possible subregions within the hemisphere, such as Central or South America. The problem is further compounded by the fact that certain regional actors, such as Upper Volta, deal with a very small number of geographically proximate states while others, such as Ethiopia, deal with a large number of states throughout a wide geographic region. It might be better to try to define a "regional environment" for each state based on the distance between it and other states that it interacts with so that, for example, Chile's regional environment would be "x" miles from its border.

Recognizing the inherent difficulties in defining regions, we present the following regional breakdown. This breakdown takes into account geographical, cultural and historical considerations and should be considered only an approximation of the domain of many regional actors.[11]

---

[11] Bruce M. Russett, *International Regions and the International System,* and "Delineating International Regions," in J. David Singer, ed., *Quantitative International Politics: Insights and Evidence* (New York: Free Press, 1968), pp. 317–52, has explored the question of the nature and shapes of international regions in great detail and from a number of different viewpoints. Also see Bruce M. Russett, J. David

(1) North and Central America: United States; Canada; Mexico; Cuba; The Carribean and West Indies; The Central American Republics (south to and including Panama).

(2) South America: All states on the South American continent.

(3) Western Europe: England; Ireland; Scandanavian states; "Free" states of continental western Europe.

(4) Eastern Europe: Russia; eastern European Communist states.

(5) North Africa: Morroco; Algeria; Tunisia; Libya; Sudan; United Arab Republic.

(6) Central and South Africa: The remainder of continental Africa; Malagasy Republic.

(7) Middle East: Arab states; Israel; Iran; Turkey; Greece.

(8) Northwestern Asia: Russia; Communist China; Mongolia; Tibet; Afghanistan; Pakistan; India; Nepal; Bhutan.

(9) South and East Asia: China (Taiwan); Japan; Philippines; Indonesia; Malaysia; Communist China; Burma; India; Pakistan; Thailand; Laos; Cambodia; Viet Nam; Australia; New Zealand.

The supraregional foreign policy actor has interests and activities beyond its immediate region. We have chosen the term "supraregional" rather than "global" because few states have interests and commitments in every part of the world. The supraregional actor is distinguished from the regional actor because it interacts frequently with regional actors in other regions while the regional actors interact only with supraregional actors from other regions. Figure 6 illustrates the different patterns of the two types of actors:

FIGURE 6

Patterns of Foreign Policy Actors

6a. Regional Actors   *6b. Supraregional Actors*

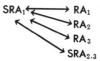

* Numbers stand for different regions.

Singer, and Melvin Small, "National Political Units in the Twentieth Century: A Standardized List," *American Political Science Review,* 62 (September, 1968), 932–52 for a categorization of all nations into broader regions than those provided in the text. This article is also important because it provides a standardized list of states with a set of code numbers which can be helpful in making data collection by different scholars more compatible.

In the 1960's, we could classify the following states as supraregional actors: United States, Soviet Union, United Kingdom, France, West Germany, Japan, and Communist China. All other states may be considered regional actors. Some supraregional actors follow broadly defined foreign policies because of past colonial tradition (France and Britain); others are motivated by interests that are economic (United States, West Germany, and Japan), military (United States and Soviet Union), and ideological (United States, Soviet Union, and Communist China). Regardless of motivation, however, the supraregional actor has made extensive commitments outside of its own region.

The classification scheme defines the general scope of a nation's foreign policy. It can be used to describe which states have relationships with other states in the system, but it says little about the nature of the relationships except whether they involve regional or global issues. Although the regional or supraregional distinction does not carry as many implications as the great power or small power distinction did, it can be used to describe the scope of foreign policy of contemporary states.

Interventionist and noninterventionist. A second classification scheme is based on how states acheive foreign policy goals—whether and to what extent a state employs interventionist versus noninterventionist modes for influencing other states. All states attempt to influence other states in their pursuit of foreign policy goals. However, some exert influence primarily by either supporting the existing regime or trying to replace it. Because they act to influence a state by determining *who* governs it, they may be viewed as interventionist. A predominantly noninterventionist foreign policy would try to influence state policies without attempting to determine governing personnel. All states use some noninterventionist strategies, but some use interventionist strategies as well. Hence, the interventionist or noninterventionist classification may be viewed as a continuum. For example, Brazil's foreign policy toward the United Kingdom may be placed on the noninterventionist end of the continuum, while United States foreign policy towards the Dominican Republic and Soviet foreign policy towards East Germany may be placed at the interventionist end.

The classification is different from the status quo or revisionist distinction because of its emphasis on means rather than goals. States supporting the existing territorial distribution, as well as states trying to revise it, may be either interventionist or noninterventionist. One need not make assumptions about the substantive goals of a state's foreign policy in order to apply the classification.

This scheme takes into account the contemporary shift away from territorial acquisition apparent in the foreign policies of many states. For example, the current trend away from colonial relationships, where the strong establish territorial control over the weak, to the neocolonial relationship, where the strong try to determine who governs the weak, illustrates the deemphasis on formal territorial control. Moreover, this classification scheme is not completely without historical foundation, since some states in the nineteenth century were classified on the interventionist continuum according to their willingness to intervene militarily on behalf of or against the existing authorities of other states.

Today, however, the classification applies to a wider set of activities. The interventionist state today seeks to influence who governs in a state through more than military intervention. Economic tools of foreign aid and trading benefits, military tools of subversion or advisory aid, and political communications of propaganda or symbolic acts (the President of the United States meeting with incumbent leaders in West Germany, for example) are all employed in an interventionist foreign policy to influence who governs in a given state by providing support for political friends within the state. The noninterventionist state may use many of these tools also—particularly economic aid and political communication—but their use is directed to influencing those who already govern or might govern.

Although the interventionist or nonintervention label can sometimes be applied to the total foreign policy of a state (for example, almost all states consider the United States and the Soviet Union partially interventionist and Canada noninterventionist), it is better to attempt to classify specific foreign policies of one state toward another. In addition to the fact that both strategies might use the same tools (propaganda, for example) frequently, a state might be interventionist with some states and noninterventionist with others. Nevertheless, some states have followed a consistent policy of intervention toward one or more states in the contemporary world. In the interventionist category, we would place the United States, the Soviet Union, the United Kingdom, the United Arab Republic, Cuba, Communist China, and France. These states attempt to manipulate the domestic political conditions of one or more states in order to determine which group of leaders governs. We might also include certain other states such as Indonesia under Sukarno towards Malaysia, North Vietnam towards South Vietnam and some of the excolonial areas (Belgium in the Congo, and so forth). However, these states are only involved in territorially-limited intervention bounded by specific issues. They would not fit the category of general interventionist. It might also be argued that the eastern European Communist states should be viewed as interventionist because their propaganda calls for changes in certain regimes. However, propaganda notwithstanding, they do not seem to follow interventionist strategies consistently.

The distinction between interventionist and noninterventionist, then, can be used to classify specific foreign policies followed by one state toward another and may be viewed as an indicator of the "style" of a state's foreign policy. The distinction implies that certain states under certain conditions are willing to pursue objectives by trying to change or support the personnel of a regime in addition to attempting to persuade existing rulers to adopt a particular foreign policy position. States pursue interventionist strategies despite the fact that rulers who have come to power through outside help have often turned their back on foreign benefactors. For example, many eastern European regimes that owe their existence to the Soviet Union have from time to time followed policies highly displeasing to that nation. Like many styles, the interventionist strategy is followed by states even though it appears to be costly and frequently unproductive (particularly in the long run).

The reasons for continued use of interventionist tactics are complex. First, the policy may be a last resort relied upon only after everything else has failed. Second, foreign policy decision makers can threaten to intervene in the domestic politics of a state as a means of "persuading" the decision makers of the threatened state to change their foreign policy. Third, some states are so involved in the political and economic life of other states that their acts automatically carry implications for the domestic politics of others. Finally, certain states (particularly the superpowers) feel that it is necessary to compete with each other for influence in third states, which often means vying for the support of competing political groups that one day might take over the government. Many of these factors operate simultaneously making interventionist foreign policies common.

Many factors contribute to a state's willingness to use interventionist tactics. One is the degree of importance a state may give to a particular dispute. For example, both the Israelis and the Arabs attach sufficient importance to their conflict to employ interventionist tactics. Another factor is the role of historical conditions. Past colonial ties provide some states with opportunity to control the economic and political life of their excolonies. In addition, states that have employed interventionist tactics in the past are more inclined to use them in future disputes, not only because decision makers and policy influencers do not find such use morally reprehensible but also because administrative machinery and trained personnel are available.

One might also want to make a distinction between interventionist tactics that directly or indirectly involve use of force (smuggling arms to revolutionaries, sabotage, and the like) and those that do not (propaganda). Although such a refinement might add additional depth to the foreign policy analysis, it should not cloud the basic difference between states that limit their efforts to influencing existing regimes and those that attempt to determine who governs in another state.

Hostility and friendship. In classifying foreign policy, it is also useful to determine a dimension of the foreign policy which can best be described as hostility and/or friendship. Because the states themselves do not classify their actions as being either hostile or friendly and, more important, often pursue foreign policies that contain elements of both, it is necessary to express this dimension as a continuum rather than as two distinct dimensions. We might, for example, construct some sort of scale between zero and one (0–1.0) with the lower end of the scale representing hostile and the higher, friendly, foreign policy. Such a scale would enable scholars to express briefly a great deal of information about the relations between states.

Two important questions must be raised when attempting to classify foreign policy along a hostility and friendship continuum. First, we must decide whether we are examining *perceived* or *actual* hostility and friendship because the actor as well as the target state might not perceive the act in the same way. Foreign aid, for example, may be viewed by the giving state as an act of friendship but is sometimes viewed by the receiving state as an attempt at manipulation and, therefore, a hostile act. For this reason, it might be better to assume that a degree of friendship or hostility is inherent in a class of acts even though the acts in question might not always be viewed in that manner. A second and related point is the necessity of assuming that state A's foreign policy toward state B might be different from the foreign policy of state B to state A. For example, the United Kingdom has followed a more conciliatory policy towards Communist China than Communist China has toward the United Kingdom.

A number of relatively available sources of data may be employed in classifying foreign policy along this dimension. Rummel has developed and employed a classification scheme to acquire data on a variety of hostile behavior ranging from written and oral communication to warfare. Using reports in the *New York Times,* Professor Rummel has generated data on conflict among nations for most years since 1955.[12] On the friendly side, one could examine trade policy, treaty agreements,[13] diplomatic exchange[14] or common membership in intergovernmental organizations.[15] United Nations voting data could be used as an indirect measure of hostility and

[12] Rummel, "Relationship between National Attributes and Behavior."

[13] Professor Peter Rohn has been collecting data on treaties reported in the United Nations Treaty Series. See "Institutionalism in the Law of Treaties: A Case of Confirming Teaching and Research," *Proceedings of the American Society of International Law* (1965), 93–98.

[14] J. David Singer and Melvin Small, "The Composition of Status Ordering."

[15] Chadwick F. Alger and Steven J. Brams, "Patterns of Representation in National Capitals and Intergovernmental Organizations," *World Politics,* 19 (1967), 646–64; as well as Russett, *International Regions,* pp. 94–122.

friendship among states.[16] Although a number of problems are associated with use of such data, they nonetheless could be and have been used by scholars to assess patterns of behavior.

The dimension of hostility or friendship is particularly important because it describes basic political predispositions among states across a wide variety of patterns. At the hostile end of the scale is warfare; at the friendly end, close cooperation if not some type of integration. Because friendship does not always produce more friendship or hostility more hostility, it is necessary to consider both aspects together in order to ascertain under what conditions basic political relationships among states change.

DETERMINANTS OF FOREIGN POLICY

Having just discussed some classifications of foreign policy behavior, we will now turn to the "causes" of that behavior. Our presentation will focus on four determinants of foreign policy behavior: the international context, the behavior of foreign policy decision makers, the impact of economic and military conditions within the state, and the role of domestic politics in the formulation of foreign policy. Since we have already established the background for the last three determinants in Chapters 2, 3, and 4, we will begin our discussion with the international context.

The International Context

Of the many explanations of why states behave as they do, none is more frequently offered than the one that focuses on international context. Analysts have traditionally emphasized that the nature of the international system and the relationship of the state to conditions in that system determine how the state will behave. Two related schools of international relations theory—geopolitics and realism—have developed this emphasis.

Theories of state behavior that emphasize the geographical context are not a modern phenomenon. In the 4th century, an Indian philosopher—Kautilya—developed a theory of state behavior partially based on geography by imagining:

> . . . a circle of states forming a kind of political solar system
> and tending to gravitate toward one another as friends or come
> into collision as enemies according to their respective positions

---

[16] This is implied in Russett, *International Regions and the International System*, pp. 59–80, where similarity and differences in UN voting can be used to infer hostility and friendship between nations.

in the circle. Thus, states adjacent to each other, and therefore in the nature of things bound to have a greater number of points of friction, are to be regarded as natural enemies.[17]

Assuming that states would try to expand their territory, Kautilya argued that neighbors are always enemies and neighbors' neighbors are friends. Although their theories are much more complex, geopoliticians around the turn of the century—Alfred T. Mahan,[18] in his emphasis on sea power, and Sir Halford MacKinder,[19] in his emphasis on land power—have underscored the importance of the geographical context

In the twentieth century, the geopoliticians' narrow emphasis on geography was broadened into the "realist" approach. Hans J. Morgenthau, a realist, argued that every state had a particular relationship with the international environment that he defined as a set of "objective" national interests.[20] These national interests were thought to determine the foreign policy of a state. Geography was still important because it had a great deal to do with definition of the national interest, but other factors of military power now entered the formula. Small states, according to this approach, could only follow policies of allying with states that were most likely to protect them. Hence, Poland, it was argued, should have allied with Britain and France in the interwar period. Large states should use their power to counter other large states. In short, what was thought to be the configuration of power was presumed to determine foreign policy.

The primary difficulty with the geopolitical and the realist positions is that they overemphasize the role of the international context for the state and correspondingly underemphasize the role of internal foreign policy-making processes—particularly, the ways in which decision makers within states perceive the international context. As a result, these scholars are frequently plagued by a dilemma. On the one hand, they argue that international conditions *as they perceive them* determine the foreign policy of states. On the other hand, they find many instances—particularly when

[17] Frank M. Russell, *Theories of International Relations* (New York: Appleton-Century-Crofts, 1936), p. 45.

[18] For discussion and bibliography on Mahan, see Robert E. Osgood, *Ideals and Self-Interest in America's Foreign Relations* (Chicago: University of Chicago Press, 1953), Chapter I.

[19] Sir Halford J. MacKinder, *Democratic Ideals and Reality* (New York: Henry Holt, 1942; W. W. Norton, 1962).

[20] In addition to his classic textbook, *Politics Among Nations,* Morgenthau's monograph *In Defense of the National Interest* (New York: Knopf, 1951), illustrates the assumptions that a state's foreign policy should be or is determined by international conditions. Nicholas J. Spykman represents a transitional figure in the scholarly literature from the narrow geopolitical approach view to the broader realist position. See his book *America's Strategy in World Politics* (New York: Harcourt, Brace & World, 1942).

analyzing U.S. foreign policy—when states do not follow policies that appear to be dictated by the international conditions. In other words, while realists claim that international conditions determine a state's policies, they also chide states for not doing what they think is necessitated by the international conditions.[21]

The reason for this dilemma is that the realists do not attribute enough importance to internal political and psychological processes, which interact with international conditions to produce foreign policies. Developing theories that see the state as a set of processes interacting with the international environment, they tend to assume the state is a monolithic actor that reacts to international conditions.[22] To avoid this dilemma, we must treat international conditions as *one* set of factors influencing foreign policy activities of states, remembering that those who make foreign policy do not always perceive the international context as the analyst perceives it. In the following analysis, we must keep in mind the limited role the international context plays in determining foreign policy.

In discussing the impact of the international context on foreign policy of a state, the three elements are geographic, economic, and political. The international environment of any state consists of the location it occupies with respect to other states in the system as well as the economic and political relationships it has with those others.

Geography continues to play an important foreign policy role although not the paramount role geopoliticians have assigned it in the past. As Russett has demonstrated in his excellent quantitative analysis of various dimensions of state behavior, geographical proximity is related to trading among states, voting behavior in the United Nations and common membership in intergovernmental organizations[23] although the relationship

---

[21] This confusion between what is and what should be is a classic illustration of the dangers of failing to make a sharp distinction between descriptive and prescriptive analysis defined in Chapter 1.

[22] This criticism of the realist is based on the assumption that the realists are describing reality when they overemphasize the international context. However, as indicated in the quotation in Chapter 1 (Footnote 3), realists like Morgenthau often confuse their normative and prescriptive positions with their descriptive analysis. Hence, they might adequately cover the role of domestic politics in their descriptive analysis of the foreign policy of a state but at the same time decry that role. However, because they do not clearly separate their prescriptions from their descriptions, they often give the impression of overemphasizing the international context. Even if we were to accept their emphasis on the international context as a prescriptive position, we might still question the appropriateness of allowing the international context to substantially shape foreign policy.

[23] See Chapter 11 in Russett, *International Regions and the International System,* for a full discussion of the relationships among geography, trade, voting in the United Nations, sociocultural characteristics, and membership in intergovernmental organizations.

is stronger for some regions (eastern Europe) than others (Latin America). In addition, alliances continue to be formed, based in part on logistical calculations of states: transporting men and supplies. Although technological conditions have revolutionized certain logistical considerations (the Soviet Union no longer needs a warm-water port; the United Kingdom no longer considers the European lowlands a prime factor in its defense), some geographical conditions remain a constant part of foreign policy decisions. For example, canals and water passages such as Suez, Panama, and Gibraltar have importance in the contemporary world although much less than in earlier periods.

Economic relationships also are an important part of the international context. The flow of goods and services as well as the flow of capital make certain states dependent upon others. As we saw in Chapter 4, underdeveloped states often depend upon developed ones for trade and aid while many developed states face pressures of different types from others in their environment.

Finally, political relationships with other states in its environment play a large role in a state's foreign policy decisions. Alliances—especially if they involve troops on foreign soil—can have a great impact on members and nonmembers. The fact that a massive troop commitment of the United States still remains in Europe creates conditions that all states must recognize and deal with when making decisions. In addition to alliances, ability to win support from other states in a given circumstance can affect the decisions of the state. This is true whether a state is trying to win support for its position in a United Nations resolution or trying to get another state to recognize an economic boycott.

It is important to realize, then, that the international context plays a large role in determination of foreign policy even though the role is not as conclusive as some geopoliticians and realists have argued. In the final analysis, the international context will allow us to explain the foreign policy of a state only partially. We might be able to explain why the United Kingdom tries to placate the United Arab Republic or why Upper Volta —a landlocked nation—will not attack Chile by sea, but we will not be able to explain particular decisions or even general foreign policies by looking only at the international context. Instead, we will have to examine foreign policy processes within the state to understand interaction with the international context.

The Decision Maker

In Chapter 2, we examined the place decision-making behavior takes in the foreign policy process. It is little wonder that many analysts have pursued what amounts to a "great-man theory" of state behavior because individual leadership has a great deal to do with foreign policy activities. Rosenau calls the role of individual personality and behavior in foreign policy the "idiosyncratic variable" because of the unpredictability introduced by the individual in the foreign policy process.[24] Unlike Rosenau, who tempers the idiosyncratic variable with other variables (very similar to the ones presented here), many scholars attempt to explain all foreign policy behavior by saying that *it is* the behavior of the leaders.

The same set of criticisms that apply to proponents of the great-man thesis in history can also apply to those who overemphasize the decision maker in the foreign-policy process. The great-man thesis does not allow room for the operation of the environment within which the great man operates. As the decision maker molds his environment, he is simultaneously molded by it. A product of his times, he is able to follow policies that break with historical tradition, but is still forced to deal with conditions as he finds them. The decision maker, whether or not he is a great man, cannot operate in a vacuum of his own making. His environment is the international system and the internal social and political processes that constrain and define the limits of his activity. When speaking of a man's activities, it is as unnatural to omit references to the field of his activities as it is to speak about patterns of activities in a field without referring to the way men react within that field.

However, if there is danger of overemphasis on the role of individual personality and leadership, there is also danger of underemphasis. Fidel Castro, for example, has revolutionized both the environment within Cuba and the relationship between Cuba and its international environment. The shifts are not always so radical, however, and one must be careful not to identify foreign policy revolutions where they do not occur. For example, the foreign policy of France from 1958 to 1968 is considered to be the product of Charles de Gaulle, when in fact many policies, such as nuclear weapons development, were started before De Gaulle took over. This is not to argue that De Gaulle did not greatly influence the course of French foreign policy. The point is that forceful leadership does not always mean revolutionary foreign policy decisions.

Therefore, we must leave room in this discussion of determinants for the role of the decision maker without falling into the trap of explaining a foreign policy entirely in terms of the peculiar behavior of a leader. We can explain the foreign policy of the United Arab Republic or Cuba by focusing our attention on Nasser or Castro, but we should neglect neither the

---

[24] James N. Rosenau, "Pre-Theories and Theories of Foreign Policy," in R. Barry Farrell, ed., *Approaches to Comparative and International Politics* (Evanston, Ill.: Northwestern University Press, 1966), pp. 27–92.

international context in which those two states exist nor the policy-influence system and economic-military conditions affecting their decisions. The idiosyncratic variable—to use Rosenau's term—is an important but nonetheless partial determinant of foreign policy decisions.

Domestic Politics

A number of ideas exist at various levels of analysis on the role of domestic politics in foreign policy making. At one level, the idea is current that the difference between autocratic and democratic political systems greatly affects foreign policy making. At another level, many writers have argued that stability of the political system plays a role in foreign policy decisions. We will look at both levels in the context of what was said about domestic politics in Chapter 3.

Despite evidence to the contrary, writers and politicians have argued that autocratic and democratic governments differ in terms of the ends and means of foreign policy. Usually, it is members of democratic states who maintain the distinction. Starting with Thomas Paine, continuing through Woodrow Wilson and including George F. Kennan, the argument that the foreign policy of a democratic state is different from the foreign policy of an autocratic state has been maintained.[25] In terms of ends, democratic states are presumed to be uninterested in territorial acquisition except to "enlighten the natives" of primitive areas; autocratic states, on the other hand, are presumed to be interested in acquiring as much territory as possible for sinister aims. In terms of means, democratic states are viewed as peace-loving, perhaps a little unrealistic in failing to understand that power must be countered with power, and interested in the development of international law and organization. In contrast, autocratic states are viewed as willing users of force who promote international law and organization only to increase their power. It should be obvious to even the most naive observer that these pictures of the two types are unrealistic.

Based on our discussion of the policy influence system in foreign policy making in Chapter 3, it appears that the distinction between democratic and autocratic states—"open" and "closed" systems—has some explanatory power; although not to the extent that paints the democratic states with halos and the autocratic states with horns. In that chapter, we found that while in an open system the foreign policy decision maker is

[25] Arnold Wolfers and Laurence W. Martin, *The Anglo-American Tradition in American Foreign Affairs: Readings from Thomas More to Woodrow Wilson* (New Haven, Conn.: Yale University Press, 1956), pp. 127, 275 and George F. Kennan, *Realities of American Foreign Policy* (Princeton, N.J.: Princeton University Press, 1954), pp. 3–31.

forced to argue in public about policies, in a closed system that individual can find consensus for his policies behind closed doors. The primary implication of this public aspect of foreign policy occurs in the bargaining relations among states. In a democracy, a major shift in policy is often preceded by extensive public debates as the decision makers attempt to build a consensus. In an autocracy, important shifts, such as the 1939 Soviet decision to sign a pact with Hitler, can occur without debate. Although one should not assume that democracies and autocracies follow completely different foreign policies, it should be remembered that the sharply different nature of their policy-influence systems has some impact on their foreign policies.

A second distinction often maintained in explaining foreign policy decisions is between stability and instability. Many writers on international politics argue that the unifying consequences of external wars often lead foreign policy decision makers who are faced with instability at home to be adventurous overseas.[26] A refinement of this argument would be that foreign policy decision makers do attempt to build domestic support for their regimes through all of their policies and that the foreign policy field represents one area where support can be gained.

Although many foreign affairs writers have traditionally offered this argument, recent empirical studies by Rummel and Tanter indicate that no clear-cut relationship appears between domestic instability and foreign policy hostility, at least for the years 1955 to 1960.[27] Data collected for most states on the degree of domestic instability (as measured by factors such as incidence of violence) and of foreign policy hostility (as discussed in previous pages) were used to show that no systematic relationship existed between the two factors. Although the studies do not take into account the effect of moderately long time periods (domestic instabilities in the early 1950's could produce foreign policy hostility in the late 1950's), they do indicate that what would appear to be the logical relationship (given the decision makers' desire to stay in office), between domestic instability and foreign policy hostility is questionable or should at least be refined.

The important thing to remember about the search for relationships between attributes of domestic political systems, such as open-closed or stable-unstable, and foreign policy behavior is that domestic politics is only one set of determinants operating on the foreign policy of states. Although the openness of a political system or the amount of domestic stability that

---

[26] Richard N. Rosecrance, *Action and Reaction in World Politics* (Boston: Little, Brown, 1963), takes this view throughout the book, especially pp. 280–93.

[27] Rudolph J. Rummel, "Relationship between National Attributes and Behavior," and Raymond Tanter, "Dimensions of Conflict Behavior."

system enjoys may shape certain aspects of foreign policy, other factors may also be operating, such as the personality of the decision maker or the structure of the international context.

Economic and Military Conditions

Although Chapter 4 indicated that economic and military capability does not provide absolute advantages for some states in dealing with other states, we did state that economic and military conditions play an important role in the foreign policy-making process by providing supports for and making demands upon the foreign policy decision makers. Lippmann expressed the idea when he said the commitments of a state must be balanced by its capabilities.[28] This statement implies that a state must have *both* ability and willingness to create the capabilities necessary to support its foreign policy.

Viewing economic and military conditions as determinants, then, we must realize they play a large role in the foreign policy of states. It is also true that given levels of economic or military capability—potential or real —do not necessarily lead to particular foreign policies. With this qualification, we can look at an attempt by Rostow to relate to the behavior of a state five stages of economic growth: (1) traditional, when the economy is stagnant, (2) pretakeoff, when growth begins primarily by a revolution in attitudes among the elite, (3) takeoff, when economic growth becomes a normal part of the condition of society, (4) maturity, when growth continues but the economy becomes more diversified and more interdependent with the international economy, and (5) high mass consumption, when growth continues but at a lower level and consumer goods and services play a dominant role in the economy.[29] A variation on these five stages was presented early in Chapter 4.

Rostow sees a clear relationship between stages of economic growth and foreign policy behavior of states. Those in the traditional and pretakeoff stages are too weak to engage in hostility. They may be dominated by a state in the stages of takeoff or maturity. Rostow states that the "nationalism" necessary to catapult a state into the takeoff stage can often lead to "regional aggression." Citing "the American effort to steal Canada during the French wars; Bismarck's neat military operations against Denmark, Austria, and France from 1864–71; the Japanese acquisition of primacy in Korea in 1895; and the Russian drive through Manchuria to Vladivostok"

---

[28] Walter Lippmann, *U.S. Foreign Policy: Shield of the Republic* (Boston: Little, Brown, 1943), pp. 9–10.

[29] W. W. Rostow, *The Stages of Economic Growth: A Non-Communist Manifesto* (Cambridge: Cambridge University Press, 1960), pp. xii, 4–17.

at the end of the 19th century,[30] Rostow argues that the need for external adventures to produce internal support at a time when economic progress creates social unrest is limited by the modest economic capabilities of the takeoff period. Takeoff conditions stimulate military adventure, but only on a limited scale—that is, regional aggression.

This leads to what the author calls the most dangerous stage of economic development, maturity; because the economic strength of the nation is now large enough "to concentrate the resources of the mature economy on a more ambitious expansion of external power."[31] Although states entering the maturity stage do not necessarily engage in large-scale expansion, this stage creates the most favorable conditions for unlimited expansion, according to Rostow. He bases this statement on the assumption that in maturity the economy is strong enough to embark on large-scale external activities (in contrast to the takeoff stage) but is not constrained by demands for mass consumption that would limit available capability for military efforts. Some states, he notes, reach the stage of high mass consumption before they achieve maturity. Such a path lessens the chances of warfare, because it tends to deprive the economy of large-scale war-making capability.

Rostow's treatment is not as deterministic as it appears. It is primarily an attempt to develop a model of the relationship between economic growth and foreign policy. Although some assumptions conflict with the work of Rummel and Tanter, the arguments appear to make good historical sense. The scheme appears useful as long as one remembers that other effects are at work, such as the existence of strong states to counter expansionist interests of takeoff and maturity states.

Marxist-Leninist theories of international politics also posit relationships between foreign policy patterns and economies. The most well known is Lenin's theory of imperialism, which argues that a certain stage in capitalist economies creates pressures for colonialism; colonies represent new markets and raw materials considered essential for the survival of the capitalist economy. As a result, writes Frank M. Russell in describing the Marxist-Leninist interpretation, "wars and militarism are . . . inevitable accompaniments of the whole expansionist process."[32] This Marxist-Leninist "theory" bears some relation to Rostow's concept that the mature economy promotes certain expansionist tendencies.

Some analysts of foreign policy behavior assign too much significance to military capability. This is particularly true of writers who use the

---

[30] *Stages of Economic Growth*, p. 113.
[31] *Stages of Economic Growth*, p. 114.
[32] Russell, *Theories of International Relations*, pp. 509–710.

concept "power" in their analysis of international politics. Although they claim that many intangible elements constitute the "power" of a state, they usually use the term as a synonym for actual or potential military capability. For example, although Hans Morgenthau defines power as the ability to control the minds and actions of men,[33] he lists "elements of national power" that are almost all related in some way to military capability. Major headings in the list are geography, natural resources, industrial capability, military preparedness, population, national character, national morale, quality of diplomacy, and quality of government. The major exception is the "quality of diplomacy," which is viewed as a qualifier of military capability. National character, national morale, and the quality of government—three factors that might not be considered direct elements of military capability—are discussed primarily in terms of their relevance to improving military efficiency.[34]

A certain mechanical quality is introduced into the discussion of the determinants of foreign policy by those writers who rely on the concept of power. For example, A.F.K. Organski's model for the "power transition" assumes that changing relationships among states in actual or potential power (defined like Morgenthau, primarily in military terms) will produce conflict among states. Hence, Organski argues that Communist China's absolute increase in power (relative to the other states) means that conflict between China and other states is likely.[35] Such an analysis fails to take into account the operation of other foreign policy determinants by positing an overly simplified relationship between military capability and foreign policy behavior.

Moreover, the course of history clearly shows that one cannot predict the outcome of a given sequence of international events merely by knowing who held the preponderance of military capability in a given situation. For example, capability analysis would not have predicted the success of Hitler in the 1930's. Starting out as a military underdog to France and Great Britain, and continuing thus until at least 1938, Hitler pursued a policy of directly challenging both states. Neither Hitler's policy nor the Anglo-French reaction to it could have been predicted purely from an analysis of the capability of the states involved. Other determinants, particularly decision makers and domestic politics of both France and Great Britain, must be considered in order to assess the proper role of military factors in foreign policy behavior.

[33] Hans J. Morgenthau, *Politics Among Nations,* 3rd ed. (New York: Knopf, 1961), p. 28.
[34] *Politics Among Nations,* pp. 110–49.
[35] A. F. K. Organski, *World Politics* (New York: Knopf, 1958), p. 334.

RELATING FOREIGN POLICY PATTERNS TO DETERMINANTS

The two sets of foreign policy concepts presented above—the patterns of behavior and the classes of determinants—can serve as a framework for descriptive analysis of foreign policy because they pose a set of theoretically interesting questions for the analyst. In this section, we will provide some suggestions on how the framework may be applied to two very different research problems. First is the analysis of specific foreign policy activities on a case-study basis; second, development of a set of propositions comparing foreign policies of nations on a general basis.

Applying the Framework to Case Studies

A case study may focus on any one of a number of foreign policy activities. It may involve the foreign policy of one state toward one or more other states (U.S. foreign policy toward Canada, toward NATO allies, toward the world). It may cover a particular period of time—from a year to a century or more. It may concentrate on a particular issue (disarmament or fishing rights). Finally, it may focus on a particular set of decisions bounded by time, space, and issue area (the U.S. decision to intervene in Korea). Employing the categories of foreign policies developed in Chapter 2, the case study can focus on general, administrative, or crisis foreign policy decisions.

Given the wide variety of forms a case study may take, how is it different from a mere descriptive presentation? Theoretically at least, the case study *should* differ because its primary purpose is to develop and test a set of concepts and propositions that can be used to analyze similar cases. Although the descriptive analysis provided in a case study may be interesting and important because of what it tells us about the particular case, the ideal goal of those performing case studies is the development of concepts and propositions that are useful across a number of cases.[36]

The concepts developed in this chapter relating to the patterns and determinants of foreign policy can provide this framework for comparative foreign policy case studies. The framework suggests a standard set of questions that all foreign policy students should attempt to answer for a specific case. Although different questions might be posed, those generated by the framework of patterns and determinants developed here should

[36] Note that statements in the text have shifted to the normative and prescriptive. Unfortunately, most case studies fail to be based on a set of concepts and propositions that will enable comparison across cases. With a few notable exceptions —an example is Glenn D. Paige, *The Korean Decision* (New York; Free Press, 1968)—most foreign policy studies are more concerned with descriptive detail than with the development and testing of concepts and theoretical propositions.

cover all basic factors and relationships considered in any foreign policy case study.

To illustrate, we will present below a series of general questions and suggest how these questions might be applied to Israeli foreign policy toward the Arabs from 1948 to 1968 and to U.S. actions during the 1962 Cuban missile crisis.

Some Theoretical Questions Applied to Two Cases

General Questions

1. How can one classify the scope, style, and substance of foreign policy actions?

2. What role does foreign policy personnel that has been responsible for the decision have, including images, ambitions for himself and his country, and risk-taking behavior.

3. What role does domestic politics play in the foreign policy?

4. What role did military and economic capability play in the foreign policy decisions?

5. What is the international context (geographical, economic, and political)?

Applied to Israel's Arab Policy

1. What is the mixture of hostile and friendly actions, including the sequence of events by Israel toward the Arab states? What states and intergovernmental organizations are involved? What type of interventionist actions were pursued?

2. How many people have been involved in the policy? What have been their images and goals? Has change in personnel led to changes in policy?

3. How have the policy influencers changed over the twenty years in terms of both relative influence and attitudes? Does political instability play a role?

4. What was the relative strength of Israel vis-à-vis the Arabs? What economic and military costs were involved with maintaining the policies?

5. How cohesive are the Arabs? What type of outside support can both sides expect under different conditions? What logical factors could affect use of military force? What type of economic ties would different policies generate?

Applied to U.S. in Cuban Missile Crisis

1. In what parts of the globe did the U.S. take actions? What was the sequence of action? What was the hostility-friendship mixture? Which actors were directly involved?

2. Who were in the decision-making group and how were decisions

reached? What were the prevailing images and goals? What affect did the intensity of the crisis have on the decisions?

3. How did the decision makers view the policy influencers' perceptions of the crisis? What impact did the coming election have? How much importance was placed on the reaction of the policy influencers?

4. What possible economic and military actions could the U.S. and the Soviet Union take toward each other? What is the likelihood of these actions, and the costs and benefits?

5. What type of support would various types of foreign policy actions receive by the U.S. from allies and neutrals? What type of support could the Soviet Union expect? What impact did geographical distance have on the military considerations?

This illustration merely suggests the types of questions that should be asked in performing a foreign policy case study. The framework developed in the chapter provides a set of guidelines or a checklist upon which the student should base specific questions he thinks are important in adequately exploring the case. Although a different checklist may be employed, a thorough case study should evaluate various dimensions of foreign policy behavior patterns as well as the role of the individual decision makers, their domestic political environment, the economic and military capability of the state, and the international context.

Developing Crossnational Assumptions About Foreign Policy

Instead of approaching particular cases, it is sometimes useful to study a large number of cases for relationships between causes and effects. Not only can we learn something about the world generally from such an approach; we can also acquire a more thorough background for exploring specific cases. The following represents one way to go about generating a set of assumptions that would apply crossnationally to foreign policy.

Let us hypothesize that the four determinants of foreign policy affect to different degrees the five categories of foreign policy behavior discussed earlier. This hypothesis might lead us to conclude that the determinants have a different order of importance to a state's stand on each category of behavior. For example, while the economic and military capability of a state might be the most important single determinant of whether a state is a regional or supraregional actor, it might be the least important determinant of whether that same state is east, west or neutral in its United Nations voting. Table 7 presents a hypothetical ranking of the four determinants for each of the five foreign policy patterns.

Although the chart represents mechanically the very complex set of

TABLE 7

**Relative Importance of Four Determinants to Categories
of Foreign Policy Behavior**

Behavior Categories	Most Important ←		→	Least Important
Scope				
Regional/ supraregional	Econ.-Mil. Conditions	Decision Makers	Intern'l Context	Domestic Politics
Issue-Content				
Rich-poor (North-south)	Econ.-Mil. Conditions	Domestic Politics	Intern'l Context	Decision Makers
East-west- neutral	Intern'l Context	Decision Makers	Domestic Politics	Econ.-Mil. Conditions
Style				
Interventionist/ noninterven- tionist	Decision Makers	Intern'l Context	Econ.-Mil. Conditions	Domestic Politics
Hostility- friendship	Domestic Politics	Decision Makers	Intern'l Context	Econ.-Mil. Conditions

conditions that we have been discussing for the past four chapters, it should serve to illustrate the types of propositions that can be applied to different cases once one has identified patterns of foreign policy behavior and the determinants of those patterns. The reader should attempt to discover the kinds of theoretical assumptions that are implicit in this chart (for example, that international context and the particular predispositions of the foreign policy decision makers have more to do with the east, west, or neutral content of a state's foreign policy than domestic politics and economic-military conditions). Even more important, he should think of ways of analyzing case studies and cross-national data to judge the validity of the propositions.

In this section, then, we have suggested some of the research implications of the framework presented in the chapter. It is important to realize that unless one approaches any research task with a framework such as the one presented here, he will be able to do little more than report information in a disorganized manner. Descriptive analysis contributes to knowledge only if it is expressed in a clearly developed set of concepts and propositions, and a framework similar to the one presented here is essential to the understanding of foreign policy.

SUMMARY OUTLINE

I.   Classifying patterns of foreign policy behavior is crucial to its analysis.
  A.   It is difficult to classify foreign policy behavior despite increasing sources of empirical data.
  B.   *The distinction between great and small power was more useful before World War II than it is today.*
  C.   *Because it was tied primarily to issues growing out of the control of territory, distinction of status quo from revisionist states was once more useful than it is today.*
  D.   *The east-west-neutral distinction is not as meaningful as it once was because of increased antagonism within blocs and lessening hostility between members of different blocs although it seems to be increasingly important in General Assembly voting.*
  E.   *The rich-poor distinction has more meaning for international politics in respect to activities at international conferences or within global intergovernmental organizations than for other aspects of international politics.*
  F.   The scope of a nation's foreign policy can be classified as differentiation between regional and supraregional actors.
  G.   The use of tools of foreign policy influence can be distinguished on a basis of interventionist (states that attempt to influence by determining who governs) and noninterventionist (states that attempt to influence existing regimes without offering support or threatening subversion).
  H.   *Some states are interventionist in their dealings with most states while other states are interventionist in their dealings with one or two states.*
  I.   *The degree of hostility and friendship in a foreign policy must be expressed on a continuum because elements of both are usually contained in any foreign policy.*
II. Factors shaping the foreign policy of a state can be analyzed in terms of four general areas: international context, decision makers, policy-influence system and economic and military conditions.
  A.   The international context involves geographical, economic, and military factors.
      1.   *Geography is important in defining a state's international context in areas relating to military logistics, trading patterns, alliance patterns, membership in intergovernmental organizations, and voting in the United Nations General Assembly.*
      2.   *Economic interdependencies create both supports and demands on the foreign policy decision maker.*

3. Political relationships such as alliances and a feeling of mutual interest represent an important part of the state's international context.

4. Even though the international context is important in shaping foreign policy, it is tempered by other factors.

5. *Geopoliticians and realists tend to overemphasize the role of the international context in shaping foreign policy.*

B. A great deal of foreign policy behavior is attributed directly to the particular behavior of the foreign policy decision maker.

1. Overemphasis on the role of the foreign policy decision maker leads to the excesses of the "great-man theory of history" because it ignores the role played by the environment of the decision maker in shaping his behavior.

2. *Change in the person occupying the role of foreign policy decision maker can often have a revolutionary effect on the foreign policy of a state but often has no effect at all.*

3. The role of the decision maker in the foreign policy of a state is tempered by the other determinants.

C. Domestic politics plays a role in the foreign policy of the state.

1. *The open-closed distinction does not explain differences in the ends and means of foreign policy.*

2. *Although many writers have argued that domestic instability leads to foreign policy hostility, empirical studies do not indicate a relationship.*

D. Economic and military conditions within a state play a role in determining its foreign policy.

1. A relationship appears to exist between a state's economic development and its foreign policy.

a. *Willingness to expand and use force for aggressive purposes is small in the traditional, pretakeoff and mass consumption stages.*

b. *A propensity for regional aggression occurs in the takeoff stage.*

c. *Global expansion, if it occurs, takes place during the maturity stage of a state's economy.*

2. Military capability alone can never be used to predict the foreign policy of a state or the results of a particular foreign policy situation.

III. By relating foreign policy patterns to the determinants of foreign policy behavior, one gains a useful framework for both case studies and crossnational studies.

A. The framework of patterns and determinants suggests a set of questions that can be useful in exploring general, administrative and crisis foreign policy decisions.

B. One set of useful crossnational questions suggested by the framework has to do with the relative importance of the four determinants in shaping each of the patterns of foreign policy behavior.

C. Without a framework such as the one presented in this chapter, it is not possible to develop understanding about foreign policy either at the case study or crossnational levels.

BIBLIOGRAPHICAL ESSAY

As Rosenau's article in (124) points out, the literature on foreign policy analysis contains very little scholarly work that attempts to develop and *apply* a theoretical framework as a basis for comparisons. This absence is particularly crucial in comparative foreign policy analysis. Most foreign policy literature is case-oriented. Although it is frequently of theoretical significance, as in Cohen (79) it fails to increase our ability to generalize across a large number of cases. Books that promise comparative orientations are Buck and Travis (60), Black and Thompson (36), and Macridis (267); these, however, are only collections of essays focusing on one state at a time. They make little or no attempt to follow a single theoretical framework. A book of essays edited by Farrell (124) and a monograph by Wilkinson (423) represent two of the few attempts in the field to develop a basis for comparative foreign policy.

It might be useful to compare the categories of determinants of foreign policy developed in this chapter with those developed by other scholars. Table 8 compares the categories developed in this chapter to those provided by Gross (142), Snyder-Bruck-Sapin (389), Frankel (128), London, Rosenau in (124), and Brody (162) by listing the major categories or factors identified by each writer in terms of those presented in this chapter. Different theoretical perspectives are obvious. Coplin and Rosenau deal with determinants and the foreign policy process as the unit of analysis. Brody and Snyder et al. focus on the foreign policy decision maker as he perceives the other factors. The others (Gross, London and Frankel) adopt a more general focus on foreign policy and international politics.

It is important to make the distinction of foreign policy output (behavior or patterns) and foreign policy determinants because in many cases a given piece of data may contain inferences for both. For example, trade may be viewed as both an output—that is, the result of a conscious decision by the foreign policy decision maker—and a determinant, or factor influencing the foreign policy decision maker. Quincy Wright (427)

TABLE 8

Factors Identified As Foreign Policy Determinants

Author	Determinants			
Coplin.	Decision maker	Policy influencer	Economic-military conditions	International context
Rosenau (124)* pp. 47–52.	Idiosyncratic role	Governmental	Societal	Systemic
Brody (162) pp. 324–27, 328–34.	Decision makers and their organizations	Special general publics	Social structure and behavior	International system as communication structure and role
Snyder et al. (389) p. 72	Decision makers	Internal setting		External setting
Gross (142) pp. 57, 92–162.	Leadership, ideology, culture	Socio-political factor	Economic, population, military	Geographic
London pp. 22–205.	Decision makers	Domestic politics	Economic, military	Geography, national security considerations
Frankel (128), pp. 20–84.	Decision makers	Domestic environment	Military, economic, intelligence propaganda, and scientific support agencies	International environment

* Numbers refer to Bibliography in this volume.

and Rudolph Rummel (352) have tried to develop the concept of "distances" to represent underlying factors determining relations between states while using elements of foreign policy output as well as natural characteristics (trade, conflict, and so forth) to measure the distance. The use of the concept of "distances" in this manner implies that certain foreign policy outputs at one point in time can be considered as determinants later on.

The great or small power distinction and the status quo or revisionist distinction are popular among historians like Taylor (399), although some political scientists have also employed them. One example is Organski's concept of satisfied and dissatisfied states (302). The east-west-neutral distinction made by some journalists continues to be used in the popular media, but the rich or poor distinction is also frequently employed by political analysts such as Ward (415). Both distinctions, moreover, have been used in studies on United Nations voting by scholars like Hovet (184) and Alker and Russett in (383). Intervention is explored by Cottam (87) under the concept "competitive interference." Also, see the entire issue of the *Journal of International Affairs,* Vol. 12, No. 2 (1968) for a discussion of intervention from a number of analytical viewpoints.

A number of attempts have been made to develop empirical measures

TABLE 9
Subject Matter and Sources of Some Empirical Studies

Author(s)—Work*	Dimension Measured	Source of Data
Alker and Russett (9)	Issue positions	U.N. General Assembly voting
Alger and Brams (7)	Common membership in intergovernmental organizations	Membership in intergovernmental organizations
Alker and Puchala (383) Russett (358)	Economic interaction	Trade data
Deutsch (100)	Communication, interaction	Mail flow, tourist, and so forth.
Rohn (319)	Cooperation	Treaties
North et al. (297)	Perception and hostility	Content analysis of documents
Klingberg (227)	Hostility and friendship	Panel of experts attributing attitudes to states
Singer and Small (385)	Status	Diplomatic exchange
Rummel (353)	Conflict output	Coding of events reported in newspapers
McClelland (383)	Crisis actions	Coding events reported in newspapers

* Numbers refer to Bibliography in this volume.

of foreign policy relations among states. Table 9 shows each scholar, the dimension being measured in the study (for example, hostility), and the source of data he used. Interested students should examine the works listed for firsthand, detailed observance of the literature. In addition, raw data can be found in the following sources: *United Nations Statistical Yearbook,* the *Statesman's Yearbook,* the *United Nations Treaty Series,* the *Yearbook of International Organizations,* and the works of Banks and Textor (24) and Russett et al. (361).

As indicated in this chapter, scholars have had some difficulty in finding empirical relationships between national characteristics and foreign policy behavior. This problem is most graphically illustrated in a study reported by Rummel in (383). Using aggregate data and factor analysis for 1955–57, Rummel found little or no relationship between foreign conflict behavior and (1) economic development and level of technology (in contradistinction to Rostow's assumptions); (2) international communication and other transactions; (3) cooperation, save for treaties; (4) "degree of totalitarianism" (contrary to those who argue foreign policies followed by democracies differ from those followed by autocracies); (5) power as expressed in economic and military resources; (6) domestic instability; (7) military capability; (8) psychological motivations expressed through achievement, affiliation, power, and other-directedness; and (9) values such as internationalism and other ideologically based values. Many of the variables Rummel used have been mentioned in this chapter as having an impact on foreign policy behavior. Rummel fails to find relationships probably because he is only measuring conflict behavior; interaction of the various determinants is so complex that any one would not show up on the basis of such highly aggregated data. A new analysis of Rummel's data by Wilkenfeld (422) controls for time and type of political system. His study found a relationship between a state's domestic instability and its foreign policy behavior. See Haas (150), Kallenberg (205), and Merritt and Rokkan (277) on problems encountered with aggregate data and comparative models.

This new information would suggest that a less highly aggregated approach might be employed. By focusing on crisis situations, as McClelland in (383) and others have done, and by doing time series or longitudinal studies, the student might find relationships that would otherwise be lost, as when testing for relationships across many states for a single time period. Also, Russett's (358) technique of defining "regions" for a number of dimensions (trade, geographical proximity, United Nations voting, and the like) appears to be more useful. He analyzed regions to see where they overlap, what type of foreign policy behavior characterizes them, and whether or not they change over time. Finally, Breecher et al. (48) have attempted to compare major policy decisions by states under a large variety of conditions.

Turning to the intuitive, if not antiempirical, wing of the literature, it is important to point out the intellectual background of the "realists." Reacting critically to what they assumed to be America's and the other western democracies' failures to cope with Hitler, the "realist" school— characterized by the writing of Morgenthau (284) and Kennan (219) in the 1940's and 1950's—tended to overemphasize the impact of the international context on foreign policy. Disliking the way in which domestic politics and the popularization of foreign policy affected foreign policy decisions, they argued that a true understanding of the national interest was based on being aware of immutable interests and conditions in the international environment. Because the realists have confused prescriptive analysis (domestic politics should not interfere with foreign policy) with descriptive analysis (the international context determines foreign policy), they have tended to adopt a monocausal approach by emphasizing power and the international system in their foreign policy analysis.

In closing, it should be emphasized that the descriptive analysis of foreign policy must be both multicausal and multilevel. The student must not only look for general relationships among foreign policy behavior and various foreign policy determinants; he must also attempt to apply his general ideas about determinants and patterns to specific foreign policy cases. By attempting to analyze foreign policy at both levels, he can develop and test better theories.

6

Intergovernmental Organizations as Actors

So far we have concentrated on the state as an actor, and if this book were describing only international politics before 1900, we would not have much cause for discussing other types of actors in the international political system. Possible exceptions might be the Catholic Church, particularly prior to the seventeenth century, or a few organizations that developed in the late nineteenth century. However, there would be no need to study in detail organizations other than the state in order to understand international politics between the Peace of Westphalia in 1648 and World War I.

In contrast, any discussion of contemporary international politics cannot ignore the tremendous growth of a new kind of organization. We call these organizations *transnational* because their membership, purposes, and scope of activity transcend national boundaries.[1] In this chapter, we will be concerned primarily with a class of transnational organizations that are sometimes called *international* organizations; for reasons cited below, we shall call them *intergovernmental organizations*. After distinguishing them from other types of transnational organizations, we will discuss their activities, membership, and policy-making structure. In Chapters 7–10, we will examine the role the organizations play as settings for interactions among states.

---

[1] Much of the information in this chapter is taken from the *Yearbook of International Organizations, 1966–1967*. (Brussels: Union of International Associations, 1966.) This includes some of the descriptions we have provided of various intergovernmental organizations as well as our more general remarks and tables on the characteristics of intergovernmental organizations. Unless another source is cited, the reader can assume that the information is taken from the *Yearbook*.

TRANSNATIONAL ORGANIZATIONS

A transnational organization has membership from and a capacity to act in more than one country. In addition to the intergovernmental organization, two other types of transnational organizations may be distinguished: *nongovernmental* organizations and *multinational* organizations. The first refers to an organization created among individuals or private organizations in different countries. It differs from intergovernmental organizations because its members are not states but private citizens and organizations. The International Red Cross, for example, does not have governments as its members (although it sometimes receives support from governments) but is operated and controlled by private citizens and organizations. The multinational organization is initially based in one country but has operations, interests, and/or employees in other countries. For example, large manufacturing corporations such as General Motors are multinational because they have sales and production facilities in many nations. Both of these transnational organizations are distinguished from the intergovernmental organization because governments are not official members.

The nongovernmental organization is composed of private citizens or groups, or both, who cooperate at the international level. As a form of institutional cooperation, it has existed since the beginning of the state system as the Catholic Church; it continues to exist and multiply whenever people of two or more nations feel they have something in common with sufficient conviction to create an organization. The best way to illustrate the diversity of nongovernmental organizations is to present the following list—a small but representative sample of the more than 1,900 nongovernmental organizations:

> African Trade Union Confederation
> Association of International Libraries
> Baptist World Alliance
> European Civil Service Federation
> European Computer Manufacturers Association
> Experiment in International Living
> Inter-American Bar Association
> International Association of Seed Crushers
> International Chamber of Commerce
> International Confederation of Free Trade Unions
> International Confederation of Midwives
> International Council of Scientific Unions
> International Criminal Police Organization (Interpol)
> International Federation of Christian Trade Unions
> International Film and Television Council
> International Olympic Committee
> International Political Science Association

International Rice Research Institute
International Society for the Protection of Animals
Lions International
Nordic Musicians' Union
Salvation Army
Scandinavian Bank Employees' Union
Union of International Fairs
Universal Esperanto Association
World Coalition Against Vivisection

A brief study of the list should clearly show that people form organizations on a transnational nongovernmental basis to pursue a wide variety of social, economic, and political goals. Some have substantial formal structures and institutions while others meet only occasionally to discuss the mutual interests of members. These organizations raise and allocate funds or gather and distribute information. Often, they attempt to exert pressure within the governmental structure of certain states either by becoming policy influencers or by trying to shape the attitudes of policy influencers. Frequently, they seek to pressure intergovernmental organizations like the United Nations. In short, their tactics and activities are as broad as their purposes.

The *multinational organization* is different from the other two transnational types because it is directed and controlled by a group of individuals in one nation. The most common multinational organization is the business whose leaders operate from a single base but whose activities are performed in foreign states. The tremendous increase in international economic activity since World War II has stimulated and been stimulated by the growth of multinational businesses such as General Motors. In addition to these, other multinational organizations attempt to pursue social-humanitarian goals. Examples are private foundations like the Ford Foundation and religious organizations like American Friends Service Committee. Like the nongovernmental transnational organizations, these multinational organizations attempt to influence policies and conditions across national lines. However, multinational organizations differ fron nongovernmental organizations because their goals are defined and policies formulated by a relatively small group of individuals usually located in one state.

We will not treat nongovernmental and multinational organizations in detail at this point because their main significance in the international political system is as a set of policy influencers attempting to pressure states and intergovernmental organizations. Although some of these organizations are powerful, they can best be understood as policy influencers of states, as discussed in Chapter 3, or as policy influencers in intergovernmental organizations as we shall discuss in this chapter.

TYPES OF INTERGOVERNMENTAL ORGANIZATIONS

An intergovernmental organization is formed when two or more states sign a treaty or charter. This document serves as a constitution for the organization; that is, a set of guidelines outlining the aims of the organization as well as the ways in which it should achieve those aims. Certain types of intergovernmental organizations grow from these initial charters. Two basic ways to classify intergovernmental organizations are by geographical scope of membership and by types of purposes they seek to accomplish.

The geographical scope of the membership can be classified as either global or regional. A global intergovernmental organization may be described as one with members in every major region of the world. The term *global* is more accurate than *universal* because some organizations have members in every region of the world but membership is not open to all states. For example, the British Commonwealth is an intergovernmental organization that has global but not universal membership. A distinction based on whether or not membership was open to all states would not be acceptable because even the United Nations, usually viewed as one of the most universal intergovernmental organizations, has not been willing to admit states that are thought to be "not peace-loving," for example, the Chinese People's Republic. The term *regional* will be used to describe organizations that do not have members in every region of the world. They may include members from a number of regions, as NATO does, or from only one region, as the Organization of American States does. Table 10 applies the global-regional distinction to forty of the more important intergovernmental organizations.

One important trend in the development of these groups has been the increase in the number of active organizations. In 1949, there were 38; by 1967 the number had increased to 199.[2] Even more significant has been the relative increase of regional over global intergovernmental organizations. Between 1949 and 1967, the latter had seen an increase of from 33 to 88 while the number of regional organizations had increased from only 5 to 111.

We can also roughly classify the intergovernmental organization according to basic purposes: pursuit of economic or social welfare goals (World Health Organization, European Economic Community); military security (NATO, the Warsaw Treaty Organization); and multipurpose organizations with social, economic, and military security goals (The Organization of American States). Forty representative intergovernmental organizations are classified in Table 10 according to these categories.

[2] These figures on the number of intergovernmental organizations are taken from the 1st and 11th editions of the *Yearbook of International Organizations*.

TABLE 10

**Forty Intergovernmental Organizations Classified
by Scope of Interest and Purpose**

Organization	Scope	Purpose
African Development Bank	Regional	Economic
African Postal Union	Regional	Social
Arab International Tourist Union	Regional	Social
Arab Postal Union	Regional	Social
Asian Development Bank	Regional	Economic
Bank for International Settlements	Global	Economic
Central Treaty Organization	Regional	Military
Commonwealth Agricultural Bureau	Regional	Social
Council for Mutual Economic Assistance	Regional	Economic
Council of Europe	Regional	Multipurpose
Danube Commission	Regional	Economic
European Civil Aviation Conference	Regional	Social
European Coal and Steel Community	Regional	Economic
European Economic Community	Regional	Economic
European Free Trade Association	Regional	Economic
European Nuclear Energy Agency	Regional	Social
European Parliament	Regional	Multipurpose
Euratom	Regional	Social
Inter African Coffee Organization	Regional	Economic
Inter American Defense Board	Regional	Military
International Civil Aviation Organization	Global	Social
International Development Association	Global	Economic
International Coffee Organization	Global	Economic
International Cotton Institute	Global	Economic
International Exhibition Bureau	Global	Economic
International Finance Corporation	Global	Economic
International Monetary Fund	Global	Economic
International Wheat Council	Global	Economic
Latin American Free Trade Association	Regional	Economic
League of Arab States	Regional	Multipurpose
Nordic Council	Regional	Multipurpose
North Atlantic Treaty Organization	Regional	Military
Organization of American States	Regional	Multipurpose
Pan American Health Organization	Regional	Social
Southeast Asia Treaty Organization	Regional	Military
United Nations	Global	Multipurpose
UN Food and Agricultural Organization	Global	Social
UNESCO	Global	Social
Warsaw Treaty Organization	Regional	Military
World Health Organization	Global	Social

These classifications give us a general notion of the types of intergovernmental organizations operating in the contemporary international political system. There are many regional and few global organizations. In addition, many more organizations are set up to deal with problems of a social or economic nature than are dealing with problems of preventing war and promoting peace. The United Nations is the only global organization designed to deal with issues of peace and war on a regular basis even though, as we will see in the following pages, the ability of the United Nations to deal with these issues is limited.

Regional organizations dealing with these problems can also be found in every region of the world, although they vary radically in character. In some regions such as Southeast Asia, as well as western and eastern Europe, they are little more than alliances directed against a state or states from outside that region. SEATO was initiated to defend against attack from China or the Soviet Union. The Warsaw Pact was established primarily to defend against attack from the United States or western European states. The major goal of NATO is to defend against attacks from eastern Europe or the Soviet Union. In Africa and the western hemisphere, organizations have been created to deal with military disturbances from within as well as outside. This is not to say that organizations such as NATO do not deal with military conflicts among members; the Greek-Turkish dispute over Cyprus has been influenced by NATO as an intergovernmental organization. Rather, organizations such as NATO were established primarily to meet what were thought to be military threats from outside the region, and their character is largely determined by their original purpose.

DECISION MAKING IN INTERGOVERNMENTAL ORGANIZATIONS

Intergovernmental organizations are rarely examined as decision-making institutions. Instead, they are more frequently studied as institutions in which states interact and through which they compete or cooperate. Although such a viewpoint may be justified, one must view intergovernmental organizations as institutions that make decisions and take actions in the contemporary world. In this section, we will do just that by employing the policy-influence system framework developed in Chapter 3 and by studying decision making in intergovernmental organizations as the interaction between decision makers and policy influencers. The first questions to be answered in using this framework are: who are the decision makers and who are the policy influencers in these organizations?

First, these decision makers may be viewed as leaders of the permanent administrative bodies of the organizations, usually called "secretariats." These leaders, such as the Secretary-General of the United Nations, are usually appointed or elected by members, but they nonetheless have authority to make certain decisions as defined by the organization charter. As we shall see, the powers and activities of decision makers as leaders of these groups are frequently limited primarily because the charter and members restrict the sphere of the organization's competence. We will think of these administrative leaders as decision makers, however, because they possess whatever authority exists to act on behalf of the organization.

Second, the policy influencers are states and nongovernmental organizations. Created in the first place by the will and resources of the state, intergovernmental organizations are frequently dominated by member states. The states may be viewed as very powerful partisan influencers because they have voting power to determine what policies decision makers can follow. For this reason the state may be viewed as the primary policy influencer in all intergovernmental organizations.

Nongovernmental organizations play a significant decision-making role in many intergovernmental organizations and therefore may be viewed as policy influencers also. As the Congress of the United States has created laws to provide a role for lobbies and pressure groups, the charters of many intergovernmental organizations give certain nongovernmental organizations official observer status. For example, the Economic and Social Council of the United Nations gives observer status to the International Federation of Agricultural Producers and others. Whether given an official status or not, nongovernmental organizations try to influence activities by pressuring not only officials but also member states of the intergovernmental organizations. Like lobbies and pressure groups in the United States, the intergovernmental organization has its main source of influence in its ability to gather pertinent information (expertise) and to argue persuasively. Although nongovernmental organizations do not vote, they play an important role in shaping the decisions of certain types of intergovernmental organization.

In our discussion of the foreign policy making process in preceding chapters, we noted that relationships between the decision maker and his policy influencers within the state could be characterized as (1) policy influencer dominant, (2) decision maker dominant, and (3) pluralized. The type of relationship between the policy influencers (states and nongovernmental organizations) and decision makers (permanent officials) in contemporary intergovernmental organizations can also be placed in the same three categories.

Before illustrating this point, it is necessary to discuss the role of the charter in the evolution of the relationship between these decision makers and policy influencers. All intergovernmental organizations are shaped by their charters but the purposes and procedures outlined in the charter often do not provide a clear picture of the way decisions are made within the organization. Sometimes the charter gives certain powers to the decision makers that they have been unable to exercise for some reason. For example, the Secretary-General of the United Nations is given authority by the UN Charter to develop a standing military force, but the states have never taken the necessary action to create that force on a permanent basis. At other times, the decision makers are able to make decisions that were never envisioned by those who first drafted the charter. The Secretary-General, for example, took actions in the Congo in the early 1960's not clearly authorized by the UN Charter. Therefore we must consider decision making within intergovernmental organizations by examining both the charter and the history of each organization.

In this context, an important characteristic of the development of many intergovernmental organizations—particularly the United Nations—is the growth of suborganizations within the larger organizational framework. The United Nations has six organs—Secretariat, General Assembly, Security Council, International Court of Justice, Economic and Social Council, and Trusteeship Council. Each performs so many complex functions that it represents a suborganization. In addition, many intergovernmental organizations establish "committees" to perform certain functions such as policy studies or the administration of aid programs. These committees also tend to become almost autonomous.

The enormous growth of intergovernmental organizations has resulted in the development of complex and poorly coordinated international bureaucracies. Unlike the bureaucracies in domestic political systems, international bureaucracies raise money from many sources, and as a result are not subject to the control national governments usually maintain over their own bureaucracies. Although attempts are made to coordinate activities, the lack of clear authority and control over financial resources by one particular body makes the coordination much more difficult. Implications of this condition will be clear as we discuss the types of relationships between decision makers and policy influencers in intergovernmental organizations.

Policy Influencer Dominance

Organizations in which policy influencers play a large role and decision makers a small role in the determination of policy are not uncommon. In these types of organizations, states are the only significant policy influencers. Nongovernmental organizations play little or no role in influencing either the state or the decision makers. Usually, the strength of the state in relation to the weakness of the permanent officials of the organization indicates an unwillingness among members to give decision makers wide latitude in policy making.

In fact, in some ways it would be reasonable to argue that the states are the "real" decision makers in policy-influencer-dominant intergovernmental organizations in the sense that they control what the organization does. However, the organization "acts" through its permanent officials who, though authorized by the states, make a large number of concrete decisions implementing the mandate given them by the state. Although the distinction between the decision maker and the policy influencer is not completely clear-cut (just as it was not always clear in the feudal period within states), it can be used as a framework for discussing the policy-influencer-dominant intergovernmental organization.

The most obvious example of this category are those parts of the United Nations that deal with issues of war and peace as distinguished from those whose domain is social and economic. The General Assembly, the Security Council, and certain upper-echelon officials in the UN Secretariat are the principal components dealing with these issues. We will discuss interaction between the states as policy influencer and the Secretary-General as primary decision maker in terms of the way the three organs deal with problems of war and peace.

In dealing with these problems, the Secretary-General is greatly limited. According to the charter, the Security Council has power to authorize the Secretary-General to take actions ranging from official United Nations statements to the use of troops and economic sanctions. Without such authorization, the Secretary-General can only act behind the scenes as a mediator or with the recommendations of the General Assembly. Moreover, the General Assembly may recommend that the Secretary-General take a wide range of actions, but these recommendations are not binding on member states. If the Security Council calls upon the Secretary-General to use force, that official can demand military support from members because they are obligated to carry out Security Council decisions. However, states are not bound to carry out recommendations of the General Assembly; this means the Secretary-General still depends upon the states' willingness to cooperate even if the General Aseembly has acted. The Secretary-General might be able to use funds voted by the General Assembly for certain policies, as he did in the Congo, but such use is not within the normal authority of his office.

The power of the states as policy influencers differs between the Security Council and the General Assembly. In the former, five states—France, the United Kingdom, Nationalist China, the Soviet Union, and the United States—have a veto over substantive questions. An additional ten members have normal voting power. The ten are elected from total UN membership for two-year terms. In the General Assembly, the formal voting power is equal, although in practice certain states are often able to control the way other members vote. The General Assembly votes on a simple majority for unimportant questions and a two-thirds majority for important questions. The decision of whether or not a given question is important is determined by a simple majority, although in many instances precedent makes the decision automatic.

According to the UN Charter, then, policy influencers dominate United Nations activities concerned with issues of war and peace. The Secretary-General must placate members and is obligated to follow the directives they make through the General Assembly and the Security Council. The Secretary-General has no troops or finances except for those given to the United Nations by its members. His position is similar in many respects to the medieval monarch who was so dependent upon his nobles that he had little autonomy in making policies.

Even though the Secretary-General and his staff are severely circumscribed by the states acting through the Security Council and the General Assembly, they have had a significant impact on certain recent conflicts. The ability to obtain information gives the Secretary-General an important role in conflict situations. With his staff strategically placed in many trouble spots, he is able to acquire information from sources not directly involved in the dispute. For example, in 1967 Secretary-General U Thant played a central role in the Arab-Israeli War because UN outposts in the embattled area allowed him to report up-to-date and relatively unbiased information to the Security Council.

Moreover, because the Secretary-General is viewed as a neutral figure, he can often play an effective mediating role in disputes. He can visit the capitals of disputing states at the height of tension to suggest a settlement or to carry messages. Having access to high-level officials, he can be useful in maintaining communication in tense situations. Although states will closely watch his behavior to make sure that he acts impartially, the Secretary-General is able to take part in delicate diplomatic negotiations if he has been able to maintain his reputation for neutrality.

The personality and values of the Secretary-General (with his close advisors) greatly affect his effectiveness in dealing with conflict situations. He must be able to find and represent a consensus among many conflicting states over a large variety of complex issues. If he has moral or political predispositions favoring one state's position over another, he must not show it as, for example, Trygvie Lie was alleged to have done as the first Secretary-General of the United Nations. Unlike U Thant (Secretary-General 1961–   ), who has avoided taking sides in any dispute, Trygvie Lie sided with the United States' position on Korea in the early 1950's.[3] Moreover, the Secretary-General must be able to manage the information he receives to further the chances of peace and the aims of the United Nations. He cannot rely on a large staff because the chances of information leakage increase as the number of people possessing the information increases. The successful Secretary-General must be resourceful and dedicated to the cause of peace and to the United Nations. Even more important, he must earn the trust of the major states. In the area of peace and war, the United Nations is clearly policy influencer dominant. The policy influencers are states that support the organization and are given a powerful role by the UN Charter. As a result of the unwillingness of the states to give wide latitude to the Secretary-General and his staff as the decision makers, he can do little that is not directly or tacitly approved by the majority or at least by the more influential members of the organization. In spite of this dominance, however, the Secretary-General still plays some role in international conflict situations, both in managing information and in mediating among conflicting parties.

Although the United Nations is in many respects different from most other intergovernmental organizations, it is strikingly similar in terms of the dominance of the policy influencers. Many intergovernmental organizations at the global and regional level are dominated by the members in the sense that their decision makers are provided with little latitude and authority. Usually, the unwillingness of states to allow the permanent secretariat wide discretionary power is a result of their distrust of each other and not necessarily of the secretariat. Where commitment to an intergovernmental organization and assumption of a common sense of interest among members is weak, the organization tends to be dominated by the states. As the organization grows and the states become aware of mutual interests, the secretariat has a better chance of gaining more authority and responsibility, although gains will always be circumscribed by members' basic beliefs. In the final analysis, however, the quality of leadership in the secretariat can have an important impact on whether decision makers will ever have a more substantial role in a policy-influencer-dominant intergovernmental organization.

Decision Maker Dominance

In contrast to this type of policy-making structure, the decision maker is dominant when the permanent organs of the organization are relatively

---

[3] For a discussion of the role of the Secretary-General in conflict situations, see Leland M. Goodrich, "The Political Role of the Secretary-General," *International Organization,* 16 (1962), 720–35.

autonomous. When policy influencers exert pressures through brief meetings convening every three or four years, the permanent staff of the organization enjoys a significant amount of freedom. This situation exists in many intergovernmental organizations.

Decision makers dominate organizations only under specific conditions. First, the scope of activities usually involves a narrowly defined purpose. Second, there must be general agreement among members that cooperation through such an organization can achieve the particular purpose. The states must clearly have more to gain than to lose from participation. Third, the specific purposes of the organization must not involve the types of interests likely to lead to open conflict among members. If these conditions exist, states seem willing to create and maintain a permanent staff to carry on the organization's purposes with a minimum of control.

Such conditions frequently exist on both global and regional levels. Many specialized global agencies, such as the Universal Postal Union or the World Health Organization, have permanent secretariats performing most of the duties with only supervisory control from organization members. To cite an extreme example, the International Union for the Publication of Customs publishes information on the tariff policies of states; it has almost no control from members and a completely independent permanent staff. Regionally, many organizations qualify as decision maker dominant. For example, the Inter-American Institute of Agricultural Sciences has a staff of over two hundred permanent employees headed by a director who is elected by the 20 member states for a six-year period.

The Universal Postal Union[4] can be cited as an illustration of the dynamics of such a decision-maker-dominant organization. The four organs of the union are: (1) Congress, comprising all members (states) meeting every five years; (2) 20-member Executive and Liaison Committee, which is elected by the Congress and meets to insure continuity and fulfillment of the wishes of the Congress; (3) International Bureau, the permanent secretariat at Berne, Switzerland; and (4) Consultative Committee on Postal Research, which is made up of interested members and which elects the Management Council to carry on its activities.

Obviously, the states play a minimal role in influencing the permanent organs; the entire membership meets only once every five years. Although the Congress authorizes the activities of the International Bureau, the long period between these meetings surely gives the Bureau a relatively autonomous position. The Executive and Liaison Committee serves as a watchdog

---

[4] For a discussion of the history and operation of the Universal Postal Union, see Charles H. Alexandrowicz, *World Economic Agencies: Law and Practice* (New York: Praeger, 1962), pp. 1–34.

to make sure that the Bureau performs its assigned duties. However, this function is limited by the technical and functionally specific duties of the permanent staff.

Although the organizational structure creates conditions in which the Bureau (secretariat) dominates, we should realize that this dominance continues as long as most members find its activities acceptable. The ultimate authority rests with the states; they are potentially very powerful policy influencers. No doubt they could reestablish their control if they wanted to, but under present conditions they are willing to let the secretariat dominate the organization.

The role of nongovernmental organizations in an inter-governmental organization where decision makers dominate is more important than in a policy-influencer-dominant one. Because the states exercise much less control, a certain vacuum exists, which the nongovernmental organization fills. The secretariat is willing to hear the opinion of the nongovernmental organizations for a number of reasons. First, it represents the views of individuals who have an interest in what the organization is doing; those views might have considerable weight because they represent the knowledge of technically competent individuals. Second, nongovernmental organizations are able to pressure national governments; they can call the attention of their governments to certain policies pursued by the secretariat. Members of the permanent secretariat of decision-maker-dominant intergovernmental organizations, prefer to be guided by nongovernmental organizations, rather than have member governments attempt to exert more authority.

Pluralized Decision Making

Somewhere between the intergovernmental organization whose members allow the permanent staff very little leeway and those whose secretariats enjoy autonomy in their given area is the third type: the organization in which the relationships between decision makers and policy influencers can be described as pluralized; that is, where both influence each other substantially. The intergovernmental organizations in this equilibrium category usually have a broader purpose than those that are decision maker dominant and a narrower purpose than those that are policy influencer dominant. In addition, members have general commitment to the organization; this includes willingness to allow the permanent body significant autonomy. In the global area, we might place the International Labor Organization in this category; regionally, many European organizations such as the European Economic Community (EEC or Common Market) would fit. In order to demonstrate the nature of the pluralized relationship between decision makers and policy influencers, we will discuss the decision-making structure of the EEC.[5]

The Community is part of a complex set of institutions that have developed in Europe since World War II. Its primary members (as distinct from associates) are West Germany, France, Italy, Belgium, the Netherlands, and Luxembourg. Decisions are made in the EEC by two bodies—the Council of Ministers, official cabinet-level officials of six countries, and the Commission, a body of nine individuals elected for staggered terms every four years. The two bodies share decision-making authority in areas specified by the 1957 treaty that established the Community.

The Council of Ministers gives members direct influence over policy making in the areas specified by the treaty. However, that influence is limited by the Commission. The election policy for members of the Commission (four-year terms at staggered intervals), leads us to assume from knowledge of the behavior of other representatives that they do not necessarily represent the official positions of their countries. Like the U.S. senator who exercises more independent judgment than the congressman partially because he serves a longer term, members of the Commission, we can assume, exercise a relatively free hand in making decisions because of their four-year terms. The Commission may be considered a collective Secretary-General that oversees the permanent staff and has significant authority in making decisions. In operation, then, organizational structure gives both the state and the decision makers important roles in EEC activities.

The Commission is also pressured by other intergovernmental and nongovernmental organizations that play a role in European politics.[6] A European Court of Justice interprets the treaty that established the Community. Also, a European parliament advises the Commission; it consists of members appointed by the national parliaments of member states. Organizing themselves around partisan rather than national lines, members of the parliament act as transnationally organized Christian Democrats, Socialists, and Liberals rather than solely as Italians, Frenchmen, Germans, Belgians, Dutchmen, and Luxembourgers.

Nongovernmental organizations also exert pressure on the Community's decision making bodies. Political and economic interests organized across national lines in Europe seek to influence decisions that are made by

[5] For a discussion of the European Economic Community see Leon N. Lindberg, "Decision-Making and Integration in the European Community," *International Organization,* 19 (1965), 58–80.

[6] See Michael Curtis, *Western European Integration* (New York: Harper, 1965).

European institutions as well as governments. Because they are often given associate roles in the intergovernmental organizations, the nongovernmental organizations exert a great deal of influence.

In the case of EEC, one must also cite the influence of multinational businesses.[7] Development of transnational economic institutions in Europe has been stimulated in many ways by the rise of businesses which had production and marketing facilities in different European states. Today, these multinational businesses exert significant influence on the individuals making decisions for Europe's economic institutions. In addition, they are the prime targets for those decisions.

Given the multitude of forces operating on the EEC Commission, and given the significant degree of authority enjoyed by the Commission in making decisions, we must consider the relationship between the decision makers and the policy influencers to be pluralized. Many "actors" have significant ability to influence, taking part in the making of decisions. In the Community, the policy influencers are not only the member states acting through the Council of Ministers (and of course the associate members) but also the other intergovernmental organizations of Europe, nongovernmental organizations and multinational business. Even though these policy influencers are powerful, the Commission has authority to make important decisions. This authority shifts under different conditions but remains substantial enough so that the structure is pluralized, dominated by neither policy influencer nor decision maker.

SUMMARY

In summary, Table 11 illustrates the relationship between types of decision making processes within intergovernmental organizations and the scope as well as purpose of the organizations. Based on the preceding discussion and the chart, we can make some general statements about that relationship.

Organizations with policy-influencer-dominant structures are primarily, although not entirely, (1) global and regional organizations that pursue both economic-social and war-peace purposes or (2) regional military security organizations. In the multipurpose group we would place the United Nations, the Organization of American States, and the Organization of African Unity. In the regional war-peace organizations, we would place NATO, SEATO, CENTO, ANZUS, and the Warsaw Pact. We can

[7] The role of multinational businesses in the development of the European Common Market is discussed in Ernst B. Haas, *The Uniting of Europe* (Stanford, Cal.: Stanford University Press, 1968), pp. 162–214 and 318–55.

TABLE 11
Decision-Making Structure of Intergovernmental Organizations

Scope	Policy-Influencer Dominant	Decision-Maker Dominant	Pluralized
Global			
War-Peace	None	None	None
Economic-social	Few	Many	Some
Multi-purpose	One (UN)	None	None
Regional			
War-Peace	Many	None	None
Economic-social	Few	Some	Some
Multi-purpose	Most	None	Few

assume that the importance of war-peace activities in the activities of both types of organizations accounts for the importance of the states as policy influencers.

In contrast, the decision-maker-dominant organizations are those that perform very specialized economic and social purposes. Either on the global or the regional level, decision-maker-dominant organizations have members who feel that the assets of an effective and dynamic organization far outweigh any burdens that might conceivably be placed on the members. Although the decision-maker-dominant organization can be transformed, at the members' discretion, into a policy-influencer-dominant one, the members are usually willing to allow the permanent staff to carry on most of the functions without restrictions.

The pluralized intergovernmental organization deals with social and economic questions, but the questions usually involve broader and more important interests than those handled by decision-maker-dominant organizations. In the case of the organizations of western Europe, almost the entire spectrum of policy concerns—including on some occasions issues relating to war and peace—is covered by some of the regional organizations. Currently, most pluralized intergovernmental organizations are European.

From the preceding discussion, a clear relationship emerges between the purpose of the organization and the amount of control states are willing to let the permanent staff exercise. As the purpose expands from specialized economic and social goals, through broad economic and social goals,

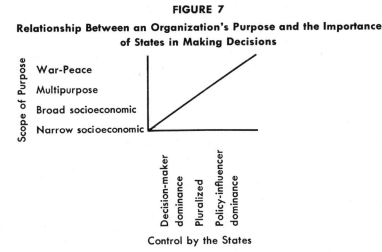

FIGURE 7

Relationship Between an Organization's Purpose and the Importance of States in Making Decisions

to questions of war and peace, the states become more jealous of their authority. This relationship is roughly illustrated in Figure 7.

History plays an essential role in the development of intergovernmental organizations, just as it does in the development of any political institution. Often beginning as policy-influencer-dominant, intergovernmental organizations sometimes evolve as pluralized or decision-maker-dominant, particularly if their members come to accept and trust its operations. Because states continue to supply most of the financial resources for the majority of intergovernmental organizations, the evolution away from the policy-influencer-dominant structure is never irreversible. At the same time, it appears that for the foreseeable future, organizations with broad social and economic purposes or war-peace concerns will not become decision-maker dominant.

We can also see that the role of nongovernmental organizations as policy influencers is clearly related to the purposes and structure of the organization. Those intergovernmental organizations with war-peace concerns and with policy influencer dominant structures appear to offer little or no place, either formally or informally, for nongovernmental organizations. In contrast, as the organizations become concerned with economic and social purposes and less controlled by the states, nongovernmental organizations play an increasingly large role as policy influencers.

In the perspective of history, it is remarkable how numerous intergovernmental organizations are today. Although their growth appears to be limited at the global level, at the regional level it appears to be virtually unlimited. Moreover, many organizations that started out with few responsibilities and a small permanent staff have become large organizations with broad authority. We will examine the impact of intergovernmental organizations in interactions among states in later chapters. It is important to remember that intergovernmental organizations play a role in relations among states in the areas of social and economic cooperation as well as war and peace, and that this role results from a complex set of interactions between decision makers and policy influencers within each organization.

SUMMARY OUTLINE

I. Of the three types of transnational organizations, intergovernmental organizations should be treated as "actors" while nongovernmental organizations and multinational businesses should be viewed as policy influencers in the policy-influence system of states and intergovernmental organizations.

II. The intergovernmental organization's scope of activity is both regional and global, and includes social and economic as well as war or peace concerns.

    A. Global intergovernmental organizations have members in every major region of the world but are not necessarily open to every state.

    B. *Intergovernmental organizations have been increasing, but regional organizations are increasing much more rapidly than global ones.*

    C. *Most intergovernmental organizations are concerned with social and economic problems, not war and peace issues.*

    D. *Except for the United Nations, only regional intergovernmental organizations are concerned with issues of war and peace.*

III. The decision-making process within intergovernmental organizations can be analyzed using the concepts of decision maker to refer to the permanent staff and policy influencer to refer to states and nongovernmental organizations.

    A. *States are crucial policy influencers because they authorize the charter of the organization and usually supply the majority of funds.*

    B. *Nongovernmental organizations may be policy influencers if they manage information and present their cases.*

    C. *The charter of an intergovernmental organization plays an important, although not the final, role in the organization's activities.*

    D. *Suborganizations—that is, agencies set up by larger established organizations—are becoming more important.*

E. *Coordination of effort has been particularly difficult among inter-governmental organizations.*

F. *Some intergovernmental organizations are dominated by the member states as policy influencers.*

G. *The United Nations in the area of peace and war issues is dominated by policy influencers.*

  1. *The Secretary-General is dependent upon the will of the states expressed through the actions of the Security Council or General Assembly.*

  2. *The permanent members dominate activities of the Security Council but not of the General Assembly.*

  3. *In spite of his weak position the UN Secretary-General can still play a critical role in certain war and peace areas if he can maintain his neutral position.*

H. Some intergovernmental organizations are decision-maker dominant.

I. Some intergovernmental organizations are characterized by a pluralized relationship between policy influencers (both states and nongovernmental organizations) and decision makers.

IV. *As the purposes of intergovernmental organizations expand from the narrow to the broad social and economic area as well as to issues of war and peace, the influence of the state in decision making increases.*

A. *Policy-influencer-dominant structures are either multipurpose or concerned with war and peace issues.*

B. *Decision-maker-dominant intergovernmental organizations deal with strictly defined social and economic aims.*

C. *Pluralized intergovernmental organizations deal with a broad span of social and economic concerns.*

D. *Even considering the fact that the older an intergovernmental organization the greater the chance that it will not be policy-influencer dominant, organizations with broad social and economic purposes and war and peace interests have little chance of becoming decision-maker dominant.*

E. *Nongovernmental organizations play a large role in decision-maker-dominant intergovernmental organizations and an even larger role in pluralized organizations but no major role in policy-influencer-dominant organizations.*

BIBLIOGRAPHICAL ESSAY

In a survey of the literature on intergovernmental organizations, Ronald J. Yalem (430) quotes the Committee on the Study of International Organizations of the Social Science Research Council (an organization that finances social science research). The committee cites the need for "comparative study of international organizations." Looking at Professor Yalem's list as well as the titles of articles published in relevant journals such as *International Organization,* one notes an almost total absence of literature that attempts to compare dimensions of intergovernmental organizations as we have tried to in this chapter. A number of studies have emphasized the importance of concepts and theories, from Potter's well-known volume (317) through Levi (246), Reuter (332), Claude (74), Haas (147), Jacob and Atherton (191), Plano and Riggs (312), and Goodspeed (141). However, these works focus on the relationships among states, intergovernmental organizations, and the international environment rather than on the dimensions of the organizations and the relationship of those dimensions to other aspects of international relations. The following remarks, therefore, will not be concerned with the comparative literature on these organizations but rather with certain attempts to describe particular intergovernmental organizations or parts thereof. Like the rest of the chapter, the essay will not deal with the role of intergovernmental organizations in relations among states.

Adequate historical documentation can be found in Mangone (268) and Luard (256). Discussions of the role of nongovernmental organizations in intergovernmental organizations can be found in White (420), Buck (59), and Lador-Lederer (237). The charters of many intergovernmental organizations are reproduced in Lawson (242) and Peaslee (309). As noted at the outset of this chapter, a great deal of valuable information —enough to write numerous papers—is located in the *Yearbook of International Organizations* which has been published since 1949. Problems and some aspects of international administration are presented in Hill (171), Loveday (255), Lengyel (244) and Langrod (241).

The United Nations is by far the most frequently studied organization. We might cite some of the more classic studies of that organization since they are related to many of the concepts and propositions discussed in this chapter. Assessments of achievements of the first twenty years of the United Nations can be found in Padelford and Goodrich (307). Also of interest are three recent books of essays by Waters (417), Kay (211), and Barkun and Gregg (27). Decision making in the United Nations is discussed in Nicholas (293) and Hadwen and Kaufmann (152), while Stoessinger (397) and Singer (378) examine financing. Bailey (20) discusses the Security Council; Hovet (183), Alker and Russett (9), and Alger in (383) examine the politics of the General Assembly; and Stoessinger (396) investigates the activities of the United States and Soviet Union in the United Nations. Decisions and activities of the United Nations in areas of peace and war are examined in Rossner (349), Burns and Heathcote (62), Lefever (243), and Wainhouse et al. (408). Kelsen (216) has examined the Charter as a legal document. Finally, the role of the United Nations Secretary-General is discussed by Miller (279), Bailey (20), and Schwebel (371).

The literature on regional intergovernmental organizations, although not as substantial, is nonetheless extensive. Regional multipurpose organizations are discussed by Lindberg (247) and Haas (146, 148) for Europe; Dreier (110) and Thomas and Thomas (403) for the Organization of American States, MacDonald (260) for the Arab League, and Korbonski (233) for Comecon. Haas's book (148) remains one of the best presentations of the nature of pluralized regional intergovernmental organizations.

Thus, despite the lack of literature comparing international organization an extensive body of literature analyzes particular intergovernmental organizations. Moreover, in recent years, as Alger points out in (314) widely varying techniques have been applied, particularly to study the United Nations. Complementing such traditional studies as Hadwen and Kaufmann (152), are works that have applied statistical analysis to United Nations voting—Hovet (183) and Alker and Russett (9)—those that observe interactions among representatives in the General Assembly—Alger in (383)—and one that researches by questionnaires to new UN representatives—Alger (6). In addition, Haas (147) has attempted to apply systems concepts to the study of international organizations using the International Labor Organization as a case. Alker and Russett (9) have applied concepts developed in the study of the legislative process of the U.S. Congress. Although a great deal remains to be done, particularly in the area of comparative intergovernmental organizations, existing literature on intergovernmental organizations is substantial. Unfortunately, only a small part has been discussed here.

Part Two

INTERNATIONAL INTERACTIONS

In the next four chapters the focus of our discussion will shift from the state and intergovernmental organization per se to how states and, to a lesser degree, intergovernmental organizations deal with each other on an official basis.[1] Our comparative analysis of the patterns and determinants of foreign policy behavior and of the decision-making processes in intergovernmental organizations will facilitate discussion of the nature of international interactions. However, the following chapters will concern themselves more with *what* the actors do to and with each other than *why* they do it.

Most discussions of government-level international interactions have focused on the way *states* deal with each other. Intergovernmental organizations are frequently viewed solely as an institutional framework in which interactions among the states take place—and for good reason. They frequently provide the setting for states' dealing, whether as a forum for discussions, as the General Assembly of the United Nations does, or as an instrument through which the will of the states as members can be realized, as the Universal Postal Union does.

However, intergovernmental organizations also serve as actors attempting to shape the behavior of the states, even though much less frequently. This is as true when the UN Secretary-General attempts to mediate a dispute between two hostile nations as it is when the permanent staff of an intergovernmental organization seeks to build necessary consensus among states in order to solve a particular problem—the spread of

[1] It should be emphasized that we are defining international interactions only as the product of actions taken by officials of states or intergovernmental organizations. Nongovernmental contact such as the flow of private citizens, for example, is not considered to be an international interaction although the rules regarding the treatment of foreign travelers may be so considered.

disease, for example. Hence, although the intergovernmental organization usually serves merely as a framework for interactions, it sometimes serves as a force in its own right.

Nevertheless, the state remains the principal actor and accounts for the basic direction of most international interactions. For this reason, our discussion of the nature of international interaction throughout the next four chapters will focus primarily upon the way states deal with each other. Where appropriate, we will discuss intergovernmental organizations either as institutional settings or as actors, recognizing, however, that for the foreseeable future the state will dominate international politics.

It might be useful at this point to outline the three basic types of interactions we will discuss. The first and by far most frequent interaction among states may be characterized as "routine," involving official regulation of the daily flow of communications, people, goods, and the like among states. The second we will call "collective problem solving" because it occurs when two or more states perceive a condition that cannot be solved by independent actions and on which the states are willing to cooperate. The third type will be called "competitive bargaining;" it involves the efforts of one or more states to have another state agree to something to which it would not otherwise agree.

The three types of interactions are related. Problems sometimes arise that cannot be resolved through routine interactions. They may range from an event in the international environment (such as a gold crisis) to a planned action by one state. This creates conditions for collective problem solving or competitive bargaining. Similarly, the failure to solve a problem cooperatively may lead to competitive bargaining.

Although the three types of interactions are highly interdependent and sometimes very difficult to separate, they will be treated here in separate chapters. After describing the overall setting for all international interactions in Chapter 7, we will examine routine interactions in Chapter 8, collective problem solving interactions in Chapter 9, and competitive bargaining in Chapter 10. The primary purpose of this section, then, is to provide a framework for understanding the way states and, to a much lesser extent, intergovernmental organizations deal with each other in the contemporary world.

7

The Setting for International Interactions

Whether it is a casual interaction, such as saying hello to a neighbor, or a highly significant and complex one, such as informing one's wife that the only solution to a problem is divorce, interactions between people do not take place in a vacuum. In addition to the always present dimensions of time and space, a variety of surrounding conditions affect the interactions among people. Past experiences and images of those experiences have a great deal to do with the way people deal with each other, as do their own psychological and physiological nature.[1] Add to these factors such conditions as the social, economic, and political events and institutions that directly or indirectly affect every individual, and one can see that the way people deal with each other is enormously affected by the environment in which they exist.

The same is true for interactions among states. States exist and interact in a time-space dimension that is shaped by tangible factors like geography and intangibles like the images of past experiences. To complicate matters, while states are interacting at the formal governmental levels

[1] One could object to this sentence by arguing that psychological and physiological character is not the setting for interactions but a factor that shapes an individual's behavior. Such a position is based on the analytical assumption that it is more useful to treat psychological and physiological factors as attributes of the actor rather than as the setting. In most cases, it would be justified. However, when looking at states as actors, the "psychology" and "physiology" of the state sometimes can be viewed as part of the environment with which the decision makers of the state must deal. It is as if we made a distinction between the "soul" of an individual and his psychophysiological makeup. Although it is not frequently useful to make such a distinction when analyzing the behavior of individuals (unless the analysis is for theological or moral purposes), it is sometimes necessary to distinguish between the decision maker and conditions within the state in order to understand certain types of international interactions.

through their officials, people within states are also dealing with each other across national lines in every imaginable dimension from marriage to trade. The flow of official interactions takes place within the context of the flow of unofficial interrelationships among the people of the world.

Our aim in this chapter is to examine the various dimensions, institutions, and interrelationships that constitute the environment for official governmental interactions among states. Remembering that it is sometimes difficult to separate the setting from interactions themselves, we are interested in examining the forces operating throughout the international environment that affect the way states deal with each other. These five aspects of the international environment will be explored: ecological factors—that is, man's relation to his biophysical environment; the flow of ideas; the flow of people; the international economy; and international law. We will see how each of these aspects creates conditions for and sets limits upon international interactions.

THE ECOLOGICAL SETTING

The ecological setting for interactions among states involves the general relationship of man to his biophysical environment. It is concerned primarily with physical and biological conditions, and how man affects and is affected by those conditions. In this section, we will trace the manner in which physical location and the distribution of resources—tempered as they are by man's ability to move from place to place and to use the resources at his disposal—provide a setting for and an influence upon official interactions of states.

The most fundamental factor is that the state is a territorially-based political organization. Its location affects how it behaves towards other states, and its boundaries define the area over which it has generally recognized control. Legal relationships among states are important factors in the way states deal with each other. In addition, as Russett has illustrated in a quantitative study, trading patterns, membership in intergovernmental organizations, instances of conflict, and even voting in the UN General Assembly are related, in some degree, to states' physical locations.[2]

Although one has to be wary of geographical determinism, the following statement by Saul B. Cohen, a political geographer, should illustrate the importance of geography in foreign policy relations among states:

[2] Bruce M. Russett, *International Regions and the International System: A Study in Political Ecology* (Chicago: Rand McNally, 1967). Also see Steven J. Brams, "Transaction Flows in the International System," *American Political Science Review*, 60 (1966), 880–99.

Two basic locational conditions characterize the geopolitical positions of the U.S.S.R. and the United States. First, these two superpowers have grown up in physical isolation from one another. They are still physically remote, save in a time-distance, air-age sense. Second, the Soviet Union lives in direct land or narrow seas contact with a large number of sovereign states; Americans have few neighbors.

The first condition may help to explain why the Cold War has not erupted into a shooting war. The second condition underscores the fact that the U.S.S.R. places a very high priority on its military relations with its neighbors, while the United States cannot find security through military hegemony over its neighbors alone.[3]

Thus, spatial relationships determined by ecology provide an important part of the setting for interactions among states at all levels.

In addition, the ecological setting also involves distribution of resources. The location of natural resources such as coal, steel, and oil, for example, greatly affects the way states deal with each other. Equally important is the location of human resources; not only the number of people but also their levels of education and skill. As we have seen in Chapter 4, economic and military capabilities affect the way states behave; this means distribution of resources also plays an important role.

Although ecological factors are significant as a framework for interaction among states, they do *not* play the *same* role over a long period. We sometimes make the mistake of assuming that location and distribution of resources are hard facts that remain static. However, such an assumption fails to take into account the dynamic nature of the interplay between man and his biophysical environment—an interplay that results not only from technological developments but also from evolving patterns of social, economic, and political life.

The impact of technological factors on modern life has altered the ecological setting. By increasing the speed of communication and transportation, technology has affected the role of location. This is manifest, for example, in the changing formulations of military strategy over the past 300 years. Control of the seas meant much more in the eighteenth and nineteenth centuries than it does today. Great Britain could protect herself through seapower until certain technological changes made air power more important than control of the seas. The contrast between United States foreign policy before World War I and after World War II is a clear example of the fluidity of geographical conditions. Prior to World War I, nonentanglement in European affairs appeared to be a reasonable policy;

[3] Saul B. Cohen, *Geography and Politics in the World Divided* (New York: Random House, 1963), p. 186.

the Atlantic was viewed—with good reason—as a protective barrier for the United States. After World War II, however, when it was apparent that the Atlantic could be spanned quickly, an isolationist policy was less easy to defend.

The overall impact of technology on these ecological factors is to lessen the constraining influence of distance for states more advanced technologically. The enormous increase in man's ability to move himself, his communications, his economic goods, and his military forces over long distances in a short time has altered the contemporary world. The growing economic and military interdependence among states in all parts of the world can partially be explained by the impact of technology on the effects of distance.

Technology has also significantly affected distribution of resources, not only by increasing the accessibility of various raw materials through improved transportation but also by making certain hitherto useless resources extremely valuable. Coal, iron, and oil did not become important until the capacity to use these resources was developed. Prior to the nineteenth century, gold and other precious metals were viewed as the primary natural resources of value. Today, energy resources challenge the importance of precious metals in the affairs of state. Similarly, educated and skilled people (human resources) were made valuable by the industrial revolution. In addition, technological developments have created new tools for discovering and recovering natural resources. The crude methods of discovery and mining of the nineteenth century have been replaced with the highly sophisticated and effective methods of today. Venezuelan oil, for example, has become important today because techniques have been developed of drilling for oil under large bodies of water.

Changing social, economic, and political patterns have altered man's relationship to his biophysical environment to such an extent that certain basic biological and physical threats have developed. The population explosion, water and air pollution, as well as the control of disease and the conservation of physical and biological resources represent problems and challenges that cannot be solved without cooperative, international interaction. In addition to changing the goals and tools of conflict, the revolution in the ecological setting has also provided a broad arena in which nations can and in fact *must* cooperate.

For these reasons, then, ecological factors are changing the setting for interactions among states. Traditional conditions have been radically altered by the impact of technology on man's relationship to his environment. Often, decision makers do not understand the changes. Using the framework we developed in Chapter 2, their *images* of the relationship between land, time, and military force or economic conditions fail to adjust to the changes produced by technological factors. For example, prior to World War II, French decision makers assumed that the military conditions were still basically the same as they were before World War I. Failing to take into account the impact of such technological changes as the airplane and mobile armored units, the French army was not prepared to resist German military might displayed in World War II. The impact of ecological factors on interactions among states, then, involves not only the way technology and other conditions affect geographical factors, but also the ability of decision makers and their policy influencers to adjust their images to the new ecological conditions.

THE FLOW OF IDEAS

Whether we define "ideas" as beliefs, images, or merely information, the increase in the exchange of ideas among the peoples of the world has increased rapidly in recent years. Foreign travel has expanded to provide greater opportunity for face-to-face exchange of ideas while mass communication has made possible the transmission of ideas to a vast number of people. Just as important, the growth in number of intergovernmental and nongovernmental organizations has provided both a public forum and a private meeting place for exchange of viewpoints.

The enormous increase in the flow of ideas may be viewed as part of the setting for interactions among states. To provide an analytical framework for looking at the flow of ideas as a setting for interactions among states, we will use the concept of world culture. Defining culture as a set of shared ideas that orients and guides behavior, we will look at the flow of ideas as emerging world cultures.[4] Neither completely homogeneous nor universally accepted, the world culture consists of certain sets of ideas or subcultures. We will identify and discuss three of these: world technological culture, world social culture, and international political culture.

The *technological culture* consists of those elements of knowledge necessary to organize and maintain agricultural and industrial production.

---

[4] The term "culture" has been used by political scientists to discuss sets of ideas or attitudes and beliefs that have sufficiently wide currency to provide a framework for political behavior. See Gabriel Almond and G. Bingham Powell, Jr., *Comparative Politics: A Developmental Approach* (Boston: Little, Brown, 1966), pp. 16–72. This usage is somewhat dissimilar from the sociologist's use, which focuses more on patterns of behavior than on attitudes, although the two usages are not completely incompatible.

Although once shared by only the countries of Europe and North America, technological knowhow is being disseminated rapidly throughout the world. Because those who must acquire the knowhow are limited to a relatively small group of individuals in each state, the ideas have not been circulated by mass media. Rather, personal contacts, transnational organizations, and official contact between states have been the prime source of transmission. Not to be confused with economic progress per se, the flow of technological ideas represents probably the most homogeneous and accepted segment of the world culture.

The *world social culture,* those ideas relating to how societies should be organized and managed internally, is less homogeneous. Transmitted through the mass media, in intergovernmental and nongovernmental organizations as well as through foreign travel, and involving social, political, economic, and moral questions, ideas on the good society are exchanged on a universal basis. However, individuals as well as governmental and nongovernmental organizations often promote conflicting ideas. The apparent conflict between Marxist and non-Marxist ideas on the organization and management of society, for example, is a recurring theme not only in the mass media and intergovernmental organizations but also in personal interchanges among foreign travelers. However, even though there are obviously contrasting social ideologies, certain shared ideas remain. For example, Marxists and non-Marxists alike agree on the need for equal opportunity or on the importance of material well-being and progress even though they disagree on how to achieve such goals. Although it is necessary to emphasize that the ideas individuals espouse are not always the ones that actually motivate them, one can nonetheless point to a set of ideas about the purposes and organizations of societies that is discussed, if not accepted, throughout the world.

Finally, the *international political culture*[5] concerns the way relations among states should be organized. Held by foreign policy decision makers and many foreign policy influencers, the international political culture is permeated by inconsistencies. Some call for the increased authority of supranational organizations at both regional and global levels while others embrace the old days of traditional diplomacy. Some say all states should unilaterally disarm while others call for the increased use of force. Again, ideas on international politics are transmitted by foreign travelers, transnational organizations and the mass media, just as the social culture is.

However, even though confusion, ambiguity, and heterogeneity exist

---

[5] For a more complete discussion of the international political culture see William D. Coplin, *The Functions of International Law* (Chicago: Rand McNally, 1966), pp. 186–95.

in the international political culture, there still appears to be an underlying sharing of ideas, especially in the light of primary foreign policy decision makers and the most powerful policy influencers. As one gets closer to the people in every state who make foreign policy decisions, consensus appears on a few basic ideas about international politics. In this consensus, the state is viewed as the primary actor maintaining a predominant amount of authority; force is viewed as an acceptable tool of foreign policy if the issues at stake are considered to be related to national security; and international cooperation through intergovernmental organization is considered a necessary alternative in many areas.[6]

These three subcultures of the world culture act as an important part of the setting for interactions among states. The technological ideas often represent a resource through which the rich states cultivate the political support of poor states. The world social culture forms an ideological battleground in which certain states engage other states not only for the political support of foreign states but also to develop political support for their own regimes. The international political culture represents a setting for the formulation of national strategies implying the limits of acceptable actions in a very general fashion.

In closing this section, it might be worthwhile to point to a famous statement by Max Weber that "the 'world images' that have been created by 'ideas' have, like switchmen, determined the tracks along which action has pushed by the dynamic of interest."[7] Without getting into a chicken-and-egg argument concerning the origin of ideas and the motivation behind human behavior, it is important to realize that ideas can have a vast impact on the future behavior of states and the role of intergovernmental organizations. If foreign policy decision makers and powerful policy influencers come to accept different ideas about the way society and relations among societies should be organized, the whole environment for international interactions could be transformed. Under such conditions, it is possible that decision makers would no longer jealously guard the authority and capability of states and that international institutions that would develop would regulate the use of force. However, although ideas can change the course of history, it is apparent from past events that alterations of basic attitudes frequently occur so slowly that the change can better be measured in centuries than in years. It is important, then, to recognize the flow of ideas for what it is—an important feature of the setting for interaction among

---

[6] The future of the international political culture is projected in Chapter 12.
[7] Max Weber, "The Social Psychology of World Religions," in H. H. Gerth and C. Wright Mills, eds., *From Max Weber: Essays in Sociology* (New York: Oxford University Press, 1958), p. 280.

states—rather than as a means for quickly transforming the way states deal with each other.

THE FLOW OF PEOPLE

A somewhat related aspect of the setting for interactions among states is the flow of people. Individuals travel to foreign countries for various reasons. They may be vacationing or traveling on business. They may be taking part in the meeting of some transnational organization to which they belong for social, political, or economic reasons, or they may be sent by their governments to fulfill an overseas duty as diplomat or soldier. Possibly, they may be moving permanently, planning to become a national of the state to which they are moving.

The factors underlying the increased flow of people in the contemporary world are similar to those underlying the increased flow of ideas. The speed of modern transportation and communication, as well as the impact of technology, has made the peoples of the world not only more dependent upon each other but also more interested in dealing with each other. In addition, the tremendous population growth of most states has increased the pressure for transnational travel primarily because individuals are in search of a better place to live.[8] In many underdeveloped states, travel to a developed country, either permanently or merely for education, represents a path to a better life and an escape from the hardship shared by an increasing number of uneducated members of his society.

While tourist and business travel is encouraged by most states and as a result has increased tremendously in recent years, immigration is frequently discouraged and consequently has diminished.[9] The primary reason for this slowing down is precisely because immigration—except to escape religious or political persecution—is pursued by individuals who want a better life but who lack the skills and education necessary to be anything but an economic burden in the receiving state. Although certain states such as Australia encourage immigration because they have a general labor shortage, most states are willing to admit only individuals who would bring needed skills; in most cases they are not the ones most likely to immigrate. In contrast, almost all states encourage influx of tourists, who usually bring

[8] For a discussion of the nature of population growth in the twentieth century, particularly as it affects international relations, see Philip M. Hauser, ed., *Population and World Politics.* (Glencoe: Free Press, 1958).

[9] Immigration is examined in Dorothy Swaine Thomas, "International Immigrations" in Hauser, *Population and World Politics,* pp. 137–62.

foreign currency that will help the host state's balance of payments. Similarly, states often encourage foreign business investments and activities within certain limits because investment capital is usually in short supply.

Given the nature and size of the flow of people among states in the contemporary world, this aspect of the international setting constitutes a source of potential interaction among governments. Tourists who find themselves in trouble in foreign lands create a potential source of negotiation—albeit on a low administrative level—between the governments. Governments also manipulate the flow of people to indicate policy positions to other states. Hostility is expressed by limiting the number of tourist visas issued for a particular country while friendship is evidenced by a willingness to exchange travel and business.

One important consequence of this flow and particularly of immigration is the growth of family and personal ties across national boundaries. These social ties can also result from the shifts in national boundaries that sometimes follow wars. In either case, people living in one state with social ties in another state often play an important role in the relationship between the states. At one level, such ties increase the number of private contacts that might give rise to disputes, legal or otherwise. At another level, groups with foreign origins often try to influence the foreign policy of their new states toward their home countries. Sometimes the pressure is for increased friendship, as with former Israeli citizens in the United States, and at other times the pressure can be for a more hostile policy, as with Hungarian and Polish refugees in the United States. At still another level, the leader of a state can use his minority in another state in political bargaining. For example, Germans in Czechoslovakia played a role in Hitler's dealings with the Czech government during the 1930's, because Hitler used the demands of Czechoslovakian nationals of German origin as a basis for his territorial claims. Today, social ties across national boundaries in such areas as sub-Sahara Africa where tribal loyalties know no boundaries affect the political relationships among the African states.

The flow of people has also had an impact on international relations, particularly prior to World War II, in terms of the quest for "living space." Traditionally, foreign policy decision makers have attempted to legitimize their claims for territorial expansion by arguing that the population growth within their state makes such expansion necessary and right. Such arguments are rarely persuasive, not only because other economic and military interests are often involved, but also because underpopulated areas in most states can be developed to alleviate the over-populated areas. Although population growth throughout the world represents a general problem all governments must face on a collective basis, within a state it never automatically produces the drive for more territory. Rather, it serves as part of the setting in which states shape their general foreign policy interactions. Since World War II the "living space" argument has rarely been seriously advanced by states pursuing territorial aims.

Like the flow of ideas, then, the flow of people provides a setting for interactions among states. It represents a source of friction in international relations, an element through which foreign policy decision makers can take policy positions vis-à-vis other states, and a component of internal pressure in the foreign policy-making process. A product of the increasing speed of transportation and communication, the expanding flow of people in the twentieth century constitutes one of the most important factors in the setting for interactions among states.

THE INTERNATIONAL ECONOMY

The term "international economy" is somewhat of a misnomer because it assumes that patterns and institutions in the flow of goods, services, and money among states are similar to those in domestic economies. However, unlike domestic economies where the government has the authority to make major decisions that affect the entire economy, the international economy is a product of *decentralized decision making*. The term refers to the fact that there is no one central authority controlling the international economy but decisions are made by the states themselves acting either unilaterally or collectively. Collective action may be taken either formally through an intergovernmental organization or informally through coordinated unilateral actions. Crucial decisions that affect the stability and future of the international economy are often made unilaterally by governments who are thinking primarily of their own economic situations. Certain intergovernmental organizations have been created to help control the international economy. More important, in recent years states have recognized the necessity of coordinating policies. However, these developments are still far from the creation of an international economy regulated by one set of central institutions.

For purposes of presentation, we may view the international economy as three complex and interdependent markets: the international trade market, the international capital market, and the international currency market. Each of these is a market in the sense that it involves buyers and sellers whose transactions form the basis for future transactions between buyers and sellers. Although these were originally free markets, with prices determined solely by interaction of buyer and seller, governments and intergovernmental organizations today have infused some regulations. Even so, compared to the degree to which states regulate their own economies, the amount of regulation in these three markets is small. There are, however, more techniques for controlling the international economy today than there were in the past.

The Trade Market

This international market consists of the flow of goods and services across boundaries, a flow determined by both economic and political considerations. Economically, the principle of comparative advantage operates so that nations can sell more of what they produce most cheaply and buy more of what they produce least efficiently. By these means each nation gains, and because nations have different material and human resources, there is usually a basis for comparative advantage.

However, this principle of comparative advantage is often moderated by political factors. The degree of friendliness among nations will affect their willingness to allow trade. Because trade involves increased interdependence and contact, states have often curtailed trade with those to which they are hostile. In addition, the states themselves often decide that it is important to protect certain industries from cheap foreign goods; protective policies using tariffs and import quotes are then used to keep cheaper goods out of the country. Often they are justified on grounds of national security or protecting the infant industries that might one day be efficient. No matter what the justification, however, the impact of these protective measures is to moderate the influence of comparative advantage in trading patterns.

In the period since World War II, some intergovernmental organizations have developed to promote the more complete operation of the comparative advantage principle. On a global basis, the General Agreement on Trade and Tariffs (GATT) has been designed to contribute to lower tariffs and the elimination of other restrictions to free trade among states. Although GATT has provided little more than a loose organization and general guidelines to aid states in mutually reducing restrictions to trade, it nonetheless has had an impact on the expansion of international trade in the post war period. In addition, regional organizations have developed to promote free trade. In Europe, the European Free Trade Association has practically abolished trade restrictions among its members (Austria, Denmark, Norway, Portugal, Sweden, Switzerland, and the United Kingdom) while the European Economic Community (EEC) has abolished restrictions among its members and has introduced a common tariff policy towards nonmembers. In other areas (Latin America and Africa) attempts have been made to introduce types of organizations to promote trade similar to those now operating in Europe.

The Capital Market

The international capital market involves the flow of investment capital across national boundaries. The buyer in this case is the recipient of the capital, and the seller is the investor. Capital investment on a private basis across national lines has been practiced for a long period of time. The United States, for example, received a great deal of investment capital from British investors in the nineteenth century. In the twentieth century, however, the increase of foreign private investment involves almost every country in the world.

Before World War II, foreign capital investment was closely tied to colonialism. Before 1945, for example, French investors usually invested in French colonies in Asia and Africa. However, with the disappearance of overt colonialism as a form of political relationship, patterns of foreign investment have become less determined by colonial ties. Investors from developed states still tend to invest money in their state's former colonies, but the tendency is much less pronounced than when the underdeveloped areas were under colonial rule. In addition, a large proportion of foreign investment capital circulates among the developed states themselves.

The actual mechanisms for foreign capital investment are varied. An investor can buy foreign stocks and bonds on the various markets. Banks in one country can loan funds to banks or businesses in another country. More recently, big corporations have made direct foreign private investment in other countries in the form of production and sales facilities.

The flow of foreign capital investment, like trade, is not as free as it would be if purely economic conditions were operating. Actually, political pressures are exerted both ways. On the positive side, many of the governments of developed states have reason to attempt to increase the flow of capital to certain underdeveloped states. This attempt can take the form of foreign aid and loans from the developed state or investment guarantees to protect the investment of its citizens in certain foreign states. On the negative side, the recipient state often follows policies that make outside capital investment unattractive. This can take the form of discriminatory taxes or even the threat to nationalize foreign businesses. Both developed and underdeveloped states frequently follow policies that discourage foreign investment even though investment may be helpful to the economy. Fear of too much outside economic and ultimately political influence is usually the motivating factor in these cases.

In recent years, regional and global intergovernmental organizations have developed and expanded into a source of investment capital. The International Bank for Reconstruction and Development, the International Development Agency, and certain agencies of the United Nations procure money through pledges from states and through traditional financial mechanisms like bonds. They lend this money to states that otherwise would not be able to borrow it. In addition, certain regional organizations such as the Inter-American Development Bank, the African Development Bank, and the Asian Development Bank have been created to provide investment capital on a regional basis, particularly for underdeveloped states.

Intergovernmental organizations provide investment capital for areas of the world that cannot attract private investment. Foreign investors want safety and a good return on their money; they usually provide capital in stable areas and for businesses that have a good chance of success. Because these conditions frequently do not exist in underdeveloped states, or because certain measures such as road building must precede them, intergovernmental organizations have been created to provide long-range developmental funds. In a sense, they represent sellers of capital who are willing to take greater risks with less return than private foreign investors. Without financial support from government treasuries, they would have difficulty keeping their organizations financially solvent.

The Currency Market

The international currency market is both a consequence and regulator of the other two markets. It exists because there is no uniform world currency regulated by an international institution. In trading from one state to another, individuals cannot rely on barter—that is, exchanging goods and services of equal value as, for example, one dozen eggs for two loaves of bread. Instead, the exchange in goods must involve exchange of currency. The buyer exchanges currency for the product. For the relationship between the buyer and seller to be on stable grounds, the currency used for the transaction must be stable. By stable, we mean that a given unit of currency will be worth approximately the same amount of another stable currency in the foreseeable future.

In international trade, the currencies of buyer and seller are usually different. To find a basis for measuring stability, international traders usually measure currencies according to an accepted standard. Before World War II, gold served as such a standard. Since that war, gold plus certain "international" currencies have served as the standard. For example, most governments and dealers in currencies have viewed the dollar as an international currency; this means that merchants and financiers have been willing to assume the dollar's stability in order to measure the worth of other currencies. Although both the dollar and the British pound—two currencies that were "as good as gold"—have become less stable in the 1960's, they still function as substitutes for gold in the international currency market. Hence, the seller looks at the amount of money the buyer offers in terms of how much it is worth in gold, or dollars; comparison makes international commerce possible. At this point, the international currency market indicates the worth of any currency in terms of gold or one of the international currencies.

The international currency market determines price primarily through supply and demand. If many people want to convert currency from country A into American dollars because A has been doing a lot of buying overseas, the worth of A's currency as measured by American dollars (and indirectly by gold) will tend to go down. If only a few want to convert country A's currency into American dollars because that country has not had a lot of overseas expenditures, the price of A's currency will go up.

As in any market, however, factors other than "natural" supply and demand determine the worth of a given currency. An important determinant of the behavior of the market is speculation. Speculators are individuals or organizations who are willing to bet on their judgment of whether the price of a given currency will go up or down. When they buy a currency, they are betting the price will go up. When they sell, they are betting the price will go down. Speculators help determine the price of currency because their behavior is keyed to what they think the market will do. As a result, their view of the country's economic position and its political stability will affect the price of the currency on the market.

Hence, speculators represent a powerful force in international economics and politics because they can affect a country's economic position by their judgments on its economic and political conditions. While there are usually underlying economic factors, such as the long-range balance of payments, determining the activities of people involved in the currency market, other factors sometimes operate too. For example, speculators might lose confidence in the leaders of a particular country or they might view with alarm the election of a particular political party. If they sell their currency holdings as a result of this loss of confidence, they can cause financial as well as political crisis.

The experience of Great Britain and the United States in the 1960's illustrates the role of politics in shaping the behavior of currency speculators. When the Labor Party became the ruling party in the United Kingdom in 1964, many speculators sold their holdings of British pounds, threatening its price on the currency market. The decision of the speculators was in part a consequence of the uncertainty about what policies the Labor Party would follow. The selling stopped only after the Labor Party followed relatively conservative economic policies. Similarly, speculators became increasingly concerned about inflation and heavy overseas U.S. expenditures. This led in early 1968 to heavy selling of the dollar for gold. The crisis that ensued forced the United States to alter its long-standing policy of guaranteeing to exchange gold for dollars to any foreign investor. Although the nation has continued to guarantee to exchange dollars for gold to governments whose banking institutions do not in turn sell to private speculators, that heavy selling of U.S. dollars led to the so-called "two-tier" system, a substantial change in policy.

In recent years, intergovernmental organizations have been developed to try to make the currency market more stable by affording states the means to protect their currency from the radical actions taken by speculators. In this area the chief intergovernmental organization is the International Monetary Fund. The Fund has reserves of the currency of each of its members (which include virtually every non-Communist state except Yugoslavia) and makes loans in gold or some other currency to countries that find the price of their currency in danger of depreciation. Although member governments finance and generally direct it, the Fund acts according to what its Board of Executive Directors (elected members) consider to be proper economic guidelines. Members receive advice on internal fiscal measures relating to stabilization of currency on the international currency market. The Fund tries to encourage and sometimes actually pressures states to follow practices which it deems desirable. Loans are short term (three to five years) and are not designed to provide permanent stability; long-run stability can only be a result of sound economic planning. The Fund attempts to keep short-term fluctuations within the currency market from harming international trade and the economic health of states.

The Fund has been relatively successful since World War II. Although it has not prevented all financial crises, it has allowed the international currency market to function continuously. In 1967, the Fund was authorized to use special drawing rights ("paper gold") in its effort to maintain the growth of international liquidity. This provision enables the Fund to operate with a new "international" currency to supplement its gold and other currency reserves in stabilizing currency fluctuations. A product of the willingness of the developed western states to cooperate in meeting changing conditions, the Special Drawing Fund is considered an important step toward maintaining stability in the international currency market.

The International Monetary Fund and contemporary practices of international public finance are a great improvement over the international economic institutions of the interwar period. However, international economy continues to be only partly regulated by central institutions. The willingness of states to follow policies designed to promote general international economic health remains the key to the international economic stability necessary to sustain current levels of trade and capital investment.

Economy as a Setting for International Interactions

The international trade, capital, and currency markets, along with activities of intergovernmental organizations and states to regulate them, constitute the international economy as a setting for interactions among states. In examining the positions of various states in terms of the ways these markets should be regulated one cannot help but note the differences between the developed non-Communist states, the Communist states, and the underdeveloped states. Each of these groups has a particular position regarding the international economic policies that states and the relevant intergovernmental organizations follow.

The developed states of western Europe, the United States, and Japan have a high stake in the smooth operation of the three markets. Their economies are heavily dependent upon overseas trade and capital investment; in turn, the stable operation of the currency market is essential to them. For this reason, the currency market consists almost totally of their activities and the activities of their citizens. Although the developed non-Communist states have cooperated extensively in regulating the currency market, they have not been able to achieve complete control because the behavior of their citizens is an important determinant over which they have only limited control. The attitude of these states has been to stimulate international trade by lowering tariff restrictions and stimulate international capital investment by providing protective mechanisms for overseas investment. In short, the policies of the developed states of the West have been to stabilize the currency market they virtually control, and to expand trade as well as overseas investment particularly in relationship to the developed countries themselves.

Members of the Communist bloc—more specifically the eastern European states including the Soviet Union—are involved primarily in the trading market. Recent trends, however, show activity in the other two markets. Trade among themselves and with states throughout the world has been increasing steadily since 1950. They have not been members of the International Monetary Fund or the International Bank for Reconstruction and Development. Not only have they viewed these institutions to be under the control of the western states, but they consider outside attempts to make economic policy suggestions an unacceptable infringement on their autonomy. The position of the Communist states toward the currency market is that of outsiders. They have found the currency market a necessary evil in dealing with other states. Businesses in non-Communist states usually accept only western currency in their dealings with Communist states. As a result, Communist states have had to acquire the currencies of western states to trade internationally. In terms of the capital investment market, the Communist states have drawn most of their resources from internal sources or from other Communist states. More recently, some Communist states have accepted investment capital from businessmen in non-Communist states, although this appears quite limited. In general, the overall position of the Communist states towards the international economic system is one of weakness because they have little influence in the currency market that serves as the basis for both trade and capital investment.

The underdeveloped states have a disadvantage in all three markets. Because their ability to pay is considerably less than their demand for imported goods, they are in the unenviable position of wanting to import more than they export. They are always buyers and never sellers of capital investments because their own population has few capital resources. In addition, they do not have the conditions to provide as stable and profitable investment opportunities as the developed states in order to attract foreign capital investment. Sometimes, they cannot get even nationals to invest in their own country. These disadvantages in trade and investment contribute to their weak position in the currency market. In addition, their domestic economies are subject to sharp fluctuations; these, in turn, make their currencies unstable on the international currency market.

In many ways, the international economic system creates class division among states. The non-Communist developed states represent the upper class: they control a major portion of productive resources, are the primary creditors, and regulate the currency market through control of the International Monetary Fund. The underdeveloped states are the lower class: they depend upon the developed states for economic concessions and developmental capital. The Communist states occupy a position somewhere in between: they enjoy some productive capability and sufficient internally-produced developmental capital, but still are not major creditors and do not control the international financial institutions. Although the wealthy states have financed and created intergovernmental organizations to give the poorer states some help, the underdeveloped countries have not been satisfied, particularly in the area of trade concessions. The creation of the United Nations Conference for Trade and Development (UNCTAD), controlled by the poorer nations but having wealthy nations as members, is a response to this lack of satisfaction with concessions. To date, however, UNCTAD has remained a relatively unproductive response as far as the underdeveloped states are concerned.

The split between the rich and poor nations over trade and aid policies is an important factor in both the international economy and interactions among states. The rich have used aid and trade as political tools in dealing with the poor nations. Resenting this, the poor nations have sought to coordinate aid and trade at the international level so the rich cannot use economic tools to achieve political objectives. In some cases, the split has been so deep that states like the United States and the Soviet Union, which are relative enemies in other fields, have cooperated with each other in dealing with the poorer states at the level of intergovernmental activities (UNCTAD).

Therefore, the international economy affects and is affected by international politics. As in domestic society, politics and economics are highly interdependent. Given the relative decentralized nature of the international economy, the various economic patterns continue to be determined by the states themselves and in many cases by the private citizens of those states rather than by central institutions. Because the lines of control are so complex and diffuse, the danger of gross instability—that is, economic disruptions causing the loss of trade and capital flow—is an ever-present fact that must be taken into account in formulating political as well as economic strategies. Although some attempt has been made to regulate the international economy, lack of a strong central institution still characterizes economic relations among nations. Moreover, the sharp division between rich and poor, with the Communist nations somewhere in between, limits the development of international economic institutions because it gives the impression that the international economy is run by the rich for the benefit of the rich. Although the poor states and even the Communist states cannot afford to "opt out" at this point, their antagonism toward the international economy and the states that dominate it limits the growth of worldwide central economic institutions.

INTERNATIONAL LAW

International law is a system of institutions and rules that aims to organize the behavior of states and intergovernmental organizations. However, in describing the actual impact of international law as a setting for interactions among states, one must be careful to examine to what extent it successfully fulfills its aim. We will attempt to do this by contrasting the nature of the highly developed legal systems of domestic societies with the nature of international law as a poorly developed *decentralized* legal system.

Any domestic legal system may be studied in terms of three traditional processes: *legislation, adjudication,* and *enforcement.* We say that domestic legal systems are "centralized" because a specific set of central institutions performs each of these three processes. In the United States, for example, legislative bodies make the law, courts adjudicate the law, and the police enforce the law. Although the distinctions between the three processes are not as clear-cut as one might assume—courts sometimes "make" law by providing new interpretations—nevertheless these three processes are performed by central institutions.

"Politics" affects these three domestic legal processes in a number of ways. The legislative process is most affected by competing interests and ideologies, at least in democratic states. Partisan groups try to control legislative bodies; interest groups try to influence those bodies after they are elected. The adjudicative and enforcement processes are only indirectly affected by political forces. Judges are elected or appointed and administrators of the police departments are also often dependent upon political support for their positions. However, after initial appointment, individuals play their roles with little open political pressure. This is not to say that political pressure is never applied to a judge or a police commissioner, but rather that there is usually no legitimate or institutionalized political force built into the legal system.

In contrast to the relationship between law and politics in domestic societies, political considerations greatly affect adjudication, enforcement, and legislation in the international society. Characterized by a lack of well-respected central institutions with broad authority, interactions among states are shaped by a decentralized legal system. This means that many of the processes of legislation, adjudication, and enforcement are not performed by central international institutions but instead by the states themselves acting sometimes unilaterally and sometimes in cooperation with other states.[10]

International Legislation

The making of international laws clearly illustrates both the decentralized nature of international law and the interrelationship between law and politics. Because there is no international legislative body, laws are made outside formal institutions. The most prevalent form of international lawmaking today is the general treaty signed by a number of states indicating mutually accepted rules in a particular area. For example, many states have agreed upon a set of rules governing the exchange of diplomats in the Vienna Convention on Diplomatic Immunities. Sometimes these general

[10] For a more complete discussion of international law employing a framework similar to the one employed here, see Coplin, *The Functions of International Law.*

law-making treaties are drafted by international institutions or *ad hoc* conferences but the treaties do not take effect until the states individually ratify them.

In addition to the law-making treaty, international laws develop from the customary policies of states. Habitually announced policies that are also reinforced by actions of the state are considered to be indications that the state is following a law. If enough states follow similar policies, an international law is said to exist. For example, states have habitually allowed innocent passage to commercial vessels in their coastal waters. Hence, there is a generally recognized international law that commercial vessels have the right to innocent passage in coastal waters of a state.

Other sources of international law are "general principles recognized by civilized nations," the opinions of publicists or scholars, and rules stated by certain international institutions—most notably the United Nations. These sources are not considered primary, although they are often used to bolster legal positions that are presented in courts or in verbal exchanges between states. A few intergovernmental organizations have the authority to formulate "laws" obligating their member states, but their authority is granted by the general treaties that originally set up the organizations.

Hence, the processes of law making in the international legal system are highly decentralized. There is no legislative body that all states agree is empowered authoritatively to state the law. States themselves still maintain the ultimate authority in creating laws they are willing to consider binding, although an intergovernmental organization might also draft a law. Given the large role played by the state, there is a great deal of confusion over what legal norms do exist in the international legal system. States present competing interpretations of the law so that conflict and disagreement can arise over the nature of the law itself, let alone what application there should be in a specific instance. Because no central institution makes international law, the formulation of the law itself often involves direct political bargaining.

International Adjudication

This leads us to the judicial institutions that are supposed to adjudicate the laws. Here also, the decentralized nature of international law is very apparent. We can distinguish three types of judicial institutions applying international law—national courts, the International Court of Justice, and *ad hoc* international tribunals. Each of these institutions is greatly affected by the decentralized nature of international law and the political pressures resulting from that decentralization.

Most international legal questions continue to be handled by domestic courts of one of the states involved. If a citizen of state A feels he has been wronged by a citizen from state B, legal recourse must come from the courts of state B; that is, unless some of citizen B's property can be found in state A. In this case he can use the courts of his own state. Such private litigations often involve questions of international law, and the domestic courts are given the responsibility of applying the international legal norms. This means the citizen is dependent upon the fairness of a court that is responsible to a foreign government. Also, it gives rise to widely different interpretations of what is supposed to be the same international legal norm.

The International Court of Justice is a judicial institution whose membership encompasses almost all of the states in the international system. One reason for this is that the Court is one of the six organs of the United Nations so that all UN members are *ipso facto* (automatically) members of the International Court of Justice. Prior to World War II, it was called the Permanent Court of International Justice.

Politics and the decentralized nature of international law greatly affect the operation of the Court in a number of ways. First, the fifteen judges of the International Court of Justice are elected by the General Assembly of the United Nations with the recommendation of the Security Council. Hence, bargaining and political interests often influence who sits on the Court. Second, the Court can render advisory opinions if the United Nations requests them. Although these opinions have no binding authority, they often involve political and constitutional questions about the United Nations. In addition, the Court can interpret treaties. Consequently, the Court is similar in some respects to the Supreme Court of the United States because it is used to interpret broad political issues. However, because advisory opinions are not binding, it does not play a significant political role in disputes among states.

Third and most important, the Court depends upon the willingness of states to submit cases to it. Some states have signed the so-called "Compulsory Jurisdiction Clause," which binds them to accept the jurisdiction of the Court if another state starts a litigation against them. However, many of the signers have made a reservation that somewhat nullifies the clause. As a result, compulsory jurisdiction rarely operates; before the Court can apply the law two states must agree to take a dispute to the Court. This is strikingly different from the operation of domestic adjudication where subjects of the legal system have to stand trial regardless of their willingness. In international law, then, politics enters even into the question of whether or not the Court can adjudicate.

Finally, states have often employed *ad hoc* tribunals of one sort or another in disputes involving international law. These tribunals are sometimes called commissions or arbitral courts. They are set up by two or more states to deal with a specific dispute or set of disputes. For example, the United States has from time to time set up *ad hoc* tribunals with Canada to deal with mutual disputes. The judges are appointed by joint agreement and the area of international law to be applied is identified. Sometimes the states agree to have the tribunal make a judgment on grounds other than legal. On such cases, it is usually called an arbitration tribunal. However, like other *ad hoc* tribunals, arbitration tribunals only operate with the consent of the states involved.

International adjudication, like international legislation, then, is affected by the lack of central institutions given authority by the states. In recent years, some regional tribunals in Europe have been given extensive authority to deal with a variety of issues and as a result more closely approximate domestic courts. However, except for the European development, the international tribunals, whether they be *ad hoc* or the International Court of Justice, depend upon the political decision of states to use them. Politics, then, determines the ability of the courts to deal with each issue as it arises.

International Law Enforcement

Enforcement of international law is also subject to a great deal of political pressure. No universal permanent police force is established to deter or punish law breakers. The closest thing to such a force are the peace-keeping operations of the United Nations. For a number of reasons, however, the UN does not enforce international law. First, only the Security Council is empowered to authorize use of force against a state (the General Assembly can only recommend it). Because five states in the Security Council have an absolute veto over any action authorized, they can stop action against themselves and their allies. Second, both the General Assembly and the Security Council are more concerned with keeping the peace than with enforcing the law. Two cases will illustrate. If state A breaks a law, but does not threaten the peace because no state is sufficiently harmed to start a war, the Security Council and the General Assembly would not take any action. If state B, on the other hand, does not break a law but threatens to use force for some legitimate purpose, action probably would be taken against state B. Even if the Security Council were able to act, then, it would probably not act to punish a law breaker unless the law breaker also happened to be threatening the peace.

This leaves enforcement of international law to the states themselves. "Self-help" is the legal principle used to describe the act of individually enforcing the law. Individuals in domestic societies resort to self-defense (a form of self-help) when the police are not around to protect them. Their position is analogous to states in international law because there is no police force available. However, individuals in domestic societies only resort to self-help under unusual circumstances. In contrast, states resort to self-help as a matter of course.

The resort to self-help can take the form of lodging a diplomatic protest, threatening or taking economic sanctions, or threatening or carrying out acts of war. In general, international law stipulates that the action should not be stronger than the wrong against which the state is reacting in the first place. For example, state A claims that state B has infringed upon its rights. Normally, state A would protest to state B. If state B then acts in a way to compensate for the wrong (apology, reparations, or the like), the matter ends there. This in itself would be a form of enforcement since state B's payment would be retribution for the wrong it committed. However, if state B refuses to compensate, state A might have to take an action that under other circumstances might be considered illegal. Such action would be considered punishment against state B as a wrongdoer, and, therefore, legal, if similar in degree to the wrongful act.

The trouble with this formulation is that the states themselves are both judges and policemen. As a result, many political factors operate on their decisions that do not operate when judge and police are centralized institutions. For example, state B might not agree that it committed a wrongful act against state A. Who is to decide, if neither state is willing to submit it to the International Court? Furthermore, state A might refrain from pursuing its legal rights because it is militarily weaker than state B. Consequently, a number of political factors affect enforcement precisely because international law is so decentralized and the state has such a large role in its operation.

Law as a Setting for International Interactions

The boundary between international law and international politics is much less clearly defined than the boundary between the legal and political system in domestic societies. At almost every point in the legislative, adjudicative, and enforcement processes, political strategies affect operation of the international legal system. The state acts unilaterally as legislator, judge, and policeman in many areas of international law, while intergovernmental institutions lack the support and authority to put the operation of the international legal system on a more orderly and regularized basis.

Because of decentralization, international law provides a relatively amorphous setting for official interactions among states. The large role assigned to independent action of states in the legislative, adjudicative, and enforcement processes leads to unevenness in the law. In areas such as navigation of the high seas or diplomatic exchange the states recognize the need for well-established, clear-cut international laws and such laws exist. In areas such as national security, where the states are unwilling to trust any external institution, international law provides few guidelines. One should neither underemphasize the importance of international law in the former areas nor overemphasize its importance in the latter.

SUMMARY

As we can see, official interactions among states occur in a setting shaped by a variety of factors. Ranging from the relatively stable impact of geography to the dynamic operation of the international economy and from daily frictions arising out of the flow of people to the amorphous long-range impact of the flow of ideas, the factors discussed generate conditions that sometimes directly produce official interactions among states and always affect international interactions in one way or another. The next three chapters will examine how the setting we have just described affects routine governmental interactions, how states attempt to solve problems collectively, and patterns of competitive bargaining.

SUMMARY OUTLINE

I.   *The large majority of official international interactions originates with the state although intergovernmental organizations sometimes act but more often serve as an institutional setting for interactions among the states.*

II.   Ecological factors play a large role as a setting for interactions among states.

    A.   *Trading patterns, membership in intergovernmental organizations, instances of conflict, and voting in the United Nations are related in varying degrees to geographical location.*

    B.   *Distribution of natural and human resources affects interactions among states.*

    C.   *The role of ecological factors varies over time as a result of changes in technology as well as social, economic, and political conditions.*

    D.   *The images of ecological conditions are almost as important in the behavior of foreign policy decision makers as the actual conditions are.*

III. The international flow of ideas serves as a setting for interactions among states.

    A.   *The flow of ideas has increased as a result of the increase in foreign travel, the power of mass communications, and the growth of transnational organizations.*

B. The flow of ideas may be viewed as an emerging world culture.

C. *Technological ideas have spread rapidly throughout the world and form a world subculture.*

D. *A world social culture is emerging although competing ideologies tend to obscure the existence of a small number of shared ideas.*

E. The international political culture also contains conflicting ideas although consensus appears to exist among foreign policy decision makers and powerful policy influencers.

F. *Ideas have a long-range impact on the setting for interactions among states, but are slow to be transformed.*

IV. The flow of people affects official interactions among states.

A. *Travel for business and pleasure on a temporary basis has been growing enormously and is encouraged by most states.*

B. *Immigration has been decreasing in recent years, and is discouraged by most states.*

C. *The flow of people creates a constant source of potential problems to be settled by official interaction.*

D. *Immigration often has an impact on official interactions among states.*

V. The international economy affects official interactions among states.

A. The international economy is decentralized because there is no set of central institutions to regulate it.

B. *The principle of comparative advantage that provides an economic basis for international trade is often comprised by political conditions.*

C. *Intergovernmental organizations like GATT and the EEC have had some success in promoting free trade.*

D. *The international flow of capital was tied to colonial patterns prior to World War II.*

E. *Although the flow of capital is still affected by past colonial relationships, other factors now play a big role.*

F. *Some political pressures dampen the international flow of capital while others encourage it.*

G. *Intergovernmental organizations tend to remove some of the political consequences of the international flow of capital.*

H. *The international currency market is both a consequence and a regulator of the other two markets.*

I. *Gold and certain international currencies have served as a standard for measuring the value of other currencies.*

J. *The value of currencies on the international currency market is determined by supply and demand, as well as the judgments of speculators.*

K. *The International Monetary Fund has attempted to provide some stability to the international currency market.*

L. *The non-Communist developed states have a high stake and a correspondingly high degree of control over the three markets that constitute the international economy.*

M. *Members of the Communist bloc are most involved in the international trade market, least involved in the international capital market, and involved in the international currency market only insofar as necessitated by their involvement in the trade and capital markets.*

N. *The underdeveloped states are in a disadvantaged position in all three markets.*

O. *The non-Communist developed states are the upper class of the international economy, the underdeveloped states are the lower class; and the Communist states are somewhat in between.*

VI. International law affects official interactions among states.

A. International law is decentralized because no central institutions have authority to legislate, adjudicate, and enforce in most cases.

B. *States acting independently, together through treaties, and in intergovernmental meetings and organizations have the authority to make new international laws.*

C. *International adjudication is performed by three types of institutions, all of which depend on the willingness of the state to accept the role of litigant or, in the case of national courts, to apply international laws.*

D. *International law is enforced primarily by the states themselves acting to protect their legal rights or to sanction wrongdoers.*

E. *International law provides a relatively uneven framework for the behavior of states because lack of a centralized structure allows states to follow only those laws they judge to be in their interest.*

F. *International law is relatively clear-cut in areas where states recognize the need for law, and extremely tentative and ineffective in areas of vital interest where basic disagreements exist.*

BIBLIOGRAPHICAL ESSAY

Because this chapter attempts to build a framework to describe relationships among a number of widely divergent areas in international politics, the relevant literature comes from divergent fields. In studying the international political setting, it is helpful to tap literature outside the strictly defined discipline of political science. The following remarks are intended as a guide to the literature most relevant to international politics.

Works defining the relationship between international politics and ecological factors fall into four categories. First are books that provide geographical information on specific cases; for example, Boyd's *Atlas* (42). Second are attempts by geographers to describe the general impact of geography on politics, such as Cole (82). Third are works of geopoliticians (see Chapter 5) such as MacKinder (263) and Saul Cohen (81), who attempt to predict and prescribe policy on the basis of geographical postulates. The final category is made up of a few contemporary political scientists who systematically relate ecological factors to international politics. Examples are Sprout and Sprout (391, 392, and 393) and, more recently, Russett (358), who uses quantitative techniques.

Works assessing the role of the flow of ideas in international politics are less easy to find. The impact of technology is analyzed in Ogburn (299) but not from the point of view of dispersion of technological ideas. The impact of travel on the transmission of ideas is examined by Pool in (215), while the role of the United Nations in changing the attending delegate's conception of international politics is empirically studied by Alger in (215). Bozeman (43) discusses culture and politics in terms of historical developments. The impact of mass communication on universal transmission of ideas is examined in Davison (95). An abstract discussion by Parsons in (348) of the role of ideological poles in international politics is fruitful, but for the dynamics of ideology in general, two radically different approaches should be consulted: Hoffer (177) and Lane (240). For political science generally the concept of political culture is developed by Almond and Powell (12); for international politics, it is developed by Coplin (84, 314).

For the impact of foreign travel, Pool in (215) looks at its effect on national and international images; Mishler, in the same volume, investigates the role of international student exchanges. In addition, a number of studies we will discuss later have attempted to show the impact of tourist trends on relations among states (see Chapter 12). Hauser (163) presents a variety of viewpoints on aspects of the impact of population growth and the flow of people on world politics.

The role of international economics in world politics has not been adequately studied by political scientists, and therefore the student must rely primarily on the writings of economists. These works can be divided into two types, both of which are important for the student interested in the interrelationships of economics and world politics. First is the textbook discussion of international economics exemplified by Kindleberger (222),

Kenen (218), and Krause (234), in the tradition of "pure economic descriptions" of international economics. Second is the growing body of "reformist" literature that attacks the subject from the prescriptive framework typical of Myrdal (290), Aubrey (19), Hansen (160), and Johnson (198). Both sets of literature, together with descriptive material from students of intergovernmental organizations such as Alexandrowicz (3), represent a valuable beginning point. This body of literature provides essential information about the nature of the international economy as well as on the resulting policy problems.

The field of international law and politics suffers from problems similar to those in other fields, although political scientists have always shown some interest in the role of law in world politics. Bibliographical analysis and suggestions for future research are provided in Coplin's essay in (314). Coplin (84) and Friedmann (129) have attempted to survey at an introductory level the general operations of law in various areas of international relations. Applications of related social science concepts to law are made by Barkun and Gregg (27) and Bohannan (40). Other discussions of the relationships of law to politics and politics to law can be found in de Visscher (108), Corbett (86), Kaplan and Katzenbach (208), Hoffmann (178), and McDougal and Feliciano (261).

8

Routine Official Interactions Among States

Within the setting of the international environment we have just described, governments of states often find occasion to deal with each other. Through their administrative officials, foreign policy decision makers communicate with and act toward other states in a wide variety of fields and an equally wide variety of ways. In this chapter, we are concerned with those official interactions which, for one reason or another, have become routine. Executed by lower-level administrative officials in the foreign policy bureaucracy of the state, routine interactions are products of decisions by both sides to maintain certain patterns of activities. They are called "routine" because the actions they involve are expected by both sides and are considered part of the general pattern of relationships the two states have developed.

It is important to note that "routine" does *not* necessarily mean "friendly." (See Chapter 5 for a discussion of hostility and friendship as foreign policy determinants.) Hostile relationships between two states can be routinized just as friendly relationships can be. Communist China's decision to avoid almost all contact with the United States is as routinized in the behavior of lower-level Chinese officials as is the decision of the United States government to maintain as much contact as possible with the United Kingdom. Similarly, interactions between the western powers and East Germany are routinized even though the two sides are extremely hostile. Although both sides have occasionally attempted to break the routine for bargaining reasons, the great importance attached to such a break indicates conscious awareness of the routinized nature of the interactions.

Whether evolving from a climate of friendship or hostility, routine interactions are developed through two processes. First, and most common before the twentieth century, routine interactions were a product of customary behavior. When a specific situation arises for the first time, decision makers of the states involved may handle it on an *ad hoc* basis. If the pattern that emerges is satisfactory to the involved parties or at least does not create too much displeasure, a precedent may be established, this precedent is followed in similar situations, and as time goes by the situation continues to be handled in the same manner. At some undefined point in time, the parties may come to accept the pattern or formula as obligatory —in which case it becomes international law. They may assume that the formula is merely customary practice, in which case it becomes international comity—that is, accepted practice. No matter how the states view the routine interaction that develops through custom, however, reciprocity or the willingness to perform activities that are mutually beneficial (although they may not be beneficial to one party at a particular time) plays a large role.

Second, interactions are routinized through explicit creation of a set of rules to maintain certain patterns of activities. A treaty may be signed and ratified that (1) spells out how governmental officials are to behave in certain circumstances or (2) establishes an intergovernmental organization to regulate the relationship. Like the first process, the second depends upon the mutual agreement among the parties based on their reciprocal interests. However, this process also involves a more conscious attempt than the first on the part of the states to find a mutually agreeable pattern of behavior. Moreover, while routine interactions established on an *ad hoc* basis may be either hostile or friendly, interactions regulated through treaty usually imply some degree of cooperation between the contracting states.

In the contemporary world, states have found it increasingly necessary to employ the second process—that is, to establish routine interactions through explicit agreements rather than through customary practice arrived at on an *ad hoc* basis. Not only have the number of formal treaties among states and the number of intergovernmental organizations increased tremendously, but the number of informal agreements among states has also risen. Sometimes called executive agreements, these informal arrangements number in the hundreds per year for many states. They are employed by foreign policy decision makers to settle pressing problems without going through constitutional procedures many states require for ratification of treaties. No matter what the form of agreement (treaties, executive agreements, or establishment of intergovernmental organizations), states have increasingly turned to explicit negotiations in the contemporary period. In many fields, customary practices provide neither the level of technical sophistication nor the flexibility of adaptation necessary for routinization of interactions in the contemporary world.

Whether developed through customary practices or direct negotiation and whether hostile or friendly, routine interactions among states are subject to change. The most frequent reason is a change in policy by one of the involved states. For example, the East German regime's decision to allow West German citizens to visit relatives in East Germany on certain holidays involved an alteration of a routine interaction. This has been interpreted as a change, albeit slight, in the foreign policy of East Germany. Because routine interactions among states are a direct product of their foreign policies, they are often employed as a barometer of the nature of the foreign policy relationships among states. (See Chapter 5.)

Another reason for this change is evolution of conditions that provide a setting for the interactions. For example, let us suppose that state A and state B administer a shared lake by allowing nationals from each country to fish in the lake as long as they return to the port from which they departed. Officials of the two states cooperate, according to agreed-upon rules, by registering departing and returning vessels and then exchanging registration lists. Let us suppose that the supply of fish in the lake begins to dwindle and that conservation methods are sorely needed. This new condition necessitates a change in international rules governing administration of the lake quite apart from the policies of the two states.

Even though continuous pressures are applied to change routine interactions between states, whether due to domestic pressures for change of the general foreign policy or to conditions in the international setting that pose new problems, certain factors conspire to maintain the existing routine. If a state's foreign policy decision makers had to apply *ad hoc* bargaining to every interaction with another state, they would waste a good deal of time and money. Moreover, negotiating anew every time would increase the chances of hostility growing and friendship diminishing between any two states regardless of their basic predispositions. Hence, in the face of pressure to change routine, there are counterpressures not to tamper with existing procedures.

Remembering that routine interactions occur between friendly as well as hostile states and that these play a large role in the way states deal with each other, we will examine a number of points related to the nature and maintenance of routine interactions among states. We will study (1) the role of international law in maintaining various areas of routine interactions; (2) the role of diplomatic missions in keeping interactions among states routine; (3) the diplomatic mission itself as a "routine instrument of foreign policy"; and (4) some patterns of routine interactions among contemporary states.

THE ROLE OF LAW

When states have agreed, through explicit or tacit means, to follow a given routine procedure, international law plays a crucial role. As we have seen, international law is not uniformly effective. Enforcement processes continue to be controlled primarily by individual states. Hence, agreement among states on a given procedure is essential for effective operation of international law just as it is for routinization of a given set of interactions. To illustrate the areas where some basic agreement exists, we will discuss a number of fields in which international law helps maintain routine interactions among states.[1]

International law assists in keeping the flow of people between states as routine as possible. It regulates travel on the high seas by stating, for example, that any ship may travel wherever its owners wish outside the territorial waters of states and that private or commercial vessels may navigate territorial waters (usually defined as the three-to-twelve mile span of water surrounding a state's coast) as long as they do not threaten the peace and tranquillity of the coastal state. These rules for sea travel make routine movement of men and commerce possible.

International law also facilitates travel in the air and on land. International laws and cooperative agencies like the International Civil Aviation Organization make air travel less hazardous, not only for the traveler, but also for the states involved. Land travel requiring border crossings is regulated by rules established by states with common borders. These rules allow for international travel without individual *ad hoc* disputes over each traveler. Whether traveling by air, land, or sea, then, the citizen is provided certain routine conditions through operation of international laws; consequently, states are spared the costs and dangers of constant bargaining over matters of international travel.

Similarly, international law stipulates that states may determine whether or not they wish to admit any given individual. This stipulation is extremely important in the movement of people across international boundaries because it allows the states to control those movements. In addition, international law indicates how aliens—that is, nationals of a

---

[1] To get an idea of the types of routine interactions international law helps to maintain, see William D. Coplin, *The Functions of International Law* (Chicago: Rand McNally, 1966), Chapter 2.

foreign state—are to be treated. It outlines procedures that aliens must follow as well as procedures the alien's nation must follow if it wishes to protect the rights of its nationals. As foreign travel increases, the need for controlling and protecting people residing in foreign lands increases.

Related to this is the problem of jurisdictional authority that arises from international travel and business. The question of which state has legal authority to regulate behavior of which persons occurs more often in the highly mobile modern world than it did in the past. International law provides certain guidelines for establishing this legal authority in a given circumstance. If, for example, a national of state A performs an illegal act in state B and flees to state C, which state has the authority to apprehend and try the criminal? International law provides guidelines in order to keep the incident at a routine level so that it does not become a source of conflict.

International law and related institutions also affect economic interactions among states. There are international guidelines for protecting foreign investors, even though these guidelines often remain ambiguous. International law indicates the ways in which an alien can receive fair treatment in economic matters from the state in which he is located. It also indicates procedures for establishing tribunals to settle economic disputes among the citizens and governments of different states. Economic disagreements of potential significance are often kept routine by the international procedures and institutions states have developed to settle them.

A final area in which international law maintains routine relations among states is exchange of governmental officials. Almost all states exchange diplomats who, as we will see in the next section, are important in maintaining these routine interactions. International law provides rules for exchange of diplomats and establishes how diplomats are to be protected from threats by the host country so they can carry on their functions. Most countries recognize that diplomats cannot be executed, jailed, or even fined for traffic violations. Not only are diplomats immune to local, civil, and criminal law, but they are also exempt from many taxes. The immunity usually extends all the way from high-ranking officials of a diplomatic mission to staff members and their families. Under the principle of diplomatic immunity, the most severe penalty a host country can impose on a diplomat is to demand his recall by declaring him *persona non grata,* but this penalty is rarely employed among friendly states. Usually, the home country can see when a given individual has outlived his usefulness and call him home before action is taken by the host country. International law establishes guidelines for handling other government officials such as members of the armed forces. The purpose of such regulations is to protect representatives of foreign governments and enable them to do their jobs as effectively as possible, which in many cases means to work to maintain routine relations among states.

THE ROLE OF THE DIPLOMATIC MISSION

The "diplomatic mission" consists of a group of governmental officials sent by one state to reside and fulfill certain duties in another state. Protected by international law from the normal civil and criminal rules of the host state, the diplomatic mission is headed by a chief who is usually but not always an ambassador. In the larger missions, there is usually a political section, an economic and commercial section, an information and cultural section, and a consular section, each of which has specialized functions. Sometimes attachés are appointed to provide coordination in areas such as military, agricultural and labor affairs. These attachés are often associated with departments in the home country other than the foreign office. The modern diplomatic mission (at least in the developed states) is large by classical standards, and often involves hundreds of officials performing a wide variety of duties.

No matter what the mission's duties, however, a prime concern of its members is to keep certain international interactions as routine as possible. The diplomatic mission does this in two general ways: (1) by gathering information that might affect relations between the two countries, (2) by handling complaints and requests that might threaten the existing routine. We will briefly discuss ways in which the modern diplomatic mission performs these functions.

Gathering Information

One major function of the diplomatic mission is to obtain and pass on information to policy makers in the home country. The ability of a state to adjust its foreign policy to meet changing conditions in other states is crucial in the contemporary world, and the diplomatic mission plays a large role in providing this ability. One should not, however, assume that the members of the diplomatic mission are "James Bond types" looking in files marked "Top Secret." Nor are they the suave dinner party hosts pouring alcoholic beverages into their guests in the hope of acquiring secret information. On the contrary, most information comes from relatively open sources. The local newspapers and public speeches by government officials provide more information about conditions that might affect the relationship between the two countries than do reports of secret agents. Although some espionage plays a role—particularly in military planning and technology—the information needed to make foreign policy is primarily acquired through conventional channels.

The functional division of the mission aids in the acquisition of information. The political section attempts to acquire information on many subjects relating to political stability and the foreign policy position of the host state, while the economic and commercial sections seek to gain information that might be of interest to governmental officials concerned with economic policy. Often, the attachés are employed to gain information from their counterparts in the host state. Thus, the labor attaché studies and establishes contact with policy influencers and governmental officials concerned with matters of labor. The military attaché investigates the views of the armed services of the host state. Frequently these attachés report to departments of the government other than the foreign office in the home country, but usually they keep their chief informed of conditions that might affect the overall political relationships between the two states.

The role of chief of mission is crucial in the acquisition and transmission of information. It is he who usually reports through regular channels any changes that might affect relations between the two states. His personal qualities and interests affect his choice of what information to provide to the home office. His ability to see the importance of specific events and to press his views on the home office often determine the ability of his country to adjust its policies to meet new conditions in the host country. The chief must be skilled not only in acquiring information, but also in channeling the information to a place where it can have the proper impact on the making of policy.

This is not always easy. The foreign policy making institutions of most states overlap and conflict. While every state has a foreign office that handles most of its foreign affairs matters, many states also direct some of these matters to other agencies in the bureaucracy. In the United States government, for example, the Department of Defense, the White House staff, the Central Intelligence Agency, the Bureau of the Budget, and the Departments of Agriculture, Treasury, Labor, and Commerce all have foreign policy staffs that accumulate and digest information. As supreme decision maker, the President receives information about a particular nation through many channels, including those just listed. Hence, the report of the mission's chief stands a good chance of getting lost within the bureaucracy itself. It might never reach those who formulate broad policy unless the chief has the qualities discussed above.

The information flow to the home foreign policy establishment is extremely complex. Sources of information overlap not only within the foreign office itself, but also within different departments of the government. The Central Intelligence Agency duplicates some work of the Intelligence and Research Bureau of the Department of State, to cite one example. Moreover, information must pass through many channels before it reaches the policy makers. The organization must decide at what level the information flow should stop. Often members of the organization have reasons for withholding or changing information because of internal political pressures. (This point is discussed in Chapter 2 from the framework of the behavior of large-scale organizations.)

At the same time, however, reports from diplomatic missions may contain certain biases. One of the most common is the tendency for members of the mission to lose sight of the perspective of the entire foreign policy of their state. The following passage from George W. Ball, Under-Secretary of State for Presidents Kennedy and Johnson for over six years, illustrates the point:

> . . . it was my responsibility and that of other officials of the State Department to put the excitement of our local missions into perspective and to recognize that not all countries were of the same size or significance to our interests. This was not always an easy point to make. I once incurred the rebuke of some of my colleagues when, informed in anguished terms of the threatened ascendancy in a tiny state of a leader who was supposed to be under the sway of Red China, I responded to a recommendation for active intervention with a memorandum noting that "God watches every sparrow that may fall, but I do not see why we need to compete in that league."[2]

There is also the danger that the reports from the mission will be biased in one direction or another. Aware of the viewpoints of higher officials in the home office, the diplomat may present information he knows the official will find "encouraging." Or, his close contact with people in the host country may predispose him to act as a "representative" of their interests in the home office.[3] Conversely, some initial negative experiences with the host state may lead him to see all events in that state with a jaundiced eye. As a result, the home office must weigh information it receives from the mission to account for possible biases.

Administering Claims and Requests

In addition to providing information the home office needs to maintain and/or adjust routine interactions, diplomatic missions also administer

---

[2] George W. Ball, *The Discipline of Power: Essentials of a Modern World Structure* (Boston: Little, Brown, 1968), p. 233.

[3] See Dean G. Pruitt. "An Analysis of Responsiveness between Nations," *Journal of Conflict Resolution* 6 (1962), 5–18, for a discussion of how desk officers in the State Department tend to "represent" the interests of the countries to which they are assigned.

claims and requests from two very different sources: (1) nationals of the home state who are visiting, involved in business, or have other interest in the host state, and (2) nationals and officials of the host state. In its capacity as administrator of claims and requests, the diplomatic mission acts as a broker for the interests of its nationals vis-à-vis the receiving country. The smooth operation of this broker function is a crucial part of maintaining stable relations between states because it prevents small incidents from becoming occasions for competitive bargaining or collective problem solving.

A major part of the work of diplomatic missions has to do with facilitating travel and business of nationals from the home state. Most of the work is highly routine, requiring only application of regulations set up by both the home and the host state. The consular service of the mission serves as a clearinghouse for its nationals on routine matters. In addition, there are generally enough complaints and unusual requests from its nationals to keep the mission busy. Such instances not only provide work for the mission but also represent a possible source of trouble between the two nations.

A long-time diplomat, Hugh Gibson, characterizes the burdens placed on the mission by its citizens when he writes,

> Americans are fond of telling each other what a simple, easy-going race we are. That doubtless holds good at home, but you would be surprised how many of your fellow citizens enter an embassy with a chip on their shoulder.
>
> As he crosses the threshold he undergoes a transformation from a simple American to an American-citizen-taxpayer-and-don't-you-forget-it. . . . And the things they want service on would fill a book. They want to be taken around at once to see the king. They want to be invited to dine at the Embassy and demand it as a right. They want you to give a party—at your expense of course—so that they can play or sing or recite, preferably before some royalties.[4]

This humorous and exaggerated picture of the plight of the mission should not obscure the potential for disruption of relations between states inherent in the complaints of nationals. The mission is bound to protect its nationals. An affront to a national in a foreign state—whether real or imagined—can give rise to international disputes. Questions frequently arise concerning fair treatment by the laws of a state. Seeking to settle and put an end to such questions without unnecessarily increasing tensions, the mission is placed in an extremely difficult position. Because members of the mission never know what factors might be unleashed by a given incident,

---

[4] Quoted in Charles W. Thayer, *Diplomat* (New York: Harper & Row, 1959), pp. 113–114.

they are continually faced with decisions that can have enormous consequences after it is too late for reversal. To compound matters, members are
subject to second guessing by officials and policy influencers such as mass
media, political parties, and so forth, not only in the host country but at
home as well.

The mission is also the initial recipient of claims and requests by
nationals and officials of the host nation. The claims by nationals can run
the gamut from attacks on the general policy of the home state to requests
for travel visas. Officials within the host nation usually will send requests or
complaints to the embassy, particularly if they are minor. The misbehavior
of a national of the sending state, for example, might give rise to a private
communication from a governmental official of one host state to a member
of the embassy staff.

The work of the diplomatic mission in the area of claims and requests
is rarely publicized, but it represents an important factor in keeping interactions routine. Located in a foreign land and separated from the home
office, the diplomatic mission filters relations between its government and
the host country. It seeks to handle potentially disrupting questions in a
manner that will prove acceptable to both sides. Paid by and subject to the
authority of the home government, the diplomatic mission frequently
stretches its command to be as accommodating to the host country as
possible. Although there is always the danger that the mission may become
too accommodating (a danger which many states minimize by regularly
rotating their staffs), a major purpose of the diplomatic mission is to ensure
that interactions that foreign policy decision makers wish to maintain as
routine be protected from conditions that might destroy the basis for their
routine quality.

THE DIPLOMATIC MISSION AS A ROUTINE INSTRUMENT
OF FOREIGN POLICY

In addition to looking at the diplomatic mission as a means for maintaining
routine interactions among states, it is also important to examine the
mission as a regularized channel for the pursuit of foreign policy goals.
Aside from its informational role the mission is a generally accepted
institution through which the sending state furthers its foreign policy aims.
It does this by carrying out specific policy decisions made by the home
office as well as by defending its state's foreign policy to the host country's
decision makers and policy influencers. Although the diplomatic mission
might be involved with the host state, in collective problem solving or
competitive bargaining on behalf of the sending state, it nonetheless repre-

sents a regularized or routine channel through which such bargaining takes place. We will treat that function briefly here.

The diplomatic mission is a clearinghouse for most of its own government's operations within the host country. Programs designed to achieve a certain purpose, such as economic aid or technical assistance, may not be run by diplomats, but they are run by governmental officials who coordinate their activities with the mission staff. The mission's role in this respect is to oversee the activities of specialized personnel so that friction between the two states is minimized. Because control is often fragmented by conflicting authority from governmental officials in the home office, the mission is not always entirely effective; nonetheless, attempts are made to ensure the smooth operation of specialized programs.

In addition, the diplomatic mission is a primary channel for communication between officials of the sending and host states. Because the method of delivery of a message to a foreign official is often a determining factor on how that message is received, the proper choice of medium is often crucial. One way state A can deliver a message to state B is to make a public statement and openly announce the message. However, because the audience would be so large, this medium would be chosen only if the sending state intended people other than the foreign policy decision makers of the receiving state to know about the message. Occasionally, mass media are employed to save time. In the Cuban missile crisis, for example, public statements and newspaper releases appear to have been employed by both sides to speed up the communication processes. As we will see in Chapter 10, actions involving competitive bargaining often take the form of public statements. However, foreign policy decision makers often use the mission instead of public channels if the general public is not a part of the bargaining strategy.

The mission also provides a routine channel for communication among states. It can be used in a number of ways. One way is for state A as sender to deliver the message to state B's diplomatic mission in state A. Or A might send the message to its diplomatic mission in B with instructions that it be delivered to the governmental officials of that state. Written messages, however, are often slow, even in this modern age of high-speed communications, because they have to be encoded and decoded. Moreover, the sender is never quite sure that the message has been received by the right individuals, properly decoded and translated.

An alternative is to have the ranking member of the diplomatic mission deliver a message orally to officials of the host country. This method also has its assets and liabilities. On the one hand, the reaction of the officials from the receiving state can be noted by the chief of mission. At the very least, he can be certain of who in the government received the message. On the other hand, one is never sure if the correct information was passed on because of the biases the chief of mission might possess. In addition, his reputation with the leaders of the host state will have a direct bearing on how the message is received.

A third alternative is for sending state decision makers to confer with the chief of mission from the receiving state who is located in the sending state. For example, Soviet leaders may call in the United States Ambassador under certain circumstances. Potential benefits and costs must be weighed; if the chief of mission has good access to officials in his home country and is likely to present the message in the most advantageous form, this is a good method. However, if the chief of mission is disliked or ignored by his own officials in the home country or he is not particularly friendly to the sending state, choice of this method is ill-advised.

In addition to administering programs and acting as a communication channel, the diplomatic mission is also responsible for certain types of negotiation. Negotiation can be viewed as a complex form of international communication in which both sides talk to each other with some particular issue in mind. Although normal diplomatic channels are employed for the preliminary stages of most negotiations, an increasingly significant trend has been the use of specially appointed representatives in major negotiations. This trend has been made possible by the availability of high-speed transportation and necessary by the technical skills required for many issues now receiving the attention of states. Experts on a particular subject such as tariff reduction or disarmament are necessary for the successful drafting of agreements between states.

Diplomatic missions also attempt to build support for the foreign policy of their state by defending the foreign policy position of their home country. Their most important task is to make sure that decision makers of the host state are made to believe exactly what the decision makers in the sending state want them to believe. Whether this involves threats or promises, the diplomatic mission can be a valuable arm of the foreign policy maker by delivering the right message at the right time.

Insofar as the activities of diplomatic missions designed to build support for the policy aims of the home state are considered to be legitimate by the host state, we can say that these activities constitute a routinized aspect of interactions among states. As a matter of routine, a member of the diplomatic mission is often assigned to explain or defend the foreign policy of his state to particular policy influencers. The labor attaché, for example, keeps in close touch with labor leaders of the host state so that he can report on their views but also so that he can build support for his state's foreign policy. The military attaché works with the military elite of the nation while the economic department of the mission tries to build support among the business policy influencers. The diplomatic mission attempts to insure that policy influencers of the host state understand and support the foreign policy of its state.

While the diplomatic mission attempts to build support for the foreign policy of its state among the host's policy influencers and decision makers, it must walk a thin line between legitimate activities in behalf of its government's policies and illegitimate activities designed to substitute more friendly decision makers in the host state. The reason for this is that the host state can and will take severe actions against a mission that is involved in anything resembling subversive activities, including the severing of diplomatic relations and the declaring of members of the mission staff *personae non gratae*. Few states are willing to run the risk of being the target of such action even under conditions of high tension.

The reason for this reluctance lies primarily in the high value most foreign policy decision makers place on the diplomatic mission as a routine foreign policy instrument. Like the common agreement on certain areas of international law, commitment to maintain diplomatic contacts even under hostile conditions is based on the realization that the benefits of regular diplomatic contact generally outweigh the costs.

PATTERNS OF ROUTINE INTERACTIONS

Although almost all states have some routine interactions with all other states (even if they are limited to common membership in an intergovernmental organization or routine refusals to establish official diplomatic contact), there is a wide variation in both the quality and types of routine interactions that characterize relations among states. In closing this chapter, we will explore the nature of and the reasons for variations in the way states deal with each other routinely.

A primary cause of variation in routine interactions is the degree of friendship or hostility that exists between states. As we have seen, hostility can be routinized just as easily as friendship. The United States, for example, interacts routinely with both Great Britain and the Soviet Union in the area of tourist traffic, even though the size of the flow to and from the United States differs greatly for the two states. However, the varying degrees of hostility and friendship experienced can lead to differences in these routine interactions.

First, friendly states usually maintain a larger number of routine interactions with each other than with hostile states. One indication of this tendency is the size of diplomatic missions. For example, in 1968 the United States sent 161 foreign service officers to the United Kingdom; it sent 65 to the Soviet Union.[5] In large part, we can assume that this size difference, as well as the difference in volume of routine interaction it represents is a product of the more friendly relations the United States maintains with the United Kingdom.

In addition to the quantity of routine contacts, the balance of hostility and friendship between states also affects the types of routine activities as well as the nature of the administrative personnel. Military alliances, for example, are prime manifestations of friendship that demand an exchange of governmental personnel. This is true even in the absence of foreign troops because contemporary military technology demands that allies co-ordinate their efforts at various administrative levels.

In addition, even the private travel of diplomats is affected by the existing degrees of hostility and friendship. Both the United States and the Soviet Union, for example, have restricted the area for legitimate travel by each other's diplomatic staff. Although these restrictions are sometimes rationalized on the grounds of "national security" and the "prevention of spying," they also are instituted to communicate a routinized hostility. An extreme example of routinization of hostility is refusal to exchange diplo-mats. Diplomatic missions are closed if this hostility leads to war, although the host state may allow the sending state to withdraw its diplomatic personnel. At the very least, it will agree not to harm them if they are interned for the duration. While some contacts may be maintained through a third party (as, for example, Communist China and the United States, who have met regularly in Poland), this refusal of diplomatic exchange is one of the most hostile routine actions a state can take against another.

A related routine act of hostility is refusal to recognize a government or the existence of a newly constituted state. One should distinguish between recognition of statehood—which applies only in the case of a colony's becoming a state, an unoccupied piece of territory becoming a state, or an independent state being established on *part* of the territory of another state—and the recognition of government that applies to any unconstitutional change in the head of state (president or monarch). The refusal of the United States to recognize the Communist regime in China is an example of withholding the recognition of a government as a rou-tinized act of hostility. Whatever the reason, the refusal to recognize a new state or government implies a general decision to refrain from most contacts with that state, and therefore constitutes a highly hostile act.

In addition to hostility and friendship, another set of factors deter-mines interactions among states. We can call this set of factors *importance*

---

[5] Department of State, "Foreign Service List, Department of State, January, 1968," Publication 7802 (Washington, D.C.: Government Printing Office).

or *salience* of the prospective host state for the sending state. The key question in this respect is: What makes one state important or salient to another state? Three of these factors are geographical location, economic relationships, and historical ties.

Geographical location is extremely important. The sharing of a common border or a common body of water creates a number of situations that have to be handled routinely. Even hostile states like East Germany and West Germany are forced to establish a large number of routine contacts because they share a common border. When there is friendship between the two states, as in the case of the United States and Canada, sharing a border produces a greater number and variety of routine interactions. Similarly, the farther away states are from each other (unless one state happens to enjoy a strategic geographical location, as for example the United Arab Republic through the Suez), the fewer the routine interactions.

Economic relationships also affect the amount and variety of routine interactions. Heavy mutual trading creates conditions for large and varied routine interactions not only because many types of administrative problems might result from a large volume of trade but also because the countries involved have a heavy stake in each other's economic policies. Moreover, attempts by underdeveloped states to cultivate markets and capital investment in developed states lead them to send diplomatic missions to those states.

Historical ties also serve to increase the number of routine interactions among states. Colonial ties, for example, have contributed to the establishment of a large variety of routine interactions for states like Great Britain and her excolonies. In fact, both Britain and France have developed loosely structured intergovernmental organizations composed of excolonial areas. The British Commonwealth and the French Community are manifestations of the heavy routine interactions between excolonies and their past masters. Other historical relationships, such as the United States in South America and the Soviet Union in eastern Europe, account for greater and more varied routine interactions with the states of that area than one might otherwise expect.

One important additional factor affecting the quantity and variety of routine interactions among states is the *economic resources* available to states. More than 150 states exist; many states cannot afford to maintain diplomatic missions and other forms of routine contact with all of them. Alger and Brams found that "fifty nations send diplomats to only ten to twenty-nine other nations."[6] Moreover, diplomats often "double up" by

[6] Chadwick F. Alger and Steven J. Brams, "Patterns of Representation in National Capitals and Intergovernmental Organizations," *World Politics,* 19 (1967), 662.

serving as the chief of mission in two or more states. Many African states, for example, have their American Ambassador also act as United Nations representative. Hence, some states maintain what amounts to half-time staff in some of the states where they have missions. The high cost of maintaining diplomatic missions, then, affects the size and number of missions states send to other states.

As Alger and Brams point out, however, the existence of intergovernmental organizations is important to those states that cannot afford to send missions to other states. The organizations themselves probably serve as something of a substitute for diplomatic missions in providing a routine instrument for interactions, although we can assume that they are not as effective as the diplomatic mission.

SUMMARY

In this chapter, we have briefly discussed the routine interactions that take place among states by examining the processes through which those interactions are developed and maintained. In addition, we have focused on the role of the diplomatic mission not only in maintaining routine interactions but also as a routinized instrument through which states deal with each other. Finally, we have discussed the factors that most affect the amount and nature of routine interactions among states.

Routine interactions comprise the overwhelming majority of events involving two or more states. In spite of the newspaper reports of instances of competitive bargaining or collective problem solving, the business of international affairs is primarily routine. Although immensely affected by competitive bargaining and collective problem solving, routine interactions create many of the preexisting conditions that shape the other types of activities. The student interested in international affairs should realize the importance of routine interactions for two reasons: if he chooses a career in this field he will be concerned with the types of routine events discussed in this chapter;[7] and in the long run what happens in the day-to-day activities of states affects and is affected by the other types of international interactions.

[7] Those interested in an international affairs career should be advised that jobs that might be considered international affairs positions demand skills in addition to the knowledge of international affairs. A diplomat ought to have administrative skills, an intelligence officer might need training in economics, sociology, a foreign language and/or statistics. Although students are often attracted to international affairs because of the glamor of foreign places or their desire to "make a better world," such a position will be open to them only if they can offer something other than an intense interest in and knowledge of international politics.

SUMMARY OUTLINE

   I.   *Routine official interactions among states are usually performed by relatively low-level administrative officials of the foreign policy bureaucracy.*

 II.   *Routine interactions occur for friendly as well as hostile states.*

III.   *Routine interactions originate either through ad hoc precedent-setting activity or the conscious and mutual effort by states to routinize a certain area.*

IV.   *Changes in routine interactions can occur if at least one involved state seeks to change them or if conditions surrounding the interactions (in the international setting) change.*

  V.   Law plays an important role in maintaining routine interactions among states.

     A.   *International law assists in keeping the flow of people between states as routine as possible.*

     B.   *International law facilitates the movement of goods, services, and capital.*

     C.   *International law aids in keeping the exchange of government officials routine.*

 VI.   Diplomatic missions play an important role in maintaining routine interactions among states.

     A.   Diplomatic missions gather information and supply it to the home office for policy-making purposes.

        1.   *The bulk of information is gathered through legitimate regular sources.*

        2.   *Diplomatic missions are divided into functional areas responsible for gathering information on a specific aspect of the host state.*

        3.   *Information provided by the mission is sometimes biased.*

        4.   *Such information often conflicts internally and with other sources when it gets to the home office.*

     B.   Diplomatic missions help to maintain routine interactions by administering claims and requests.

        1.   *Nationals from the home state, whether vacationing or on business, often make demands the mission seeks to satisfy.*

        2.   *The mission is placed in the middle of a set of conflicting demands: from the home office, from the nationals, and from the host state.*

        3.   *Nationals and officials of the host state often make demands that are channeled through the diplomatic mission.*

VII.   Diplomatic missions also operate as routine instruments of foreign policy.

A.   *The mission is the chief clearinghouse for the home government's policies.*
B.   *The mission provides a communications channel between the home government and host government.*
   1.   *The mission provides a regularized, relatively "quiet," means of high-level governmental contact.*
   2.   *The diplomatic instrument provides a number of alternatives for sending messages.*
C.   Diplomatic missions attempt to build support for the home government's foreign policy.
   1.   *They present their policy to the officials of the host governments.*
   2.   *They present their policy to important policy influencers.*
   3.   *Their general behavior can have an impact on support for their home government's foreign policy.*
   4.   *Diplomatic missions are usually careful not to openly attempt to advocate or take actions to overthrow the host government because the host government can retaliate.*

VIII.   Routine interactions among states vary in both quantity and type.
A.   *The degree of hostility and friendship between two states will affect both the quantity and types of routine interactions.*
   1.   *Hostile states will exchange fewer governmental representatives than friendly states (all other things being equal).*
   2.   *Hostile states will exchange governmental representatives that perform a smaller variety of activities than friendly states (all other things being equal).*
   3.   *Refusal to recognize a state or its regime and refusal to maintain diplomatic representation are routinized ways of expressing hostility toward a state.*
B.   Other factors that can roughly be called the "importance" or "salience" of a state affect the quantity and type of routine interactions among states.
   1.   *Geographical proximity and especially sharing a common border increases the quantity and varitey of routine contacts (other things being equal).*
   2.   *Economic relationships—whether equally interdependent or one-sided—affect the quantity and variety of routine interactions (other things being equal).*
   3.   *Historical ties—such as colonial relationships in the past —affect the quantity and variety of routine interactions (other things being equal).*

C. *The high cost of maintaining diplomatic missions has led a large majority of states in the world to refrain from sending missions to states that are not important to them.*

D. *Intergovernmental organizations have helped to supply some of the contact that is lost by the absence of diplomatic exchanges among states.*

BIBLIOGRAPHICAL ESSAY

Except for a few recent empirical studies, the bulk of the literature on routine official interactions is historical and/or prescriptive. Among a number of works that trace the evolution of modern diplomatic institutions are Nicolson (294) and (296). Numelin (298) uses an anthropological approach. The standard work on the nature of diplomatic activities and the rules governing them is Satow (365) in any of numerous editions. Craig and Gilbert (89) and Thayer (402) focus on the behavior of diplomats per se. Instructive works on American diplomatic practices are Poole (316), McCamy (258), Stuart (398), Westerfield (418), Jackson (190), Barnet (28), and Plischke (313). Some modern developments in diplomatic practices, including the role of intergovernmental organizations, are discussed in Cardozo (66), McCamy (259), Merchant in (197), Waters (416), and Lall (238). Students interested in the role of international law in routine interactions among states may consult Brierly (49), Friedmann (129), and Coplin (84).

Five recent works that examine various dimensions of diplomatic activities should be mentioned. Singer and Small (385) trace patterns of diplomatic representation among states between 1815 and 1940 as an indication of the relative status of states in the system, while Alger and Brams (7) study these patterns in contemporary states. McClelland (383) uses quantitative techniques to study routinized hostile behavior. Keller (214) examines diplomacy as an instrument for communication while Pruitt (320) applies the concept of "responsiveness" to routine interactions among states. Although these works represent a promising beginning of knowledge, many aspects of routine interactions among states remain unknown. The area is open for further, original study.

9

Social, Economic, and Political
Problem Solving Among States

One reason states break existing routine interactions is to create new routines that better serve their mutual aims. As a result, a certain class of official interactions among states involves neither routine interactions nor competitive bargaining. Although it is sometimes difficult to distinguish this class of interactions from the other two, we will deal with these interactions as collective problem solving activities. Occurring both bilaterally and multilaterally, collective problem-solving interactions consist of cooperative undertakings between and among states to meet problems that confront them. The difference between the collective problem solving type of inter-actions and the competitive bargaining type (discussed in Chapter 10) lies in the attitudes of the parties toward each other. In the former situations, the states agree that a mutual problem confronts them although they may offer different solutions and competing interests; in the latter, the states see each other's behavior as the basic problem. Therefore, each is more concerned with changing the other's behavior than with mutually solving the problem. With this definition, it is apparent that any given set of interactions between the same states can involve elements of both collective problem solving and competitive bargaining. As in the case of other categories employed throughout the book, we make the distinction for purposes of discussion. It is up to the reader to judge the utility of the distinctions.

In this chapter, then, we are interested in the types of interactions in which the participants—whether two states or a hundred—feel that co-operation is necessary to deal with a mutually perceived problem. The problems may range in complexity and scope from an attempt by United States and Canada to maintain effective border control to a campaign by most of the nations in the world to stop the spread of a particular disease. Remembering that we are attempting to cover a large variety of types of official interactions, we will discuss collective problem solving among states by examining (1) the origins of problem-solving behavior among states, (2) bilateral and multilateral cooperation, (3) the scope of current cooperation, and (4) the role of politics in collective problem solving among states.

ORIGINS OF COLLECTIVE PROBLEM SOLVING

As pointed out in Chapter 7, the setting for interactions among states creates the initial conditions for all types of interactions among states including collective problem solving. However, it is important to emphasize that problem solving does not occur among states unless the states agree a problem exists. Either on their own or as a result of pressure from intergovernmental organizations, states must perceive a mutual problem before initiating collective problem-solving behavior. In examining the origins of collective problem solving among states, then, we must identify not only environmental conditions that create the problems but also the processes through which these problems become identified as targets for collective problem solving.

States have attempted to resolve two basic types of social, economic, and political problems through international cooperation. The first type concerns conditions in the international environment which, if left unregulated, would harm those states involved. At the bilateral level, patrolling shared bodies of water or aiding in the capture of fugitives who have fled across boundaries have stimulated cooperative interactions. At the multilateral level, the world narcotics traffic, which cannot be effectively controlled through unilateral policies and laws or bilateral activities of states, has been met by multilateral activities. The earliest attempts at international cooperation involving travel on the high seas and modern international postal and telegraph service also fall into this category.

The second type includes certain domestic social, economic, and political circumstances that are assumed to have such a systemwide consequence that they are perceived as mutual international problems. Social conditions such as low literacy rates or poor health, economic conditions such as lack of developmental capital, and political conditions such as human rights have been considered to be so significant that they warrant general international cooperation. Sometimes this cooperation is bilateral but most often it occurs on a multilateral basis. Although international cooperation has not so far been notably effective in improving domestic conditions, these conditions are increasingly becoming targets for international cooperation as the lives of states become more closely intertwined.

Two related assumptions motivate cooperation among states. First, it is often thought that a problem cannot be solved at all unless some form of international cooperation takes place. Examples of bilateral cooperation can be found in the Canadian-American agreements to regulate fishing and hunting in the northern Pacific. Multilaterally, regulation and facilitation of international travel and communication cannot occur unless states cooperate at least to the extent that they agree under what conditions travel and communication can be permitted. International cooperation is also necessary for dealing with highly communicable diseases that know no international boundaries. The need for some minimal standardization in such fields as medicine and communication cannot be satisfied by the uncoordinated behavior of states. In regions such as Europe, where the people have made a commitment extensively to coordinate their economies, international cooperation is a universally recognized prerequisite.

The second assumption stimulating cooperative behavior among states is that the pooling of resources can eliminate wasteful duplication of effort as well as improve the general efficiency of the operation in any field, even one as complex as international cooperation. Scarcity of certain resources —whether of skilled technicians and educators, capital, or raw materials —creates problems that can best be met through collective action. For example, intergovernmental organizations have been created to assist the underdeveloped countries. It is assumed that the scarce capital and technical resources necessary for such assistance can be better used if they are collected and coordinated by global and regional intergovernmental organizations. Private resources are still distributed through the traditional market mechanisms discussed in Chapter 7. However, intergovernmental organizations have been effective in acquiring resources that probably would not have been distributed to underdeveloped states through the market mechanisms. Such pooling of resources is a prime stimulus to extensive international cooperation.

Discovering that a problem exists often determines whether or not international cooperation will result. As already noted, agreement among states that a problem exists is not always an automatic result of the conditions themselves. In many cases, the people affected by a condition might not assume that the condition can or should be altered. For example, large parts of the populations of underdeveloped states do not consider lack of economic development to be a problem because they either are unaware of better conditions or consider it inevitable. In contrast, certain conditions that do not threaten survival nevertheless stimulate problem-solving behavior. For example, many recent developments toward social, economic, and political integration within Europe are not absolutely necessary; it is highly unlikely that without them social, economic, or political chaos would result. Nevertheless, many Europeans both within and outside governmental circles feel that problems that do exist in these areas ought to be met with international cooperation.

Whether or not a given condition gives rise to problem-solving behavior depends on the attitudes of those who can do something about the condition. This means that decision makers within states and policy influencers that support them, as well as decision makers within intergovernmental organizations must believe that conditions need to be altered. Usually, the problem is initially identified by relatively powerless individuals or groups, such as specialized interest groups or bureaucratic influencers within states, or officials in nongovernmental or intergovernmental organizations. These agents may call attention to a particular problem they feel needs collective action. If action is to occur, the initiators must mobilize individuals who will more directly influence the decision makers within states and intergovernmental organizations. Such mobilization depends on two factors: the ability of the initiator to educate policy influencers and their ability to enlist political support from the decision makers.

Conditions surrounding the initiation of international cooperation to solve social, economic, and political problems can be likened to the conditions surrounding the origins of governmental action in a domestic society. In the United States, for example, a problem that is localized in one particular geographical region is usually identified at either the state or federal level by an interest group, a legislator, or an influential group of officials within the executive branch of the federal government. If people within the region agree that some governmental action is necessary they are the ones to pressure for that action. However, if they feel the status quo should be maintained—as, for example, white southerners have felt about racial issues in the past—the pressure for change comes from outside the region. A more geographically dispersed problem such as air pollution usually stimulates a more geographically dispersed set of legislators, interest groups, and lower administrative officials. In either case, however, the initiation of pressure for governmental action starts among a few and, if successful, spreads to a large enough group to make governmental action more probable.

Similarly, the development of forces for multilateral international cooperation starts with a few and may spread to a sufficiently large number of states to make some type of international cooperation possible. The process is more complex on the international level. First, while certain individuals might perceive the need for cooperation, to have a chance for success they must gain the support of a few states and perhaps an intergovernmental organization. Nongovernmental organizations are also important in mobilizing opinion across various nations. Again, those who attempt to pressure for international cooperation might be within the target (European states in pursuit of economic integration), or outside the area (African states in their attempts to mobilize international cooperation to end apartheid in South Africa and Rhodesia). Sometimes, worldwide realization of the need for cooperation greatly facilitates development of international cooperation, as in the case of the Universal Postal Union. But even when this occurs, the responsibility for the initial development usually lies with a small group of dedicated individuals.

Bilaterally, the process of generating support for collective problem solving is not as complex. It is only necessary that key policy influencers and decision makers within two states identify a mutual problem and press for cooperation. Many bilateral cooperative activities among contemporary states involve a relatively small group of policy influencers, since issue areas are likely to be related to narrowly defined problems such as conservation of resources or control of smuggling. This means that the primary actors in the collective problem-solving process are bureaucratic and interest influencers whose concerns are focused on specific problems.

Whether bilateral or multilateral, however, the ability of a small, narrowly-based set of policy influencers in the states concerned to generate broad political support is crucial for collective problem solving among states. Figure 8 clearly illustrates the process. Although we might speculate that as the world becomes increasingly interdependent, more broadly-based policy influencers will become interested in questions likely to lead to collective problem solving among states, it appears that for the immediate future the genesis of collective problem-solving behavior between and among states will depend upon policy influencers committed to such activities.

PATTERNS OF INTERNATIONAL COOPERATION

Collective behavior among states to solve social, economic, and political problems has taken three forms. First, as the problem is initially identified, *ad hoc* or stopgap measures are taken by the states most closely concerned. If these measures prove unsuccessful or too limited, states often form intergovernmental organizations. Finally, if the problems are highly complicated and there is a tendency for many intergovernmental organizations to become involved, some attempt is made to coordinate the activities of

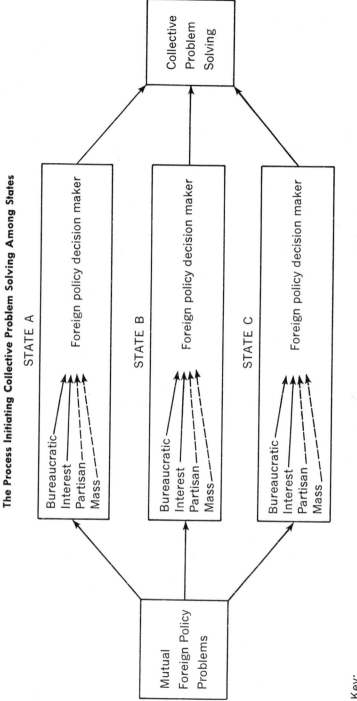

Figure 8

The Process Initiating Collective Problem Solving Among States

Key:

——— Primary lines of influence

– – – Secondary lines of influence

the intergovernmental organizations. These three forms are highly interde-pendent although the first does not necessarily lead to the second or the second to the third.

Ad hoc solutions to mutual problems have been sought and found by states throughout the entire history of international politics.[1] This continues to be the states' primary mode of cooperation in dealing with their interna-tional environment, particularly for the many problems that are settled on a bilateral basis. Ranging from questions of health, control over businesses, and the enforcement of domestic laws to questions of military cooperation and national honor, problems unique to two states that happen to border each other or are related to each other for some other reason (historical, ideological, or economic) are resolved daily through international agree-ments. Although states also employ the *ad hoc* approach multilaterally, the problems most often dealt with in an *ad hoc* manner are bilateral ones.

To apply the *ad hoc* approach to world problems the states must agree upon a set of rules governing their behavior. These rules do not necessitate intergovernmental organizations because they are directed strictly at the behavior of the states themselves. They indicate exactly what actions states will and will not take in relation to a clearly defined problem. In effect, they supply a form for coordinating national policies and laws in order to create mutually beneficial international conditions. For example, the United States and Canada have laws governing the behavior of their fishermen so that fish resources in the international waters along their respective coasts can be conserved. Thousands of treaties and executive agreements on both bilateral and multilateral bases aid contemporary states in solving mutual problems.

Although a large share of the collective problem-solving activities performed by states have been developed through custom, treaties, and less formal written agreements, the *ad hoc* approach is effective as long as the problem can be identified and the solution agreed upon. As problems become more complex and more urgent and the interests conflict increas-ingly, the *ad hoc* approach has proven to be both slow and difficult. It is slow because it depends upon the development of favorable opinion in each country separately, and difficult because the technical nature of the prob-lem as well as internal political pressures preclude easy solution. States continue to handle most problems, and particularly bilateral problems, through *ad hoc* cooperation. However, the increase in the number of multilateral questions and the complexity of the problems have rendered

---

[1] Information for the examples and lists of organizations used through this chapter comes from the *Yearbook of International Organizations,* Eyvind S. Tew, ed. 11*th* ed. (Brussels: Union of International Associations, 1966).

the *ad hoc* approach less satisfactory than it was when the international setting was less complex and interdependent.

In response to the growing complexity and urgency of mutual social, economic, and political problems and as a natural development of the *ad hoc* approach, states have employed intergovernmental organizations to facilitate their collective problem solving. The type of organization used varies from the single-purpose commission of representatives from two states (such as the Mexican-American Claims Commissions established in the 1930's to deal with treatment of American property in Mexico), to the multipurpose World Health Organization with its large staff and complex organizational structure. The organization may be permanent, so it can treat the specified problem as well as related problems on a long-range basis, or it may be temporary, to disband as soon as it can find a lasting solution and embody that solution in a set of rules. No matter what the structure and purpose, however, intergovernmental organizations have certain distinct advantages over the *ad hoc* approach in solving problems that confront states.

First, states often agree to create intergovernmental organizations to study and deal with a problem without agreeing on the substantive solution to the problem. Because the organization exists in the absence of a solution, the states themselves need not explicitly agree on a solution. The organization provides permanent staff as well as negotiating machinery to arrive at a substantive solution among its members. Hence, details do not have to be negotiated prior to the explicit commitment of states to solve the problems that have been identified. There is no guarantee that the organizations may not be prevented from acting by the same conflicts that would have blocked substantive agreements. There is, however, a greater chance that some solutions will be tried if an organization is set up to find agreeable substantive solutions.

Second, the intergovernmental organization creates the conditions for a set of people whose technical and career backgrounds become harnessed to the drive for the identification and solution of the problem. This applies not only to the permanent staff of the organization whose technical experience over a period of time will create a resource in itself to solve the problem, but also to the representatives from the member states. Although these representatives are officials of the member states, they often develop personal involvement with the goals of the organization. This in turn can result in pressure on the home government to provide more support for the organization.

Third, certain types of problems cannot be solved through substantive legislation. What is often needed more than a set of rules to guide behavior is an independent body to take actions to meet changing conditions. For example, the International Monetary Fund helps keep the international economic system stable not by making rules of behavior but by taking certain actions at the right time to stabilize certain currencies. Day-to-day, on-the-spot decisions cannot be handled by a static set of rules; they must be made by an intergovernmental organization on a flexible basis.

Fourth, many problems that take one form at one time may arise in another form at another time. A permanent intergovernmental organization constitutes a "continuous search committee" for identifying new conditions that might relate to their problem area. For example, the International Telecommunications Union, originally set up in 1865 to deal with problems posed by the telegraph, now deals with related problems growing out of the use of telephones and radio. Although two or more intergovernmental organizations sometimes compete to handle the same problems because of overlapping functions, the pressure to find and solve related problems is built into the structure of most organizations. Hence this approach is a flexible tool for collective international action.

Finally, the intergovernmental organization represents a more effective approach to problem solving than the *ad hoc* approach in certain areas because a large variety of activities and rules might be related to one general problem area but could not possibly be handled by *ad hoc* treaty making. The activities of the World Health Organization, for example, include such diverse administrative and norm-creating programs that most of its problem-solving impact would be lost if states acted together on health problems only through substantive agreements. The intergovernmental organization can help to integrate the efforts of states in one problem area by performing a number of related operations.

At both the global and regional levels, then, states have cooperated through intergovernmental organizations in approaching mutual economic, social, and political problems. The desire to maintain higher and more complex levels of cooperation than are possible through *ad hoc* agreements has stimulated the creation of approximately two hundred intergovernmental organizations in the world today. (For a discussion of their nature and structure, see Chapter 6.) This large number has some drawbacks, however. Proliferation of all types of intergovernmental organizations at global and regional levels has led to difficulties in coordinating their activities so that they do not duplicate or cancel out each other's efforts.

Conflict occurs between regional and global intergovernmental organizations in relatively similar functional areas. The pursuit of economic developmental objectives, for example, by agencies of the United Nations is not always compatible with policies of the regional organizations in the economic development field. Because the global and regional organizations have different sources of funds resulting from differences in membership, coordinating their efforts is not easy. Even though most charters of regional organizations call for cooperation with other intergovernmental organizations, no central authority maintains this cooperation because there is no central source of funds for all the organizations.

There is also conflict among those organizations with similar aims and geographical scope. For example, a study of land reform has been carried on simultaneously by the Food and Agricultural Organization and the International Labor Organization. Both have financed similar reports and symposia in the 1960's.[2] Acting in what may be viewed as an imperialistic style, intergovernmental organizations jealously guard their existing responsibilities, autonomy, and budgets while seeking to expand their operational scope. This behavior results in conflict among intergovernmental organizations just as it results in bureaucratic conflict within any large-scale organization.

In an effort to overcome some of the waste inherent in this kind of competition, certain institutions have been designed to coordinate the various activities of intergovernmental organizations. The Economic and Social Council of the United Nations, for example, has attempted to coordinate the activities of global and regional organizations. Empowered to coordinate activities of specialized agencies by Articles 57 and 63 of the United Nations Charter, the Council makes recommendations on the basis of reports the organizations submit periodically. However, because the Council has authority only to recommend, it can be successful only insofar as the decision makers in the organizations are willing to coordinate their activities.

The Council also tries to provide regional coordination through its regional commissions in Europe, Asia, the Far East, Latin America, and Africa. These commissions provide technical advice and sometimes financial resources to various regional intergovernmental organizations. At the same time, they seek to promote efficient use of the organizations as tools for collective problem solving among nations.

Certain regional intergovernmental organizations also seek to promote cooperation among various organizations within their region. The Organization of American States in the western hemisphere, the Council of Europe in Europe, the Arab League in the Middle East, and the Organization of African Unity, particularly in sub-Sahara Africa, all attempt, with varying degrees of success, to foster the most advantageous uses of intergovernmental organizations within their respective areas by serving as coordinators. Although this sometimes results in conflict with coordinating

[2] Gerard J. Mangone (ed.), *United Nations Administration of Economic and Social Programs* (New York: Columbia University Press, 1966), p. 127.

activities of the United Nations, it has had some effect in eliminating conflict.

Despite the growth of these intergovernmental organizations designed to promote coordination, difficulties in achieving such coordination appear to be increasing. The enormous growth in the number and scope of intergovernmental organizations, particularly in the period since World War II, and the desire of many permanent staffs to maintain their organizations as going concerns has led to unnecessary duplication and waste of what are admittedly scarce resources. The lack of a unified financial structure to channel funds through one control point has made tight coordination impossible. No Congress, no President, and no constitutional guidelines exist to force coordination on the intergovernmental organizations. In that respect, it is worth noting that even with these sources of authority, administrative conflict and duplication is not unknown in the American government itself. In many ways, the intergovernmental organizations that have been created to meet social, economic, and political problems of international significance are similar to the nations that have spawned them. They guard their own financial base and functional autonomy while attempting to expand—even if expansion means the destruction of other intergovernmental organizations.

THE SCOPE OF CURRENT INTERNATIONAL COOPERATION

Because of the exceedingly broad scope of activities now performed through the international cooperation of states, it would be impossible to present detailed information given the purpose of this book. Therefore, we will attempt to provide the reader with a rough idea of the broad scope of activities performed by intergovernmental organizations in the social, economic, and political fields by a combination of tables and commentary. While the discussion will focus primarily upon collective problem solving among states through intergovernmental organizations, it should be remembered that many of the areas discussed are also handled through *ad hoc* problem solving at the bilateral level.

Cooperation in the Social Field

At both the global and regional level, intergovernmental organizations attempt to deal with social problems through international cooperation. These organizations operate in the related fields of health, research and education, transportation and communication, social welfare, legal advisory, and law enforcement. Some of the organizations most concerned with each of these areas are listed below:

Health

World Health Organization
International Agency for Research on Cancer
European Commission for the Control of Foot-and-Mouth Disease
Institute of Nutrition for Central America and Panama
International Committee for Military Medicine and Pharmacy
Pan American Health Organization
International Office Epizootica

Research and Education

UN Education, Science and Cultural Organization
European Space Research Organization
Inter-American Institute of Agricultural Sciences
International Board of Education
International Council for the Exploration of the Sea
International Institute for Educational Planning
Joint Institute for Nuclear Research
Latin American Center of Physics
Latin American Educational Film Institute
Nordic Advisory on Films for Children
Commonwealth Advisory Aeronautical Research Council
Commonwealth Education Liaison Committee

Transportation and Communication

International Civil Aviation Organization
Universal Postal Union
International Telecommunications Union
African Postal and Telecommunications Union
African Postal Union
Arab Postal Union
Asian-Oceanic Postal Union
Central Commission for the Navigation of the Rhine
Commonwealth Telecommunications Board
European Civil Aviation Conference
European Conference of Ministers of Transportation
European Conference of Postal and Telecommunications Administrations

Social Welfare

Interamerican Childrens Institute
Inter-American Conference on Social Security
Inter-American Indian Institute
International Children's Centre
Tripartite Commission on the Working Conditions of Rhine Boatman
Office of UN High Commissioner for Refugees

Legal Advisory and Law Enforcement

Asian-African Legal Consultive Committee
International Union for the Protection of Industrial Property
Permanent Court of Arbitration
International Union for the Protection of Literary and Artistic
  Works

Cooperation in the Economic Field

International economic cooperation also occurs on global and regional levels. Many intergovernmental organizations attempt to promote economic development within states. In addition, organizations are concerned with increasing trade, regulating commodity markets, stabilizing international financial conditions, and promoting economic integration. The last —economic integration—is particularly important in Europe. The European Coal and Steel Community and the European Economic Community are organizations that have been established to coordinate economic policies not only to increase trade but also to improve general economic conditions of participating countries by raising levels of productivity and employment. The following list indicates the general scope of activities in the economic area.

Regional Economic Development

African Development Bank
Asian Productivity Organization
Central American Research Institute for Industry
Inter-American Committee for Agricultural Development
Inter-American Committee on the Alliance for Progress
Inter-American Development Bank
Inter-American Nuclear Energy Committee
Latin American Institute for Economic and Social Planning
UNESCO Research Centre on Social and Economic Develop-
  ment in Southern Asia
Organization of American States
Afro-Asian Rural Reconstruction Organization

Global Economic Development

United Labor Organization
Food and Agriculture Organization of the UN
International Bank for Reconstruction and Development
International Bank for Economic Cooperation
Organization for Economic Cooperation and Development
International Development Association
United Nations Development Program Contributing Govern-
  ments
Council for Mutual Economic Assistance

Increasing Trade

Commonwealth Economic Committee
Commonwealth Secretariat
Customs Cooperation Council
Latin American Free Trade Association

Regulating Commodities

International Cotton Advisory Committee
International Coffee Organization
International Cotton Institute
International Olive Oil Council
International Rice Commission
International Sugar Council
International Tea Committee
International Tin Council
International Vine and Wine Office
International Whaling Commission
International Wheat Council
North Pacific Fur Seal Commission
Organization of Petroleum Exporting Countries
South West Atlantic Fisheries Advisory Commission

Stabilizing Financial Condition

International Finance Corporation
International Monetary Fund
Tripartite Commission for the Restitution of Monetary Gold
West African Monetary Union

Economic Integration

Organization for African Unity
Council for Mutual Economic Assistance
Council of Europe
Benelux Economic and Social Consultive Council
Benelux Economic Union
Danube Commission

Cooperation in the Political Field

Collective problem solving has not been as widely employed in the field of politics as in the social and economic fields. Unwilling to entrust intergovernmental organizations with issues that might be unpopular at home, foreign policy decision makers have been reluctant to surrender their political problems. In fact, the only two areas of international cooperation that can be cited as having clear political significance are self-determination and human rights.

Self-determination is related to the question of colonialism. Starting with the period following World War I and culminating in the early 1960's, the vast colonial empires that had been maintained for centuries by Great Britain and France were dismantled. This change resulted partly from the objection of the people within the colonies to colonialism and partly from decisions among the colonial powers that continuance of the system was not worthwhile. With both the master and the colony agreeing upon the goal, international institutions were designed to handle the process. As we shall see, however, the institutions operated only for the colonial areas that belonged to the losers in the two world wars.

Under the League of Nations the Mandate system[3] was created, not for the purposes of decolonialization but to dispose of colonial holdings taken from Turkey and Germany as a result of World War I. Although a number of states wanted to annex these territories, President Wilson's commitment to end colonialism as well as the neutral position of the British resulted in the Mandate system. Nevertheless, the system was closer to the colonial system than to the Wilsonian ideal. Article 22 of the Covenant of the League of Nations states that the well-being and development of people in the Turkish and German colonies should be preserved by entrusting "to the advanced nations" the "tutelage" of these areas.

The machinery of the League of Nations for ensuring that the mandatory powers were performing their duties properly was weak. An annual report presented by the mandatory to the League of Nations Council was to be analyzed by a Committee of Experts, who would then advise the Council. This group in turn would make recommendations to the mandatory power. Neither the Committee nor the Council, however, had authority to enforce the recommendations. Although the Mandate system was significant because it represented an attempt to solve a political problem (what to do with the colonies of the defeated powers) it had only a limited impact on the question of self-determination.

After World War II, the Trusteeship system of the United Nations was created to take over where the Mandate system left off. In some ways it was merely an extension of the Mandate system. The Trustees and the trust territories were virtually the same as the mandatory powers and the mandated territories except that the United States replaced Japan and became Trustee for many Japanese colonial holdings. Although the mandated territories in the first class under the League of Nations were all given their independence early in the period after World War II, the rest of the territories were merely transferred to the new system except for Southwest

---

[3] The discussion of the Mandate and Trusteeship systems is based primarily on Jack C. Plano and Robert E. Riggs, *Forging World Order: The Politics of International Organization* (New York: Macmillan, 1967), pp. 355–77.

Africa whose mandatory power, South Africa, refused to complete the transfer. Finally, despite the stipulation that other colonial powers could turn their colonial holdings over to the Trusteeship system in order to make the road to self-determination less difficult, only Italy "accepted" the option by putting Italian Somaliland under the system. It took the action primarily because it was forced to by its World War II conquerors. The Trusteeship system, like the Mandate system, was used to solve postwar problems connected with the capture of the losing side's colonial holdings rather than to promote self-determination through international cooperation.

There was one important difference between the two systems. The international machinery under the Trusteeship system was much more elaborate and powerful than the Mandate machinery. The United Nations Charter created the Trusteeship Council, a permanent organ of the United Nations, to watch over the relationship between the Trustee and the trust territory. The council consisted of government representatives instead of private experts. The representatives consisted of Trustee states, the permanent members of the Security Council, and enough elected members so that there were as many Trustees as non-Trustees on the council. The most important powers of the Trusteeship Council were those relating to the procedures for investigating the Trustees' administration of the trust territory. Instead of an annual report, the Trustee had to provide information on a questionnaire. In addition, the council could accept oral and written petitions from individuals living in the trust territory. Moreover, the council could send visiting missions to gain firsthand knowledge; unlike the League's Mandate system, the Trusteeship system could investigate the trustee's behavior. Although the council could not order changes in this behavior, it was not solely dependent upon the Trustee's open report, and at any rate could make public the way the Trustee was administering its territory.

It should be clear that while the attempt to use intergovernmental organizations to bring self-determination to colonial areas never materialized, states were able to cooperate through the League of Nations and the United Nations to handle a potentially volatile political question—what to do with conquered colonies. Some of the states used the Mandate and Trusteeship systems to achieve their aims of controlling territory. For example, South Africa acquired Southwest Africa, and the United States has acquired control over certain Pacific territories for "strategic reasons." On the whole, however, the systems allowed states to avoid the normal competition that might otherwise result from the distribution of the losing side's colonial holdings. Obviously, the two systems did not cause decolonialization. Many of the areas not under the Trusteeship system became independent just as soon as if not sooner than the trust territories following World War II. In addition, areas still under colonial rule, such as Angola and Mozambique, do not appear to have been affected by the general movement toward self-determination. Although international cooperation did not and has not produced self-determination, it did provide a collective solution to an important political problem.

A more recent but related development in the field of political action is the pursuit of human rights within nations through international machinery.[4] Following World War II, the horror many people felt for Nazi activities during the 1930's stimulated a movement to establish a code of minimum standards of treatment for humans within states. Although international law had traditionally assigned to the state the authority to deal with its people as it saw fit, the postwar movement sought to partially remove that authority by establishing universal standards. At both the global and the regional level, some effort was made to promote human rights through international cooperation.

At the global level, the development of a Declaration of Human Rights in 1948 listed a number of principles that were considered to be part of the way states should treat their citizens. This Declaration, which was to have only a voluntary effect, was to be followed by a treaty obligating states to maintain certain human rights. However, dissension over the substantive principles has led to prolonged discussion with little chance of fruitful settlement.

Also at the global level certain states have attempted to use organs of the United Nations such as the General Assembly or the Security Council, to apply the norms established in the Declaration of Human Rights. These attempts by certain African states have been directed against Rhodesia, South Africa, and Portugal; they have failed because the major powers have been unwilling to allow such actions. They do not want interference in the domestic affairs of states to be established as a precedent.

Finally, at the global level the activities of the International Labor Organization should be mentioned. In its attempt to protect and improve the living standards of laborers throughout the world, the ILO has established not only standards of treatment of laborers but machinery to judge whether or not states are maintaining labor standards. Based on reports from member countries, detailed analyses of the degree to which labor standards are maintained are prepared by the Committee of Experts and

---

[4] The discussion of human rights is based on Philip R. Jacob and Alexine L. Atherton, *The Dynamics of International Organization* (Homewood, Ill.: Dorsey, 1965), pp. 570–603, and William Korey, "The Key to Human Rights—Implementation," *International Conciliation,* 570 (November 1968).

published annually. Although no overt sanctions are connected with them, states do attempt to receive favorable ratings.

The operations of the Committee of Experts of the ILO represent the only continuous operation to implement a program of human rights at the global level, and its operation is quite limited. In contrast, a remarkable development at the regional level was the creation and operation of the European Convention on Human Rights. Signed in 1950 and in force since 1953, the convention comprises 15 European nations. These nations have agreed to submit disputes among themselves concerning questions of human rights to the organs established by the convention. Ten of the fifteen states have also granted to their own nationals and private organizations the right to make claims against them. The complaints are filtered through a Human Rights Commission, which seeks to evaluate the authenticity of the claim as well as its relevance to the convention. In addition, the commission attempts to act as an agent on behalf of the claimant to seek redress. If redress is not possible or satisfactory, the individual claimant and his state are obligated to submit the case to the European Court of Human Rights. Although the number of cases that have reached that stage are small, the establishment of such machinery must be considered a milestone in the protection of basic human rights. Although other regions such as the western hemisphere have proposed and discussed similar machinery, only Europe at this time enjoys it.

Summary of the Scope of International Problem-Solving Activities

We have briefly surveyed some extremely broad areas where some international cooperation exists to solve problems. If we included in our discussion the subjects that are treated through *ad hoc* agreements, we would have to consider the thousands of treaties on almost every conceivable subject in force among states throughout the world. Such a study would reveal that collective problem-solving activities have an even broader scope than those handled through intergovernmental organizations. In this respect, the activities of intergovernmental organizations provide an imperfect idea of the actual scope of collective problem solving.

A final word might be said about the role of this type of organization in collective problem solving among states, particularly in terms of the framework outlined in Chapter 7. In that chapter we said that intergovernmental organizations frequently act as a setting for interactions among states and sometimes behave as relatively independent actors. This is particularly true in the area of international cooperation. In many cases, the organization is merely a tool through which states develop and administer a consensus on how to solve a particular problem. In other cases, the organization initiates action either by identifying a problem and generating support for a particular course of action or by taking specific administrative actions far removed from the initial intentions of states.

THE ROLE OF POLITICS IN COLLECTIVE PROBLEM SOLVING

Because collective problem solving involves cooperation among states, the reader should not make the mistake often made by political scientists of assuming that the activities are *apolitical*. On the contrary, many aspects of the way states cooperate with each other contain politics. There is a politics of international cooperation just as there is a politics of welfare, education, or fiscal policy in the United States. Like bureaucratic or administrative politics anywhere, the politics of international cooperation involves how the bureaucrats (permanent staffs of intergovernmental organizations) deal with each other as well as how actors outside the bureaucracy (states and nongovernmental organizations) relate to, deal with, and act through the bureaucrats. If we use Lasswell's definition of politics—the determination of who gets what, when and how[5]—the set of interactions we have described as collective problem solving among states certainly is politics.

We have already seen how intergovernmental organizations compete among themselves for increased budgets and organizational authority. This results in the same type of organizational politics that exists in other large-scale organizations. (This subject is discussed in Chapter 3.) Competition among bureaucratic units within General Motors, the U.S. government executive branch, and United Nations agencies are strikingly similar. The goals and strategies of the people involved are related to career ambitions in all three, just as performance of those institutions is a product of the complex interaction of many pressures.

Politics is also a part of the way states deal with each other when they solve problems collectively. To say that the states have certain mutual interests in resolving a specific problem is not to say that they have no conflicting interests. Hoping to cooperate, a state will also attempt to convince other states to act in a way most compatible with its interests. If the problem solving takes the form of an *ad hoc* agreement, the terms of the treaty or tacit agreement designed to solve the problem are subject to the push and pull of the political process. If the problem solving involves construction of an intergovernmental organization, the conflicts of interests

[5] Harold Lasswell, *Politics: Who Gets What, When and How* (Cleveland and New York: World, 1958).

and differences of opinion that are a part of the formation of any constitution take place. If the intergovernmental organization already exists, the processes involving the making of decisions as outlined in Chapter 6 will occur. (See pages 166–75.) No matter what the circumstances, however, collective problem solving among states involves conflict of interest and competitive bargaining (to be described in the next chapter) normally associated with the term "politics."

Perhaps the clearest evidence of these political implications is the way the states themselves approach collective participation. Political enemies are not as likely to undertake collective activities as political friends. In terms of the distinction made at the beginning of this chapter, unfriendly states are more likely to see each other as the *problem* rather than to view the *situation* as a *mutual* problem. On the *ad hoc* level, the impact of political relationships among states is manifested in the fact that more cooperative treaties are likely to be in force among friendly states than among hostile ones. Similarly, at the level of collective problem solving through intergovernmental organizations, common membership in the organizations will be greater among friendly states than unfriendly states. The members of the Communist bloc except for Yugoslavia, for example, have boycotted a number of global intergovernmental organizations, particularly in the economic realm (for example, International Monetary Fund). A certain degree of willingness to cooperate, which is usually based on the entire political relationship between states, is essential for collective problem solving.

In addition, states often use intergovernmental organizations as part of their own policies. The United States has established them to coordinate alliance activities (for example, NATO, SEATO, OECD). In the 1960's the Alliance for Progress was not a military alliance but a forum for meetings among governments in the western hemisphere to use American aid more effectively. The British have done a similar thing with the Columbo Plan (an economic development plan directed at former British colonies in Asia). The United States created the Organization for European Economic Cooperation (OEEC) to aid in administering the Marshall Plan in the late 1940's. These organizations were created to help solve social, economic, and political problems through collective action but they also have implications for the general position of the United States in its relationship with states like the Soviet Union. Similarly, the Soviet Union has employed such organizations as COMECON to pursue collective action for economic goals in eastern Europe.

The underdeveloped states have also found intergovernmental organizations to be useful not only for attacking problems collectively, but also for marshalling political support in dealing with the developed states. Enjoying a numerical superiority over the developed states, they have been able to cooperate with each other to bring limited amounts of pressure on the developed states, particularly in the area of economic development. For example, against the initial wishes of the major powers, the underdeveloped states were successful in establishing the United Nations Committee for Trade and Development (UNCTAD). Although there have been few tangible benefits from the establishment of the institution, the underdeveloped states have viewed it as an instrument for focusing pressure on the developed states for economic concessions.[6]

This brief survey should illustrate that the study of collective problem-solving behavior among states is an important part of the study of international politics. Such behavior is no more apolitical than the processes through which the bureaucracies of the U.S. government reach decisions. Moreover, just as political actors within the United States view governmental institutions as an instrument for pursuing their goals, states and even policy influencers within states view intergovernmental organizations as instruments for pursuing their general goals. Moreover, as the scope and intensity of collective problem solving among states increases (as it must, given current social, economic, and political trends), it appears that its political implications will also increase.

SUMMARY

This chapter has examined a wide variety of international interactions from a number of different angles. We have emphasized that a class of interactions we have called collective problem-solving activities overlaps significantly with other types of activities, but we have also argued that it is important to realize that many routine interactions and competitive bargaining situations both affect and are affected by the attempts of states to cooperate. Noting that the predominant mode of collective problem solving is *ad hoc* and bilateral, we have maintained that there appears to be an increasingly significant emphasis on intergovernmental organizations and multilateral activities. For these reasons, a satisfactory conception of international politics must include an understanding of the many ways in which contemporary states seek collectively to solve problems.

---

[6] For a discussion of the trials and tribulations of UNCTAD, see Branislav Gosovic, "UNCTAD: North-South Encounter," *International Conciliation*, 568 (May 1968).

SUMMARY OUTLINE

I. One class of interactions among states can best be described as collective problem solving.

II. The origin of any collective problem solving among states lies in the nature of the setting for state actions as well as in the attitudes of actors within both states and intergovernmental organizations.

  A. *States are motivated to collectively solve a problem if they assume there is no other way to solve the problem.*

  B. *States are motivated to collectively solve a problem if they assume there will be a large economy of scale through cooperation.*

  C. *Although the initiators of collective problem solving may be a small, unpowerful group in the state or the intergovernmental organization, their success depends upon their ability to mobilize some support from powerful policy influencers within states, foreign policy decision makers, nongovernmental organizations, and the permanent staff of intergovernmental organizations.*

  D. *Usually, the foreign policy decision makers and bureaucratic influencers of certain key states are the most important actors to mobilize.*

III. Collective problem solving among states exists at both the *ad hoc* and intergovernmental organization levels.

  A. Ad hoc *solutions involving formal or tacit agreement are the most frequently used type of collective problem-solving activity.*

  B. *The* ad hoc *approach is limited in terms of flexibility and speed, and as a result is being replaced by intergovernmental organizations.*

  C. Intergovernmental organizations are used to solve problems collectively for a number of reasons.

    1. *States will more easily reach agreement on a procedure to determine how a problem will be solved than they will solve the problem directly.*

    2. *Development of a specialized permanent staff in a given area makes the intergovernmental organization a specialized resource for solving problems in that area.*

    3. *Solving certain types of problems requires an on-going institution.*

    4. *Intergovernmental organizations can deal with a set of problems that might take different forms over the years.*

    5. *Intergovernmental organizations can be the focus for a*

number of types of actions (legislative, regulatory, and the like) that cannot be solved by a treaty.

D. Intergovernmental organizations tend to multiply without sufficient central control or planning.
   1. Geographical overlapping often occurs.
   2. Functional overlapping often occurs.
   3. Although the Economic and Social Council of the United Nations attempts to coordinate activities of many intergovernmental organizations, lack of a central source of finance and the complexity and enormity of problem-solving activity have hindered this attempt.

IV. Collective problem solving among states has been most extensive in the economic and social fields and least extensive in the political fields.
   A. It has occurred in health, research, education, transportation, communications, social welfare, legal advisory, and law enforcement in the social fields.
   B. International economic cooperation has worked toward increasing trade, regulating commodity markets, stabilizing international financial conditions, and promoting economic integration.
   C. In the political field, limited cooperation has occurred in the areas of self-determination and human rights.
      1. In the area of self-determination, the League and the United Nations have been most effective in helping the victors to deal with the colonial holdings of the losers in the two world wars.
      2. The League machinery was less elaborate than the United Nations machinery in managing the systems established to administer the colonial areas handed over to it.
      3. Although the development of machinery to protect human rights has been extensive in western Europe, global attempts have been unsuccessful.
   D. Bilateral collective problem solving outside the domain of intergovernmental organizations is extremely extensive.

V. Collective problem solving among states involves "politics."
   A. Competitive bargaining and conflicts of interest arise out of the way these organizations deal with each other.
   B. Competitive bargaining and conflicts of interests occur when states deal with each other in solving problems collectively whether they take the ad hoc path or they use intergovernmental organizations.
   C. States employ political strategies and consider political relationships in working with other states on mutual problems.

D. *Some states create intergovernmental organizations as a part of their general foreign policy.*

E. Collective problem solving among states is no more *apolitical* than is interaction between bureaucracies and political actors in any domestic political system.

BIBLIOGRAPHICAL ESSAY

The literature is extensive on the subject of international cooperation through intergovernmental organization. The area of nongovernmental international cooperation, however, is not covered quite as well. In general, existing literature can be classified as general (treatises) or specific (case studies). Like the literature on intergovernmental organization we reviewed in Chapter 6, the literature we are discussing here is frequently devoid of middle-range theoretical discussions.

General treatises on problem solving through intergovernmental organizations can be divided into attempts to look at all activities of all such organizations and attempts to look only at those in the social and economic areas. In the first class, Jacob and Atherton (191) and Plano and Riggs (312) are two texts that approach the entire field of intergovernmental organizations from the point of view of problem solving. Other valuable texts are Levi (246) and Goodspeed (141).

Many works focus on the operations of a few institutions in only a few areas. In addition to articles in the periodical *International Organization* and short monographs in *International Conciliation,* we will suggest a *small* sample of works that might be read by an interested student. General activities of the United Nations in social and economic areas are discussed in Asher (18); Sharp in (268), and Mangone (268), examine organizational problems we have discussed—problems such as overlapping and coordination. Operations of the Trusteeship Council are studied in general by Murray (289), and in a specific situation by Chidzero (70). Chowdhuri (71) discusses both the Mandate and Trusteeship systems. Alexandrowicz (3) studies global intergovernmental organizations that are concerned with economics, while Friedmann, Kalmanoff, and Meagher (130), examine organized aid to underdeveloped states. Just a few of many case studies of particular organizations can be mentioned: Codding (76) studies the International Telecommunications Union; Briggs (50), the International Law Commission; and Landy (239), studies the ILO. Cattel (69) and Kaser (209) examine intergovernmental organizations in eastern Europe, and western European organizations are examined in such works as Haas (148) and Robertson (340).

In addition, Friedmann (129) has looked at both international law and intergovernmental organizations in terms of problem solving. Beckhoefer (31) examines the bargaining that led to creation of the International Atomic Energy Agency. Cardozo (66) investigates the impact of international cooperation on the foreign policy bureaucracy of the state. Finally, Galtung (135) systematically examines factors contributing to success or failure of summit meetings.

10

Competitive Bargaining Among States

A final class of official interactions among states may be classified as competitive bargaining interactions. Motivated by their goals and guided by their views of others, states try to influence each other in acquiring those "payoffs" they consider important. Although competitive bargaining can be a part of routine interactions (Soviet and American routine behavior over Berlin is part of a competitive bargaining strategy) as well as collective problem solving (formation of the United Nations Charter involved a great deal of bargaining), we have decided to discuss it as a separate class of interactions because it characterizes much of international politics.[1] Bargaining behavior and the patterns of activities associated with that behavior constitute a significant segment of what observers have traditionally termed "international politics."

In this chapter, we will develop a model of bargaining behavior. Like the model of foreign policy decision making in Chapter 2, the bargaining model will be illustrated by familiar examples and then applied to international politics. Similarly, because the bargaining model assumes that states act according to rational calculations on the best way to achieve objectives, it sometimes fails to describe adequately the actual patterns of competitive interactions among states.[2] Hence, while using the bargaining model to

[1] We have previously used the term "competitive bargaining" to distinguish it from collective problem solving and routine interactions although, as we have pointed out, it can be a part of the other two types of interactions. In this chapter, we will discuss how states bargain with each oher. The competitive element is implicit in the notion of bargaining although bargaining situations also involve varying degrees of cooperation (usually tacit). Therefore, we will not use the qualifying adjective "competitive" throughout the chapter. It is an artificial distinction, employed in other chapters only to maintain the distinction for purposes of discussion.

[2] In the case of the bargaining model to be employed in this chapter, one of the problems in the general international literature is that the scholars are unclear

describe international interactions, we will point out situations in which the model does not adequately explain the way states deal with each other in conflict situations.

SOME GENERAL ATTRIBUTES OF BARGAINING IN DOMESTIC SOCIETIES

Bargaining refers to a process in which two or more actors try to influence each other—that is, to change each other's behavior—in relation to a particular object. Bargaining situations arise when actors find it necessary to influence each other's behavior in order to achieve objectives. For example, the buyer of a used car finds it necessary to influence the seller of that car just as the seller finds it necessary to influence the buyer; the benefit one receives from the final transaction is interdependent with the benefits received by the other. One of the key concepts in analyzing bargaining situations is *payoff,* the value to be received from a certain condition. (See Chapter 2.) Bargaining among the actors will determine the payoffs each will receive.

Let us say that our potential buyer and seller are bargaining over the price of a used car. The seller has asked for $1,000; the buyer has offered $500. In addition, we assume that prior to the bargaining interaction the seller would be satisfied with $750 but dissatisfied with the $500 price. He might, therefore, be willing to take $600. Assuming for the sake of argument there are only four possible prices, we could assign to each price a "payoff utility"—that is, a numerical indicator of relative subjective value —to represent the seller's attitude toward the prospective sale:

Price	Payoff Utility
$500	−1
$600	0
$750	1
$1000	2

In contrast, the buyer feels that the $500 price is the best, would be satisfied with the $600 price, ambivalent towards the $750 price, and unhappy with the $1,000 price. Hence, his utilities would be:

over whether they are presenting a description of how states behave or a normative model of how they should behave. Like the author quoted in Chapter 1 (Footnote 3), many who employ bargaining models confuse description with normative and sometimes with prescriptive analysis. See also Footnote 17, this chapter.

Price	Payoff Utility
$500	2
$600	1
$750	0
$1000	−1

These payoff utilities only "represent" the general feeling about certain bargaining outcomes. They tell us that one price is more appealing than another although they do not necessarily constitute indicators that can be ascertained through empirical investigation. In this case, they are intuitively assigned for illustrative purposes.

Considering the payoff utilities, we can detect a conflict of interest between the buyer and seller; the buyer cannot receive a positive payoff unless the seller accepts a zero or minus payoff. Hence, the two actors must bargain, because the payoff each receives will be directly related to that received by the other.

One can distinguish two types of bargaining situations by looking at the payoff *matrices* (tables) of actors in a given situation. The bargaining situation in which only one party receives a positive payoff—that is, only one party is not dissatisfied with the results—is the first type, and is represented by the example above. Either the seller or the buyer, but not both, will be happy with the outcomes designated in the tables. In contrast, in some bargaining situations more than one actor will receive a positive payoff. In the above example, a $700 price would please both buyer and seller if both would receive a positive payoff of .5.

Students of bargaining behavior have developed a twofold category of games similar in some respects to the distinction above. They have distinguished between *zero-sum* games and *non-zero-sum* games. The former occurs when the winner wins as much as the loser loses, that is, positive payoff for the winner will be equivalent to negative payoff for the loser. A life-and-death struggle between two people is an example of a zero-sum game.

Actually, because payoff values are internally produced by the actors themselves, conditions of a zero-sum bargaining situation are extremely rare. A college student and a first grader pitching pennies certainly would attach different values to the loss of a penny. As a result, the concept of the non-zero-sum game has more applicability to human behavior. A non-zero-sum game assumes that there can be winners and losers, but their positions are always relative rather than absolute. Moreover, it assumes that both actors can receive negative payoffs or positive payoffs, even though one actor may gain more or lose more than the other. There is a winner and loser in the World Series, for example, but even the members of the losing team still gain (about $5,000 apiece) for their efforts. Hence, even in the most competitive situation, the results are rarely zero-sum; both sides may gain or lose even though unequally.

As two actors involved in a bargaining situation, a buyer and seller consciously or unconsciously follow a bargaining strategy, that is, a pattern of activities or tactics designed to influence each other. Four types of tactics —arguments, promises, threats, or coercion—can be part of any bargaining strategy.

First, the bargainer may use *arguments*—that is, the manipulation of symbols that will convince the other to make a decision he might not otherwise make. For example, the buyer might persuade the seller to let the car go for a lower price by saying, "I'm broke but I am really a hard-working kid supporting my mother and four sisters." The use of verbal arguments may be viewed as an attempt to change the payoff values of the other actor. By appealing to the actor's sentiment, sense of morality, or whatever, it is possible to make him change the values he has attached to certain outcomes. In the example we have been using, a good-natured car salesman might receive added benefits from selling the car cheaply to a "hard-working kid"; thus raising his utility for the $600 price from 0 to 1.

A second tool or tactic of any bargaining strategy is *making promises*. The impact of such promises would be to change the payoffs associated with bargaining outcomes. In our example, the buyer could promise to get his friends to buy from this particular salesman or the seller could offer a 90-day warranty on all parts. Many factors relating to particular circumstances and to attitudes of the actors determine the effectiveness of promises, so we will discuss them only in terms of bargaining among states.

The third tactic—the converse of the second—is *making threats*. Like promises, threats are communications among bargainers about future conditions. Unlike promises, threats involve future actions unpleasant to the actor being threatened. Threats change payoff utilities by promising to make the value of a given outcome lower than it was prior to the threat. In our example, the buyer can threaten to go elsewhere with his business while the seller can threaten by intimating that there is another buyer or that prices will go up in the near future. Threats and promises are only effective if they are believed. The actor making the threat or promise may have no intention of carrying it out, but if the other is not willing to take the chance that the first actor is bluffing, the threat might work. Determining the credibility of a given threat or promise is a crucial part of successful bargaining. Because the factors determining credibility are closely related to the particular condition and actors, we will examine them later in the context of bargaining among states.

The final tactic is *coercion;* that is, direct application of force. The buyer, for example, might steal the car (even though he is a hard-working kid) or the seller might take the money but not deliver the car. Although the alternative of coercion is not frequently employed in the type of bargaining which normally occurs in domestic society, it still remains a possibility in almost every bargaining situation.

In addition to understanding the payoffs and types of strategies available, it is also necessary to study the setting in which bargaining takes place. In our example, the buyer and seller are affected by relevant conditions in their respective environments. Our system of law and order, for example, makes strategies of direct coercion so hazardous that the ordinary buyer and seller never contemplate theft or fraud. Moreover, the market conditions or, to be more precise, the relationship of price to supply and demand, shape the behavior of actors. The buyer could easily threaten to buy from another source if used car dealers in general had too many cars and prices were depressed. Under the same conditions, the car salesman might be willing to make more promises of extra benefits and less threats of remaining inflexible on the price. While the rule of law minimizes the use of coercion, market conditions surrounding the bargaining process affect the types of threats and promises that will be made.

The environment will also determine the effectiveness of arguments as part of the bargaining strategy. In the example we have been using, the seller cannot live solely on sentiment—his wife cannot buy a new dress with the knowledge that her husband helped out a poor working kid. The attitudes of people in the social environment will greatly affect the use of arguments as a bargaining strategy. Also involved in the bargaining process is the behavior of the actors. What factors determine the way they will act in a given bargaining situation? We can roughly divide those factors into three interrelated aspects—values, capabilities, and images.

The values of an actor determine the payoff utilities he will assign to different bargaining outcomes. In formulating one's strategy, it is necessary to determine not only his evaluation of certain possible outcomes but also the values his opponent attaches to those outcomes. As we noted in Chapter 2, decision making involves making choices which in turn are based on the application of one's goals to specific courses of action. To decide on the proper strategy, the actor must know what his goals are so he will know what outcome he likes. In addition, his knowledge of his opponents' goals will enable him to choose the tactic best suited to getting his opponent to do what he wants.

Capabilities play a large role in his bargaining behavior because, among other things, they represent the basis for threats and promises. In order for a threat or promise to be credible, the actor making it must convince the other actor that he has the ability to back it up. In our example, the *money* of the buyer and the *used cars* of the seller represent their respective capabilities. Capabilities are also directly related to values of the actors. One does not have capability unless he has something, or the control over something, that someone else wants.

A final influence on behavior is the bargainer's image of the environment and of the others involved in the bargaining process. As noted in Chapters 2 and 3, an image is information that guides individuals' behavior. Images affect the payoff utilities one attaches to bargaining outcomes. The used car buyer's image of the market, for example, has a great deal to do with what he considers a good price. At the same time, images affect the choice of strategies made by the bargainers. The seller's image of the buyer, based on selling experience and hunches, will determine whether he wants to make the hard sell (clear threats and promises) or the soft sell (arguments based on what the seller purports to be detached objective opinion, with threats and promises implied).

To briefly summarize the concepts and propositions contained in our bargaining model: (1) Payoffs are products of interaction among values, capabilities, and images and involve the actors in a bargaining relationship; (2) Bargaining strategies include the mixture of four tools—arguments, promises, threats, and coercion—and are formulated as a result of the actors' estimates of each other's future behavior; and (3) The setting in which the bargaining interaction occurs affects payoffs as well as bargaining strategies. These interrelated concepts and propositions loosely form a bargaining model that can be useful in understanding bargaining among states.

THE SETTING FOR THE INTERNATIONAL BARGAINING PROCESS

The bargaining environment of the buyer and seller of used cars differs greatly from the bargaining environment for interactions among states. The economic, legal, and social conditions shaping the behavior of buyer and seller contrasts sharply, as we saw in Chapter 7, with the economic, legal, and social setting for bargaining among states.[3] In the buyer-seller situation the economic system provides clear indicators of success because the issue is primarily the price of the car. In contrast, states rarely try to influence each other over price as defined by a given currency because most of their

[3] It is suggested that the reader review Chapter 7 before reading this section (perhaps by rereading the Summary Outline following that chapter).

objectives have no price tags. The domestic legal system that makes the use of force too risky between buyer and seller is much different from international law, which hardly affects the calculations of decision makers in assessing alternatives of using force. Domestic social conditions also provide pressures in the form of personal and cultural relationships that are influential in determining the behavior of the buyer and seller. The international flow of people and ideas, as we have seen, provides only a fragmented framework with few pressures on the behavior of states.

The factors in the setting for bargaining interactions among states affect the bargaining process at its origin, at the determination of payoff utilities, at the choice of bargaining strategies, and finally at the determination of who gets what payoffs. Each of these aspects of the international bargaining process contrasts sharply with bargaining in a domestic marketplace.

In discussing the origin of any bargaining process, it is useful to make a distinction between prebargaining relations among actors and those relations that involve bargaining. An analogy with bargaining in domestic society can be instructive in illustrating the distinction. The prebargaining stage in the relationship between citizen A and citizen B exists when A inquires into B's willingness to comply with A's wish. This inquiry might be explicit (Would you mind keeping your dog off of my lawn) or tacit (Two cars approach an intersection at the same time and one must go first). If B complies, bargaining between the two does not occur. However, if B communicates a lack of willingness to comply, the bargaining process begins.

In domestic society, the highly developed structure of the economic, legal, and social systems contributes to the existence of many relatively stable prebargaining relationships. Prices are not determined every time a sale occurs, but become fixed on a semipermanent basis. One does not bargain with the bus driver over the price of a ride. The legal system defines reciprocal rights and duties so that citizens have mutual expectations about which wishes will be complied with and which will not. Property rights, for example, are protected by law. Finally, the existence of complex social institutions and conventions enables citizens to enter many relationships with each other without engaging in continuous bargaining. People form lines when waiting to get on a bus so they do not have to bargain for positions when the bus arrives.

In the interaction among states, however, the economic, legal, and social institutions are weak, as indicated in Chapter 7. This limits the frequency and scope of prebargaining interactions. To be sure, numerous types of prebargaining interactions exist in which state A makes requests that are handled automatically by state B. These comprise the routine interactions discussed in Chapter 8. Although there are many such routine interactions, however, the setting for bargaining is characterized by uncertainty over whether a given act will be handled routinely or will give rise to bargaining among the involved states.

In any setting, bargaining occurs when the behavior of one actor represents sufficient disutility to another to stimulate the latter to seek a change. The domestic environment for bargaining differs from the international setting because of laws and social conventions that reduce uncertainty over how individuals will behave. These conventions minimize the likelihood of unanticipated responses that will lead to a bargaining situation. Moreover, domestic societies have the institutional machinery to channel bargaining situations, when they occur, into certain prescribed paths. Judges and lawmakers intervene to regulate and resolve many bargaining situations. In contrast, in the international setting, law and social attitudes do not limit the occasions for bargaining situations as extensively and clearly as they do in domestic societies. Every issue can be a cause for bargaining among states because the processes for creating, adjudicating, and enforcing laws are not as effective as they are in domestic societies. While the domestic social institutions identify the issues that constitute areas of legitimate bargaining, the international setting leaves the choice of issue up to the states in a comparatively large number of cases. Hence, a dispute over distribution of territory between two states can be a stimulus for bargaining just as easily as can an insult by a public official.

If international bargaining differs from bargaining in domestic society because the distinction between prebargaining and bargaining activities is not clearly identified by law and social convention, it also differs in terms of the number of actors and the roles they perform. In domestic bargaining situations, whether a buyer-seller relationship, a litigant-respondent relationship, or a political dispute, there are usually two major actors; their opposing interests constitute the basis of the bargaining relationship. If a third actor is involved, it is usually some central institution of the society. The occasion for bargaining between private citizens often leads to the use of the courts (either directly or indirectly, as a threat). Political actors bargain with each other to form coalitions so that political institutions will make authoritative decisions by determining who wins a political office or whether a particular law is passed.

A primary characteristic of the international bargaining process is the absence of common institutions to intervene. Except in the case of actions by the UN Security Council to impose conditions on bargaining among states—something which it rarely does because it cannot get agreement among its permanent members—intergovernmental organizations can intervene in bargaining among states only if both parties are willing to allow such intervention. As we have seen, the World Court does not provide compulsory jurisdiction in most cases, and states usually choose the alternative of not using the Court. Nor can the UN General Assembly and regional intergovernmental organizations intervene without the consent of the parties because their acts do not have binding authority on the states. Moreover, the acts of such international institutions as the General Assembly do not constitute laws; bargaining over what those will be has little relationship to the end results of the bargaining process. For example, Israel and the Arab states bargain in the General Assembly to have favorable resolutions passed on their behalf, but such bargaining is only tangentially related to settlement of the real issues between the antagonists.

Although intergovernmental organizations rarely determine bargaining outcomes and then only when the states allow them to they do provide a setting through which states bargain with each other in at least two distinct ways. First, intergovernmental organizations provide communication among states. At the public level, state A's address to the General Assembly could really be intended to affect the behavior of state B and its allies. On the private level, many intergovernmental organizations provide the officials of states numerous occasions on which informal discussions can take place without public exposure. The most famous instance of private contact is when Soviet officials indicated privately to American officials at the United Nations that it was ready to consider lifting the Blockade.[4]

Intergovernmental organizations also provide a setting for bargaining among states by providing opportunities over which "deals" or exchanges of promises can be made. Electing officials, creating committees, and passing resolutions occupy much of the delegates' time in many intergovernmental organizations and particularly the United Nations. These functions provide numerous areas in which states can make tradeoffs. For example, some writers argue that some states take certain voting positions in the United Nations in return for the receipt of foreign aid.[5] Intergovernmental organizations, then, provide states with opportunities they would not otherwise have for bargaining over many objectives.

In addition to serving as a setting for bargaining, these organizations —particularly the United Nations—sometimes intervene as actors in a bargaining situation between states. As noted in Chapter 6, the Secretary-General of the United Nations frequently plays a role in mediating disputes

[4] See K. J. Holsti, "Resolving International Conflicts: A Taxonomy of Behavior and Some Figures on Procedures," *Journal of Conflict Resolution* (September, 1966), 285.

[5] See Robert Owen Keohane, "Political Influence in the General Assembly," *International Conciliation* (March, 1966), 18–20.

by providing a relatively direct communications channel between the two bargaining states. (See p. 183. The distinction between organizations as actors and as settings was developed in Chapter 6.) Because the Secretary-General maintains some independently derived prestige vis-à-vis almost all the states, he often serves to represent the pressure of the majority in a bargaining situation. For example, he usually symbolizes the desire of most states for peace when a bargaining interaction threatens to break into war.

States also frequently become involved in a bargaining situation even though they are not the major antagonists. Unlike domestic bargaining, where opposing sides tend to polarize, international bargaining always involves interested third parties. Frequently, this is because one way to convince a state to change its policy is to convince other states to join in pressuring that state. Just as frequently, most of the states not directly involved in a bargaining situation will be concerned with the danger that violence might start and involve them. Hence, they attempt to pressure the bargaining states to refrain from the use of force, if not the threat, by acting as a mediating communication channel (similar to the Secretary-General of the United Nations) or by threatening to oppose the first state that uses force. No matter what the strategy of the state that plays the role of third party in a bargaining situation, however, the fact that such a role is frequently played by many states is a clear feature of the international bargaining process.

Not only is the international bargaining process different from bargaining in domestic society regarding the origins of the situation as well as the number and role of bargainers, it is also different in terms of payoff determinations. Although the domestic buyer and seller are only responsible to themselves (and perhaps families and friends), a number of factors affect payoff utilities for foreign policy decision makers. We have seen how difficult it is to determine and rank foreign policy goals. We have also seen how many internal pressures from policy influencers must be considered when making foreign policies. These two conditions make determination of payoff utilities extremely difficult. Cross pressures, lack of precise goals, and complex conditions make payoffs amorphous. In most cases, states lack criteria by which to evaluate clear success and failure, so they often bargain with vaguely defined payoff utilities.

Given the nature of foreign policy goals and the alternatives available, negative payoffs are much stronger than positive ones. As noted in Chapter 2, foreign policy decision makers attached negative values to "loss" of national security but found it difficult to measure "increase" in national security. In addition, decision makers also attach negative value to the dissatisfaction of important policy influence groups. They are frequently criticized but rarely applauded by groups trying to influence decisions. A loss of "prestige" or national honor is often felt by policy influencers but a gain is rarely felt. Positive payoffs are difficult to discern because it appears easier to know when you are losing than when you are winning.

There are also differences in the effect of the environment on the choice and effectiveness of bargaining strategies. Economic, legal, and social systems within domestic society significantly shape the use of arguments, threats, promises, and coercion in bargaining between a buyer and seller, but the environment for bargaining among states is much less constraining. The nature of the international setting for bargaining gives a different role to the four elements of strategy.

Attempts to influence states through arguments frequently occur. Appeals to morality, law, ideology, peace, or the interests of the "world community" are frequently found in public statements of leaders of many states. However, the absence of substantial agreement on social and political ideas limits the basis for argument as an effective bargaining tool. Only the appeal to peace seems to influence payoff utilities of states, but this appeal is often viewed as a ploy. Despite opportunities to engage in lengthy if not endless discourses, argumentation is a weak tool in the pursuit of foreign policy goals.

Promises are as important in the international bargaining process as they are in any bargaining situation. If politics is the art of compromise, promises constitute the road to compromise. In the domestic political system a stable environment exists for making and keeping promises. The legal system creates and enforces conditions for contracts; individuals making contractual promises break them only at the risk of punishment from the system. Furthermore, routinized behavior and use of laws to implement policy decisions provide opportunity for bargainers to make useful promises across a wide range of issues.

In contrast, the international setting does not provide a stable environment for promises. The treaty is similar to the contract in that it states promises in legally binding terms. However, the ineffectiveness of the legal system in enforcing compliance renders many treaties inoperative, especially those that are likely to be made in political bargaining. Stalin is said to have remarked that "treaties are like piecrust, made to be broken."[6] This statement should not be taken as an indication of the bad faith of Stalin, Russians, or Communists but rather as an example of the general aware-

---

[6] I am unable to cite a source for this quotation. However, it is not dissimilar from the attitude held by many decision makers and writers. It can be traced back to the Thomas Hobbes statement: "Covenants, without swords, are but words, and of no strength to secure a man at all." (*Leviathan,* Chapter 17).

ness that promises represented in treaties are binding only so long as they are acceptable to the states that made them. At the same time, however, it is important to realize that the state that habitually breaks its promises will not be able to use promises as an effective bargaining tool in the future. In addition, the desire for reciprocity often leads states to make good on their promises even if they are unhappy about it.

Furthermore, the lack of a centralized legislative process to implement policy decisions made by the states limits opportunity for making promises that are specific enough to be judged. Unlike the domestic politician, who can see if a promise to vote for a bill he favored is in fact kept, the state that has been promised political support often finds it difficult to know if that support has been forthcoming. Except for specific economic promises or for votes in intergovernmental organizations, promises among states involve amorphous commitments. They can be made in very general terms that render the promised state unable to assess whether the promises were in fact kept.

Threats are extremely important in the international bargaining process. Absence of a centralized legal system creates conditions allowing for a broad range of threats. In the domestic political system, there is a sharp distinction between legal and illegal threats. For example, it is legal to threaten a fellow politician with public denunciation, but it is illegal to threaten his life. In contrast, a weakness of international law is that it fails to make a clear-cut distinction between legal and illegal tactics in practice; no central institutions exist to apply and enforce the law. Hence, states frequently employ the threat of force.

Use of force is not the only act threatened by states when bargaining with each other. Economic threats play a role, although as even the most one-sided economic relationship usually gives rise to mutual dependence; this makes economic threats risky and only partially effective. (See Chapter 6.) If, for example, the United States wishes to threaten to withdraw aid from an underdeveloped state, it must face the possibility that the state might nationalize American business or might look to the Soviet Union or another developed state for aid. Threats are also made at the level of acts that will affect the policy influencers of the threatened state. For example, decision makers in state A might threaten to reveal the nature of certain negotiations between it and state B that will cause an uproar in state B.

Finally, we must note that direct use of force to achieve an objective continues to have a quasi-acceptable role in the international political system—quasi-acceptable because the situation is unclear. On the one hand, a number of international legal documents such as the UN Charter, the Kellogg-Briand Pact, and the Nuremburg Trials clearly outlaw the use of force except for self-defense. In addition, decision makers and policy influencers in most states hold that peace must be preserved and force should be used only as a last resort. On the other hand, instances of the use of force have not diminished sufficiently since these documents have been promulgated to warrant our assuming that the prohibition is accepted. To qualify, the use of force as a means of directly achieving objectives has diminished slightly and the use of force as part of a strategy of threat has increased, but the limitations placed by the system itself on the use of force are still weak.

Bargaining activities among states, then, are greatly affected by the international setting as described in Chapter 7. The autonomy enjoyed by the state is a corollary of the lack of centralized political, social, economic, and legal institutions that characterize the system. The line between prebargaining and bargaining interactions among states is continuously shifting so that the states themselves usually decide which issues will stimulate bargaining relationships. The payoffs states attach to bargaining outcomes are also continuously shifting so that tactics that worked in one situation might not work in another. The tactics themselves are also affected by the lack of accepted, authorized international institutions. As a result, threats and coercion play a larger role in international political bargaining than they do in domestic political bargaining.

DYNAMICS OF BARGAINING TACTICS

In this section, we plan to discuss factors affecting the choice and effectiveness of these four general bargaining tactics. As we have already indicated, each tactic aims at changing the payoff utilities of the actors. Arguments are used to convince the bargainer that, given his own values, his initial evaluation of payoffs was wrong. Promises introduce extra benefits to change the initial payoff utilities. Threats introduce added costs. Direct coercion also changes payoff utilities because if presented as a *fait accompli,* the actor must deal with new conditions. If engaged in as a prolonged military encounter, new payoffs are introduced in the form of costs of continuing or benefits of ending the war.

In assessing the effectiveness of various bargaining strategies, we must not only take into account the capabilities, values, and images of the actors, but we must also examine the role of communication. Each of the four tactics involve both verbal and tacit (in the sense of the meaning attached to specific actions) communications. Although it would be a mistake to assume that the medium of communication constitutes the entire message, it would be equally serious not to assume that the form of communication often directly affects the substance of the message.

Arguments

We have already indicated that lack of shared values and images among members of the international political system weakens the role of arguments in the bargaining process. The domestic politician can appeal to patriotism or national security to convince policy influencers that a given policy is less undesirable than they might think, but foreign policy decision makers cannot appeal to decision makers and policy influencers in other countries on the basis of allegiance to a world state. There is no strong feeling of common destiny or even a tie to a common past to serve as unifying symbols for bargaining arguments.

Two related themes have served in recent years, however, as a common focal point for arguments that might be used in bargaining situations. The first is the common danger of widescale war which, as we will see in Chapter 11, represents an important factor in contemporary international politics. Appeals to international peace and security, when not used as a threat or a promise by the appealing state (in which case they are not considered arguments) are a part of the rhetoric of almost every contemporary foreign policy decision maker. Although it is difficult to judge how much impact the rhetoric has on the foreign policy decisions, international peace is a common symbol often used when a state tries to convince another to change its payoff utilities in a specific situation.

The other theme that has recently become a frequent part of foreign policy speeches is the unity of mankind. The emphasis is not only on international security but also on the social and economic implications of the interdependence of all mankind in the contemporary world. Again, the rhetoric probably does not have much of an impact, but it does represent a common symbol decision makers might use in making arguments. It probably has greater appeal for some of the policy influencers of states than for the decision makers themselves. Given the substantial inequality among the different states in the system, it usually is a symbol employed by those wanting basic social and economic changes.

As a bargaining tactic, decision makers may direct their arguments to two different targets within any given state. They may try to change the payoff utilities of decision makers by trying to convince them of a need to reevaluate the situation. Or they may try to convert policy influencers to their position so that they in turn will try to force the decision makers to reevaluate. The choice of target is related to the type of issue involved in the bargaining situation. If state A is trying to get state B to adopt a more supportive policy towards A and a less supportive policy toward state C, the decision makers in A would probably try to change the minds of both decision makers and policy influencers in B. However, in a narrower issue, such as the need to reach an agreement on administering a common body of water, arguments would be directed to the decision makers and more specialized policy influencers.

One important element in the use of arguments is the ability to have the message reach groups and individuals it should reach. In addition to normal diplomatic channels, public statements both within and outside intergovernmental organizations can be used to accomplish this goal. Propaganda in the form of radio broadcasts or published material can also be disseminated, particularly in reaching the policy influencers. In addition, if a state wishes to use an intergovernmental organization as a platform, it must be a member to present arguments to a number of states simultaneously.

One can change a person's payoff utilities through arguments either by changing that person's image of a given situation or by altering his interpretation of his values. British decision makers, for example, might highly value the protection of the Suez Canal as long as they maintain an image which views the canal as an essential part of British national security. If their image of the world is changed, as it appears it has been in recent years, Britain's commitment to maintenance of the canal will change. Similarly, their conception of the value of national security might also change. Some policy influencers in Great Britain, particularly partisan leftwing groups, do not consider national security the highest priority value. In fact, some consider it a negative value. If British decision makers also felt this way, they would assign very different payoffs to given conditions.[7]

Despite the fact that decision makers continue to use arguments in dealing with each other as well as with each other's policy influencers, arguments play only a subsidiary role in the foreign policy strategies of states. Often when the officials of a state use arguments alone—without threats, promises, or coercion—it is assumed that the state is only half-heartedly pursuing the objectives involved. The lack of common symbols to provide a universal, influential reference for men throughout the world, lessens the impact of arguments as a bargaining tactic. Most decision makers and many policy influencers do not take foreign policy propaganda very seriously. Even more than the bargaining between the buyer and seller, then, arguments that appeal to sentiment, morality, or law and that do not imply threats or promises play only a secondary role in the final outcome of bargaining situations.

[7] For a representation of British attitudes leading to the Suez crisis of 1956, see Leon D. Epstein, *British Politics in the Suez Crisis* (Urbana, Ill.: University of Illinois Press, 1964).

Promises

In dealing with states, leaders often use promises to change payoffs. Promises can involve economic commitments, military support, or political support in the form of alliances or voting in the United Nations. As pointed out earlier, sometimes these promises are formalized in treaties while at other times they are based on tacit understanding. The term "quid pro quo" has been long used to indicate the important role played by the exchange of promises in international politics, and is as much a part of the international scene as it is of domestic politics.

Techniques for communicating promises are extremely important. Often the nature and conditions of promises are such that decision makers try to prevent their own policy influencers and/or other states from knowing about them. For this reason, they are often made on a personal level, as (it is assumed) for example, the promises exchanged by President Kennedy and the Soviet Union's Premier Khrushchev to resolve the 1962 Cuban missile crisis.[8] Other promises might be openly expressed and formalized in treaties. Open negotiation may precede the making of final promises while treaties may be employed to try to ensure that promises are carried out in the way intended by the parties. Many treaties are now registered with the Secretariat of the United Nations. Even so, as we have already noted, they are not always considered binding.

Promises are not always offered and made through negotiation or even explicit discussion. Under certain conditions, promises may be suggested and even agreed upon in the bargaining process by each side making certain interpretations of the words and actions of the other side. In the Korean war, for example, China and the United States tacitly agreed not to attack certain areas.[9] Although it was never explicitly stated during the war, both sides came to act as if such an agreement had been reached.

Tacit bargaining in offering and making promises is used for a number of reasons. First, if the tacitly made promise is not accepted by the target state, the rebuff can also be made tacitly so the state that made the promise is not openly slighted. This factor is particularly important when decision makers offer promises that are unpopular with their policy influencers. Second, by tacitly communicating promises, the initiating state can leave what almost amounts to a blank check open to the target state. The blank can be filled in by the bargaining state so that the offering state need not

---

[8] For information on the Cuban missile crisis, see our discussion in Chapter 2. See also David L. Larson, *The "Cuban Crisis" of 1962* (Boston: Houghton-Mifflin, 1963) and Elie Abel, *The Missile Crisis* (New York: Lippincott, 1965).

[9] Discussion of the nature of limited warfare, particularly in terms of the limitations during the Korean war, can be found in Morton H. Halperin, *Limited War in the Nuclear Age* (New York: Wiley, 1963).

overestimate what is necessary. If the target state asks for too much, the tacit conditions of the offer allow the initiating state to "tear up the check." In short, tacit promises involve less commitment and are less binding than explicit promises.

Whether or not the promise will be effective in changing the target state's behavior in the bargaining situation after it receives the message depends on two other factors. First, will the promise be believed by the target state; second, will the promise have enough appeal to convince decision makers to reassess the payoff they initially attached to a particular bargaining outcome?

The question of the degree to which a promise will be believed may be viewed as a question of credibility: How credible is the promise? Credibility depends upon two things—the capability and the willingness of the state making the promise *as perceived by the target state.* If state A promises foreign aid to state B in exchange for support in the United Nations, B (the target) must believe that A is both capable and willing to give the foreign aid. Hence, B's image of A's capability to make good on its promise as well as B's image of A's willingness to keep the promise will determine the credibility of the promise as seen by B. B's belief in A's capability and willingness is more crucial to success than A's capability and willingness to keep the promise.

Therefore, the key to credibility of a state's promise depends to a great extent on the image other states maintain, and past experience has a great deal to do with that image and with actual credibility of a state's promises. If A has a reputation for failing to carry out promises, its use of promises as a bargaining tool will be limited. For this reason, most states seek to make good on the majority of their promises. Bad faith can be just as damaging to the bargaining strategy of a state as poor credit can be to the bargaining power of a buyer in a market situation.

Even if a promise is credible, however, it might not produce the kind of behavior the promising state aims at. The promise must involve something valued by decision makers and/or policy influencers of the target state. One key to successful political strategy at any level is the ability to judge what is needed to get people to do what is wanted. This is as true for local politicians as it is for foreign policy leaders. However, it is frequently easier said than done. States might not have the capability to provide what is really desired by a state they wish to influence—even if they were able to ascertain what that would be. Sometimes, decision makers make promises aimed at certain policy influencers rather than at the decision makers. Even this action, however, does not always provide a basis for offering promises that will have the desired effect.

It might be useful to illustrate the types of promises often made between states. Economic promises of aid, trade, and investment are frequently used, particularly in bargaining between developed and underdeveloped states. Promises of military support can be both defensive and offensive. Examples are the Warsaw Pact and the North Atlantic Treaty Organization, which are supposed to be designed to counter an attack from outside the respective pacts, and the agreement among Frederick the Great of Prussia, Catherine the Great of Russia, and Joseph II of Austria to "partition" Poland in the late eighteenth century. Promises in relation to voting and general "politicking" in intergovernmental organizations have become more important in recent years with the growth of such organizations. The United States, for example, has been accused of "buying" voting support for its position on Communist China in exchange for a more anticolonialist stand vis-à-vis Portugal in General Assembly voting. Political promises can also be exchanged in relation to policy influencers. For example, a state visit by a high dignitary can sometimes enhance the popularity of the regime in the host state. Finally, promises between two states relating to a third state have an important role particularly in the formation of alliances and counteralliances in the contemporary world.

The question of timing and commitment is also important. In a quid pro quo situation, the state that makes good on its end of the bargain first has certain disadvantages. Primarily, it must depend on the good faith of its counterpart. For this reason, states often attempt to fulfill promises simultaneously so that the question of trust is not so crucial. However, certain promises involve future behavior and preclude simultaneous promises. To reduce the risk associated with long-term promises, states often make commitments to insure the keeping of their promises. For example, the United States backed its promise to defend Europe when it placed troops there. An attack on Europe would presumably result in the loss of American lives so that the United States would automatically maintain its commitment. This commitment is viewed as insurance that the United States will keep its promise to defend western Europe.

A final point, particularly in the dynamics of the quid pro quo, is the nature of the promises to be exchanged. Generally speaking, a quid pro quo that involves a specific promise for one state and a very general promise for the other is unstable. In the 1930's, for example, France and England made a number of immediately effective deals that involved tangible events when they allowed Germany to remilitarize the Rhineland and partition Czechoslovakia.[10] In exchange, Hitler made vague promises

[10] For a discussion of international politics in the 1930's, see E. H. Carr, *International Relations Between the Two World Wars, 1919–1939* (New York: St. Martin's Press, 1947).

to maintain the peace. The exchange, by Great Britain and France, of a specific, self-executing promise for Germany's general, ill-defined promise was doomed to failure at the outset. In effect the two democracies got nothing in return for very important gifts, but to take them back would have resulted in the war they were seeking to avoid. Therefore, when promises are exchanged, the terms of the promises greatly affect the final outcome.

Threats

Threats are very similar to promises in the international bargaining process because they must be credible and they must affect the values of the target state. Because the use of force in the international system is only slightly and, at best, imperfectly restricted, the role of threats is important. Threats of force are, of course, cheaper than the use of force because they involve communication rather than coercion; they are often used. Again, the means of communication and the interaction of capabilities, values, and images are extremely important.

Techniques for communicating threats are complex and numerous. The direct verbal statement made in private or public is often chosen as the instrument to communicate a threat. The statement itself may tacitly make a threat or it may state clear conditions of the threat, including under what circumstances it will be carried out. Sometimes, leaders address each other when making threats, as in the Cuban missile crisis. At other times, they address some audience of policy influencers or allies. Infrequently, the threats are made before an intergovernmental organization. The choice of audience is often important because it indicates the seriousness of the threat. A bellicose statement made before members of a military group would have different implications than the same statement made before the UN General Assembly.

Threats are also communicated through specific actions. Military activity such as the mobilization of troops is often employed to communicate a military threat, even though in the context of modern military technology mobilization has more symbolic than operational significance. The act of sending troops to an ally is also often used to communicate to potential enemies of the alliance that the alliance represents a credible threat. The axiom "actions speak louder than words" is just as true in international bargaining as it is in any human relation.

The way a threat is communicated—that is, the words and actions used to communicate it—often has an impact on credibility. The key element in this respect is the degree of precision and specificity used in the terms of the threat. A threat involves a statement of what the threatening state will do to the target state if the target state does not do what the threatener wants it to do. Hence, the state that makes the threat has the option of being specific or general about (1) what it wants the target state to do and (2) what it will do if the target state does not do it. In addition, the time element is often important. A threat with no time limits creates much less tension and is perhaps less credible than a threat with limits.

In fact, the more general the terms, the less seriously the threatened state is likely to take the threat. For example, threats made by England and France toward Hitler in the period between the wars were not as precise as those the United States has made to the Soviet Union over conditions in postwar Europe. As a result, Hitler took his threateners a lot less seriously than decision makers in the Soviet Union have taken the United States. Although all general threats are not inappropriate, however, as it would appear that John Foster Dulles' doctrine of "massive retaliation" indicates, we should assume that specifically stated threats are inherently more credible because the threatener cannot easily back down.

The reason for this is that identification of specific conditions creates a firmer commitment. It then becomes more difficult to interpret events that might occur as not being contrary to conditions posited by the threatener. For example, if the United States were to threaten that "Soviet interference in Latin America will result in a serious increase in tension," the general nature of the threat would allow hedging by the American government. Certain Soviet actions could be excused as noninterference; conversely, the United States could "increase tension" by moving a few ships rather than actually engaging the Soviet Union in combat. Threats which state only general conditions, then, allow the threatening state a great deal of flexibility but at the same time tend to reduce the credibility of the threat.

If a state can increase the credibility of its threats by increasing the degree of precision in the conditions of the threats, it also runs the risk of cutting down the flexibility necessary to bargain. If, in an attempt to preserve the territorial status quo, state A threatens against state B's acquisition of territory, B might successfully gain control over the territory in question by establishing a puppet regime. Because the United States clearly identified territorial acquisition as unacceptable, the Soviet Union appears to have abstained from direct territorial aggrandizement following World War II. At the same time, however, the Soviet Union did succeed in gaining indirect control over many eastern European states through puppet regimes. Hence, the gain in credibility a state receives by making threats with specific conditions is frequently balanced by a loss in flexibility to deal with different conditions.

The credibility of a threat is also affected by the capability of the threatening state. With increased capability, the costs of executing the threat usually diminishes; in turn, credibility increases. The capability behind a threat is determined not only by the economic-military strength of a state but also by support from its policy influencers and from other states in the system.

The strength of a state's economic-military system (see Chapter 4) has a direct impact on its ability to carry out threats. The stronger its military and economic capability, the greater its ability to make a wide range of threats with some credibility. Although credibility also depends on the target state to *perceive* the capability of the threatening state, one can assume that the stronger the state, the greater the likelihood that it will be perceived to be stronger.

The support policy influencers give to decision makers also has an impact on the decision makers' ability to carry out threats. If economic and military resources are tied down by the demands of the policy influencers, the decision makers will not have the resources for threats directed outside the country. For example, Indonesia has a large army but has not been able to seriously threaten its neighbors—partly because the army has been busy keeping internal order. In addition, substantial opposition from policy influencers will weaken the ability of decision makers to carry out the threat. Lack of internal support, either for the regime generally or for specific foreign policies, can have an adverse effect on the credibility of threats made by foreign policy decision makers.

Political support from other states is another crucial factor. When a state is surrounded by enemies, as for example Germany has been since the end of the nineteenth century, its ability to make and carry out threats is weakened. In addition, alliance patterns have a great deal of impact on economic and military capability. On the one hand, the threatening state's allies can contribute to its overall economic and military capability as a product of alliances. On the other hand, the target state is deprived of potential political, economic, and military support it might receive if it could get the threatening state's allies into its camp. Because the economic, military, and political support accruing from alliances add to the capability of a state, the formation and maintenance of alliances is an ever-present aspect of the international bargaining process.

Of course, capability is only part of credibility. Threats, like promises, are credible only if others perceive the threatener to be both able and willing to carry out the threat, and willingness is even more difficult to ascertain than capability. It depends on relative values attached to different outcomes as well as the decision maker's ability to carry out a threat. We might assume the greater the capability the greater the willingness, but that is not always the case. States whose capabilities are diminishing and whose decision makers have poor support from their policy influencers will often be more determined to carry out a threat than those with increasing capabilities and policy influencer support. In short, weakness does not always detract from credibility. If the decision makers have little to lose because of weak political support, or the state has little to lose because of a precarious international position or a weak economy, they might be willing to take greater risks by carrying out threats than decision makers enjoying a relatively strong position. Rousseau's comment that slaves have nothing to lose but their chains illustrates this point quite well at the domestic level. The saying often holds true for the weak at the international level.

It is often difficult (but not impossible) to make threats credible because negative payoffs usually exist for both sides. When state A threatens state B in order to increase B's risk of increased costs if it does not comply with A's demands, A also incurs risks of increased costs. An economic boycott, for example, will not only harm the target state; it may also harm the boycotter. To threaten such a boycott increases the risks of high costs for both target and threatening states. Consequently, the state making the threat has to convince the target state that it is willing to incur the cost if the threat has to be carried out.

Because the credibility problem confronts every state that tries to use threats, many decision makers attempt to make the carrying out of a threat as automatic as possible through the act of commitment. Commitments involve actions made in the past or present that appear to bind the state for future actions. A self-executing commitment, that is, one that forces the threatening state to follow through, cuts down on the flexibility of the decision makers but at the same time makes their threats more credible. The most obvious example in the contemporary world is the United States troop commitment to western Europe. By placing American troops on western European soil, the United States is making a commitment which, it is assumed, will force her to come to the defense of Europe in case of attack. Whether or not this commitment is as much of a "trip-wire" as some assume is open to question; it is possible (although highly improbable for the foreseeable future) that the United States would not respond to an attack on its armed forces in western Europe.

Commitments reduce the degree of control the threatening party has over the consequences of the target state's ignoring the threats. While commitment to western Europe, for example, makes American threats more credible because it implies that American decision makers would have no option but to protect western Europe if it were under attack, it also involves a substantial reduction in flexibility because it tends to place the responsibility for control on the shoulders of the target state. The Soviet Union, for example, can "force" (or to be more precise, almost force) America to make good on its commitment.

Credibility of threats is also greatly affected by the history of the threatening state. Failure to carry out a threat at one point in time is often viewed as an indicator that the state will not carry out future threats. For example, the failure of Britain and France in 1936 to back up their pledge to keep the Rhineland demilitarized indicated a general weakness that Hitler exploited in succeeding years. At the same time, however, it is important to point out that foreign policy decision makers would be mistaken to assume that prior failures to keep commitments automatically means that future commitments will not be kept. Austrian and German decision makers in the early twentieth century found this out the hard way. When the 1914 crisis occurred with the death of the Archduke of Austria, Austria—backed by Germany—threatened to attack Serbia in spite of Russia's guarantees to protect the small Slavic nation. Assuming that Russia's previous failures to protect the Balkan states in eastern Europe was a good indication of what she would do in 1914, Austria and Germany did not consider the Russian commitment credible. However, precisely because Russia had failed to make good on previous commitments to the Slavic states, she felt compelled to uphold her commitment in 1914.[11] Although the record of events has a definite bearing on the credibility of threats, one can never be sure how the record will affect both the threatener and the target. Credibility is a complex phenomenon, and images of the past possessed by the parties involved play an important, but difficult to predict, role.

Even if the credibility of the threat is high, however, the threat can be effective only if it changes the payoffs of the target state. The threatening state must make a credible threat to the target state involving an action the target state would find unsatisfactory. Moreover, the negative payoff for the target state must be greater than the negative feeling resulting from compliance with the terms of the threat. For this reason, as the stakes of the bargaining process increase, the number of situations in which decision makers are susceptible to threats decreases. If state A wants a small concession from state B, it can make threats that involve negative costs much greater than those of the concession. However, if state A wants three-quarters of state B's land, there is little that state A can threaten that would have more negative payoff for state B than the actual achievement of the objectives.

The dynamics of escalation are relevant here. As one threat fails, the natural tendency is for the threatening state to employ a threat with greater negative consequences. If that threat does not produce the desired behav-

---

[11] For analysis of events leading up to World War I, see A. J. P. Taylor, *The Struggle for Mastery in Europe* (New York: Oxford University Press, 1954).

ior, the threatening state may have to carry out the threat or cease making threats. Again, the natural tendency is for the threatening state to make another threat that has more negative payoff than the earlier ones. Knowledge of this tendency does not always prevent the leaders of states from falling into the trap; this is clearly illustrated by United States bombing of North Vietnam from 1965 to 1968.[12] In those years, the United States alternately threatened and then executed bombing raids on Vietnam of increasing severity and scope hoping to convince North Vietnam to stop its support of and intervention in the war against South Vietnam. Each time the threat failed, the United States threatened more severe actions.

Threats need not involve only the use of force, although they ultimately depend on some coercive capability. Economic threats such as trade or aid restriction, retaliation against property of aliens within the threatening state, and embargo—that is, trying to prevent the passage of any economic goods into the country—have been used by states in different situations. In the military area, the use of alliances, troop mobilization, and force itself are all employed to indicate military attack. The attack itself can take numerous forms. Air strikes, sabotage, and conventional or subversive warfare can be threatened. Of course, the nuclear powers can also threaten to use nuclear weapons, but the high risks involved have led them in recent years to reserve nuclear threats for only the most vital issues. In the political area, decision makers of states can threaten to withdraw support of alliances, to withdraw support of policy positions within intergovernmental organizations, or to join the opposing side. Pakistan has threatened the United States with each of these moves in efforts to get American help in its dispute with India. In addition, leaders have often threatened to take action to weaken political support for the regime within the state. Withdrawal of foreign aid is sometimes more of a threat to lessen the domestic support for the regime than it is to harm the target state as a whole.

Although threats are intended to make a state do something it would not otherwise do, as Schelling has pointed out, threats can be used either to deter or to compel.[13] In deterrence, state A threatens state B by saying, "If you do 'x,' I will do 'y.' " State A only has to carry out the threat if state B takes action on "x." This is usually called deterrence because the threat is used to deter or prevent the other state from acting in a particular manner. In contrast, some threats are used to force the threatened state to change its present policy. It involves the proposition, "If you do not stop

---

[12] For an analysis of the bargaining implications of United States policy in Vietnam, see Thomas C. Schelling, *Arms and Influence* (New Haven, Conn.: Yale University Press, 1966).

[13] *Arms and Influence*, pp. 69–91.

doing 'x,' I will do 'y.' " This has been called compellance because the target state must actually alter its present policy in order to avoid retaliation.

Contemporary U.S. foreign policy has employed threats to compel as well as to deter. In the Cuban missile crisis, the United States was successful in compelling the Soviet Union to remove its missiles from Cuba. In the Vietnam situation, however, the United States has attempted with little success to compel the North Vietnamese regime to change its existing policy and withdraw from participation in the war in South Vietnam. The use of threats to deter other states has also been a part of contemporary American foreign policy. In fact, the general policy of containment may be viewed as a massive attempt to deter or prevent certain actions of the Soviet Union.

Whether employing threats to compel or deter, however, foreign policy decision makers find threats a necessary part of their foreign policy. Threats are products of interaction of numerous factors ranging from capabilities and values to images held by the other party; they represent an essential element of the international bargaining process.

Use of Force

We have already discussed how the use of force affects the other three tools of foreign policy bargaining. The common fear of warfare plays a major role in the rhetoric of statecraft while promises in the form of alliances and counteralliances, and threats of using force or increasing the intensity of its use continue to play a major role in international politics. In this section, we will examine how the actual application of force is employed by states by examining its use as (1) a way of communicating a bargaining position, (2) a way to radically alter an existing situation by presenting a *fait accompli*, (3) a means of inflicting punishment to alter bargaining utilities, and (4) a means of destroying the enemy completely.

States frequently make a limited application of force to communicate a bargaining position. The Israelis, for example, after their defeat of the Arab coalition in June 1967, countered an isolated attack by the United Arab Republic on an Israeli military vessel with a strike aimed only at Egyptian oil refineries. This limited strike was designed to communicate to Egypt that Israel was not going to accept further military attacks without severe retaliation. In cases of this type, it appears that actions speak louder than words because they effectively deterred further UAR attacks in the following months, although not indefinitely.

The use of force to communicate a bargaining position does not always mean that the state using the force is seeking to make threats more credible. Frequently, states employ force on a ritualized and limited basis to indicate their willingness to accept the *status quo* for the time being. The heavy guard placed on both sides of the borders between eastern and western Europe, for example, indicates the firmness of the United States and the Soviet Union as well as their willingness to accept given conditions. Similarly, the sporadic firing with no clear increase on Quemoy and Matsu by the Red Chinese can be interpreted as indication that the Chinese are willing to accept conditions for the time being although, as Charles McClelland has indicated, China occasionally increases the firings to provoke a crisis or communicate additional concern.[14]

Because consistent application of force over time indicates a willingness to accept conditions even while appearing to protest them, it is often necessary for the threatening state to escalate military actions as a way of communicating the threat. Applying the same amount of force over time, without escalating either by extending the geographical scope of attacks or increasing the intensity of the attack, might be interpreted as a tacit willingness of the state to accept existing conditions. Hence, escalation is a natural tendency when states use force to communicate threats unless, of course, the threats are initially successful.

The use of force to achieve a *fait accompli* is a tactic states frequently use. When attempting to achieve a limited objective, especially acquisition of control of a relatively small piece of territory, states will strike unannounced, hoping to catch the enemy off guard. For example, India's takeover of Goa in 1962 involved the quick and decisive move of Indian troops into Goa with no resistance from the Portuguese authorities that had controlled Goa for over five centuries. Hitler also used the technique effectively in the period between world wars when he remilitarized the Rhineland, took over Austria, and absorbed what was left of Czechoslovakia after the partition of 1938.

The *fait accompli* is an extremely limited tool because it can be used in few instances. The primary consideration is that the objective must be small; victory can be so swift that the other state does not have time to form opposition to the move. More than a day or two can be too long, particularly with the speed of modern communication and transportation.

The *fait accompli* should not always be considered the end of the bargaining process over a particular issue. Rather, it should be examined as a technique for changing the bargaining positions of both sides. India, for example, could only threaten Portugal if the latter failed to pull out of Goa —that is, a threat to achieve compellance—while Portugal still controlled

---

[14] Charles A. McClelland, "Action Structures and Communications in Two International Crises: Quemoy and Berlin," *Background,* 7 (February 1964), 68–77.

the enclave. However, once India successfully occupied the area, she then only had to threaten Portugal against coming back, that is, a threat to deter rather than compel Portugal. Although the military capability of the two states was not particularly affected by the change in territorial control, the different conditions radically altered the position of the two states as bargaining agents over Goa. In this case, the *fait accompli* only changed conditions surrounding the bargaining, giving India a decisive edge.

The third use of force is the attempt to inflict punishment on a state or states which cannot otherwise be persuaded to comply with the wishes of the attacking state. Whether attempting to acquire a piece of territory or merely defending against an attack by another state, the use of force to inflict punishment can be effective in convincing the target state to change its policy. When both sides engage in hostilities, the damage each is doing to the other becomes a factor in determining which side will comply with the other's wishes first. An attacking state seeks to inflict sufficient punishment to force the target state to accept its terms; the defending state has the option of counterattacking—in effect, inflicting punishment on the attacker so he will refrain from attacking. Or the defender may defend against the attack to limit its destructive effect. No matter what the tactics, however, the use of force to punish still remains an essential part of the international bargaining process.

In contemporary times, three types of warfare—conventional, subversive, and nuclear—have become possible. Each has a particular effect on the payoff structure of any bargaining situation. (Military capability is discussed in Chapter 4.)

In the traditional, conventional use of force the attacking side may use land, sea, and air capability to destroy as much of the enemy as possible. In the case of massive attacks, the attacking side is usually engaged in direct combat with the defending side. Both civilian and military targets may be involved, not only because the civilian sector provides economic capability for the military, but also because punishment directed at the civilian sector might raise the cost sufficiently to change the bargaining payoffs. A conventional war may be limited almost solely by military capability as, for example, World War II. Limitations on geographical scope and military intensity may result from tacit political agreement, as in the Korean war.

Subversive warfare, in contrast to conventional war, is employed when a military disadvantage or other conditions make conventional warfare difficult or undesirable. Subversive warfare benefits the weaker military power because it minimizes the risk of a direct military confrontation, but it is also used by strong states that, for one reason or another, do not want open warfare. Because it minimizes military confrontation, however, it inflicts punishment at a slower rate than conventional warfare. States using guerrilla tactics, then, are trading time and intensity for the safety of their small military forces. Subversive warfare is most often used by a military force within the state seeking to overthrow the regime. For example, underground forces in France during World War II used guerrilla tactics against German occupying authorities just as Vietnamese nationalists used subversive warfare against French authorities in the late 1940's and early 1950's. Subversive warfare is a slow, but relatively effective tool for weaker military powers. Its success depends upon the loyalty and endurance of the fighting men as well as the logistic support it can receive from sources within and outside the fighting areas.

Nuclear warfare is similar to conventional warfare because it is a technique for inflicting a great deal of punishment in a very short period of time; it represents an immense increase in the destructive power of military weapons. Together with its ability to demolish large areas and the second-ary effects of the destruction of human life through radiation, nuclear war constitutes a serious threat to all of mankind. Some analysts, in fact, consider it to have completely changed the role of force as a bargaining tool.[15] The Soviet Union or the United States could destroy so much of any given nation within hours that the decision makers of the target state would almost have to capitulate on any terms. Nuclear weapons can be aimed at civilian targets or military targets, or both, although the effects of radiation and flash fires would make it difficult to pinpoint destruction accurately. Despite the hope that a nuclear exchange can be limited to certain targets, and despite the great military efficiency resulting from the use of nuclear weapons, the nuclear powers so far have refrained from using these weapons ever since the first atomic bombs were dropped on Hiroshima and Nagasaki to end World War II. Aside from moral implica-tions, the basic reason for abstention is that no effective defense against nuclear attack exists. Both the United States and the Soviet Union have ability to punish each other severely no matter which state strikes first. Fearing nuclear retaliation, neither the superpowers nor the lesser nuclear powers have been willing to use nuclear weapons against each other or against any other state.

The role of warfare in affecting the payoff utilities of decision makers is not as clear-cut as one might expect. It appears certain that the emo-tional strain and excitement resulting from any war usually hamper the decision makers' ability to weigh alternatives. Hence, decision makers on the winning side tend to use more destructive power than is necessary to

---

[15] One such analysis is Walter Millis and James Real, *The Abolition of War* (New York: Macmillan, 1963). Most contemporary arguments are foreshadowed in the writings of Norman Angell. See *Arms and Industry* (New York: Putnam, 1914).

win the initial objective. Similarly, the losing side has a tendency to hang on longer than is necessary even when collapse is certain. The behavior of the United States in World War II illustrates the first tendency, while the behavior of the Japanese and Germans illustrates the second.

Although warfare is a bargaining tool, it often becomes a bargaining objective. Winning a war frequently becomes more important than the achievement of certain objectives. Military goals are frequently separated from political goals under wartime conditions not only because military men play a larger role in national decision making during war than in peacetime but also because the sense of national commitment and loyalty usually stimulated by warfare leads decision makers to view military victory as the supreme political goal. When this happens, the war itself becomes a bargaining objective as well as a bargaining tool. No bargaining solution is then possible except unconditional surrender of one side, unless a stalemate forces decision makers to seek compromise.

Bargaining Patterns

In closing this section, it might be useful to describe briefly the bargaining patterns that characterize contemporary international politics. For purposes of discussion, we will distinguish three bargaining patterns: resolution, escalation, and freezing.

The vast majority of bargaining situations among states are resolved with both parties feeling somewhat satisfied. Bargaining over the formulation of the United Nations Charter, for example, involved a prolonged set of multilateral bargaining situations in which the final product was a set of compromises that benefited the parties that "had" to be benefited. In addition, Panama and the United States have bargained over the status of the Panama Canal on a number of occasions. Because of Panama's weak bargaining position (in the form of relative capabilities) the outcomes have tended to favor the United States. One of the most important bargaining episodes in contemporary history was the Cuban missile crisis. Two extremely powerful states were willing to resolve a conflict situation as a result of a series of threats and, we can assume, promises regarding Soviet missiles in Cuba. In this case, resolution occurred because the United States convinced the Soviet Union that the risks were not worth the benefits, and because this country was able to create conditions that allowed the other to pull out gracefully.[16]

These well-publicized examples of bargaining resolution are interlaced among thousands of less momentous but significant bargaining resolutions

[16] See Roger Hilsman, *To Move a Nation* (Garden City, N.Y.: Doubleday, 1967), pp. 226–29.

that are a part of international politics. Treaties of all types and activities within intergovernmental organizations, discussed in Chapters 8 and 9, constitute everyday bargaining activities among states. While these activities rarely make newspaper headlines, they crucially shape the events that do. As states seek to protect their citizens and their industries in an increasingly interdependent world, the compromises necessary to make a mutually beneficial environment are the product of the resolution of a large number of bargaining situations.

The second pattern of bargaining among states, escalation, might be viewed as the opposite of resolution. Instead of reaching an "acceptable" state of events, states enter into a spiral which leads them from rhetoric and promises to threats and the use of force. Although much fewer in number than the bagaining resolutions that occur in international politics, bargaining escalations have a tremendous impact on the course of international politics. For example, in 1914 both sides made commitments they found themselves unable to break; in 1939 the western democracies became convinced that warfare was the only way to stop Hitler. Unable to break the cycle of mutual suspicion, hostility and fear, states involved in a bargaining escalation are swept into full-scale warfare.

It should be made clear, however, that inability to reach a bargaining solution does not inevitably lead to war. In fact, unlimited escalation is not even the predominant pattern of unresolvable bargaining situations. Rather, states tend to "freeze" bargaining situations that they find unresolvable. The Soviet-American "disagreement" over how central Europe, particularly Germany, should be divided is a classic example of prolonged disagreement over high stakes that, while threatening to escalate to open warfare, has yet to do so. In fact, the threat to escalate itself serves as a freezing device because it gives both superpowers high motivation to maintain the status quo even while proclaiming status quo unacceptable. Sporadic increases and decreases in tensions notwithstanding, the modern world has lived with prolonged high-conflict bargaining situations not only in Berlin but also in the China Straits, Kashmir, Cyprus, and Israel. Even occasional outbreaks of military activity have not produced extensive and unlimited warfare.

For reasons we will elaborate in Chapters 11 and 12, bargaining situations for which no agreement among parties can be found do not usually lead to prolonged warfare in the contemporary world. In fact, before World War II (dating back to the classical system) warfare rarely became an end in itself. Even while bargaining for each other's territory, foreign policy decision makers were usually able to keep conflicts limited and military devastation small. At the same time, however, the possibility of large-scale warfare existed then as it exists today. As recent experience *within* the United States indicates, violence and politics are never totally separated. In relations among states, the separation is even more fragile because the conventions, laws, and force of habit that militate against the occurrence of violence in relatively stable domestic societies are much weaker in the international bargaining setting.

SUMMARY

Throughout this chapter we have identified similarities and differences between bargaining that occurs in a stable domestic economic situation and bargaining among states. We have noted that the setting for bargaining as well as the goals and tactics of the bargaining states are different in a number of ways for foreign policy decision makers. We have made the assumption that it is useful to approach conflict and cooperation with other states as bargaining situations and implied that the behavior of the states corresponds to the calculations of the rational decision maker weighing alternatives and taking actions specifically designed to achieve objectives.

However, because we know that foreign policy decision makers behave like human beings and not like rational problem solvers, we should expect that the interactions of states cannot always be described as the product of two rational players attempting to maximize payoff utilities. In fact as we have noted in our discussions on the use of force, during wartime states often act contrary to their own payoff utilities and contrary to what might be considered reasonable estimations of reality. Even under conditions not approaching war, foreign policy decision makers frequently act out of sentiment rather than out of clear calculations. For example, American foreign policy leaders often are characterized as unnecessarily concerned with either Europe or China and the Far East. This overconcern with one area to the exclusion of another is frequently a product of previous experiences or a particular cultural predilection rather than of a clearly evaluated foreign policy position.

In the final analysis, the view of the state as a bargaining entity is only partially adequate just as the view of man as an economic being is limited. The individual combines his economic sense with other facets of his character when acting. So the state's action in any given foreign policy decision is the result of interaction of various individuals who play a large number of social and political roles and are motivated by many conflicting goals. Although we can usefully analyze a state's behavior by assuming that its foreign policy decision makers conceive of themselves as bargainers, we should remember that it is frequently possible to picture the foreign policy decision maker of a particular state as a religious missionary (Alexander II of Russia), a political reformer (President Woodrow Wilson), or as a tough guy who isn't going to be pushed around (President Harry Truman). It is possible that decision makers do not see arguments, promises, threats, and the use of force as tools for international bargaining but rather as acts ordained by God, truth, or righteousness. Although some would hold with Schelling that it is more healthy for the future of mankind to view these tools as instruments in the international bargaining process,[17] this normative judgment should not cloud the fact that the leaders of states do not always see themselves as manipulating bargaining tools. We must conclude therefore that the bargaining model provides only a partial explanation of the way states deal with each other in competitive situations. In a general way, however, it serves as a framework for studying interactions among states.

SUMMARY OUTLINE

I. Bargaining occurs when two or more actors try to change each other's behavior in relation to a particular object.
    A. *The outcome of any bargaining process affects the payoffs the bargainers receive.*
    B. *Most bargaining situations are non-zero sum.*
    C. Four tools are used in bargaining—arguments, promises, threats, and force—and each is used to change the payoff utilities of the bargainers.
    D. *The setting for bargaining greatly influences the way the various tools are used.*
    E. *Values held by the actors are important because they determine the payoffs they will assign to different bargaining outcomes.*
    F. *Capabilities are important because they provide the basis for the use of the four tools.*
    G. *The image held by the bargainers of the general setting as well as the specific intentions of each other have a direct impact on the bargaining process.*
II. The setting for international bargaining contrasts sharply with the setting for domestic bargaining processes.
    A. *The distinction between prebargaining (routine) interactions and bargaining interactions are blurred in the international*

---

[17] The normative character of Schelling's bargaining model is clearly indicated in *Arms and Influence*. The book does not describe the role arms have played in influence as much as it prescribes how they should play such a role. Schelling does not clearly distinguish his descriptive from his prescriptive analysis. He assumes if states bargain with each other, more stable international politics will occur. Although implicitly admitting that states *do not* always view force as a bargaining tool by systematically arguing that they should, Schelling does not provide a clear description of how the use of force is actually related to influence.

bargaining process because of the fragmented nature of international law and social ideas.

B. *Lack of central institutions as a focal point of bargaining strategy characterizes international bargaining.*

C. *A large number of actors intervene in bargaining among states.*

D. *Payoffs are less clear-cut in international bargaining than they are in other bargaining processes.*

E. The setting for bargaining among states affects the use of the four bargaining tools.

　1. *Arguments are limited as a tool because of the lack of a commitment to transcendent values and symbols.*

　2. *Promises are important, but opportunities for making and keeping them are not abundant in the international bargaining process because of the absence of strong central institutions.*

　3. *Threats play a correspondingly larger role in international bargaining because an ambiguous distinction exists between legal and illegal threats and there is no authority to enforce the distinction even if it were not ambiguous.*

　4. *Force has a quasi-acceptable role in international bargaining because it is simultaneously outlawed (except for self-defense) and employed by states (in non-self-defense situations).*

III. The dynamics of the international bargaining process can be analyzed in terms of the operation of the four bargaining tools.

A. *Arguments are frequently used by states particularly in referring to the aims of peace and the "unity of mankind" although they appear to have little effect.*

B. Promises can involve economic, military, and political actions.

　1. *The way in which promises are communicated has an impact on the effectiveness of the promises.*

　2. *Tacit promises are less binding than explicit promises, but they also stand less of a chance of being believed than explicit ones.*

　3. *Credibility, or the degree to which a promise is believed, is important to the effectiveness of the promise.*

　4. *Images of the state determine whether or not its promises will be believed.*

　5. *To be effective, promises must involve something the target state values.*

　6. *Quid pro quo, or the exchange of promises, is an important aspect of all politics, including international politics.*

　7. *Conditions affecting the effectiveness of a quid pro quo*

        include timing and the level of specificity of the things being promised.

C.   Threats can also involve economic, military, and political actions.

    1.   *The way in which a threat is communicated affects its chances of success.*

    2.   *Threats can be expressed verbally or implied through actions.*

    3.   *The seriousness with which a threat is taken (credibility) depends in part on the degree of specificity in the communication of the threat.*

    4.   *Credibility is also affected by the image the target state has of the willingness and capability of the state making the threat.*

    5.   *Political support at home and from other states affects credibility of threats.*

    6.   *Weakness does not always mean a lack of credibility.*

    7.   *It is difficult to make threats credible because they usually involve costs to the threatening states.*

    8.   *Commitments are employed to reduce the threatener's flexibility so that a threat will be "automatically" followed through and therefore will be credible.*

    9.   *Past performance of a threatening state is part of its image and has a bearing on credibility of its current threats.*

   10.   *Threats are only effective if they change the payoffs of the target state in relation to given decisions.*

   11.   *Threats that fail tend to lead to threats of a more intense nature.*

   12.   *Threats do not always involve force directly although they usually imply the use of force indirectly.*

   13.   *Threats either deter or compel.*

   14.   *Threats of deterrence are usually more easily made effective than threats of compellance.*

D.   Force is used in international bargaining for a number of purposes.

    1.   *Force can serve as a basis for promises.*

    2.   *Force is often used to increase the credibility of other threats.*

    3.   *Force is often used to communicate a bargaining position.*

    4.   *The* fait accompli *is the limited application of force under certain conditions that changes the basic bargaining situation.*

    5.   *Conventional warfare can be limited or unlimited, and aims to punish and/or destroy the target state.*

6. *Subversive warfare is most often employed by weaker states that seek to punish without running the risk of large-scale defeat.*
7. *Nuclear warfare enables men to punish others with a great deal of severity in a short period of time.*
8. *Warfare changes the bargaining payoffs by increasing costs for both sides.*
9. *The emotional strain of warfare usually creates conditions where decision makers on both sides do not clearly assess relative payoffs involved.*

IV. Three general bargaining patterns can be identified: resolution, escalation, and freezing.

A. *The ˙vast majority of bargaining situations are resolved when both parties feel somewhat satisfied.*
B. *Significantly few bargaining situations escalate into large-scale warfare.*
C. *Inability to resolve a bargaining situation does not lead automatically to war.*
D. *A number of high-tension bargaining situations are frozen into prolonged, sporadically increasing and decreasing, tense situations.*

V. The bargaining model provides only a partial explanation of competitive interactions among states because in many cases foreign policy decision makers fail to think of their actions in terms of bargaining strategies.

BIBLIOGRAPHICAL ESSAY

Strategic interaction or bargaining among states has received a good deal of attention in recent years. Always of interest because of its obvious relevance to policy prescription, bargaining has been studied along a number of dimensions. Stimulus has also come from the application of game theory concepts in both economics and psychology to the general discussion of human behavior. A pioneering figure is Thomas C. Schelling, whose book *The Strategy of Conflict* (368) has already become a classic. Building on the development of mathematical game theory, concepts and propositions related to the study of international politics have come from a number of areas including Schelling and Becker (32) in sociology; Boulding (41) and Russett (359) in economics; Rapoport (326) and Rapoport and Guyer (328), between psychology and mathematics; and Morton Deutsch in (381) in psychology. Also, Riker (339) has applied mathematical concepts relating to game theory to coalition formation. All these writers have applied their findings to the study of bargaining among states. To acquire adequate grounding in the basic game theory concepts, the student should read Snyder in (54), Karl Deutsch (101), Shubik (374), and Rapoport and Guyer (329).

Attempts to apply bargaining concepts and theories to interactions among states have been numerous. Although the works cited above fail to provide a systematic application, other works at least attempt to apply such a framework. They include Iklé (188), Sawyer and Guetzkow in (215), a later work of Schelling (369), and Young (432). Empirically oriented studies are much scarcer; something of a beginning is represented by Russett (355), Fink (125), and Jensen (194, 195).

A number of writers have viewed the United Nations as a setting for bargaining. Included are general framework essays such as Alger (5), Claude (74), Alger in (264), and Alker and Russett (9). Also, a number of writers have looked at the interaction between the UN and strategies of states: Stoessinger (396), Riggs (338), and Bloomfield (37). In addition, Bloomfield (39) has examined the role of the United Nations in territorial disputes. Finally, Young (431) has studied different types of intermediaries in bargaining crises among states.

Work on the role of norms, either formal international laws or tacit conventions of behavior, in shaping bargaining activities is less easy to find, as Coplin notes in (314). Evaluations of the World Court's position in bargaining among states can be found in Schlachter (367) and Coplin in (28). More general discussions are found in Corbett (86), Barkun (25), McWhinney (265), Fisher (126), and Coplin (84).

The various capabilities and activities that might be used in the bargaining strategy are examined, although not necessarily in a bargaining framework. War and the use of force has received the primary amount of attention. Kahn (202), Quester (324), Halperin (154), and Schelling (368) use some bargaining concepts. Wright's work (428) remains the classic discussion of war while Earle (111) surveys traditional (before nuclear energy) ideas of military strategy. A major thread through much recent literature on military strategy is the role of limited war as seen by Osgood (304), Kissinger (224), Brodie (51), Taylor (401), Kahn (202, 203), Halperin (154), and Kaufmann (210). Most of the current ideas on the relationship between force and bargaining strategy appear in these books. Other forms of bargaining activities are not so clearly examined. Negotiating tactics are discussed by Lall (238) and Iklé (188) as well as by diplomats like Acheson (1). Alliance dynamics are examined in Osgood (304) and Liska (252). The use of foreign aid is examined by Wolf (426) and Liska (253). Important, but less spectacular and violent, bargaining actions include diplomatic protest described in McKenna (262) and economic sanctions studied by Galtung (136) and Wallensteen (409).

Bargaining styles and principles is another area that has received some investigation. Lerche (245) compares the Soviet to the American style; scholars who have looked at the "communist" or "totalitarian" styles include Joy (200), Campbell (64), Craig in (364), and Kecskemeti (212). Hsieh (185) has investigated Communist China's strategy with some reference to style. Bell (33) has examined the relationship between military capability and negotiating behavior.

A number of studies deserve mention because of the importance of the cases included. Among them are Russett's (359) work on Pearl Harbor; Kecskemeti's (212) on Allied behavior in World War II; Davison's (94) on the Berlin blockade; McClelland in (383) on Berlin in general; and the Wohlstetters (424) on the Cuban missile crisis.

Because it is difficult or impossible to acquire relevant data on bargaining interactions among states (perceptions, attitudes, and strategies), many social scientists have tried to generalize from situations they consider relevant. As we mentioned above, they draw their principles from economics, sociology, mathematical game theory, and psychology. Of particular importance has been the study of bargaining in two-person games. Employed primarily by psychologists to assess the interplay of perceptions, attitudes, and strategies, these experiments are performed to determine how personality and environment interact in competitive situations. Examples of such work are Rapoport (327) and Rapoport and Guyer (329). Although no systematic attempt has been made at this date to apply these findings to more traditional case analysis, scholars hope that the findings can eventually be made relevant to analyses of particular bargaining situations among states. Some work by economists—Olson (301)—may interest the student, although this book and others lack the empirical foundations of the psychologists. One study of bargaining does employ experimental techniques and apply Olson's concepts: Burgess and Robinson in (348).

In spite of the excellent framework provided by Schelling and others, the study of bargaining among states still suffers from a predisposition to examine only those bargaining situations that involve the use of force. Not only does this predisposition limit the attention paid to bargaining that does not lead to war; it also is part of the general failure to develop a comparative analysis of bargaining behavior. Comparison is one of the best ways to learn about the phenomena one is studying. However, no attempt has been made to develop an explicit framework built on bargaining concepts and models from which comparisons across cases can be made. Although a number of scholars have looked at conflict situations in quantitative and comparative frameworks—McClelland in (383) and Russett (355)—there have been too few attempts to analyze cases using bargaining concepts and theories.

Part Three

THE INTERNATIONAL POLITICAL SYSTEM

We are now ready to look at the totality of events and processes that we have described in a piecemeal fashion throughout Parts One and Two by introducing a new concept—the *international political system*. If this were a textbook on American politics, we would have introduced the idea of a political system much earlier. In American politics certain institutions like the Presidency, Congress, or the Supreme Court permeate all political activities to such a degree that it would be futile to describe American politics without describing the American political system first. In withholding the discussion on the international political system until the last part of the book, we have assumed that a great deal about international politics can be understood by looking at the actors and their interactions without first discussing the nature of the international political system.

At some point, however, it is necessary to apply the general concept of political system as it is now employed throughout the political science discipline. As we might expect, the international political system differs radically, in a number of crucial areas, from most domestic political systems; nevertheless, the general concept of political system can be useful in considering certain aspects of international politics that we have not as yet discussed. The last two chapters of the book describe certain features of the past, present, and possibly future international political system. First, we will offer a brief description of the term international political system.

The international political system may be viewed as a set of semi-autonomous—in law and in fact—political units organized on a territorial basis. Called nations or states, these political units that now encompass the earth act independently and collectively toward each other in a large number of issue areas. The state is a particular kind of political organization; it claims control over a specific piece of territory and it interacts with other states in a number of ways, one of which is to maintain its own territorial integrity or control. *The international political system is a system of states, each of which claims control within its boundaries and acts to maintain that control domestically and internationally.* Whether or not a particular state seeks to expand its control over the territory of another state is not relevant to the definition of the system, although it appears that for many years a significant number of states have attempted to do just that. While the definition does not assume that states necessarily compete, it also does not assume that each state will respect the territorial integrity of others—only that each will claim the right to control and protect its own territory.

Our description of this system almost sounds as if we are describing a nonsystem because it focuses on actors in the system rather than on the laws and institutions that shape the actors' behavior. Our emphasis is on the state because the international political system is *decentralized.* In Chapter 7, we noted that the legal, social, and economic settings for international interactions were decentralized and fragmented and that the states acting independently still made many of the crucial decisions affecting international law and the world economy. Similarly, political conditions among states are determined by decisions made by the states acting both individually and collectively. Although central institutions like the United Nations or the World Court do exist, their authority is limited by the will of the states.

While central authority is weak in the international political system and the activities of the states determine the major conditions within the system, it is still valuable to look at international politics through the concept of the international political system. Certain patterns of activities have occurred regularly for hundreds of years. For example, threats to the system (as a set of semi-autonomous territorially organized political units) have been met by the states acting collectively. We will discuss these activities in Chapter 11. Other factors also make it valuable to look at the totality of events among nations as a political system. In addition to the growth of a number of intergovernmental organizations such as the United Nations, the penetration of states into each other's affairs makes the concept of the international political system useful. This interpenetration may in the long run change the entire structure of the international political system by making the state less viable as a form of political organization, or it may produce more elaborate international institutions. No matter what the implications, however, these factors—as we shall see in Chapter 12—make international politics more than just the anarchic activities of a number of competing states.

In the remaining two chapters, then, we will attempt to put together the analytical pieces we have so far developed within the context of the international political system. Building on our study of the foreign policy-making process as well as the behavior of intergovernmental organizations and on our presentation of the nature of interactions among states, we will discuss the international political system from two different angles. First, Chapter 11 will examine the ways states have attempted to maintain the international political system in the face of serious threats to the system as a form for politically organizing the world. Chapter 12 will examine contemporary trends in the system, particularly those that affect the way states will deal with each other in the future, as well as the role the state as a form of political organization will play in future world politics.

11

Maintaining the International Political System

Some might argue that the history of international politics appears to be a long string of unrelated events in which states attempted to build empires by eliminating each other. It is possible, however, to argue the contrary: there appears to be a continuous thread running at least as far back as 1648 that shows that states have acted together to maintain the international political system. Either argument can be made with some plausibility (which is usually the case with broad historical arguments). This chapter will accept the latter argument as its premise and will attempt to show how states have in the past acted and continue to act today to preserve the international political system as a form of world political organization.

In discussing maintenance of this system, we are faced with an analytical problem. In domestic politics, it is not particularly difficult to decide when a political system is maintained; all one has to do is decide whether or not certain central institutions are operating—institutions that function to preserve the system from both internal disruption (police and the courts) and foreign attack (armed forces).[1] Threats to the domestic political system can be readily discerned by looking for organized and unorganized forces both inside and outside the society that might destroy the operation of these institutions.

In contrast, the international political system has no central institutions whose continued operation are considered to be the *sine qua non* for

---

[1] The position here is not that it is easy to tell when a domestic political system is changing or becoming more vulnerable to internal or external threat. Rather, we maintain that destruction of certain central organizations may be considered the same as the destruction of the political system as a whole. The political system has become so shaped by central institutions that the life of the system and the institutions are almost one in the same.

its existence. Although the disappearance of the United Nations might eventually lead to the destruction of the international political system, it would not necessarily mean the end of the system. In contrast, elimination of the United States armed forces and police would mean the end of the United States as an effective political system. Since international institutions are only weak and fragmented, we cannot use their continued existence and operation as an indication of the maintenance of the international political system.

Instead, we must focus on the central structural feature of the international political system—the state as an autonomous territorially-based political organization. If we assume that the basic nature of the international political system has been the existence of a group of states relatively free to regulate internal matters, we can analyze the way in which the system has been maintained by examining the threats to the system of states as a form of political organization. Our discussion of the maintenance of the international political system, then, will be set in terms of the threats to a world composed of a large number of independent political entities.

We will argue that two general threats are posed to the maintenance of the system. The first has been the threat of empire or the extension of total control over the system by one state. The fear that one state would become powerful enough to control all others has persisted from the beginning of the international political system; in recent years, it has become somewhat muted and altered. The second threat has been the danger of a war so destructive that men would only be able to organize as small, decentralized, and agrarian units or as roving bands of nomads. Although this threat has always existed for foreign policy decision makers, it has become increasingly real as recent technological developments have increased man's capability to destroy.

In the following pages, we will discuss the ways in which these two threats to the maintenance of the international political system have stimulated certain patterns of behavior in three historical periods: the classical system, 1648–1815; the transitional system, 1815–1945; and the contemporary system, 1945 to the present. Because historical trends do not neatly divide themselves into clear-cut periods of time, the dates used to signify historical periods should be viewed only as general guidelines.

MAINTAINING THE CLASSICAL SYSTEM

The classical international political system existed in Europe from the middle of the seventeenth century to the French Revolution and Napoleonic wars in 1815. Some aspects of the classical period predated as well as postdated this time span. Nevertheless, it is useful to fix some point in time as a common reference point. During this period, the prime threat to maintenance of the international political system was perceived to be empire building; large-scale war was then viewed as a secondary threat. We will discuss some basic characteristics of this period as well as the activities that are thought to have been essential to maintaining the system.

First, and most important, the major actors of the classical international political system were European. The United States and other nations of the western hemisphere were preoccupied with internal development. They sought to be politically although not necessarily economically, isolated from Europe. Non-European areas of the world were either ignored by European states or treated as pawns in the struggle among them because they were neither sufficiently organized politically nor developed economically and technologically to pose a serious threat to the European states. Even the American victories against the British in the 1770's and her relative success in the War of 1812 were more a result of British involvement in Europe than they were of American military might. In both encounters, French opposition to Britain played a major role.

For all practical purposes, then, the international political system during the classical period consisted of patterns of interactions among European states. The great powers were France, Russia, Austria, and Great Britain. Spain, Sweden, the Netherlands, Turkey, and Prussia aspired to great-power status although they never really attained it for any length of time. The great powers controlled the affairs of the international political system. Not only did they treat non-European areas as pawns in their own competition with each other, but they also treated the hundreds of small states within Europe in the same way. (The distinction between great and small powers is discussed in Chapter 5.)

Second, the major powers did not always directly attack each other, but would often try to dominate the smaller states in the system and would compete for territorial gains outside Europe. Embroiled in direct conflict on their homelands as well as overseas, each major power continued to perceive all others as threats to its own security. Although they did not always fear total dominance by one state, they did fear that their own security would be compromised by other states in the system. In the classical international political system, then, the European states lived in constant fear of each other, and as a result they felt it was necessary to compete for any and all objectives even remotely related to security.

Third, the internal structure of most states in the system gave decision makers a free hand in dealing with international affairs. As we saw in Chapter 3, conditions of decision-maker dominance prevailed in most states during the classical period. Democratic forms of government were only beginning to develop, and the industrial revolution had not transformed the political system into its modern form with a large number of demanding policy influencers. Hence, very flexible foreign policies could be followed during the classical period because there were only a few policy influencers, and they had limited power over the decision makers.

Fourth, sociocultural factors tended to limit the degree of violence that foreign policy decision makers felt was permissible in the system. Because the system consisted of European states, there was a general attitude that something tied all of the states together, at least in relation to the rest of the world. In addition, the relative smallness of the European continent and the crisscrossing of family lines created alliances among the elites of Europe. Consequently, decision makers in different countries often felt more at home with each other than with their own lower-class countrymen. Fear of social revolution *within* each nation acted as a brake on the tendencies of leaders to wage war *between* nations. These sociocultural factors contributed to a general desire among the leaders of most states to avoid prolonged war and to make few moves that would jeopardize the entire system.

Fifth, technological factors tended to limit the amount and geographical scope of violence in the system. The mobility of armies was limited by the speed of the horse on land and the speed of the sailing vessel on the sea. The steamboat and the railroad did not emerge as important military factors until the latter half of the nineteenth century. In addition, firepower was small, especially by contemporary standards. Small firearms were not capable of rapid fire, and artillery was difficult to move, unreliable to fire, and relatively weak in terms of destructive power. The overall impact of these factors was to make wars relatively limited in terms of geographical scope and destructive power. Inability to control disease often took a heavy toll in human life.

Characteristics of the classical international political system contributed to certain typical patterns of behavior. States pursued the goals of security and increased territorial control by following highly flexible foreign policies. Limitations on their ability and willingness to become involved in large-scale conflict resulted from the sociocultural and technological conditions coupled with the relative autonomy of the foreign policy decision maker to produce a system of ever-shifting coalitions. States joined coalitions to increase their chances of survival as well as to gain territory from another state. The powerful states directed their ambitions to the capture of small states or colonial territory, but even these ambitions were limited by the growth of opposing allies to protect the small states.

The most prevalent pattern of activity directly related to maintenance of the classical international political system is often referred to as the *balance of power.* As indicated in the bibliographical essay following this chapter, the term has been used a number of different ways. We will use it to mean the maintenance of conditions within the system that would prevent one state from controlling the territory of all other states in the system. In the classical period, this meant preventing one state from controlling all of Europe.

As methods of preserving the system, two patterns of balance-of-power activities predominated. The first occurred when a state that threatened to control the entire system was met by a coalition of the others. The counter-coalition, or balancing alliance, was formed to protect any state that was under attack by the empire-building state. The second occurred when a state adopted the role of balancer by withholding support from two evenly matched states or coalitions and by giving its support to the side that was threatened by a state that appeared to be getting the upper hand. No matter which of the two patterns was followed, however, the balance of power signified forms of international alliance behavior that were designed to preserve the international political system.

During the classical period, threats of empire building came primarily from France. Under Louis XIV[2] and Napoleon[3] France was thought to be following a policy designed to establish a European empire. In both cases, England led the balancing alliance. Napoleon clearly was attempting to replace the international political system with an empire. Whether Louis XIV had the same ambition is debatable; the facts, however, are not as important as England's ability to convince other states that Louis XIV aimed to control Europe, and on this basis to form an alliance to stop his expansion.

By the middle of the eighteenth century, England had become so successful in acquiring overseas territory that states began to consider her the prime threat to the international political system. A coalition was led by France and joined by the Netherlands and Spain to challenge British dominance. The coalition supported the Americans in their War of Independence; this support severely hampered growth of the British Empire.[4] Although the real aim of the English was not clear, and it was unlikely that

---

[2] The foreign policy of Louis XIV is discussed in John B. Wolf, *Louis XIV* (New York: W. W. Norton, 1968).

[3] Napoleon, in Geoffrey Brunn, *Europe and the French Imperium* (New York: Harper, 1928) and Harold C. Deutsch, *The Genesis of Napoleonic Imperialism* (Cambridge, Mass.: Harvard University Press, 1938).

[4] The role of European diplomacy in the American Revolution is examined in Samuel Flagg Bemis, *The Diplomacy of the American Revolution* (Bloomington, Ind.: Indiana University Press, 1957) and Richard B. Morris, *The Peacemakers* (New York: Harper, 1965).

England contemplated continental adventures, important states in the system considered it necessary to form an alliance to counter her expansion.

The British experience indicates that it was frequently difficult to identify the state that threatened to control the entire system because mutual suspicions were high. Alliances proved extremely short-lived once the common danger was defeated, and for good reason: It was feared that yesterday's protector might be tomorrow's conqueror. In addition, members of a balancing alliance had to convince prospective alliance members that their aims were to balance rather than take over the system. Wooed by both sides, each claiming that the other threatened dominance, neutral states frequently waited until the last moment before joining a balancing coalition.

As a result, the formation of a balancing alliance was far from automatic, although as a state's threat to the system became stronger, the probability that a balancing coalition would be formed became greater. But even then, clever diplomacy on the part of the balancing states and promises of valuable "booty," usually in the form of territory, were often necessary to build a coalition strong enough to stop the state threatening to control the system. As it became obvious that a state was not merely rounding out its territorial domain and that eventually all of the states would fall, the balancing states had less difficulty gaining support of neutrals and even of members of the opposing alliance. However, this process often took a long time. England, for example, stood alone against Napoleon for many years before the European states realized the necessity of a strong balancing alliance.

When one looks at the history of the classical system as a whole, however, it seems clear that the balance-of-power pattern worked well in maintaining the international political system. The underlying forces that characterized the system in the classical period contributed a great deal in this respect. Flexibility of decision makers allowed frequent shifts in alliances that were necessary to check extensive expansion of states. The limitations on using force imposed by technological, cultural, and social conditions also contributed by preventing the complete destruction of the major powers. These two factors combined to create a system of competing states that would band together to check any state or group of states that appeared to threaten the international political system. Foreign policy decision makers followed flexible policies so they could form a balancing alliance. Although this required them to forgo certain short-range gains, they could see that maintenance of the system contributed to their own security. States that were strong enough to threaten the system and followed such a policy were eventually checked by a balancing alliance. Although a balancing alliance was never formed automatically, strong pressures acted to produce it, particularly when the aims of a threatening state became clear.

While the threat of system dominance was met by states acting in concert, the threat of large-scale war with widespread social, economic, and political destruction was contained by the basic features underlying the classical international political system. Flexibility in alliances made it dangerous for states to engage in long and mutually destructive wars because an outside power might intervene. Flexibility in foreign policy making enabled decision makers to avoid extreme antagonisms that might produce "crusading wars" like the religious wars that raged throughout Europe during the first half of the seventeenth century. The relative ineffectiveness of weapons coupled with fear of social revolution made decision makers less willing to endure long and costly wars. Therefore, while the threat of empire in Europe seemed to preoccupy decision makers during this period, they still managed to avoid large-scale destructive warfare. Even though it was extremely decentralized, then, the classical international system was maintained by patterns of international interactions and by social, economic, political, and technological conditions that reinforced those patterns.

MAINTAINING THE TRANSITIONAL SYSTEM

We have designated the years from 1815 to 1945 as the transitional international political system. Under the twin impact of the French Revolution, which symbolized the growing importance of the middle class in the affairs of state, and the Industrial Revolution, which has altered almost every conceivable aspect of human life, the classical political system underwent a series of radical transformations. We will examine the basic features of these changes and discuss their consequences for the maintenance of the international political system.

The first point of transition was universalization of the system. In 1815, all members of the system were European except for an occasional intrusion by the United States. By 1945, members could be found all over the world, not just as colonies but as powerful states that had to be dealt with as relative equals. Although it was not until twenty years after World War II that almost every area of the world was controlled by an independent state and, conversely, that colonialism—at least in its classic overt form —had virtually disappeared, by 1945 every major region of the world had at least one or two independent states.

The second point of transition was the evolution of policy influence systems within states. Prior to the French Revolution, almost every state was ruled by a small group of decision makers who depended on relatively few policy influencers for support. However, as the Industrial Revolution increased the interdependence and importance of the various segments of society, a large variety of social forces developed. They had to be brought into the political system. Although the importance of decision makers increased, policy influencers also became more numerous and more powerful. By the middle of the twentieth century, pluralized policy-influence systems characterized virtually every state in the international political system. (Pluralized policy-influence systems are described in detail in Chapter 3.)

Third, social and cultural conditions that accompanied these changes contributed to an increase of nationalistic considerations in foreign policy. Decision makers no longer felt more loyalty to each other than to their own people. Fewer social and cultural ties united decision makers of different countries, and correspondingly more social and cultural ties grew between each country's decision makers and its general populace. The willingness to use more force and less restraint against other states increased as members of the system became geographically dispersed and culturally heterogeneous. Increases in speed of transportation and communication in the transitional period did more to tie nations together internally than it did in promoting cooperation among states. Xenophobia, the fear and hatred of foreign states, became a force among many policy influencers if not decision makers in almost every state. Where the classical decision maker had difficulty in engendering patriotism among nationals, the decision maker in the transitional period had difficulty in controlling patriotism in order to follow a flexible foreign policy.

Finally, technological factors increased the ability of states to harm each other. Mobility of military capability was greatly increased by the steam engine, the internal combustion engine, and the airplane. Ability to destroy was also increased to proportions undreamed of even as late as the mid-nineteenth century. During the classical period the civilian population was able to avoid direct military harm, whereas in the transitional period military technology made it increasingly possible to punish civilians as well as the military. The means of mass destruction generated by the Industrial Revolution along with the mass army introduced in the French Revolution and perfected in World War II combined to increase the destructiveness of military encounters.

These four factors—universalization of the system, pluralization of foreign policy-making processes, growth of nationalism, and increased destructive capacity of military weapons—had a profound impact on the two traditional threats to the international political system. On the one hand, they made systemwide empire more complex; as the system expanded, regional balances became more important. On the other hand, they increased the chances of highly destructive wars.

In response to this universalization, decision makers started to think about regional empires—that is, control of a particular geographical region by a state from either inside or outside the region. Around the turn of the century, for example, British Asian policy was not based solely on concern for her colonies, but also on concern for the balance between Russia and Japan. Although not always explicitly stated, regional empire was frequently viewed as a prelude to universal empire. In both world wars, for example, Germany threatened Europe with dominance but the threat also carried global implications. No doubt these played a role in the United States decision to intervene in World War I and to concentrate its efforts on Hitler in World War II. Hence, the response to changing geographical dimensions of the international political system produced a more complicated set of considerations for foreign policy decision makers who maintained the system.

Flexibility in foreign policies also diminished during the transitional period. As decision makers received growing pressures from powerful policy influencers, their ability to shift alliances and to threaten but not necessarily use force diminished. A. J. P. Taylor's analysis of German foreign policy prior to world War I is instructive on this point:

> Each group in Germany had a single enemy and would have liked to make peace with the other. . . . Tirpitz and his capitalist supporters wanted a naval conflict with Great Britain and deplored the hostility to France and Russia; the professional soldiers and their capitalist supporters wanted a continental war, especially against France, and deplored the naval rivalry with Great Britain: the mass parties—the social democrats and the Roman Catholic Centre—were friendly to both Great Britain and France and could be won only for the old radical programme of war against Russia. . . . The feeble rulers of Germany, William II and Bethmann, preferred a ring of foreign enemies to trouble at home.[5]

Changing military technology and strategy also lessened the flexibility of foreign policy decision makers. Use of large armies created demand for long-range planning, which in turn limited the number of alternatives open to the decision makers. Once Germany mobilized in 1914 for a major attack against France, for example, she could not shift her plans for a major attack against Russia first without losing weeks or months. More-

---

[5] A. J. P. Taylor, *The Struggle for Mastery in Europe, 1848–1918* (New York: Oxford University Press, 1954), pp. 519–20.

over, to be effective an alliance demanded prior military coordination. Not only did such demands diminish the flexibility of decision makers in making and breaking alliances; it also meant that the intended target of the alliances would be forewarned by military consultation.

Coincidental with loss of flexibility, many limitations on the use of force that existed in the classical period were removed during the transitional period. The growth of nationalist sentiment, particularly after hostilities broke out, lessened the ability of decision makers to fight limited wars. Populations were fed nationalistic propaganda to increase their ability to meet the war effort; this in turn limited the autonomy of the decision makers when it came to ending the war. Policies of unconditional surrender and "fighting to the last man" were a byproduct of the nationalistic sentiment stimulated during wartime. Even in peacetime, the nationalistic fervor of certain policy influencers could push hesitant decision makers to war.

With the lessening of limitations on the use of force, the threat of destructive wars with widespread social, economic, and political consequences greatly increased. In fact, the threat was realized in the two world wars. Although the first war involved extensive devastation only on the European continent, the second caused destruction on three continents— Europe, Asia, and Africa. Both had severe political, economic, and social consequences in virtually every region of the world. Fear of war became widespread, particularly after the first world war; this fear became a prime concern in foreign policy decision making.

In fact, the fear of large-scale war began to conflict with the traditional concern for countering the empire-building state. Because traditionally the system had been maintained by forming alliances to counter states that threatened to dominate, and if necessary to use force against those states, war had traditionally been considered a necessary tool for maintenance of the international political system. However, as the potential destructive consequences of war increased in both intensity and scope, warfare became a less acceptable alternative. Preoccupation with the balance of power slowly began to be replaced by preoccupation with avoiding war. A dilemma that developed still confronts the leaders of states in the contemporary period: If one takes action to counter a state that threatens to extend its empire, he increases the danger of widespread warfare.

Nothing illustrates this dilemma better than the course of events between the world wars. The phrase "peace is indivisible" or the "indivisibility of peace" gained wide currency during this period. It symbolized the attitude that the use of force anywhere, for any reason other than self-defense, would result in a breakdown of order throughout the international political system. Such an attitude implied that wars designed to check the expansion of a state that attempted to dominate the system were not justified unless they involved direct self-defense.

The course of disarmament negotiation also indicated the tension between the fear of system dominance and of general war during the period between the wars.[6] On the one hand, leaders and scholars verbally acknowledged the need for disarmament to end the arms race and eliminate the chances of large-scale war. Some token forms of disarmament occurred, although the spirit if not the letter of the agreements was rarely carried out. On the other hand, decision makers could not bring themselves to act according to the disarmament proposals they discussed and even occasionally espoused. Their behavior can be attributed to the severe fear of war produced by World War I compromised by their deep-seated attitude that they could not trust each other sufficiently to make disarmament work.

Development of the League of Nations was perhaps even more symbolic of the conflict between those who felt that dominance by one state was the primary threat to the international political system and those who felt that the primary threat was large-scale war.[7] Embodying the principle of *collective security*—a principle that calls for united action among all states to stop any aggressor—the League was an intergovernmental organization that sought to abolish war. It was based on the premise that informal balancing alliances were no longer adequate to check states that threatened to take over the system. World War I was thought to have resulted from failure of the balance of power. Given the increasing destructiveness of military might and the lack of flexibility in making foreign policy, many felt that it was necessary to establish a central international institution to maintain the international political system.

The collective security principle, therefore, had one of the same general purposes as the balance-of-power principle: to preserve the international political system from the threat of universal empire. It proposed to achieve that aim through a formal international institution. However, in making certain assumptions about what type of central institution should be created and how that institution should operate, the collective security principle—or, to be more precise, the *theory* behind the collective security principle—differed quite radically from the balance-of-power principle.

In theory at least, the principle of collective security differed from that of balance of power in three ways. First, any act of aggression under a

[6] For a discussion of disarmament during this period see G. M. Gathorne-Hardy, *A Short History of International Affairs, 1920–1939* 4th ed. (New York: Oxford University Press, 1950), pp. 175–98 and 338–57.

[7] The evolution and subsequent record of the League of Nations is chronicled in F. P. Walters, *A History of the League of Nations* (London: Oxford University Press, 1952).

collective security system was to be "punished" by the other states. This contrasts with the principle that only those acts of aggression that threatened universal empire were to be met by a counter-coalition to maintain balance of power. Second, under the collective security formula *all* member states were to form a coalition against the aggressor or aggressors, in contrast to the balance-of-power principle that stipulates that only enough states should join the coalition to stop the threatening state. Finally, the collective security principle implied that an intergovernmental organization like the League of Nations would identify aggressive acts and organize member states against the aggressor. This also contrasts with the *informal* coalition-formation processes implicit in the balance-of-power principle. In these three ways, then, the collective security principle differed substantially from that of balance of power, indicating the altered attitudes many individuals had come to hold about maintenance of the international political system.

If the principles differed in theory, their politics were almost identical in practice. Save for different rhetoric, international politics of the interwar period was classical in many respects. Whenever a state committed what appears to have been a clearly nondefensive use of force (as Japan did in 1931 and 1937, and Italy did in 1936), the counter-coalition of the members of the system never formed. As a result, neither the threat of universal empire nor the threat of widespread war was eliminated through the efforts of the League of Nations. On the contrary, by confusing the distinction between preventing universal empire and preventing largescale war, the League of Nations made both empire and war more probable.

The tension between the two threats to the international political system was apparent not only in the history of disarmament and the development of the League, but also in the foreign policy of Great Britain and France in the 1930's.[8] Abhorring war, the decision makers and policy influencers of those countries could not bring themselves to use force in countering the German threat to Europe. The sentiment against war placed severe limitations on the leadership of the two western democracies in dealing with states like Italy and Germany that piece by piece expanded their territorial control. Hitler was able to play upon the fear of large-scale war in getting away with acts that in an earlier period would clearly have been countered by war.

Thus, the period between the early nineteenth and the mid-twentieth century was clearly transitional. Universalization of the state system put the

---

[8] For a discussion of British and French foreign policy between the world wars, see the Gathorne-Hardy work cited previously and Arnold Wolfers, *Britain and France Between the Two Wars* (New York: Harcourt, Brace, 1940).

threat of universal empire in different dimensions because it made regional balances more important. The flexibility of decision makers that character-ized the classical period was lost as technology made long-range military planning necessary and as domestic political conditions narrowed possible policy alternatives. At the same time, the threat of large-scale war in-creased, not only because more military capability was available but also because social and cultural conditions provided fewer limitations on the use of force. Although the fear of war added some limitations, it did not apply universally. Some decision makers (like Hitler and Mussolini) were still willing to use force for reasons other than self-defense. In the interwar period, these decision makers enjoyed a distinct advantage when dealing with those states where fear of war was great. With neither the League of Nations nor disarmament able to eliminate war, the decision makers were left with little else than the traditional means of balancing alliances and threatening war to prevent either universal and regional empire or wide-spread war. However, it was not until after the beginning of the second world war that this situation became clear.

MAINTAINING THE CONTEMPORARY SYSTEM

Over 50 million people were killed in the second world war at a direct cost exceeding one trillion dollars. The war ended with the detonation of atom bombs over Hiroshima and Nagasaki, marking the transition from the classical to the contemporary international political system. The ability of first the United States and then the Soviet Union to destroy each other and a good part of mankind in the post-1945 world has radically altered the balance between the two traditional threats to the maintenance of the international political system. The need to prevent nuclear powers from fighting each other directly has made widespread warfare the primary threat to the maintenance of the international political system if not to human life as we know it. It would do the United States or the Soviet Union little good to prevent the other from establishing universal empire if in the course of the preventive action large-scale warfare broke out.

Universalization of the international political system was virtually complete by the early 1960's, and has had an impact on the maintenance of the system. Even though the two superpowers continue to charge each other with world domination attempts it has become clear that the threat of universal empire is more fantasy than real. Although the threat of regional dominance is real, the idea of one state controlling the entire world is difficult to take seriously. The reason for this lies not as much in geography as in the inability of states with superior military and economic strength to maintain political control where the indigenous population firmly opposes them. Guerrilla warfare has played a major role in the withering away of the concept of universal empire because it makes conquest of territory less profitable. In addition, recent history reveals that ideological affinity or economic support does not mean political control. Communist Cuba is not a part of the Chinese or Soviet "empire" in spite of its ideological sympathy and economic dependence. Although the superpowers as well as some lesser states attempt to expand their political control, it appears clear that the possibility of one state controlling all other states in the system is remote.

Thus the fear of universal empire is no longer a real threat to the maintenance of the international political system—no matter what the rhetoric of some foreign policy decision makers. Fear of regional empire, however, continues to motivate the activities of a number of states. Either they perceive themselves to be direct targets of regional expansion or they are concerned with preventing control by a state from outside the region. Consequently, regional wars have been common in the contemporary period. Small states with regional interests have often fought. India and Pakistan as well as the Israelis and Arabs have engaged in warfare periodically since World War II. In most cases, warfare between members of a region has been limited in duration and intensity. The two superpowers, along with other states, have usually brought pressure on the antagonists to keep the conflict limited. This is done by either refusing to take sides or counseling if not forcing the antagonists to stop fighting.

Regional warfare and the threat of it have involved the superpowers directly. Although the superpowers attempt to apply pressure indirectly when two states of a particular region engage in warfare (India-Pakistan and UAR-Israel), they sometimes become directly involved, as the United States did when it intervened directly and massively to restore the status quo in Korea in 1950. Each fearful that the other will gain influence and control by changes in the various regional balances throughout the world, both superpowers attempt to keep one antagonist from gaining the upper hand in regional conflict situations. This usually means that both will attempt to end open hostilities as soon as possible.

In addition, the superpowers often become involved in regional affairs prior to warfare. One technique has been the development of regional "security organizations" which appear to be more like regional alliances. The United States has established such organizations as the North Atlantic Treaty Organization, the Southeast Asian Treaty Organization, the Central Treaty Organization, the Organization of American States, and the Anzus Council; the Soviet Union has organized the Warsaw Pact. The superpowers have also become involved in maintaining regional balances by providing arms for antagonists within specific regions. Sometimes the superpowers supply arms to both sides (as in the India-Pakistan conflict) while at other times they support competing sides (in the Arab-Israeli war the Soviet Union supported the former and the United States provided arms for both). The motivation behind the superpowers' participation in regional alliances and regional arms races is the traditional desire to prevent one nation from dominating the region.

The superpowers have also become involved in regional politics at the level of civil or internal warfare. Both states have intervened directly in civil wars. The United States intervened diplomatically in Cyprus when civil war between the Greek and Turkish minorities erupted in the early 1960's and militarily in the Dominican Republic in 1965 when it asserted that a leftist insurrection was about to occur. The Soviet Union intervened in Hungary in 1956 and less credibly in Czechoslovakia in 1968 on the grounds of threatened civil war. Acting upon the classical assumption that a state in civil turmoil represents a weak spot against which expansionist states might gain control, the superpowers have attempted to create political stability within states threatened by civil war.

In areas where both superpowers feel that one has a special interest, the intervention is one-sided. For the United States, civil turmoil in any state in the western hemisphere is usually enough of a stimulus for unilateral intervention. The intervention might be as direct as the sending of troops to the Dominican Republic in 1965 or as indirect as the pressure brought upon countries like Brazil and Venezuela during their frequent periods of instability. For the Soviet Union, eastern European states are closely watched for evidence of civil disorder or other forms of "deviance." Russian troops have intervened in Hungary, Poland, and East Germany·in the 1950's and in Czechoslovakia in 1968. There seems to be mutual agreement between the two superpowers that any threat of domestic political instability in their respective regions (western hemisphere for the United States and eastern Europe for the Soviet Union) should be handled alone even though both sides make public statements to the contrary.

Civil instability in other areas and probably in western Europe usually creates conditions for disagreement and conflict between the two superpowers. Occasionally, they cooperate through the United Nations as they did in the Congo in 1960. Even that cooperation, however, was short-lived because the Soviet Union felt that the United Nations was not following a neutral path in dealing with political forces there. It is more typical for the United States to defend status quo forces within the threatened state and for the Soviet Union to back revolutionary forces. For example, the United States gave aid to Greece and Turkey in the late 1940's because political stability was threatened by what were thought to be political groups sponsored by the Soviet Union.

The Vietnamese conflict in the 1960's illustrates the same pattern. The United States began to intervene actively on behalf of the South Vietnam government in the early 1960's. The decision to intervene was based on past United States policy to maintain stability within a regional system by defending the existing regime. Although the Soviet Union was not directly involved at the outset, the United States' decision to carry intervention to the point of using force against the North Vietnamese regime resulted in the predictable Soviet reaction of supporting the revolutionary forces.

In addition to the contemporary shift from concern with universal dominance to concern for regional dominance, the lack of flexibility in foreign policies that began in the transitional period has increased in the contemporary one. A prime reason for the increasing inflexibility of foreign policies in areas of national security is the development of alliance commitments involving the exchange of troops and other forms of military cooperation. American troops, for example, are stationed in almost every state having a military alliance with the United States. This and other forms of military cooperation (mutual strategic planning, and so forth) have made alliances more stable than they were in the classical period. Continuously shifting alliance patterns are less likely in an age where the exchange of thousands of men and millions of dollars worth of equipment are involved.

The inflexibility that appears to be a product of contemporary alliances is a two-way street for the states involved. The state hosting the foreign troops is constrained in any military response they might make while the nation sending the troops may be "dragged" into a war by the actions of the host state. To illustrate the latter point, it is not impossible to conceive of the West German regime's prefabricating an attack by East Germans or even "forcing" the East Germans to attack West Germany. Because American troops could receive the major damage from the attack, the United States might feel compelled to retaliate. Given the commitments that are part of contemporary military alliances, many foreign policy alternatives that were available to the classical decision maker are not available to the contemporary one.

In addition, flexibility is also limited by policy influencers and by economic-military conditions within states. Almost every state today has a pluralized policy influence system—decision makers are faced by conflicting demands from their policy influencers when making foreign policy. In addition, economic and military conditions within states tend to tie allies closer together and to separate enemies even more because of the natural tendency towards a division of labor. Nations become economically and militarily interdependent. This in turn limits the alternatives open to their decision makers in forming alliances. Although contemporary military alliances are not absolutely binding (particularly if no troops are exchanged), radical shifts are more difficult now than in the classical period. For example, the French decision to lessen its involvement in NATO has not had the radical effect it might have had in an earlier era because of the long-term effects of the NATO pact.

Lack of flexibility limits the operation of both the balance of power and collective security. Balance of power is maintained by informal balancing alliances that counter any state that threatens to dominate the system. If the alternatives of decision makers are limited by economic, military, and political conditions, the chances of forming such a coalition are more remote. The principle of collective security also implies a certain degree of flexibility; in this case, the freedom to join a coalition of all states against the one aggressive state. It too fails when states are closely tied together because the aggressor always has certain allies that cannot afford to join a counteralliance even if they did perceive the aggressive tactics (a highly unlikely circumstance). As a result, neither mechanism is likely to prove effective if a major power threatens regional dominance.

What has emerged is a system of universal surveillance by the United States and the Soviet Union to prevent regional empires, whether the threat is made by one of the superpowers or by a state within the region. When the threat is not from them, the two superpowers have cooperated through the United Nations or in behind-the-scenes diplomacy. When the threat is from one of the superpowers, the result has usually been a deadlock. For example, the outcome of the Korean war was in large part a return to prewar conditions. The various threats by the Soviet Union and the United States concerning Berlin have resulted in counter threats but no real change in the territorial distribution. In the Vietnam situation, both sides have attempted to stabilize conditions they assume the other has attempted to change.

The United Nations has served as an important institutional setting for Soviet-American cooperation in preventing regional dominance by other states.[9] Through the offices of the UN Secretary-General, measures are usually applied to make a cease-fire practicable. This has occurred in Cyprus; in the Middle East in 1948, 1956, and 1967; and in periodic India-Pakistan flareups. Although the United Nations has yet to settle a dispute in a way "acceptable" to both sides through the actions of either the Security Council or the General Assembly, it has in many instances

---

[9] The role of the United Nations in limiting regional conflicts is discussed in Linda B. Miller, *World Order and Local Disorder* (Princeton, N.J.: Princeton University Press, 1967); Arthur L. Burns and Nina Heathcote, *Peace-Keeping by UN Forces* (New York: Praeger, 1963); and Inis L. Claude, Jr., *Swords Into Plowshares* 3d ed. (New York: Random House, 1964), pp. 94–111 and 285–304.

limited the duration and intensity of fighting. The most effective UN measure has been to place a peace-keeping force there; although token in size, it serves to keep the two sides clearly separated. As the conflict situations more directly involve the Soviet Union or the United States, the United Nations becomes less effective primarily because it takes United States and Soviet support to make it effective in the first place. In the Cuban missile crisis, for example, the United Nations provided only a setting for communication (both public and private) rather than a vehicle for international action.

While the existing patterns of international activity appear to be relatively successful in preventing regional dominance, there is continued and justified concern about the possibility of widespread war involving the use of nuclear weapons. As contemporary decision makers make moves and counter moves to keep each region balanced, the threat of a large-scale war resulting from military confrontation among nuclear powers hangs over their heads. In closing this discussion of maintenance of the contemporary international political system, therefore, it is necessary to examine the factors affecting whether or not a large-scale confrontation will occur in the future. These factors fall into two categories: (1) relationship of the superpowers to each other and (2) conditions in the international political system.

Relationship of the Superpowers to Each Other

So far, we have discussed the relationship between the Soviet Union and the United States in terms of the extent to which they have been able to cooperate—either tacitly or openly—to minimize threats to the maintenance of the international political system. It is necessary, however, to consider factors in their relationship that might lead to direct military confrontation. Given their mutual fear of nuclear war and apparent belief that neither side would start such a war as long as the possibility of nuclear retaliation was strong, nuclear war between them could only result from an accident or a top-level decision that fails to take into account the probability of immense loss.[10]

Accidental war between the United States and the Soviet Union is possible even though it may be quite remote. Modern nuclear weapons are harnessed to complex information and transportation systems that are subject to breakdown. Although great care has been taken (in the United States and we must assume also in the Soviet Union) to provide alternative

[10] The chances of what J. David Singer calls "unintended" nuclear war are examined in his book, *Deterrence, Arms Control and Disarmament* (Columbus: Ohio State University Press, 1962), pp. 89–109.

information and transportation components in case of breakdown, the possibility of a mistake always exists. Even barring mechanical failures, the danger of human error is real. Breakdown in command systems under conditions of stress are not uncommon; and the command of a nuclear arsenal may engender a great deal of stress, especially under crisis conditions.

To counter the dangers of accidental nuclear war, the Soviet Union and the United States have set up a high-speed communication system between their two capitals. The "hot-line" is a direct telecommunications line between Washington and Moscow. If a missile carrying a nuclear warhead were accidentally launched, the launching state could call the leader of the other state to warn him and inform him that the attack was unintentional. There is no guarantee he would believe that it was accidental because such a claim could be made to delude the attacked state. Moreover, leaders of the attacked state might feel forced to retaliate in order to placate irate policy influencers. Nevertheless, the hot-line does represent the realization that nuclear weapons necessitate close cooperation between the two superpowers, particularly in times of crisis such as the Arab-Israeli War of 1967.

The second type of condition that could result in large-scale nuclear war between the two superpowers is failure of their decision makers to recognize that a nuclear attack would involve immense loss for both sides. This failure could result either from the belief that a nuclear retaliation by the attacked state would not be too costly for the initiator or from the feeling that political conditions surrounding their relations makes nuclear war the only alternative. The first belief is related to technology and the arms race while the second is related to the decision maker's perceptions and calculations of the objectives involved.

Ever since the middle 1950's the Soviet Union and the United States have maintained sufficient second-strike capability;[11] that is, the protection of nuclear attack facilities so that nuclear retaliation would be possible even if the other side struck the first blow. Second-strike capability is maintained with systems of mobile and stationary launching facilities, some of which would be left after a full-scale nuclear attack. The existence of second-strike capability minimizes the advantage of striking first, since such a strike would not eliminate a counterattack. For the first time in history, a

---

[11] Nuclear capabilities of the two superpowers are compared in Herman Kahn, *On Thermonuclear War* (Princeton, N.J.: Princeton University Press, 1961), pp. 453–523, and in Glenn H. Snyder, *Deterrence and Defense* (Princeton, N.J.: Princeton University Press, 1961). See also Herbert F. York, "Military Technology and National Security," in Morton A. Kaplan, ed., *Great Issues in International Politics* (Chicago: Aldine, 1970), pp. 371–98.

preemptive attack stands little chance of providing a significant overall advantage.

These conditions continue to exist today although each side is working to insure its own second-strike capability while eliminating the other's. In the 1960's, the emphasis shifted from developing enough capability to knock out the other side's nuclear capability by preemptive attack to developing a defense system to destroy the other side's weapons once they were launched, thus blunting the second-strike capability. Various techniques such as antiballistic missile systems and satellite surveillance systems have been employed. Barring some unforeseen technological developments, however, it does not appear that either side will develop a sufficiently efficient defense against nuclear attack to insure "adequate" protection.

Even though an "adequate" defense system may not be developed, however, it is still possible that leaders of either or both states will believe that such a defense system has been developed. History is full of instances where leaders have overestimated their own states' military capability, and we cannot assume that the leaders of the two superpowers are immune to such mistakes. We also know from history that such mistakes are likely to be made if hostility between the two countries increases. For example, in World War I the German leaders overestimated their military strength as their hostility to the French, Russians and English increased.[12] This raises the second condition between the two superpowers that could result in a nuclear war—the assumption by either or both that war is inevitable given existing political conditions.

This danger is often phrased in terms of the concept of "escalation." This concept has two aspects; hostility can escalate from verbal threats to the use of force or from a regional conflict bounded by time, intensity, and geography to a worldwide conflict. As discussed in the last chapter, escalation plays a role in bargaining among all states and particularly the superpowers. (Escalation as a bargaining pattern is treated in Chapter 10.) However, the important question is whether the superpowers' use of escalation as a strategy will get out of control and reach a point at which one or both of the leaders decides large-scale war is the only alternative.

Some escalation has been employed in bargaining interactions between the Soviet Union and the United States. Starting in 1948 and recurring periodically ever since, for example, the Soviet-American disagreement over Berlin escalated on a number of occasions into both implicit and explicit threats of nuclear war. The powers have not only made verbal

[12] This point is made in Dina Zinnes, Robert C. North, and Howard E. Koch, Jr., "Capability, Threat and the Outbreak of War," in James N. Rosenau, ed., *International Politics and Foreign Policy* (New York: Free Press, 1961), pp. 469–82.

threats but also have taken symbolic actions to increase the credibility of their threats. The Berlin blockade, in which the Soviet Union blocked land access to Berlin, and the Berlin Wall (which was built in part to stop the flow of refugees but also as a symbolic act) involved Soviet actions designed to communicate the intractability of the Soviet position on Berlin.[13]

However, despite the tendency of Soviet-American bargaining to escalate on the level of threats and symbolic acts, the two superpowers have been able to avoid direct warfare. In the past, foreign policy decision makers in both states have been able to perceive clearly the dangers involved and to act with caution. Although this caution has not produced a resolution of the conflict, it has led to a gradual easing of tension and movement away from the brink of nuclear war.[14] Whether the inevitable future crises between the two can be handled successfully remains to be seen. Since the 1962 Cuban missile crisis, however, the superpowers have appeared to be able to avoid this type of confrontation completely. One might speculate that they have considered making even direct military threats too risky, but such speculation would assume the pattern of political interaction between the two has been radically transformed.

Escalation of regional conflict also appears to be a serious threat to avoidance of nuclear and large-scale war. Remembering how World War I started with a regional crisis in the Balkans between a small state, Serbia, and an ally of a major power, Austria, students of international politics fear that regional conflicts that periodically occur throughout the world could lead to a buildup of tension to a point where decision makers are unable to weigh alternatives in clear perspective and avoid taking steps that might lead to nuclear war.

In discussing this possibility, it is necessary to make a distinction between regional conflicts in which the two superpowers are relatively independent third parties and those in which they are more substantially involved. If we look at recent examples, we can identify the India-Pakistan dispute as one in which both superpowers played a complementary role by

[13] For an excellent quantitative analysis of the interaction between the Soviet Union and the United States over Berlin, see Charles A. McClelland in Singer, ed., *Quantitative International Politics: Insights and Evidence* (New York: Free Press, 1968), pp. 159–87.

[14] The term "brink" is probably a journalistic overstatement developed to describe Secretary of State John Foster Dulles' tendency to raise the nuclear threat and therefore bring the world to the brink of nuclear war. In retrospect, it is possible to argue that neither the Secretary of State nor the Russians perceived the situation to be as dangerous as they publicly stated it to be. For an analysis of brinkmanship and the foreign policy of John Foster Dulles, see P. Peters, *Massive Retaliation: The Policy and its Critics* (Chicago: Henry Regnery, 1959), and Maxwell D. Taylor, *The Uncertain Trumpet* (New York: Harper & Brothers, 1960).

trying to enforce peaceful conditions between the two states. Such a role greatly diminishes the chances of the escalation from a regional to a worldwide conflict. If either side changes its role, the danger of escalation increases. In the Arab-Israeli conflict, for example, cooperation between the Soviet Union and the United States appears to be diminishing. In the 1956 flareup both powers worked together to enforce peace. In the 1967 crisis, however, it appears that the Soviet Union and the United States have taken positions favoring opposing sides. Although the United States has not openly backed the Israeli regime, the Soviet Union has supported the Arabs. The result of this shift has been to increase the danger that the middle eastern situation will lead to greater hostility and tension between the two superpowers. The final variation of superpower involvement in a regional conflict is the situation in South Vietnam. Since 1964 the United States has supported the existing regime with troops and has attacked North Vietnam; the Soviet Union has actively supported the North Vietnamese regime with weapons. With both superpowers clearly on opposite sides and the United States following a policy of escalation, the South Vietnam situation has represented a dangerous regional conflict with the potential of leading to worldwide conflict.

The key to whether or not regional conflict leads to worldwide conflict is difficult to find. Many students of world politics cite the Korean war as an example of how a regional conflict can remain limited.[15] In that war, both sides limited the geographical scope of their attacks. The Red Chinese and North Koreans could have attacked American shipping as well as bases outside of Korea while the United States could have invaded China. However, both sides refrained from expanding the war even though some of their policy influencers called for such expansion.

There is no question that the Korean war exemplifies the ability of the two superpowers to limit regional conflicts in which they are involved. However, the degree to which it enables the student to assess the ability of states to maintain similar limitations in the future is questionable. Special circumstances that surrounded the Korean war have not surrounded regional conflicts since then, and probably will not surround other regional conflicts in the future. During the war, Red China and the Soviet Union were vulnerable to nuclear attack from the United States because they did not have nuclear weapons and delivery capability. Hence, they had more to gain from limiting the war than the United States did. In contrast, today the Soviet Union has substantial nuclear capability, and Red China has a slowly increasing arsenal. In addition, the Korean war was conventional to

[15] For example, Morton Halperin, "The Limiting Process in the Korean War," *Political Science Quarterly*, 78 (1965), 13–39.

the degree that formal enemy lines were defined. In contrast, the South Vietnamese war involves unconventional warfare; this means, among other things, enemy lines are not clearly drawn. The condition of civil war is much more difficult to contain in terms of geographical targets than conventional wars where both sides are clearly distinguished. Because regional conflict in the future will probably be closer to the South Vietnamese example than to the Korean one, the possibilities for preventing escalation of regional conflicts will probably be substantially reduced.

At the same time, however, it appears that both the Soviet Union and the United States realize the dangers inherent in limited regional conflicts. In its attacks on North Vietnam, for example, the United States has attempted to avoid targets involving Soviet personnel, although it has not been completely successful. By the same token, the Soviet Union has not given North Vietnam full military support and has held back certain offensive military equipment. While danger of the expansion of regional conflict exists, then, the superpowers do not fail to recognize it.

Conditions in the International Political System

In addition, conditions in the international political system that might grow beyond the control of the two superpowers are often cited as increasing the threat of large-scale nuclear war. Such conditions include the spread of nuclear weapons (proliferation) and the impact of alliance patterns on world peace.

Nuclear proliferation appears to be inevitable, particularly in the 1970's.[16] During the 1950's and 1960's, only the Soviet Union and the United States had substantial nuclear capability and delivery systems. Capability of France and Great Britain, while not insubstantial, is still quite small in relation to that of the two superpowers. Red China has developed a few nuclear weapons, but its delivery systems are crude. However, by the middle of the 1970's Red China will probably have some delivery capability, particularly in terms of reaching her neighbors (which include the Soviet Union, Japan and India). By this time also, many states will have the wealth and capability as well as the inclination to produce nuclear weapons and moderately effective delivery systems. Because prospects for an *effective* nonproliferation pact do not appear good, we must assume that a dozen nations or more may have nuclear weapons by the end of the 1970's.

---

[16] See Richard N. Rosecrance, ed., *The Dispersion of Nuclear Weapons: Strategy and Politics* (New York: Columbia University Press, 1964) for a discussion of the role of nuclear proliferation in contemporary world politics.

Arguments concerning the threats posed by the spread of nuclear weapons can usually be classified into two types. The first argument is that while the United States and the Soviet Union as well as France and Great Britain are satisfied states with few bitter international grievances, the new nuclear powers will probably be much more intent upon changing certain international situations. Red China, particularly in its relationship with Taiwan; West Germany, particularly in its relationship with eastern Europe; India and Pakistan, particularly in their relationships with each other; and Israel are states that could produce nuclear weapons by the mid-1970's and that have definite grievances concerning certain international situations. Moreover, all these states have shown indications of the desire to acquire nuclear capability. As weapons spread, it is argued, more aggressive states, probably motivated by their grievances, will acquire nuclear weapons. Because these states will have a greater stake in changing international conditions, it is argued, they will be less hesitant in employing threats of nuclear force, if not the force itself.

One could counter this first type of argument by pointing out that acquisition of nuclear weapons might produce greater caution on the part of decision makers and their policy influencers. As long as Red China cannot seriously threaten the U.S. mainland, she might be extremely anti-American. However, if Red Chinese decision makers thought U.S. decision makers had a basis for taking her threats seriously, they might be less inclined to threaten. Moreover, third parties, including the United Nations and the superpowers, would apply greater pressure on the actors in a regional situation if one or both states had nuclear weapons. The relative ease with which regional actors can now engage in limited, contained warfare will no doubt diminish if nuclear weapons become more widespread. This will occur because other states will not accept the risks of having nuclear powers locked in direct combat.

The second argument concerning the dangers of nuclear proliferation is that the increase in the number of nations possessing nuclear weapons automatically increases the dangers of war regardless of which states get the weapons. The spread of nuclear weapons, it is argued, means that chances of a mentally unbalanced leader getting control of mass-destruction weapons also increases. Many political analysts agree. We can assume that policy influencers and those around the decision makers might be more careful in selecting and pressuring a decision maker if the use of nuclear weapons is a possibility. We must also assume, however, that the probability a leader will make an irrational decision to use nuclear weapons increases as the number of states acquiring the weapons increases.

An added probability is that chances of accidental nuclear war will increase as the number of states with nuclear weapons increases. The poorer states will not have sufficient resources to devote to safeguards for preventing accidental firing. Even with maximum protection, the chances of an accidental firing—resulting from mechanical or human error—would still increase with the spread of nuclear weapons.

Finally, nuclear proliferation creates a condition where the origin of a nuclear attack might not be easily discovered. A desperate nation could launch an attack against one of the superpowers. If the attacked were unable to discover the origin of attack, blame might be mistakenly placed on the other superpower. The spread of nuclear weapons would no doubt increase mutual suspicion and distrust between all states given the inevitable increases in stress. Pressure for preemptive attacks would probably increase, and even a minor spark could cause the dreaded nuclear war. Hence, it is argued that the spread of nuclear weapons could create an environment conducive to miscalculation because it would be difficult to discern the origins of attack.

The nature of alliance systems is the second condition affecting chances of widespread nuclear or conventional war. In the 1950's, the superpowers headed coalitions of closely-knit blocs. Members of the blocs willingly allowed the superpowers to formulate policy, particularly regarding relationships between the blocs. In the 1960's, however, cohesion within both blocs has diminished. Open hostility between the USSR and Red China as well as between France and the United States clearly indicates this tendency. Moreover, lesser members of both blocs have been following independent policies.

There is disagreement over whether this disintegration within blocs increases or decreases the threat of widespread war. In the classical period, it was clear that flexibility in alliances was essential to keep wars short and prevent dominance by one state. In the contemporary period, the evidence is not so clear. On the one hand, one might assume that because the flexibility that characterized the earlier system was the determining factor in maintaining the system, flexibility will also contribute to the maintenance of the system today. Such an assumption would lead to the conclusion that the independence of France, China and lesser states is a healthy development because it increases this flexibility. In addition, the neutral states may be viewed as a stabilizing factor restraining the two major blocs. Using the classical system as a model for analyzing the contemporary one, we might assume that more than two major actors are necessary to the maintenance of the international political system, and therefore that the current lessening of bloc cohesion contributes to stability.

On the other hand, it has been argued that internal cohesion of the two blocs is essential for maintaining the stability of the international political system. Emphasizing the major differences between the contemporary and the classical international political system, we might see the tendency of bloc disintegration as weakening the deterrent capability of both sides. We might then assume that maintenance of the international political system depends upon the ability of the superpowers to threaten each other with nuclear weapons so that neither would risk nuclear war. Any weakening in alliances might be viewed as an indication that the will to deter by threatening and using nuclear weapons also is weakening because the superpowers will not have consensus within their own camp. Hence, the loss of bloc cohesion is viewed as a step toward the breakdown in the nuclear deterrent of both sides.

Although the two positions just presented have different predictive and prescriptive implications, they are based on a common descriptive assumption about the contemporary international environment. The assumption is that cohesion within the two major blocs has been diminishing at least for the last decade. Such an implicit assumption does not appear to be warranted, however. Except for Communist China and Albania, which probably would not have supported the Soviet Union under any condition in recent years, members of both blocs have exhibited support for their respective bloc leaders when the threat from the other bloc appears to have substantially increased. In the succession of Berlin crises and in the Cuban missile crisis the threat of nuclear or large-scale conventional warfare appeared to be immediate and real; then members of each bloc supported their respective leaders. The important point in assessing the cohesion of the two blocs is to distinguish between questions of national security, where both blocs appear to be as cohesive as ever, and nonsecurity questions such as economic or ideological issues, where substantial disagreement exists. Although the bloc leaders appear to act as if they demanded support on all issues, it is apparent today that bloc cohesion is readily generated only when the threat of war is imminent and real.

All these dangers of large-scale warfare have stimulated increased emphasis on the role of disarmament and other forms of arms control. Like their pre-World War II predecessors, contemporary decision makers look to disarmament as a way of lessening the chance of war.[17] However, in contrast to earlier decision makers, contemporary ones have focused on piecemeal arms control rather than extensive disarmament. Hence, a prohibition on the atmospheric testing formalized in the Test Ban Treaty of

---

[17] For a discussion of disarmament in the contemporary world, see Singer, *Deterrence;* Claude, *Swords into Plowshares*, pp. 261–85; John W. Spanier and Joseph L. Nogee, *The Politics of Disarmament* (New York: Praeger, 1962); Richard J. Barnet and Richard A. Falk, eds., *Security in Disarmament* (Princeton, N.J.: Princeton University Press, 1965); and Charles A. Barker, ed., *Problems of World Disarmament* (Boston: Houghton Mifflin, 1963).

1963 has been accepted by most states including the superpowers (although excluding Communist China and France). More recently, attempts to prevent the spread of nuclear weapons have been formalized in a treaty that has been signed by many states but not ratified as of early 1969. Although gains have been modest, contemporary states have attempted to reach some agreements on methods of controlling nuclear weapons. Current arms control activities are consequences of widespread fear of nuclear warfare and willingness of the superpowers to cooperate with each other; they manifest general awareness of the threat warfare represents to the international political system.

Another manifestation of the desire to maintain the system if not to preserve mankind is the use of the United Nations. Although failing to guarantee world peace, the United Nations has provided an instrument through which to limit regional wars. As pointed out earlier the United Nations has been successful in a number of regional conflict situations not in eliminating the dispute but in promoting a cease-fire and a gradual relaxation of tensions. The superpowers have found the United Nations a valuable forum to minimize both hostility and involvement, if both seek these goals, in regional conflict situations.

When the two superpowers are more directly opposed, the United Nations has served to reduce hostility and tension between them. By providing a place for quick, informal, and relatively unpublicized communication channels for high-level officials, as it did during the Berlin blockade, the United Nations provides a setting where preliminary negotiations can be easily started. Moreover, the Secretary-General and other officials of the Secretariat can serve as mediators during times of high tension between the superpowers. They can transmit information between the two states as well as open up opportunities for negotiation in case of a stalemate.

The United Nations also aids in reducing tension and hostility by providing a public forum in which the superpowers can engage in "verbal conflict." While developing public statements and ironing out proposals, the superpowers frequently are able to "cool-off." The United Nations provides a platform where their spokesmen and their policy influencers can experience verbal exchanges that have many of the symbolic manifestations of conflict. Although it is possible to argue that the United Nations as an arena for verbal conflict exacerbates rather than diminishes tensions, contemporary events like the Cuban missile crisis appear to show the opposite.

SUMMARY

The two threats to the international political system, then, appear to have changed their relative positions of importance from the classical to the contemporary period. In the classical period, fear of universal empire was the primary threat while the threat of large-scale warfare appears to have been secondary. However, as mankind has progressed through the nineteenth and into the twentieth century, the threat of warfare not only to the system but to mankind has become paramount, while universal empire appears remote if not impossible. These conditions result from the inability of man to maintain effective controls over large-scale empires and the effectiveness of guerrilla warfare in weakening long-term military control. The fear of regional empire still motivates activities within the system, but these activities are constrained by the fear of large-scale warfare.

The chances of preserving the international political system and mankind from large-scale warfare appear to be mixed. The superpowers seem to have control over conditions as they now exist in the system. They have been successful in limiting regional conflict by forcing regional actors to limit the scope and intensity of their conflict or by following limited interventionist policies themselves. In controlling regional conflict and in dealing with each other, the superpowers have sought to maintain communication networks that would facilitate the resolution of any crisis situation.

At the same time, however, the spread of nuclear weapons, the danger of accidental war, and the possibility of escalation still exist. Although it is not clear to what extent these dangers have been minimized, we can be certain that they are still real in the contemporary world. The most that we can say at this time is that the dangers do not appear to be an unbearable strain on decision makers or a prelude to disaster.

We must conclude, therefore, that the threats to the contemporary international political system are real. While the threat of universal empire appears remote especially as long as both sides act to prevent even regional empires, the threat of a widespread war continues to preoccupy the leaders of states. Future conditions will no doubt increase their preoccupation, although it does not seem likely that any radical arrangement such as general disarmament will emerge. In the immediate future, then, men will live in a world where fear of nuclear war is the major fact of international political life. Their ability to handle the conditions surrounding this fear will determine the ability of both the international political system and mankind to survive.

SUMMARY OUTLINE

I.   The formal and informal patterns of interactions among states may be viewed as an international political system.

    A.   The international political system is decentralized because the central international institutions that exist have little authority.

    B.   Interactions among states produced the patterns that characterized the international political system.

C. Maintenance of the international political system means maintenance of a system of autonomous states.

D. The central international institutions (United Nations, for example) play only a small role in maintaining the international political system.

E. Two major threats to the international political system have been universal empire and large-scale war.

II. A number of conditions characterized the classical international political system.

   A. *Members of the system were located in Europe.*

   B. *The great powers dominated the small powers in the system.*

   C. *Major powers rarely attacked each other directly but instead fought over colonial holdings and the control of small powers.*

   D. *Decision makers dominated policy influencers.*

   E. *Sociocultural ties limited the intensity of warfare.*

   F. *Technological factors limited the intensity of warfare.*

   G. *The classical pattern of maintaining the system against the threat of one powerful state was to form a balancing coalition or alliance.*

   H. *The balancing pattern worked well because the foreign policy decision makers could follow flexible foreign policies.*

   I. *Flexibility in foreign policy along with sociocultural and technological constraints tended to prevent large-scale warfare.*

III. The period between 1815 and 1945 can be viewed as transitional.

   A. *Membership in the system was spreading beyond Europe.*

   B. *Foreign policy decision makers had to deal with more internal pressures from their policy influencers.*

   C. *Sociocultural limitations on the use of force disappeared.*

   D. *Technological progress increased the ability of states to harm each other.*

   E. *Concern with universal empire began to be replaced by concern for regional empire.*

   F. *Flexibility in foreign policy decision making decreased.*

   G. *Fear of large-scale war played a large role after World War I as indicated in the phrase, "peace is indivisible," in the attempt to develop disarmament, and in international institutions that were developed to regulate use of force.*

   H. *The principle of collective security was in effect an argument for institutionalization of the balancing coalition.*

   I. *Despite the collective security principle, balancing coalitions were slow to form during the interwar period.*

   J. *Foreign policies of England and France indicated the extent to which fear of war inhibited the formation of a balancing coalition to stop Hitler.*

IV. The contemporary international political system is relatively different from both the classical and the transitional period.

A. *Use of nuclear weapons at the end of World War II introduced a new factor into maintaining the international political system by intensifying fear of war.*

B. *The state system has become completely universalized.*

C. *Regional empire has become a more active concern of the major states than universal empire primarily because it is assumed that the former must precede the latter if the latter is at all possible.*

D. The superpowers play a large role in maintaining the contemporary international political system.

1. *In areas where they feel they have a sphere of interest, they maintain stability by themselves.*

2. *In some areas, they cooperate in preventing conflict and regional empire.*

3. *In some areas, they are involved in competition with each other by backing opposing sides.*

E. *Much less flexibility exists in foreign policy decision making today not only because of the expanded role of policy-influencers in the foreign policy-making process but also because technological conditions tend to make alliances more static.*

F. *Military alliances tie the hands of all members of the alliance.*

G. *The United Nations has served as an institutional setting for the superpowers to prevent regional empire and widespread conflict.*

H. *Accidental nuclear war is a possibility (albeit remote) in the contemporary world.*

I. *The second-strike capability enjoyed by both superpowers appears to be relatively stable and to serve as a deterrent to preemptive attacks.*

J. *Danger exists that a conflict will escalate to nuclear war.*

K. *The superpowers have often followed escalating strategies but have never become directly involved in a war with each other.*

L. *The limitations that operated in the Korean war will not necessarily operate in other wars.*

M. Nuclear proliferation is viewed by some as increasing the danger of a large-scale war; however, except for the fact that it will increase the chances of accidental war, the evidence is not clear.

N. Loss of cohesion in the two major blocs is assumed to have an effect on the chances of avoiding war.

   1. Some assume that lack of cohesion will diminish the chances
      of widespread war.
   2. Some assume that lack of cohesion will increase the chances
      of widespread war.
   O. *Although some loss of cohesion appears in areas such as eco-*
      nomic cooperation, clear threats from the opposing bloc seem to
      produce a significant amount of cohesion in the bloc being
      threatened.
   P. *Disarmament has followed a more moderate pattern in the con-*
      temporary world than it did in the interwar period.
   Q. *The United Nations has had some impact in reducing the dangers*
      of large-scale wars by keeping communication channels open for
      states and by serving as a public forum for "verbal conflict."
V.   Although the threat of universal empire is sometimes identified as a
     possibility, it is highly remote in the contemporary world.
VI. The primary threat to the contemporary international political system
     is widespread warfare, the occurrence of which appears to be neither
     inevitable nor impossible.

BIBLIOGRAPHICAL ESSAY

Literature relevant to maintenance of the international political system can
be divided into four categories. First, historical writers trace evolution of
patterns of interactions among states, particularly in relation to international stability. Second, certain writers have examined ideas pertaining to
maintenance of the international system. Third, some have attempted to
develop propositions that describe the dynamics of maintenance of the
system through a set of explicitly developed concepts and relationships. In
the final category, some works assess implications of contemporary trends.

A great deal has been written in the first category, the history of
international politics. We will discuss only those works that endeavor to
build a theoretical framework. In addition to the work of Aron (15 and
16), at least four other writers have evaluated the history of the international political system in an explicit theoretical framework. In 1955 Gulick
(143) defined the "balance of power framework" and applied that framework to the politics of the period following the Napoleonic era. This work
is still a good starting point. Osgood and Tucker (306) trace technological,
military, political, moral, and ethical trends to analyze the maintenance of
the international system. Finally, Rosecrance (343) surveys the history of
international politics through nine international systems corresponding to
the rise and fall of various states and coalitions in the context of general

conditions. These works, together with more conventional historical works including Petrie (311), Taylor (399 and 400), Mattingly (273), Nicolson (295), and Thomson (405) provide an excellent overview of this history.

A number of works deal with the second category, ideas concerning how the international political system should be maintained. Surveys are found in Gareau (137), Maurseth (274), and Seabury (372). Ernst Haas (144 and 145) considers various ways the term balance of power has been used. He concludes that it has served both as an analytical concept for scholars and as an ideological position for policy makers. The student is advised, in addition, to read Carr (68) for a classic discussion of the ideas of system maintenance during the interwar period. Waltz (414) surveys the history of western thought on the question of causes of war while Claude (73 and 74) has evaluated a number of major conceptions relating to what he calls "management of power," including balance of power and collective security.

In the third category, attempts to construct sets of propositions or models of the international political system have been numerous. Wight's short 1946 essay (421) built the essential framework for later writers who studied the idea of the balance-of-power system. Morton Kaplan (207) presents six models of the international system, two of which correspond to historical periods. Liska (252) applies to the system the concept of equilibrium developed by economists while Masters (272) applies a model of "primitive political systems." Finally, Modelski (282) has erected models that contrast international political systems based on agrarian economics with those of industrial states.

Simulation models have also proven useful in studying patterns of international interactions. Brody (52), in examining the impact of the spread of nuclear weapons on alliance politics, developed the Internation Simulation to test propositions in the literature. Hermann and Hermann (167) use the same model to study conditions surrounding the outbreak of World War I. Closely related, but at a higher level of abstraction, is the work of Riker (339), who applies principles of coalition formation through gaming experiments and game theory to international politics.

Works that generalize from explicit assumptions about future conditions in the international political system can also be found. On one side, Waltz (412, 414) argues that the bipolar structure is not as unstable as some assume. The opposing view is taken by Masters (271) and Burton (63), who opt for the stability of multibloc conditions; Deutsch and Singer (107) illustrate the stability of a multipolar situation with a simple mathematical model. Michael Haas (150) has subjected these competing propositions to empirical tests. Writers who discuss the role of alliances in the maintenance of the international political system include Liska (254),

Singer (382), and Singer and Small (384). Implications of arms races are subject matter for Richardson (334).

Contemporary conditions that create the threat of large-scale warfare and how nations endeavor to meet these conditions are examined from a number of angles. Writers in the final category are Fox in (299); Herz (170); Hekhuis, McClintock, and Burns (165); Aron (16); and Osgood and Tucker (306). Underlying conditions they discuss are threats to the contemporary international political system. In addition, nuclear proliferation is discussed in Brody (52) and Rosecrance (344). Disarmament and arms control is examined in Singer (379) and in Edwards (114). Claude (74), Wainhouse et al. (408), and Bloomfield (38) examine the role of international organizations in crisis situations. Finally, the student should read Pruitt and Snyder (321) for a relatively up-to-date synthesis on current theory and research into the causes of war.

12

Trends in the International Political System

In this chapter, we will examine major trends—past, present and future—in the evolution of the contemporary international political system. In discussing these trends and especially in projecting them into the future, we will be forced to rely on many of the concepts and propositions presented throughout this book. For this reason, review of the propositional outline summaries following Chapters 2 through 11 is recommended before reading this chapter, and also pay close attention to references in this chapter to material in earlier chapters.

When describing trends, one of the most intriguing questions is whether processes or structures are being changed. Actors in a political system (political parties in a democratic system or states in the international political system) may employ different strategies and seek different goals without significantly altering the role of institutions or the lines of authority that characterize the political system. More than once, analysts have assumed that certain changes in characteristic behavior have produced a revolution in the system when in fact the basic features of the political system have remained intact. To cite an example presented in the last chapter, many assumed that the birth of the League of Nations signified the dawn of a new era in the very structure of the international political system. Hindsight suggests, however, that changes that brought about the League had more to do with the rhetoric of statecraft and the focus of some bargaining activities than with lines of political authority.

Our basic concern in this chapter is whether and to what extent contemporary trends represent changes in structure rather than process in the international political system. If we see the international system as a decentralized political system dominated by competing, relatively autonomous, territorially-based political organizations, how much has it been affected by interactions at governmental and nongovernmental levels across national boundaries? (Chapter 11 defines the basic structure of the international political system.)

Given the nature of our purpose in this chapter, our primary interest will be to examine present trends and speculate on their impact in the future. We will discuss three factors: (1) trends in the way states bargain with each other; (2) types of governmental and nongovernmental activities often referred to as international integration, which some writers assume will have a revolutionary impact on the structure of the international political system; and (3) attitudes about the nature of the system that orient foreign policy decision makers and their influencers in international behavior (In Chapter 7 this was defined as the "international political culture").

TRENDS IN THE INTERNATIONAL BARGAINING PROCESS

In comparing international politics today to classical international politics, it is clear that competitive bargaining among states has been radically transformed by the many conditions cited in preceding chapters. The international political system continues to be a system in which states compete with each other in order to determine who gets what, when, and how with only minor influence from international institutions. Even so, the ways in which they competitively bargain with each other and the very issues over which they bargain have changed radically since the classical period. In our discussion, we will cite three of the most important areas of change, particularly in terms of the future: the importance of regions, the fragmentation of issue areas, and the use of force.

Regionalization

One of the most important trends in the international bargaining process is its regionalization, that is, its fragmentation along regional lines so that a number of bargaining issues concern only those states within a particular region. In the classical period, the European states were the primary, if not the only members of the international political system. Although bargaining situations arose among the members of the classical system in virtually every corner of the globe, the actors were European. In the seventeenth and early eighteenth century, for example, the "politics of North America" was really one aspect of the international politics of European states and the American war for independence was as much a product of European politics as it was a colonial uprising.[1]

Today, however, one can speak of the "politics" of a particular geographical area (for example, western Europe, eastern Europe, the Middle East, sub-Sahara Africa, Latin America). Each of these regions serves as a bargaining arena in which states of those regions deal primarily with each other over a number of issues. Although states continue to be involved in bargaining situations with states in other regions, there is an increasing trend for bargaining interactions to occur more frequently and across a larger number of issues within specific geographical regions.

This trend toward regional fragmentation of bargaining is a natural outgrowth of the universalization of the international political system. (See pp. 309–310.) With over 150 states spread all over the globe, geographical conditions tend to tie the interests of states within geographical regions closer together and hence create conditions that result in bargaining situations. Although there are also economic and other conditions creating dependencies across regions, the basic nexus between geographical proximity and competing interests still exists.

One of the prime consequences as well as "causes" of the trend toward regionalization is the enormous growth of regional intergovernmental organizations. (See pp. 234–252.) The Organization of African Unity, the Organization of American States, the Arab League, and the Council of Europe provide a stage upon which the politics of their respective regions can be acted out. In addition to the multipurpose organizations mentioned above, a large number of more specialized economic and social organizations create conditions for bargaining among states within a particular region.

Global intergovernmental organizations like the United Nations have an ambiguous impact on fragmentation. On the one hand, they bring states throughout the world together and provide a stage for bargaining across regions. On the other hand, there is a distinct tendency for states of the same region to interact more frequently and to vote together in the United Nations.[2] In any case, global intergovernmental organizations do not completely counteract the growing geographical fragmentation of the international bargaining process.

---

[1] See Samuel Flagg Bemis, *The Diplomacy of the American Revolution* (Bloomington, Ind.: Indiana University Press, 1957) and Richard Morris, *The Peacemakers* (New York: Harper, 1965) for the role of European politics in the American revolutionary war. Also, see Oran R. Young, "Political Discontinuities in the International System," *World Politics,* 20 (1968), for a general analysis of the role of regional systems in contemporary international politics.

[2] See, for example, Bruce M. Russett and Hayward R. Alker, Jr., *World Politics in the General Assembly* (New Haven, Conn.: Yale University Press, 1965).

Given the growing regional bargaining arenas, patterns are also evolving concerning (1) which states bargain with each other, (2) what issues they bargain over, and (3) what types of bargaining tools they employ. We will discuss each of these patterns, remembering they represent general trends that appear to be an aspect of future international bargaining.

Perhaps the greatest consequence of regionalization of the international bargaining process is that many states are likely to have very few occasions for direct bargaining with each other. For example, Gabon, a small sub-Saharan African state, and Guatemala, a small Central American state, maintain no regular diplomatic contact and rarely bargain with each other except in global intergovernmental organizations. For the bulk of states in the contemporary system, the opportunities for extraregional bargaining situations are few, especially outside of global intergovernmental organizations.

Consequently, the types of issues that involve members of the same region usually differ from the types of issues involving states in different regions. Members of the same regions become involved in a wide variety of issues ranging from territorial questions and stability of specific regimes to economic development and maintenance of communications. Members of different regions, unless they happen to be supraregional actors (as discussed in Chapter 5), rarely become involved in these questions of territory or internal stability, since most of their interactions occur through global intergovernmental organizations. Notwithstanding supraregional actors that, for reasons of "promoting peace" or trying to control global events, intervene in a wide variety of bargaining situations in different geographical regions, regionalization of the international bargaining process implies that bargaining issues will be different for members of the same region than they will be for members belonging to different geographical regions.

In addition, the geographical location of two states will affect the types of bargaining tools they employ. (See discussion of bargaining tools, pp. 269–287.) Bargaining among states within a given region could involve arguments, threats, promises, and force while bargaining between members of different regions—assuming they are not supraregional actors—will rarely involve either the threat or the use of force. Gabon and Guatemala, for example, would have no occasion to threaten or use force against each other, because if they interact at all, they do so through the United Nations or other global intergovernmental organizations. Although supraregional actors, particularly the superpowers and the excolonial states, have used force on a global scale in the contemporary period, they threat and use of force by regional actors is usually directed at other states in the same region.

Regionalization appears to be increasing in the contemporary international political system. While global intergovernmental organizations and the activities of many of the developed states (especially the superpowers) tend to tie regions together, the increasing complexity and intensity of politics within international regions continues to be an important trend in international bargaining. Moreover, should one or both superpowers decide to adopt a less globally oriented foreign policy, as it appears foreign policy decision makers in both the United States and the Soviet Union have contemplated for the 1970's, the international bargaining process will become even more geographically fragmented. In addition, although we can assume there will always be issues that will stimulate states to bargain with each other on a global basis, the international bargaining process will probably become increasingly geographically fragmented within that set of global interactions.

Fragmentation of Issue Areas

If one compares contemporary to classical international politics, a primary difference is the increase in the number and diversity of issue areas over which states bargain. (See pp. 266–286.) During the classical period, states bargained with each other primarily over control of territory which in turn often represented their physical security. Concern about alliances and about the makeup and intention of particular regimes, which were as important to the classical state as they are to the modern one, were clearly related to questions of preserving territorial control and national security. Although dynastic questions (that is, who should marry whom) often intruded, the prime issue area for the classical state—great and small—was territorial control.

In contrast, contemporary states bargain with each other in a wide range of issue areas, many of which are not related to questions of territorial control. Bargaining among states can involve questions of the makeup and activities of intergovernmental organizations, policies of economic development, dealing with the transnational flow of people, solving problems created by economic and social conditions in the international setting, and even internal social policies of certain states (apartheid in South Africa). To be sure, questions of territorial control and national security still occupy a large segment of bargaining interactions among states, particularly within specific regions. However, they are now complemented by a large variety of issue areas which have little or no national security connotation for the states involved.

Even those bargaining situations involving territorial control and national security have become more complex and in a sense fragmented. Alliance policy, for example, involves much more than the transitory agreement among a few states to achieve some territorial objective or to protect themselves from another state or coalition of states. Today, alliances like the North Atlantic Treaty Organization, the Warsaw Pact, and the Southeast Asian Treaty Organization imply extensive commitments that raise issues concerning stationing of foreign troops, allocation of support from alliance members, appointment of administrative personnel, and location of bases.

Similarly, the question of bargaining to influence the types of regimes that exist in certain crucial states also involves complex issues. (The role of intervention in foreign policy is examined in pp. 136–139.) The ideological position of the regime and the question of outside intervention become part of the bargaining strategies of the states trying to influence the makeup of the regime. Civil war—whether threatened or actual—raises bargaining conditions for nearby states as well as for interested supraregional actors. Although questions of intervention have always been important, the increasing interdependence of contemporary states, the continuous conditions of governmental instability throughout the world, and the concern of the superpowers with regional empires makes intervention a frequent, intense, and complex issue area for international bargaining.

Another issue area growing out of national security politics is arms control and disarmament. (See pp. 323 and 326.) In the twentieth century, foreign policy decision makers have frequently discussed disarmament although they have not often acted upon their discussions. Particularly since World War II attempts have been made to control certain aspects of modern military technology. Meeting in different types of international conferences ever since the end of that war, major military powers (except, for Communist China and at times, France) along with lesser states have bargained over various issues. Although many measures that would lead to extensive disarmament have never been seriously considered, a number of important arms control agreements have been reached. In 1959, a treaty was signed for demilitarization of Antarctica under mutual inspection. In 1963, the Nuclear Test Ban Treaty prohibited testing nuclear weapons in the atmosphere. In 1968, a nonproliferation treaty was signed by virtually all states except France and Communist China. Limited as these agreements are, however, they represent the importance of arms control and disarmament as an issue area for bargaining.

While issues relating directly and indirectly to national security have become more complex in contemporary international bargaining, nonsecurity issues like economic development, social welfare, and health have also increased in complexity. Interdependence is increasing and the transnational flow of people and ideas is growing; these factors have posed ever more vital and complex issues in social and economic fields. Realizing that control of social and economic factors on a regional or global basis is mutually beneficial, contemporary foreign policy decision makers have found it necessary to bargain in a larger variety of social and economic issue areas.

The growth of intergovernmental organizations has also increased the number of issue areas. Questions of the politics of the organizations, including constitutional changes, election of officials and states to positions in the organization, and budgetary allocations, constitute large sets of foreign policy issue areas. Moreover, intergovernmental organizations provide an arena for verbal conflicts over such ideological issues as human rights, communism versus capitalism, and colonialism versus anticolonialism. In a variety of ways, then, intergovernmental organizations that serve as a framework for interactions among states have also contributed to fragmentation of the international bargaining process into issue areas.

Related to this issue area fragmentation—both as a cause and an effect—is a growing specialization and fragmentation of the foreign policy-making process within states. (See pp. 72–87.) This is true for the foreign policy bureaucracy as well as the influencers that pressure the decision maker. While mass influencers tend to ignore all issue areas except those somehow involving national security (threats of war, space race, arms race, and UN Security Council activities) other foreign policy influencers often develop specialized interests. Interest, partisan, and bureaucratic influencers frequently have special interests such as tariffs, health, and transportation—as a result they help contribute to the activities of states in nonsecurity issue areas. In the foreign policy bureaucracy in particular, lower-level administrative officials frequently operate relatively autonomously in dealing with some of the more specialized intergovernmental organizations like the World Health Organization.

As a result of issue area fragmentation, the bargaining strategies of states will differ for various issue areas. The types of arguments, threats, and promises as well as whether and in what manner force will be used varies for different issue areas. For example, while France might threaten to use force against the Soviet Union if she felt the Soviet Union were contemplating an attack on western Europe, she would probably not threaten to use force over an economic issue within the Common Market. This does not mean France will never make any threats in economic issue areas but rather that the threats will not involve the use of force. In general, states will use force and threats of force in those issue areas relating directly to territorial control and national security; they will not use force for issues involving politics of intergovernmental organizations, general economic policies, or other nonsecurity issue areas.

One of the most significant aspects of the proliferation of issue areas is that any two states might be implacable enemies in one set of issues but allies in others. Like political actors within domestic societies, states are not involved in continuous absolute conflict. Rather, they are able to find areas of mutual compatible interests around which they can build various bargaining strategies. For example, the Soviet Union and the United States compete bitterly in a number of issue areas (Cold War issues in the United Nations, allegiance of underdeveloped states, German settlement) but they also cooperate in such areas as the peaceful uses of outer space and disarmament. India and Pakistan, to take another example, are bitter enemies over Kashmir but continue to cooperate in at least minimal ways on matters of economic development. Although the relationship between states in different issue areas is not always kept separate, as when Arabs and Israelis refused to deal with each other at a Conference of UNCTAD (a United Nations committee attempting to promote economic development) following the 1967 Arab-Israeli War, many states maintain different positions vis-à-vis each other for the various issue areas.

Like regionalization of the international bargaining process, issue area fragmentation appears to be growing. Increasing complexity in the definition of national security issues combined with more social and economic competition and cooperation are creating a larger number of issue areas. In the future, then, we can expect more variety in bargaining strategies as well as a greater number of combinations of "allies" and "enemies" in the international political system.

Trends in the Use of Force

In the classical period, warfare served as a final arbiter in disputes among states. War functioned like a court or a legislature does—as a decision-making institution determining which states received what payoffs. Although force was also used, as it is today, to communicate threats and to change payoffs, war functioned as "trial by combat"—that is, a fight to determine, not who was right, but who won what the states were bargaining over. Given the technological conditions that made it politically feasible to occupy a captured piece of territory and the political conditions that would permit foreign policy decision makers to lose a limited amount of territory without losing all internal support, war as a court of last resort was a viable but costly institution in the classical period.

Today, conditions have so radically changed that war is no longer employed effectively as a final arbiter in bargaining among states. Although legal institutions do not forbid all war and have not prevented frequent recourse to violence among states, they do represent a consensus that institutions other than warfare should be employed in determining bargaining outcomes. Today force is still a quasi-acceptable instrument of foreign policy especially if used in a limited fashion, but it is not used to stage trial by combat whenever deep-seated disagreements occur over existing situations.

Instead, force is exploited in contemporary bargaining primarily to change payoffs by punishing the target state. Except in the case of civil wars, where policy influencers in the same state decide to engage in trial by combat, force is used by one state to increase the costs of a given policy. For example, American bombing raids on North Vietnam are designed to punish North Vietnam for intervention in the civil war in South Vietnam. Frequently both sides decide to punish each other with sporadic acts of violence (as the Israelis and Arabs). In any case, however, the use of force is part of a general bargaining strategy rather than a battle to determine which state controls what piece of territory.

The basic reason for this is the enormous cost of modern warfare. Nuclear, conventional, and even extensive subversive warfare can produce severe punishment for the winner as well as the loser of a trial by combat. Moreover, the fear of nuclear warfare between the two superpowers has led them to limit violence between regional actors. Fearing escalation from regional to global warfare, the superpowers have disallowed trial by combat as a way of settling local disputes. Finally, it is extremely costly to capture and hold a piece of territory because occupation costs are so high. This is true for occupying powers that seek to dominate the occupied territory, as the Soviet Union did in East Germany after World War II, as well as for those that follow a more benign policy, as the United States did in postwar West Germany.

In addition, the consequences of the tremendous destructive power of modern warfare technology are compounded by the role policy influencers now play in warfare. A foreign policy decision maker who contemplates the use of force must mobilize the strength of his nation, not only to provide economic and military resources but also to engender sufficient political support for his policies. In the process of mobilizing this support, he is often forced to overstate the reasons for the use of force. In turn, this creates a dogmatic resolve on the part of his policy influencers. If he chooses to pursue a moderate military course and to sustain support for his policies over a long period of time, he is faced with the dilemma of generating too much dogmatism on the part of his policy influencers or risking growing opposition to his war policies. In either case, his available alternatives are seriously reduced. Too much commitment from his policy influencers will force him to fight an unlimited crusading war in which moderation is viewed as cowardice; too little commitment will weaken the war effort and strengthen enemy morale.

In addition to limiting the flexibility of the foreign policy decision maker vis-à-vis his own policy influencers, the use of force also reduces the flexibility of his counterparts in the target state. Evidence from the League's economic sanctions against Mussolini in 1936, those of the United States against Cuba in the 1960's, and those of the United Kingdoms against Rhodesia in the middle 1960's indicates that outside sanctions do not always alter the course of a state's foreign policy, but often increase policy influencer support for the regime and lead to a more dogmatic policy.[3] American bombing of North Vietnam in the middle 1960's is an example of this effect. Striking the first blow can often force foreign policy decision makers in the target state into a position they would not have chosen.

A related aspect of the general role of policy influencers in foreign policy making is extremely important. In the contemporary world, particularly among the developed states, there appears to be a trend away from achieving clear-cut victory or defeat. Foreign policy decision makers realize that severe foreign policy reversals for even their bitterest enemies could stimulate more, not less, recalcitrance, from policy influencers in the losing state. In the Cuban missile crisis, for example, President Kennedy offered Soviet leadership various opportunities to withdraw its missiles from Cuba without making withdrawal look like a severe policy defeat.[4] Because clear-cut victory at one point in time can lead to undesirable behavior on the part of one's adversaries at another point in time, foreign policy decision makers—even among the most antagonistic states—attempt to limit their successes as well as their losses. Unwilling to have their hands tied by their own policy influencers and fearing that the hands of decision makers in other states will be similarly tied, most foreign policy decision makers have found it necessary to search for substitutes for victory in the contemporary world.

Even though extensive use of force has become extremely costly and is generally avoided, the foreign policy decision maker still has the capacity to threaten and promise. In the classical international political system threats and promises were related in one way or another to the use of force. In contrast, the international bargaining process provides regionalization and issue-area fragmentation—conditions for extensive threats and promises without the direct threat of force. The Soviet Union might promise to

---

[3] See Johan A. Galtung, "On Effects of International Economic Sanctions, With Examples from the Case of Rhodesia," World Politics, 19 (1967), 378–416, for a discussion of the domestic impact of sanctions against Rhodesia.

[4] There is some evidence that President Kennedy was acutely conscious of the need to leave the Soviet decision makers room to back down. See Roger Hilsman, To Move A Nation (Garden City, N.Y.: Doubleday, 1967), pp. 202–212 and 228.

withdraw from territory in one region with the understanding that a settlement would be reached in the territory of another region. Or, the United States might refrain from public pronouncements on Soviet difficulties in eastern Europe in exchange for Soviet acquiescence to American policy in Latin America. Similarly, Soviet threats to refuse to accept a treaty concerning military uses of outer space might be employed as part of an opposition strategy to U.S. policies in Vietnam.[5]

In the contemporary international bargaining process, states are so involved in each other's affairs in such a wide variety of fields that they have a rich environment in which they can threaten to hurt or promise to help each other. Moreover, as social and economic ties increase and modern technology creates conditions necessitating widespread cooperation, opportunities for threatening and promising will increase. In such fields as water pollution, weather control, and disease prevention, states will be able to harm or help not just their neighbors but other states halfway around the world by policies they pursue within their own territory. Weather control in Japan, for example, could radically alter weather patterns in the United States. Or the failure to eliminate a disease in tropical Africa could jeopardize the health of the entire human race. These are not idle speculations about a science-fiction future, but foreseeable conditions that states will have to deal with in the next decade.

The importance of this growing interdependence for the international bargaining process should not be minimized. First, it means that the survival of existing living standards in one part of the world will be dependent upon various conditions in other parts of the world. This has implications not only for the activities of intergovernmental organizations as collective-problem-solving entities but also for the foreign policies of the developed states and particularly the superpowers who have the wealth—but not necessarily the influence—to do something about it.

Second, coming technological factors appear to provide states that are weak economically with the increasing capacity to harm the developed states—either consciously and directly or unconsciously and indirectly. (See Chapter 7.) It is not inconceivable, for example, that a small state in a remote area could take action to control weather within its territory that could cause a drought or a flood in a rich state a thousand miles away.[6] A small state in the not-too-distant future may be able to threaten not only to

---

[5] These examples of possible tradeoffs in threats and promises between the two superpowers can only be speculative, because the individuals involved have a stake in not revealing whether or not they did in fact occur.

[6] In the area of weather control, for example, see Thomas F. Malone, "Weather," in Foreign Policy Association, *Toward the Year 2018* (New York: Cowles Education Corporation, 1968), pp. 61–75.

nationalize the property of a developed state's nationals, but also to deprive it of its health or good weather. Interdependence among nations then, not only breeds the need for collective problem solving, it also breeds conditions for a wide variety of threats and promises.

This leads to a final consequence of the change in the use of force—the loss of a hierarchical pattern of influence. In the classical period, the powerful was clearly distinguished from the weak, and this distinction was based on a combination of factors. The most important of these were territory, economic strength, and military capability. States that possessed these factors enjoyed the ability to influence states that did not.

In the current system, however, the relationship of military economic capability to the ability to influence other states appears to be rapidly diminishing. (See the discussion of the concept of power in Chapter 4.) Even though the superpowers and the developed states possess high influence—by classical standards—as a result of economic and military strength, they do not command the general ability to influence the "lesser" states that they once enjoyed. For example, the actions of Castro's Cuba have continually been contrary to the wishes of the United States, despite American military and economic superiority and the relatively clear acknowledgement by the Soviet Union (particularly before the Cuban missile crisis) that the United States may treat Cuba as part of the American sphere of influence. One would never have predicted on the basis of traditional criteria of patterns of influence that the United States would permit the government of Cuba to behave as it did in the 1960's.

The reasons for the breakdown in the "pecking order" of the international bargaining process can be found in many of the trends we have just discussed. Most important is the changing role of force from final arbiter to part of a large set of bargaining tools. No longer effective in deciding who should get what in its capacity as final arbiter, force and the ability to use it provide a less meaningful key to distribution of influence in international bargaining than they once did.

Moreover, it is probably a mistake to talk about one pattern of influence, given the fragmented nature of the international bargaining process. Some states enjoy relatively important positions in specific regions —such as India in Asia and the United Arab Republic in the Middle East —even though they are less influential in terms of global bargaining patterns. Similarly, the Swiss and French governments and economies play a much larger role in issues relating to the world economy than they do, for example, in questions concerning the uses of outer space. Hence the relative influence of a state varies according to the region and the issue area that is relevant to the particular bargaining situation. As some observers have found in examining domestic politics, influence in the international political system is becoming increasingly pluralized according to issue area and region.[7]

It also appears that ability to threaten harm will become even less the preserve of the economically and militarily strong as technology continues to provide a great impact in the contemporary world. The spread of nuclear weapons and the ability of states to cause harm in social and economic areas will make the underdeveloped states better able to threaten seriously as the world speeds to the twenty-first century. It is and will continue to be no mistake to refer to the United States and the Soviet Union as super-powers because they have and will continue to have an enormous impact around the globe and across many issue areas, particularly when they are working together. It *would* be a mistake, however, to assume that those who are strong militarily and economically can easily get their way in most bargaining situations and will have an even easier time of it in the future.

It might be argued that the breakdown in patterns of influence is a consequence of Soviet-American competition, that is, that because the superpowers oppose each other, they cancel out each other's ability to influence third parties. Such an argument could be based on the relative success they enjoy when they cooperate. In 1956, for example, they cooperated in checking British, French and Israeli activities against Egypt. However, the argument neglects the difficulties the superpowers have had in dealing with recalcitrant allies—United States with France; the Soviet Union with Romania—and also in dominating the activities of small states close to their borders—United States in Cuba; the Soviet Union in Hungary and Czechoslovakia). Given the superpowers' inability to dominate clearly in areas where their activities would not cancel each other out, we must assume that the breakdown in hierarchical patterns of influence that have so long characterized international politics is more deep-seated than is the current conflict between the Soviet Union and the United States.

INTEGRATION AND THE STRUCTURE AND PROCESS OF THE INTERNATIONAL POLITICAL SYSTEM

Interdependence among the people of the world as we have discussed it throughout the book has affected relationships among nation-states in a number of ways. It has increased the demand for routine official interactions and collective problem solving among states. At the same time, it has profoundly affected the ways in which states bargain with each other as well as the issues over which they bargain. Moreover, it has intensified a

[7] Robert Dahl, *Who Governs?* (New Haven: Yale University Press, 1961).

feeling of interdependence and mutual destiny among states not only within a particular region but also all over the globe.

The fact that individuals and institutions of one state are becoming more involved in the lives of individuals and institutions of other states has challenged the structure of the international political system as a way of organizing the societies of the world. As we have already noted, the basic feature of the international political system is the large role played by semi-autonomous territorially based political organizations called states. The primary question posed by the growing interdependence of the contemporary world is: Can the state as the central political organization in the international system survive?

Such a question introduces the concept of "integration." This concept has been employed in a very general way to describe the merging of various national communities into larger communities. Neither the exact nature of the merging process nor whether the final product of the process will be a bigger state can be clearly predicted. For this reason, we will avoid an exact definition of the concept of integration at this time. Instead, we will look at three types of integration: (1) Socioeconomic integration—the economic and social ties (including language and attitudes as well as the exchange of ideas and people) among the nationals of two or more states (see Chapter 7 for socioeconomic setting); (2) policy influencer integration—the extent to which policy influencers in two or more states cooperate with each other and/or identify intergovernmental institutions as targets for mutual activities (see Chapter 3 for policy influences); and (3) institutional integration—the existence of intergovernmental organizations to pursue common goals (see Chapter 9). We will briefly explore each of these three types of international integration by examining the Common Market or inner-six countries (France, West Germany, Italy, Belgium, the Netherlands, and Luxembourg) as an example of an area where a high level of all three types of international integration exists.

Socioeconomic integration in Common Market countries is high. With few if any restrictions on travel, the people of the six western European states freely cross national borders. In the field of economics, trade within the Common Market has become increasingly larger than trade between the six members and the outside world.[8]

Policy influencer integration is also extensive among Common Market states. In fact, it has been argued that a set of "inner-six" partisan, interest, bureaucratic, and mass influencers now exists.

---

[8] Hayward R. Alker, Jr., and Donald Puchala, "Trends in Economic Partnership: The North Atlantic Area, 1928–1963," in J. David Singer, ed., *Quantitative International Politics: Insights and Evidence* (New York: Free Press, 1968), pp. 287–318.

The character of decision-making (for the inner-six organizations) stimulate interest groups to make themselves heard; it spurs political parties in Strasbourg and Luxembourg to work out common positions; it creates enormous pressure on high national civil servants to get to know and establish rapport with their opposite numbers.[9]

In addition, the mass media in European states allocate substantial time and space to European matters. Therefore, policy influencers within the inner six not only pressure their own governments for more international cooperation, but also cooperate across national boundaries to pressure common European institutions.

Institutional integration in the Common Market states is also substantial. In addition to the European Economic Community, which has directed the merging of the inner-six economies, the European Coal and Steel Community, Euratom, and the European Investment Bank have contributed importantly to European economic cooperation. Furthermore, a European Parliament and a Court of Justice provides institutional services to the other inner-six institutions. All of these institutions have developed since World War II.

Now that we have briefly indicated the three types of integration, we can provide some tentative evaluations of their impact on the structure of the international political system by dealing with the following questions: (1) how do the three types of integration affect each other; (2) how does integration and particularly institutional integration in one issue area affect integration in other issue areas; (3) how does the degree of integration vary for different groups of states (bilaterally, regionally, and globally); and (4) is the final product bigger states, a world state, or something else? We will deal with each of these questions in the order stated.

How are the three types of international integration related to each other? It is sometimes assumed that an increase in social and economic ties among states leads to greater policy influencer cooperation on a transnational basis and also to more intergovernmental organizations with greater areas of competence. A better assumption would be to view the three types as interdependent; that is, as causing as well as being affected by each other. Just as increased social and economic contact between state A and state B might predispose policy influencers in the two states to cooperate more, the attitudes of policy influencers within A might pressure for increased or decreased social and economic contact with state B. In the United States, for example, certain anti-Communist partisan and interest

[9] Ernst B. Haas, "International Integration: The European and the Universal Process," *International Political Communities* (Garden City, N.Y.: Doubleday, 1966), p. 100.

influencers have been instrumental in curtailing trade with the Soviet Union and Eastern European states even in the face of the foreign policy decision maker's views to the contrary. Similarly, intergovernmental organizations can stimulate increased policy influencer transnational cooperation as well as more social and economic contact. Trade among the inner six, for example, has been stimulated by creation of the Common Market.

The important point is that increased social and economic contact will not inevitably produce the other two types of integration and in fact may be limited by lack of integration at these two levels. The simplistic notion, as illustrated in Figure 9a, that the growing social and economic interdependence of the modern world will automatically produce other forms of integration is not as satisfactory as the assumption that the three types of integration mutually affect each other as illustrated in Figure 9b.

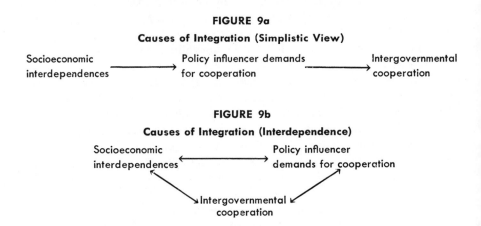

FIGURE 9a

Causes of Integration (Simplistic View)

Socioeconomic interdependences ⟶ Policy influencer demands for cooperation ⟶ Intergovernmental cooperation

FIGURE 9b

Causes of Integration (Interdependence)

Socioeconomic interdependences ⟷ Policy influencer demands for cooperation

Intergovernmental cooperation

This leads to a related point Haas has called "spill-over."[10] It is assumed that activities of intergovernmental organizations in one functional area (such as transportation) will create conditions for the activities of intergovernmental organizations in other functional areas, (such as communication). Part of the spill-over assumption is based on the view that as foreign policy decision makers and policy influencers learn to trust their counterparts in other states, they will be more willing to cooperate in a larger variety of functional areas. In addition, it is assumed that to coordinate one functional area it might be necessary to organize other functional areas on an international basis. Another aspect of this assumption is that

[10] "International Integration," p. 96.

once intergovernmental organizations are created, their own staffs will attempt to expand their domain of activities. Given these factors, it is assumed that spill-over will lead to the increasing importance of intergovernmental organizations.

To some extent, the spill-over assumption seems to be warranted, particularly but not solely in the experience of the western European inner six. Their experience in attempting to cooperate on economic matters indicates that ever increasing spheres of economic as well as social policy matters (migration, for example) become coordinated by intergovernmental organizations. However, even the inner-six experience indicates that spill-over is far from automatic especially in areas relating to national security. In 1954, for example, these six states came close to signing a treaty that would have established the European Defense Community with a single integrated armed force.[11] The treaty was defeated, although by an extremely close margin. It is possible that European states were not ready for such a bold move because the short period in which other European institutions had existed had not allowed for adequate spill-over, but it is also possible that the area of national defense is not within what foreign policy decision makers and policy influencers consider acceptable areas for international integration. Taken together with the failure of intergovernmental organizations to establish little more than a framework for alliance negotiations (NATO) or competitive bargaining (United Nations) in areas relating to war and peace, the latter possibility appears more likely.

So far, we have discussed the three types of integration in terms of the European Economic Community of the inner six. However, varying degrees of integration also exist outside of the six. In fact, it is possible to examine the degree of all three types of integration for any pair of states, for a particular group of states, or even for the world as a whole.

The degree of integration for any two states ranges from the highly integrated conditions of Canada and the United States or Belgium and Luxembourg to the conditions of virtual nonintegration for the bulk of states around the globe (for example, Gabon and Guatemala). One can trace degrees of interaction, both social (migration, mail flow, student exchanges, and the like) and economic (trade, aid, and investment); amount of contact among policy influencers such as members of the legislature; and degree of intergovernmental contact, Russett has done this for the United States and the United Kingdom in the twentieth century.[12] Such a study

---

[11] For a discussion of the history of this attempt, see Raymond Aron and Daniel Lerner, eds., *France Defeats the EDC* (New York: Praeger, 1956).

[12] Bruce M. Russett, *Community and Contention: Britain and America in the Twentieth Century* (Cambridge, Mass.: M.I.T. Press, 1963).

could indicate bargaining patterns or prospects for future integration between the two states. It could seek critical thresholds in all three types that might indicate a marked change in willingness to go to war against each other or, for that matter, to defend each other.

In addition to examining the degree of integration for any given pair of states, it is also important to look for groupings of states. Some groupings are geographically dispersed. For example, the Commonwealth contains a group of states dispersed all over the globe that have extensive economic and social contacts as well as intergovernmental cooperation because of previous colonial relationships. Most groupings, however, have some geographical locus but are poorly developed when compared to the inner-six region. In areas like Central and South America, sub-Sahara Africa, and Asia, some integration occurs, particularly at the level of intergovernmental institutions. In East Africa and Central America, for example, institutional integration is quite high.[13] However, social and economic contacts as well as policy influencer cooperation does not match the extensive progress made at the institutional level. Whether or not increased institutional integration will stimulate the other two types remains to be seen.

The same is true for global integration. Cutting across increasing integration among various sets of states—whether bilateral or regional—are the trends of global integration. General levels of economic and social contact have increased throughout the world just as globally-oriented policy influencers have also developed. However, more substantial and important for the long-run has been the growth of a relatively small (when compared to regional) but nonetheless significant group of global intergovernmental organizations. These organizations, as we noted in Chapter 9, operate for the most part in the social and economic area, aiming to coordinate activities of states and regional organizations in collective problem solving. It appears that the spill-over effect will be limited globally, more so than regionally, and in addition, that the degree of social and economic as well as policy influencer contact will also increase at a slower rate. Hence, despite some progress at the level of intergovernmental integration on a worldwide basis, it does not appear that other levels of integration will provide much of an impetus at least for the near future.

With this background, it is now necessary to assess the implications of integration for the structure of the international political system: Will the state as the primary form of political organization continue to remain the predominant structure of the system? To answer this question, we must attempt to determine what international integration is leading to.

[13] Joseph S. Nye, "Central American Regional Integration," in Nye, ed., *International Regionalism* (Boston: Little, Brown, 1968), pp. 378–79.

Two alternative definitions of integration have been given:

> . . . the attainment, within a territory, of a "sense of community" and of institutions and practices strong enough and widespread enough to assure, for a "long time," dependable expectations of "peaceful change,"[14]

or, the

> . . . process whereby political actors in several distinct national settings are persuaded to shift their loyalties, expectations and political activities toward a new and larger center, whose institutions possess or demand jurisdiction over the pre-existing national states.[15]

In these terms, the three types of integration become a form of nation-building; that is, steps to a unified state encompassing the territory of two states, a region, or the world.

To view the three types of integration as a process leading to bigger nations leaves much to be desired. Perhaps it makes sense when discussing such advanced relationships as those that exist between Belgium, the Netherlands, and Luxembourg. However, even when looking at states that enjoy high degrees of socioeconomic, policy influencer, and institutional integration—such as Canada and the United States or the states of western Europe—one is struck by the apparent remoteness of the possibility of formation of larger political entities. When we look at the bulk of states in the international political system, we can only assume that the major effect of the three types of integration we have discussed will not be the growth of regional states or a world state in the foreseeable future.

When examining the three types of integration one should not make any assumptions about whether integration will transform the state as the prime political unit or even result in the formation of larger states. A better way is to look at the impact of integration on the international bargaining process. Because we have already discussed how factors in the contemporary world have affected which states bargain with each other, the issue areas in which they bargain, and the tools they are likely to use for various issue areas, we have already indicated in part the impact these levels of integration have on the international bargaining process. Nevertheless, it is useful to summarize the role of each level on bargaining interactions among states.

At the level of social and economic contact, the greater the integration

---

[14] Karl W. Deutsch et al., "Political Community in the North Atlantic Area," *International Political Communities* (Garden City, N.Y.: Doubleday, 1966), p. 2.

[15] Haas, "International Integration," p. 94.

the greater the basis for both threats and promises. Two or more states intricately tied to each other socially and economically will bargain with each other more often than those with few ties. They will be more vulnerable to each other across a large variety of issues. Understanding this vulnerability often increases cooperation and friendly relations among states, but it can occasion competition and hostility. However, because socioeconomic integration makes states more vulnerable to each other's hostile actions, foreign policy decision makers often attempt to minimize social and economic contact with states they view as enemies.

The relationship of socioeconomic integration to alliance politics indicates how bargaining between states is affected. In a study of deterrence situations since World War I, Russett has illustrated that allies are better able to deter a threatening state if they share social and economic ties.[16] Alliances for defense between states with high levels of socioeconomic integration (such as the United States and western Europe) appear to be more credible than those between states with low levels (such as the United States and Southeast Asia). In addition, trading patterns appear to shape and be shaped by alliances. Trade within NATO and Warsaw Pact alliances is much greater than trade among those countries and others, although the recent increase in trade across alliances may be interpreted as indication of a loosening of alliance structure.

Policy influencer integration also has had a profound impact on the international bargaining process. (See policy influencer discussion in Chapter 3.) On the one hand, it means that bureaucratic, interest, partisan, and even mass influencers will cooperate with each other across national boundaries. One striking example occurred in the mid-1960's. Throughout the world policy influencers opposed to American participation in the Vietnamese war began to pressure foreign policy decision makers. Although there is no worldwide conspiracy organizing this opposition, partisan influencers in various states have communicated with each other and responded similarly to American policy and their governments' pressure on that policy. On the other hand, policy influencer integration has helped to create specialized issue areas on a crossnational basis. Groups and organizations interested in a particular area such as water pollution, air traffic, or resource conservation have communicated and cooperated with each other not on the basis of national interest but rather on the basis of mutual transnational interests. Hence, transnational policy influencers not only affect the way foreign policy decision makers bargain with each other by opposing or supporting specific policies, but also aid in defining and

[16] Bruce M. Russett, "The Calculus of Deterrence," *Journal of Conflict Resolution,* 7 (1963), 97–109.

highlighting specialized issue areas in which states might make joint decisions.

Finally, integration at the level of the formation and operation of intergovernmental organizations also profoundly affects the international bargaining process. We have frequently indicated this throughout the book. (See pp. 239–242.) Intergovernmental organizations serve as institutions for cooperative and competitive bargaining among states; they also serve as arenas in which bargaining positions can be communicated and support for specific policies can be generated among other states. In addition, constitutional issues and election of officeholders create important issue areas in which bargaining among states can take place. As in the case of the other two types of integration, we can generalize that the higher the degree of integration—that is, the larger the number of intergovernmental organizations within a region—the more specialized and complex the issue areas in which the members can bargain.

We must conclude, therefore, that what scholars have called integration in the international political system appears to have a greater effect on the bargaining process than on the structure of the political system. For the foreseeable future, we must conclude that the state as a territorially-based form of political organization will survive, although some regional and bilateral consolidation may occur. Profound changes, however, will continue to mark the way states deal with each other as each of the three types of integration increases.

TRENDS FOR THE FUTURE

In closing both this chapter and this book, it is useful to look at the structure of the international political system in a long-range framework. One way of doing this is to employ the concept "international political culture" first developed in Chapter 7. We defined the international political culture as a set of ideas concerning the organization of relationships among the people of the world, pertaining especially to the way in which values were allocated among the states. Viewing the structure of this system in terms of a culture or set of attitudes will enable us to evaluate long-range changes, because such changes always involve shifts in the attitudes of people.

In the historical development of the international political culture, two factors stand out. First is the persistence of states as the primary form of political organization. (See Chapter 11.) For more than three centuries preservation of the state has been the primary concern of foreign policy decision makers. Attachment to the state as the only acceptable form of political organization appears to be strong today—even though it has been transformed from a European institution to a universal political form. Second is the flexibility in attitudes relating to the way states should behave. Except for the commitment to the preservation of the state, those who have been responsible for interactions among states have been willing to explore institutions and create norms ranging from the development of diplomatic institutions to the creation of the United Nations in order to deal with social, economic, and political issues. (Chapter 9 is particularly relevant to these observations.) Once willing to accept few limitations on the autonomy of the state either internally or externally, states today have created intergovernmental organizations and international laws that imply enormous restrictions, particularly in social and economic issue areas.

Attitudes in the international political culture concerning the use of force illustrate the tension between desire to preserve the state and desire to promote cooperation. Realizing that unfettered and frequent use of force will only result in greater danger of worldwide conflagration, foreign policy decision makers have attempted to ban the use of force except for defense. Moreover, because of the universally agreed-upon need to preserve the right to use force in self-defense, intergovernmental organizations that could effectively prevent nondefensive use of force have not been developed. As we pointed out in Chapter 10, force is considered a quasi-acceptable tool of foreign policy—neither prohibited nor condoned. Hence, although attempts have been made to eliminate force from international politics, the attachment to preserving the state has been strong enough to doom those attempts to failure.

In addition to trends we have noted in the substantive assumptions, of certain tendencies weaken and fragment the international political culture. One important factor is the pluralization of the foreign policy-making process. As we noted in Chapter 3, the role of policy influencers has become increasingly important in the twentieth century. This increase has meant among other things that individuals with a large variety of ideas about how the world should be organized politically have influenced foreign policy decision makers. Pressures from policy influencers have included calls for a world state, the renunciation of force, unilateral disarmament, an international policy force, and the increased use of force. These contradictory pressures originate in part from different assumptions about the nature of the system and indicate a general lessening in agreement within states about the international political culture. These pressures are rarely appreciable (except perhaps for a short period after a major war) because as pointed out in Chapter 7, the more powerful the policy influencer the more likely that it supports the current international political culture. Nonetheless, they represent a divisive factor that tends to weaken the international political culture.

The other factor that tends to fragment the international political culture is closely related to its historical origins. This culture, as we have noted, has evolved along with the international political system from the European state system. The western developed states, therefore, have been associated with both the culture and with the system; antiwestern feeling sometimes takes the form of rejection of the international political culture. Communist writers and official statements have frequently pointed out that the state as a political institution and the international political system are a product of capitalism and therefore should be eliminated. Anticolonial states in the underdeveloped world have also voiced criticisms of the ideas that support the international system.

One should not, however, overemphasize criticisms based on antiwesternism, although in the long run it may play some role in transforming the international political culture. The Communist states jealously guard the preservation of the state as a political form not only by protecting themselves but also by attempting to restrict certain forms of intervention by intergovernmental organizations (as by the United Nations in Hungary in 1956). Similarly, the underdeveloped states have acted very much like nineteenth-century states, not only by using force for territorial gain and self-defense but also by limiting the authority of intergovernmental organizations. Therefore, in spite of the discordant notes in statements of the leaders of Communist and underdeveloped states about the international political system, there does not appear to be any concerted effort to change the structure of the system.

From this brief analysis of the international political culture, we might assume that the international political system will continue to be characterized by a set of competing territorially-based political organizations cooperating in social and economic issue areas through intergovernmental organizations but preserving the right to act unilaterally when questions of the use of force and national security arise. Change would require a revolution in the attitudes of individuals who now or will in the future possess authority and influence within states. How this revolution might occur is the subject of speculation on how the cultural assumptions are initially acquired and how they are passed on to future generations of foreign policy decision makers and policy influencers.

These questions bring us to the study of what sociologists and political scientists have called "socialization."[17] Usually employed with the concept

[17] The concept of socialization in the study of domestic politics is discussed in Richard E. Dawson, "Political Socialization," in James A. Robinson, ed., *Political Science Annual,* Vol. 1 (Indianapolis: Bobbs-Merrill, 1966), pp. 1–84.

of political culture, political socialization is the process through which members of a political system come to accept the basic ideas and values that characterize the political system. In recent years, political scientists have come to learn a great deal about the way individuals acquire political attitudes. For example, they have established that childhood experience and education play a role in political attitudes. However, we know very little about the socialization process that leads to attitudes about the international political system. Although we have some knowledge on the types of general attitudes people hold about international politics, we know very little about the formation of detailed ideas and values of individuals who are important in the making of foreign policy.

Nevertheless, we can speculate that childhood experience and education probably have less to do with attitudes about the international political system among individual foreign policy influencers then with attitudes toward domestic politics. We might speculate that career patterns that lead individuals into foreign policy positions produce learning experiences about the international political system that lead to relative acceptance of the system's structure. This is probably true whether the career patterns led through the bureaucracy or through political office. In addition, because the people who have made past foreign policy decisions frequently choose those who will make such decisions in the future, individuals recruited into foreign policy positions often share similar ideas about the structure (if not particular strategies) of the international political culture.

In discussing ways a revolution might occur in attitudes about the international political culture we might examine two routes. The first is recruitment of individuals who do not share the accepted cultural assumptions to foreign policy decision-making positions and to the roles of powerful policy influencers. The second is collective learning of a new political culture by future generations of foreign policy decision makers and policy influencers.

The first path appears highly unlikely. Although it is possible for an individual who rejects the existing international political culture to achieve a major foreign policy-making role, it is highly unlikely that he will have a long-run effect. For example, Woodrow Wilson might be viewed as such an individual (although there is evidence to the contrary),[18] but even he as President of a victorious state in a dominant military position was unable to revolutionize the international political system as envisioned in his statements. The reason for his failure, aside from his lack of political wisdom, was that powerful policy influencers within the United States and many

---

[18] Debate continues over how revolutionary Wilson really was. See Edward Buehrig, *Woodrow Wilson and the Balance of Power* (Bloomington: Indiana University Press, 1955). Also see our discussion of Wilson as a risk-taker in Chapter 2.

decision makers in other states took actions to prevent the international political culture from being violated by Wilsonian ideals. The example illustrates vividly how difficult it is to change international politics by recruiting individuals with different views of the proper structure of the international political system. If a revolution in the international political culture were to occur through this first route, individuals with new, homogeneous views would have to occupy important decision making and policy influencing positions in major states throughout the globe.

The second path appears to be less improbable, especially if one thinks in terms of centuries rather than decades. It would include the collective learning by succeeding generations of foreign policy decision makers and policy influencers of a new culture concerning the ways should organize their relationships with each other throughout the world. What might emerge is a *world* political culture rather than an *international* political culture—if people learn that the existing arrangement of competing territorially-based states is inadequate to meet the demands made on that structure by the environment of the international political system. For this to happen, however, future events must illustrate the inadequacies of the existing arrangement. They must not create so much anxiety that they prevent collective adaptation throughout the world.

Such an evolutionary change presupposes that existing organizations based on territory could not allow for changes in policies and activities that might result from current technological, ecological, economic, social, and political changes throughout the world. One should not accept such a presupposition too readily if only because our political system as a way of organizing international relationships appears to have provided at least minimal satisfaction over a relatively long history and in the face of enormous transformations in almost every aspect of human life. Those who have been responsible for the life and development of the international political system have often acted poorly in terms of both their own narrowly defined interests and the interests of mankind generally, but it would be a mistake to assume from the record that the system is unworkable. Moreover, some evidence seems to indicate that centralization of authority territorially and functionally (that is for all issue areas) produces as many problems in making and implementing policies as it solves. From the standpoint of creating and maintaining large organizations, it might be best to keep the framework of semi-autonomous geographical units that cooperate regionally and globally in certain specified issue areas but maintain authority in such areas as law and order, protection of civil rights, and education. Like every political system, then, the international system is a mixed bag that holds as much promise as danger for the future of mankind.

SUMMARY

In this chapter, we have attempted to look at the international political system in a dynamic framework by identifying broad trends and estimating their consequences for the future. We have underlined the complexity of the system, including how foreign policy decision makers interact with their internal environment (policy influencers and economic-military factors) and their external environment (the setting for international interactions, the international interactions themselves, and the international political culture). Because the many social, economic, and political forces we discussed interact in a large variety of ways, one can never be sure of the long-range impact of existing trends. As students of international politics, however, the only thing we can be sure of and—if this book has done its job—should be sure of is that simple solutions to international political problems are unacceptable because simple propositions are not likely to be true. As human beings, we should want to make a better world, but unless we apply all of our intellectual power to understanding the world we now have, our hope for improvement will produce only despair.

SUMMARY OUTLINE

    I.   An important distinction between structure and process should be made in analyzing trends in any political system, including the international political system.

   II.   Three major trends in the international bargaining process are regionalization of that process, issue area fragmentation of the process, and changes in the use of force.

       A.   *In contrast to the classical international political system, contemporary international bargaining is becoming fragmented into geographical regions.*

       B.   *The growth of regional intergovernmental organizations has promoted this fragmentation.*

       C.   *Global intergovernmental organizations operate to increase extraregional ties among states and to increase intraregional cohesion.*

       D.   *Regionalization of the international bargaining process means that states of different regions rarely bargain with each other, and tools employed within regions differ from those used across regions.*

       E.   *Factors appear to be evolving that will increase regionalization in international bargaining.*

F. *Issue area fragmentation is occuring in both security and non-security issue areas.*

    1. Questions of national security are no longer tied closely to the distribution of territory and the building of alliances and counteralliances to affect that distribution.

    2. Alliance politics, the arms race, and even the makeup of domestic regimes are considered part of the national security issue area and are more complex than they were in the classical period.

    3. *Nonsecurity issue areas in the social and economic field have become increasingly important as social and economic contact among peoples of the world grows.*

    4. *The "politics" of intergovernmental organizations have also become important issue areas in themselves.*

G. *Issue area fragmentation in the international bargaining process is related to issue area specialization of interest among policy influencers within states.*

H. *Bargaining strategies of states will differ according to the issue area involved.*

I. *Allies and enemies tend to be different in different issue areas.*

J. *Greater issue area fragmentation may be expected in the future.*

K. *In the classical period, warfare served as a final arbiter in the bargaining process, while today it is used as a tool for punishment and communication of threats and promises.*

L. *The shift in the role of force is partially a result of the high costs for both sides of any type of warfare.*

M. *Policy influencers play a large role in the use of force by tying the hands of the foreign policy decision maker in the attacking state as well as in the target state.*

N. *Because foreign policy decision makers do not want to eliminate alternatives even for their enemies, they refrain from winning clear-cut victories of major proportions in the contemporary international bargaining process.*

O. *The geographical and issue area fragmentation of the international bargaining process has provided additional areas for making threats and promises without directly involving the use of force.*

P. *The growing interdependence of the peoples of the world has increased the dependence of the living standards of people in one nation on conditions throughout the world.*

Q. *The growing interdependence of the peoples of the world has made all states more vulnerable to all others' actions.*

R. *Because of factors now operating on the use of force in the international bargaining process, the hierarchical patterns of influence that used to be part of the classical system are disappearing.*

III. Integration may be examined in terms of its effect on both the structure and the process of the international political system.

A. *Social and economic contact among nations is growing.*

B. *Policy influencer coordination among nations is growing.*

C. *Intergovernmental cooperation among nations is growing.*

D. *The three types of integration mutually affect each other.*

E. *Although there is some spill-over effect within specific functions or issue areas, there does not appear to be a spill-over effect (at least in the short run) from nonsecurity to security issue areas.*

F. Levels of integration may be examined for any pair of states, for any group of states or for the world as a whole.

G. *The range of degree of integration varies greatly for pairs of nations.*

H. *Outside of western Europe, international integration among groups of states appears to be more on the level of intergovernmental cooperation than increased socioeconomic and policy influencer contact.*

I. *Globally, international integration appears to be weak except for the growth of a small number of relatively powerful (within their functional area) intergovernmental organizations.*

J. *If we view international integration as a process leading to the growth of bigger nations, the prospects appear to be quite dim for most pairs of states, most regions and the world as a whole.*

K. *The major impact of international integration is in the area of changing the international bargaining process (rather than the structure of the international political system).*

IV. *Long-range structural change, if it is to occur at all, will take place first in the evolution of the international political culture.*

A. *Tracing the development of the international political culture, there is on the one hand an immense attachment to the state as the primary form of political organization, and on the other a willingness to experiment with extensive forms of cooperation especially but not entirely in nonsecurity issue areas.*

B. *Some weakening of the international political culture, in terms of general acceptance, appears to be occuring as a result of the growth of policy influencers within states.*

C. *The Communist and newly-emergent states tend to reject the structure of the international political system at the verbal level but appear to accept it at the action level.*

D. *A revolution in the structure of the international political system and the international political culture will take place when new ideas are accepted by foreign policy decision makers and policy influencers about organizing relations among societies.*

E. The international political system as an organizational form is not unworkable and could conceivably be the best form given the conditions existing now and in the future.

BIBLIOGRAPHICAL ESSAY

Like every field in which men are deeply involved, the field of international politics is heavily populated by scholars who try to predict the future. From the intuitively based and often policy prescriptive writings of scholars such as Carr (67) and Burton (63) and of statesmen such as Ball (22) to the projections of existing trends from a firm empirical foundation as in Russett (357), most writers make at least one effort to write about past, present, and future trends. Systematic attempts to investigate alternative futures—"relevant utopias"—have been undertaken by Clark and Sohn (72) and Falk and Barnet (123).

For a view of future technological conditions, see the Foreign Policy Association's book, *Toward the Year 2018* (127). Kahn and Weiner (204) project social, economic, and political dimensions for the year 2000. Questions of war and peace are examined by a number of writers in Wright, Evans, and Deutsch (429). These representative samples are only a few of many works for the attention of the interested reader.

The integration literature, particularly in the area of regional integration, in the field of international politics, is extremely extensive. In an excellent volume, Jacob and Toscano (192) discuss integration of political communities at various levels. They indicate that the term "integration" means many things to many scholars, especially in the field of international integration. In addition to arguments revolving around the concept of functionalism, as in Mitrany (281), Haas (147), and Sewell (373), a number of different approaches are evident. One major approach is found in the work of scholars who use Karl Deutsch's nation-building framework developed in his 1953 work (99). Examples are Deutsch (100), Russett (355), Deutsch et al. (106), Merritt (276), and Alker and Puchala in (283). The work of Ernst Haas (147) also represents a unique approach, although it shifts somewhat from integration as a process of political unification to integration as the development of different systems of political organization. Another approach uses the general viewpoint of the sociology of organization. This is employed by Etzioni (119, 120, 121), but his emphasis is primarily on the development of political unions among states. Finally, some writers have treated integration as a theory or ideology. Mitrany (281) for example, argues for certain types of integration; Claude (74) examines the theoretical assumptions made by many writers in the field. In addition, for a general view of the literature of regional and global integration, the student is advised to read Yalem (430) as well as collections of essays found in *International Political Communities* published in 1966. Also, *International Organization,* the *Journal of Common Market Studies,* and similar journals contain a great deal on integration.

A number of studies have attempted to trace the relationship between various types of integrative relationships (trade, mail flow, and the like) and bargaining behavior. Richardson (333, 334, 335) and Smoker (386, 387) show patterns of trade and the outbreak of conflict. Russett (355, 356, 357) investigates the effects of social and economic interactions on foreign policy strategies. In addition, Alger in (215) defines the effect of intergovernmental organizations on bargaining behavior among states while Holsti and North in (277) trace the relationship between political activity and economic trends such as gold flow in the events leading up to World War I.

Finally, a number of works try to describe and project the impact of regional fragmentation on the political system. Young (433) treats this fragmentation within the context of the evolving global international political system, although many scholars analyze particular regional systems. Among them are Breecher (46, 47), Zartman (434), Robinson (342), and Sigler (375). Cantori and Spiegel (65) offer generalizations that apply to the international politics of a number of regional systems. Many of the above-mentioned works on regions in the international systems along with two that are not mentioned here appear in Volume 13, Number 4 of *International Studies Quarterly.*

Bibliography

1. Acheson, Dean. *Meetings at the Summit: A Study in Diplomatic Method.* Durham, New Hampshire: University of New Hampshire Press, 1958.
2. Adler, Kenneth P.; and Bobrow, Davis. "Interest and Influence in Foreign Affairs." *Public Opinions Quarterly* 20 (Spring 1956): 89–101.
3. Alexandrowicz, Charles Henry. *World Economic Agencies: Law and Practice.* New York: Praeger, 1962.
4. Alexis, Marcus; and Wilson, Charles Z., eds. *Organizational Decision-Making.* Englewood Cliffs, N.J.: Prentice-Hall, 1967.
5. Alger, Chadwick F. "Non-Resolution Consequences of the United Nations and Their Effect on International Conflict." *Journal of Conflict Resolution* 5 (1961): 128–45.
6. ———. "United Nations Participation as a Learning Experience." *Public Opinion Quarterly* 27 (Fall 1963).
7. Alger, Chadwick F.; and Brams, Steven J., "Patterns of Representation in National Capitals and Intergovernmental Organizations." *World Politics* 19 (July 1967): 646–64.
8. Alker, Hayward R., Jr. "The Long Road to International Relations Theory: Problems of Statistical Nonadditivity." *World Politics* 18 (1966): 623–56.
9. Alker, Hayward R., Jr.; and Russett, Bruce M. *World Politics in the General Assembly.* New Haven, Conn.: Yale University Press, 1965.
10. Allison, Graham T. "Conceptual Models and the Cuban Missile Crisis," *American Political Science Review* 63 (1969): 680–718.
11. Almond, Gabriel A. *The American People and Foreign Policy.* New York: Harcourt, Brace & World, 1950.
12. Almond, Gabriel A.; and G. Bingham Powell. *Comparative Politics: A Developmental Approach.* Boston: Little, Brown, 1966.
13. Angell, R. C.; Dunham, V. S.; and Singer, J. David. "Social Values and Foreign Policy Attitudes of Soviet and American Elites." *Journal of Conflict Resolution* 8 (December 1964).

14. Argyris, Chris. "Some Causes of Organizational Ineffectiveness Within the Department of State." *Occasional Papers,* Center For International Systems Research, U.S. Government Printing Office, 1967.

15. Aron, Raymond. *The Century of Total War.* New York: Doubleday, 1954.

16. ———. *Peace and War: A Theory of International Relations.* Translated by Richard Howard and Annette Baker Fox. Garden City, N.Y.: Doubleday, 1966.

17. Ash, Maurice A. "An Analysis of Power With Special Reference to International Politics." *World Politics* 3 (1951): 218–37.

18. Asher, Robert E., et. al. *The United Nations and Economic and Social Co-Operation.* Washington: Brookings Institution, 1957.

19. Aubrey, Henry B. *The Dollar in World Affairs.* New York: Praeger, 1964.

20. Bailey, Sydney D. *The Secretariat of the United Nations.* Rev. ed. New York: Praeger, 1964.

21. Baldwin, William L. *The Structure of the Defense Market, 1955–1964.* Durham, N.C.: Duke University Press, 1967.

22. Ball, George W. *The Discipline of Power: Essentials of a Modern World Structure.* Boston: Little, Brown, 1968.

23. Banfield, Edward C. "The Decision-Making Schema." *Public Administration Review* PS-11 (1957): 278–85.

24. Banks, Arthur S.; and Textor, Robert B., eds. *A Cross-Polity Survey.* 2d ed. Cambridge, Mass.: MIT Press, 1963.

25. Barkun, Michael. "Conflict Resolution Through Implicit Mediation." *Journal of Conflict Resolution* 8 (1964): 121–30.

26. ———. "International Norms: An Interdisciplinary Approach." *Background* 8 (1964): 121–29.

27. Barkun, Michael; and Gregg, Robert W. *The United Nations System.* Princeton: Van Nostrand, 1968.

28. Barnet, Vincent M. Jr., ed. *The Representation of the United States Abroad.* New York: Praeger, 1965.

29. Bauer, Raymond A.; Pool, Ithiel de Sola; and Dexter, Lewis A. *American Business and Public Policy.* New York: Atherton, 1964.

30. Beard, Charles A. *The Idea of National Interest.* New York: Macmillan, 1934.

31. Beckhoefer, Bernard G. "Negotiation, the Statute of the International Atomic Energy Agency." *International Organization* 13 (1959): 38–59.

32. Becker, Howard S. "Notes on the Concept of Commitment." *American Journal of Sociology* 66 (1960): 32–40.

33. Bell, Coral. *Negotiating From Strength.* London: Chatto & Windus, 1962.

34. Berelson, Bernard; and Steiner, Gary A. *Human Behavior: An Inventory of Scientific Findings.* New York: Harcourt, Brace & World, 1964.

35. Bishop, Donald G. *The Administration of Foreign Affairs.* Syracuse: Syracuse University Press, 1961.

36. Black, Joseph E.; and Thompson, Kenneth W., eds. *Foreign Policies in A World of Change*. New York: Harper & Row, 1963.
37. Bloomfield, Lincoln P. *The United Nations and U.S. Foreign Policy*. 2d ed. Boston: Little, Brown, 1967.
38. ————, ed. *International Military Forces*. Boston: Little, Brown, 1964.
39. ————. *Evolution or Revolution? The United Nations and the Problem of Peaceful Territorial Change*. Cambridge, Mass.: Harvard University Press, 1957.
40. Bohannan, Paul, ed. *Law and Warfare: Studies in the Anthropology of Conflict*. Garden City, N.Y.: The Natural History Press, 1967.
41. Boulding, Kenneth E. *Conflict and Defense: A General Theory*. New York: Harper & Row, 1962.
42. Boyd, Andrew. *An Atlas of World Affairs*. New York: Praeger, 1964.
43. Bozeman, Adda B. *Politics and Culture in International History*. Princeton, N.J.: Princeton University Press, 1960.
44. Braybrooke, David; and Lindblom, Charles E. *A Strategy for Decision: Policy Evaluation as a Social Process*. New York: Free Press, 1963.
45. Brecht, Arnold. *Political Theory: The Foundations of Twentieth-Century Political Thought*. Princeton, N.J.: Princeton University Press, 1959.
46. Breecher, Michael. "International Relations and Asian Studies; The Subordinate State System of South Asia." *World Politics* 15 (1963): 213–35.
47. ————. "The Middle East Subordinate System and Its Impact on Israel's Foreign Policy." *International Studies Quarterly* 13 (1969): 117–39.
48. Breecher, Michael; Steinberg, Blema; and Stein, Janice. "A Framework for Research on Foreign Policy Behavior." *Journal of Conflict Resolution* 13 (1969).
49. Brierly, J. L. *The Law of Nations*. 6th ed. Edited by Humphrey Waldock. New York: Oxford University Press, 1963.
50. Briggs, H. W. *The International Telecommunications Union: An Experiment in International Cooperation*. Leyden: A. W. Sijthoff, 1963.
51. Brodie, Bernard. *Strategy in the Missile Age*. Princeton, N.J.: Princeton University Press, 1959.
52. Brody, Richard A. "Some Systematic Effects of the Spread of Nuclear Weapons Technology: A Study Through Simulation of a Multi-Nuclear Future." *Journal of Conflict Resolution* 7 (December 1963): 663–753.
53. Bronowski, Jacob. *The Common Sense of Science*. Cambridge, Mass.: Harvard University Press, 1953.
54. Brookings Institution. *Research Frontiers in Politics and Government*, Washington, D.C.: The Institution, 1955.
55. Brzezinski, Z. K.; and Huntington, S. P. *Political Power: USA/USSR*. New York: Viking, 1963.
56. Brzezinski, Z. K. *Ideology and Power in Soviet Politics*. New York: Praeger.
57. Buchan, Alastair. *Crisis Management: The New Diplomacy*. Paris, France: Atlantic Institute, 1966.

58. Buchanan, William; and Cantril, Hadley. *How Nations See Each Other.* Urbana: University of Illinois Press, 1953.
59. Buck, E. A. *Representation of Non-Governmental Organizations at the United Nations.* Washington, D.C.: Public Administration Clearing House, 1955.
60. Buck, Philip W.; and Travis, Martin, Jr. *Control of Foreign Relations in Modern Nations.* New York: W. W. Norton, 1957.
61. Bull, Hadley, et al. *International Political Communities: An Anthology.* New York: Doubleday Anchor, 1966.
62. Burns, Arthur L.; and Heathcote, Nina. *Peace-Keeping by U.N. Forces: From Suez to the Congo.* New York: Praeger, 1963.
63. Burton, John W. *Peace Theory.* New York: Knopf, 1963.
64. Campbell, John C. "Negotiating with the Soviets: Some Lessons of the War Period." *Foreign Affairs* 34 (1956): 305–19.
65. Cantori, Louis J.; and Spiegel, Steven L. "International Regions: A Comparative Approach to Five Subordinate Systems." *International Studies Quarterly* 13 (1969): 361–81.
66. Cardozo, Michael H. *Diplomats in International Cooperation.* Ithaca: Cornell University Press, 1962.
67. Carr, Edward H. *Nationalism and After.* London: Macmillan, 1945.
68. ————. *Twenty Years, Crisis. 1919–1939: An Introduction to the Study of International Relations.* 2d ed. New York: St. Martin, 1946.
69. Cattel, David. "Multilateral Cooperation and Integration in Eastern Europe." *Western Political Quarterly* 13 (1960).
70. Chidzero, B. T. *Tanganyika and International Trusteeship.* New York: Oxford University Press, 1961.
71. Chowdhuri, R. N. *International Mandates and Trusteeship Systems.* The Hague: Martinus Nijhoff, 1955.
72. Clark, Grenville; and Sohn, Louis. *World Peace Through World Law,* 2d ed. Cambridge, Mass.: Harvard University Press, 1960.
73. Claude, Inis L., Jr. *Power and International Relations.* New York: Random House, 1962.
74. ————. *Swords into Plowshares: The Problems and Prospects of International Organization.* 3d ed. New York: Random House, 1964.
75. Cleveland, Harlan. "Crisis Diplomacy," *Foreign Affairs* 41 (1963): 638–49.
76. Codding, G. A., Jr. *The International Telecommunications Union: An Experiment in International Cooperation.* Leyden: A. W. Sijthoff, 1953.
77. Cohen, Bernard C. *The Political Process and Foreign Policy: The Making of the Japanese Peace Settlement.* Princeton, N.J.: Princeton University Press, 1957.
78. ————. *The Influence of Non-governmental Groups on Foreign Policymaking.* Boston: World Peace Foundation, 1959.
79. ————. *The Press and Foreign Policy.* Princeton, N.J.: Princeton University Press, 1963.

80. Cohen, Morris R.; and Nagel, Ernest. *An Introduction to Logic and Scientific Method.* New York: Harcourt, Brace, & World, 1934.

81. Cohen, Saul B. *Geography and Politics in a World Divided.* New York: Random House, 1963.

82. Cole, John P. *Geography of World Affairs.* Rev. ed. New Orleans: Pelican; Baltimore: Penguin, 1963.

83. *Conflict Resolution.* Vol. 3 (June 1959), The Bobbs-Merrill Reprint Series in the Social Sciences, pp. 120–31.

84. Coplin, William D. *The Functions of International Law.* Chicago: Rand McNally, 1966.

85. Coplin, William D.; and Kegley, Charles, Jr., eds. *A Multi-Method Introduction to International Politics: Observation, Explanation and Prescription.* Chicago: Markham, 1971.

86. Corbett, P. E. *Law in Diplomacy.* Magnolia, Mass.: Peter Smith, 1959.

87. Cottam, Richard W. *Competitive Interference and Twentieth Century Diplomacy.* Pittsburgh: University of Pittsburgh Press, 1967.

88. Crabb, Cecil V. *Bipartisan Foreign Policy, Myth or Reality?* Evanston, Ill.: Row Peterson, 1957.

89. Craig, Gordon A.; and Gilbert, Felix, eds. *The Diplomats: 1919–1939.* Princeton, N.J.: Princeton University Press, 1953.

90. Cyert, Richard M.; and March, James G. *A Behavioral Theory of the Firm.* Englewood Cliffs, N.J.: Prentice-Hall, 1963.

91. Dahl, Robert A. *Congress and Foreign Policy.* New York: Harcourt, Brace & World, 1950.

92. D'Amato, Anthony A. "Psychological Constructs in Foreign Policy Prediction," *Journal of Conflict Resolution* 11 (September 1967): 294–311.

93. Davison, Walter Phillips. "Political Significance of Recognition via Mass Media—An Illustration from the Berlin Blockade." *Public Opinion Quarterly* 20 (1956): 327–33.

94. ———. *The Berlin Blockade: A Study in Cold War Politics.* Princeton, N.J.: Princeton University Press, 1958.

95. ———. *International Political Communication.* New York: Praeger, 1965.

96. Dawson, R. H. *The Decision to Aid Russia, 1941: Foreign Policy and Domestic Politics.* Chapel Hill: University of North Carolina Press, 1959.

97. De Rivera, Joseph. *The Psychological Dimensions of Foreign Policy.* Columbus, Ohio: Charles E. Merrill, 1968.

98. Deutsch, Karl W. "Mass Communications and the Loss of Freedom in National Decision Making." *Journal of Conflict Resolution* 1 (1952): 200–11.

99. ———. *Nationalism and Social Communication.* 2d ed. Cambridge, Mass.: MIT Press, 1953.

100. ———. "Shifts in the Balance of International Communication Flows." *Public Opinion Quarterly* 20 (Spring 1956): 143–60.

101. ———. *The Nerves of Government.* New York: Free Press, 1963.

102. Deutsch, Karl W. *The Analysis of International Relations*. Englewood Cliffs, N.J.: Prentice-Hall, 1968.
103. Deutsch, Karl W.; and Eckstein, Alexander. "National Industrialization and the Relative Decline of Foreign Trade, 1890–1957." *World Politics* (1960).
104. ———. "National Industrialization and the Declining Shares of the National Economic Sector." *World Politics* 13 (January 1961), 267–99.
105. Deutsch, Karl W.; and Edinger, Lewis J. *Germany Rejoins the Powers: Mass Opinion, Interest Groups, and Elites in Contemporary*. Stanford, Calif.: Stanford University Press, 1959.
106. Deutsch, Karl W.; Edinger, Lewis J.; Macridis, Roy C.; and Merritt, Richard L. *France, Germany and the Western Alliance*. New York: Scribner, 1967.
107. Deutsch, Karl W.; and Singer, J. David, "Multipolar Power Systems and International Stability." *World Politics* 16 (April 1964): 390–406.
108. deVisscher, Charles. *Theory and Reality in Public International Law*. Princeton, N.J.: Princeton University Press, 1957.
109. Djilas, Milovan. *The New Class*. New York: Praeger, 1957.
110. Dreier, John C. *The Organization of American States and the Hemisphere Crisis*. New York: Harper & Row, 1962.
111. Earle, Edward Mead, ed. *Makers of Modern Strategy*. Princeton, N.J.: Princeton University Press, 1948.
112. Easton, S. C. *The Twilight of European Colonialism*. New York: Holt, Rinehart & Winston, 1960.
113. Edinger, Lewis J. "Military Leaders and Foreign Policy-Making." *American Political Science Review* 57 (June 1963): 392–405.
114. Edwards, David. *Arms Control in International Relations,* New York: Holt, Rinehart & Winston, 1968.
115. Erhmann, H. S., ed. *Interest Groups on Four Continents*. Pittsburgh: University of Pittsburgh Press, 1958.
116. Elder, Robert. *The Policy Machine*. Syracuse, N.Y.: Syracuse University Press, 1960.
117. Emerson, Rupert. *From Empire to Nation*. Cambridge, Mass.: Harvard University Press, 1960.
118. Epstein, Leon D. "British M.P.'s and Their Local Parties: The Suez Cases." *American Political Science Review* (1960): 374–90.
119. Etzioni, Amitai. "Dialectics Supranational Unification." *American Political Science Review* LVI (1962): 927–55.
120. ———. "The Epigenesis of Political Communities at the International Level." *American Journal of Sociology* (1963).
121. ———. *Political Unification: A Comparative Study of Leaders and Forces*. New York: Holt, Rinehart & Winston, 1965.
122. Fagen, Richard. "Some Assessments and Uses of Public Opinion in Diplomacy." *Public Opinion Quarterly* 24 (1960): 448–57.
123. Falk, Richard A.; and Barnet, Richard J., eds. *Security in Disarmament*. Princeton, N.J.: Princeton University Press, 1965.

124. Farrell, R. Barry, ed. *Approaches to Comparative and International Politics*. Evanston, Ill.: Northwestern University Press, 1966.

125. Fink, Clinton F. "More Calculations about Deterrence." *Journal of Conflict Resolution* 9 (March 1965): 54–66.

126. Fisher, Roger, ed. *International Conflict and Behavioral Science*. New York: Basic Books, 1964.

127. Foreign Policy Association, *Toward the Year 2018*. New York: Cowles, 1968.

128. Frankel, Joseph. *The Making of Foreign Policy*. New York: Oxford University Press, 1963.

129. Friedmann, Wolfgang C. *The Changing Structure of International Law*. New York: Columbia University Press, 1964.

130. Friedmann, Wolfgang C.; Kalmanoff, George; and Meagher, Robert F. *International Financial Aid*. New York: Columbia University Press, 1966.

131. Fuchs, Lawrence H. "Minority Groups and Foreign Policy." *Political Science Quarterly* 74 (1959): 161–75.

132. Fuller, J. F. C. *The Conduct of War 1789–1961*. New Brunswick, N.J.: Rutgers University Press, 1961.

133. Furniss, E. S. *DeGaulle and the French Army*. New York: Twentieth Century Fund, 1964.

134. Galbraith, John Kenneth. *The New Industrial State*. Boston: Houghton Mifflin, 1967.

135. Galtung, Johann. "Summit Diplomacy." *Journal of Peace Research* 1 (1964): 36–53.

136. ———. "On the Effects of International Economic Sanctions With Examples from the Case of Rhodesia." *World Politics* 19 (April 1967): 378–416.

137. Gareau, Frederick H. *The Balance of Power and Nuclear Deterrence*. Boston: Houghton Mifflin, 1962.

138. George, Alexander L. "The 'Operational Code': A Neglected Approach to the Study of Political Leaders and Decision-Making." *International Studies Quarterly* 13 (1969): 190–222.

139. George, Alexander; and George, Juliette. *Woodrow Wilson and Colonel House*. New York: John Day, 1956.

140. Goldwin, Robert A., ed. *Why Foreign Aid?*. Chicago: Rand McNally, 1963.

141. Goodspeed, Stephen S. *The Nature and Function of International Organization*. 2d ed. New York: Oxford University Press, 1967.

142. Gross, Feliks. *Foreign Policy Analysis*. New York: Philosophical Library, 1954.

143. Gulick, Edward V. *Europe's Classical Balance of Power*. Ithaca, N.Y.: Cornell University Press, 1955.

144. Haas, Ernst B. "The Balance of Power: Prescription, Concept, or Propaganda?" *World Politics* 5 (1953): 442–77.

145. ———. "The Balance of Power as a Guide to Policy-Making," *Journal of Politics* 15 (1953): 370–98.

146.   Haas, Ernst B. *Consensus Formation in the Council of Europe.* Berkeley: University of California Press, 1960.

147.   ———. *Beyond the Nation State: Functionalism and International Organization.* Stanford, Calif.: Stanford University Press, 1964.

148.   ———. *The Uniting of Europe: Political, Social and Economic Forces, 1950–1957.* Stanford, Calif.: Stanford University Press, 1968.

149.   Haas, Ernst B.; and Whiting, Allen S. *Dynamics of International Relations.* New York: McGraw-Hill, 1956.

150.   Haas, Michael. "Aggregate Analysis." *World Politics* 19 (1966): 106–22.

151.   ———. "International Subsystems: Stability and Polarity." *American Political Science Review* 64 (1970): 98–124.

152.-   Hadwen, John; and Kaufmann, Johan. *How United Nations Decisions Are Made.* 2d rev. ed. Leyden: A. W. Sijthoff, 1962.

153.   Hagen, E. E. *On the Theory of Social Change: How Economic Growth Begins.* Homewood, Ill.: Dorsey, 1962.

154.   Halperin, Morton. "The Limiting Process in the Korean War." *Political Science Quarterly* 78 (1965): 13–39.

155.   Hammond, Paul Y. "The National Security Council as a Device for Interdepartmental Coordination: An Interpretation and Appraisal." *American Political Science Review* PS-120 (1960): 899–910.

156.   ———. *Organizing for Defense: The American Military Establishment in the Twentieth Century.* Princeton, N.J.: Princeton University Press, 1961.

157.   ———. "Foreign Policy-Making and Administrative Politics." *World Politics* 17 (July 1965): 656–71.

158.   ———. "The Political Order and the Burden of External Relations." *World Politics* 19 (April 1967): 443–64.

159.   Hamzeh, Fuad S., ed. *International Conciliation.* New York: Humanities Press, forthcoming.

160.   Hansen, Alvin H. *The Dollar and the International Monetary System.* New York: McGraw-Hill, 1965.

161.   Harvey, O. J., ed. *Experience Structure and Adaptation.* New York: Springer Pub., 1966.

162.   ———. *Creativity, Adaptibility and Flexibility.* New York: Springer Pub., 1966.

163.   Hauser, Philip, ed. *Population and World Politics.* New York: Free Press, 1958.

164.   Heilbroner, Robert L. *The Making of Economic Society.* Englewood Cliffs, N.J.: Prentice-Hall, 1962.

165.   Hekhuis, D. J.; McClintock, C. G.; and Burns, A. L., eds. *International Stability: Military, Economic, and Political Dimensions.* New York: Wiley, 1964.

166.   Hempel, Carl G. *Fundamentals of Concept Formation in Empirical Science.* Chicago: University of Chicago Press, 1952.

167.   Hermann, Charles F.; and Hermann, Margaret G. "An Attempt to Simu-

late the Outbreak of World War I," *The American Political Science Review* 61 (June 1967): 400–16.

168. Hero, Alfred O. *Studies in Citizen Participation in International Relations.* Vols. 1–4. Boston: World Peace Foundation, 1959.

169. Herz, John H. *Political Realism and Political Idealism.* Chicago: University of Chicago Press, 1951.

170. ———. *International Politics in the Atomic Age.* New York: Columbia University Press, 1959.

171. Hill, Norman. *International Administration.* New York: McGraw-Hill, 1931.

172. Hilsman, Roger. *Strategic Intelligence and National Decisions.* New York: Free Press, 1956.

173. ———. *To Move a Nation.* Garden City, N.Y.: Doubleday, 1967.

174. Hilsman, Roger; and Good, Robert C., eds. *Foreign Policy in the Sixties: The Issues and the Instruments.* Baltimore: Johns Hopkins Press, 1965.

175. Hirschman, Albert O. *National Power and the Structure of Foreign Trade.* Berkeley: University of California Press, 1945.

176. Hitch, Charles; and McKean, Roland. *The Economics of Defense in the Nuclear Age.* Cambridge, Mass.: Harvard University Press, 1960.

177. Hoffer, Eric. *The True Believer.* New York: Mentor Books, 1962.

178. Hoffmann, Stanley H. *Contemporary Theory in International Relations.* Englewood Cliffs, N.J.: Prentice-Hall, 1960.

179. ———. "International Systems and International Law." *World Politics* 14 (1961): 205–37.

180. Holsti, Ole R. "The Belief System and National Images: A Case History." *Journal of Conflict Resolution* 6 (September 1962): 244–52.

181. ———. "Cognitive Dynamics and Images of the Enemy." *Journal of International Affairs* 21 (1967): 16–40.

182. Horowitz, Irving Louis. *Three Worlds of Development: The Theory and Practice of International Stratification.* New York: Oxford University Press, 1966.

183. Hovet, Thomas, Jr. *Bloc Politics in the United Nations.* Cambridge, Mass.: Harvard University Press, 1960.

184. ———. *Bloc Voting in the United Nations.* Cambridge, Mass.: Harvard University Press, 1961.

185. Hsieh, Slice Langley. *Communist China's Strategy in the Nuclear Era.* Englewood Cliffs, N.J.: Prentice-Hall, 1962.

186. Huntington, Samuel P. "Interservice Competition and the Political Roles of the Armed Services," *American Political Science Review* 55 (1961).

187. ———, ed. *Changing Patterns of Military Politics.* New York: Free Press, 1962.

188. Iklé, Fred C. *How Nations Negotiate.* New York: Harper & Row, 1964.

189. Institute for Social Studies. *The Military Balance 1966–1967.* London: The Institute, 1967.

190. Jackson, Henry M., ed. *The Secretary of State and the Ambassador.* New York: Praeger, 1964.

191. Jacob, Philip E.; and Atherton, A. L. *The Dynamics of International Organization*. Homewood, Ill.: Dorsey, 1965.
192. Jacob, Philip E.; and Toscano, James V., eds. *The Integration of Political Communities*. New York: Lippincott, 1964.
193. Jensen, Lloyd. "American Foreign Policy Elites and the Prediction of International Events." *Peace Research Society (International) Papers* 5 (1966): 199–209.
194. ———. "Soviet-American Bargaining Behavior in the Postwar Disarmament Negotiations." *Journal of Conflict Resolution* 7 (September 1963): 522–41.
195. ———. "Military Capabilities and Bargaining Behavior." *Journal of Conflict Resolution*, 9 (June 1965): 155–63.
196. Jervis, Robert. "Hypotheses on Misperception." *World Politics* 20 (1968): 454–80.
197. Johnson, E. A., ed. *The Dimensions of Diplomacy*. Baltimore: Johns Hopkins Press, 1964.
198. Johnson, Harry B. *The World Economy at the Crossroads: A Survey of Current Problems of Money, Trade, and Economic Development*. New York: Oxford University Press, 1965.
199. Johnson, J. J. *The Military and Society in Latin America*. Stanford, Calif.: Stanford University Press, 1964.
200. Joy, Admiral C. Turner. *How Communists Negotiate*. New York: Macmillan, 1955.
201. Juviler, Peter H.; and Morton, Harry W., eds. *Soviet Policy-Making*. New York: Praeger, 1967.
202. Kahn, Herman. *On Thermonuclear War*. Princeton, N.J.: Princeton University Press, 1961.
203. ———. *Thinking about the Unthinkable*. New York: Horizon, 1962.
204. Kahn, Herman; and Wiener, Anthony J. *The Year 2000*. New York: Macmillan, 1967.
205. Kallenberg, Arthur L. "The Logic of Comparison: A Methodological Note on the Comparative Study of Political Systems," *World Politics* 19 (1966): 69–82.
206. Kaplan, Abraham. *The Conduct of Inquiry*. San Francisco: Chandler Pub., 1964.
207. Kaplan, Morton A. *System and Process in International Politics*, New York: Wiley, 1957.
208. Kaplan, Morton A.; and Katzenbach, Nicholas DeB. *The Political Foundations of International Law*. New York: Wiley, 1961.
209. Kaser, Michael. *Comecon: Integration Problems of the Planned Econoies*. New York: Oxford University Press, 1965.
210. Kaufmann, W. W. *The McNamara Strategy*. New York: Harper & Row, 1964.
211. Kay, David A., ed. *The United Nations Political System*. New York: Wiley, 1967.

212. Kecskemeti, Paul. *Strategic Surrender*. Stanford, Calif.: Stanford University Press, 1958.

213. ———. "The Soviet Approach to International Communication." *Public Opinion Quarterly* 20 (1962): 98–110.

214. Keller, Suzanne. "Diplomacy and Communication." *Public Opinion Quarterly* 20 (Spring 1956): 176–82.

215. Kelman, Herbert C., ed. *International Behavior: A Social-Psychological Analysis*. New York: Holt, Rinehart & Winston, 1965.

216. Kelsen, Hans. *The Law of the United Nations*. New York: Praeger, 1964.

217. Kemp, Geoffrey. "Arms Traffic and Third World Conflicts." *International Conciliation* 577 (March 1970).

218. Kenen, Peter B. *International Economics*. Englewood Cliffs, N.J.: Prentice-Hall, 1964.

219. Kennan, George F. *Realities of American Foreign Policy*. Princeton, N.J.: Princeton University Press, 1954.

220. Kent, Sherman. *Strategic Intelligence for American World Policy*. Princeton, N.J.: Princeton University Press, 1966.

221. Kerlinger, Fred N. *Foundations of Behavioral Research*. New York: Holt, Rinehart & Winston, 1964.

222. Kindleberger, Charles P. *International Economics*. Homewood, Ill.: Richard D. Irwin, 1958.

223. ———. *Foreign Trade and the National Economy*. New Haven, Conn.: Yale University Press, 1962.

224. Kissinger, Henry A. *Nuclear Weapons and Foreign Policy*. New York: Harper & Brothers, 1957.

225. ———. *The Necessity for Choice: Prospects of American Foreign Policy*. New York: Doubleday, 1962.

226. ———. "Domestic Structure and Foreign Policy." *Daedalus* 85 (Spring 1966): 508.

227. Klingberg, Frank L. "Studies in Measurement of the Relations Among Sovereign States." *Psychometrika* 6 (1941): 335–52.

228. ———. "The Historical Alternation of Moods in American Foreign Policy." *World Politics* 4 (January 1952): 239–73.

229. Knorr, Klaus. *The War Potential of Nations*. Princeton, N.J.: Princeton University Press, 1956.

230. Knorr, Klaus; and Rosenau, James N., eds. *Contending Approaches to International Politics*. Princeton, N.J.: Princeton University Press, 1969.

231. Knorr, Klaus; and Verba, Sidney, eds. *The International System: Theoretical Essays*. Princeton, N.J.: Princeton University Press, 1967.

232. Kogan, Norman. *The Politics of Italian Foreign Policy*. New York: Praeger, 1963.

233. Korbonski, Andrzej. "Comecon." *International Conciliation* 549 (September 1964).

234. Krause, Walter. *International Economics*. Boston: Houghton Mifflin, 1965.

235. Kriesberg, Louis. *Social Processes in International Relations: A Reader.* New York: Wiley, 1968.
236. Kuhn, Thomas. *The Structure of Scientific Revolutions.* Chicago: University of Chicago Press, 1962.
237. Lador-Lederer, J. J. *International Non-Governmental Organizations and Economic Entities: A Study in Autonomous Organization and Ius Gentium.* Leyden: A. W. Sijthoff, 1963.
238. Lall, Arthur S. *Modern International Negotiation.* New York: Columbia University Press, 1966.
239. Landy, E. A. *The Effectiveness of International Supervision: Thirty Years of I.L.O. Experience.* London: Stevens, 1966.
240. Lane, Robert Edwards. *Political Ideology.* New York: Free Press, 1962.
241. Langrod, G. *The International Civil Service.* Dobbs Ferry, N.Y.: Oceana, 1964.
242. Lawson, Ruth C., ed. *International Regional Organizations.* New York: Praeger, 1962.
243. Lefever, Ernest W. *Crisis in the Congo: A UN Force in Action.* Washington, D.C.: Brookings Institution, 1965.
244. Lengyel, P. "Some Trends in the International Civil Service." *International Organization* 13 (Autumn 1959): 520–37.
245. Lerche, Charles O. "Contrasting Strategic Styles in the Cold War." *U.S. Naval Inst. Proc.* 88 (May 1962): 23–34.
246. Levi, Werner. *Fundamentals of World Organization.* Minneapolis: University of Minnesota Press, 1950.
247. Lindberg, Leon N. "Decision-Making and Integration in European Community." *International Organization* 20 (1965): 56–80.
248. ———. "The European Community As a Political System." *Journal of Common Market Studies* 5 (1967): 344–88.
249. Lindblom, Charles E. "The Science of Muddling Through." *Public Administration Review* PS-169 (1959): 79–88.
250. Lindholm, Stid. "Aspects on Goals and Values in Swedish Foreign Policy Making." *Peace Research Society (International) Papers* 6 (1966): 37–50.
251. Lippmann, Walter. *Public Opinion.* New York: Macmillan, 1922.
252. Liska, George. *International Equilibrium: A Theoretical Essay on the Politics and Organization of Security.* Cambridge, Mass.: Harvard University Press, 1957.
253. ———. *The New Statecraft: Foreign Aid in American Foreign Policy.* Chicago: University of Chicago Press, 1960.
254. ———. *Nations in Alliance: The Limits of Interdependence.* Baltimore: Johns Hopkins Press, 1962.
255. Loveday, Arthur. *Reflections on International Administration.* New York: Oxford University Press, 1956.
256. Luard, Evan. *The Evolution of International Organizations.* New York: Praeger, 1966.

257. MacBean, Alasdair I. *Export Instability and Economic Development.* Cambridge, Mass.: Harvard University Press, 1966.

258. McCamy, James L. *The Administration of American Foreign Affairs.* New York: Knopf, 1950.

259. ———. *Conduct of the New Diplomacy.* New York: Harper & Row, 1964.

260. MacDonald, Robert W. *The League of Arab States: A Study in the Dynamics of Regional Organization.* Princeton, N.J.: Princeton University Press, 1965.

261. McDougal, Myres S.; and Feliciano, F. F. *Law and Minimum World Public Order.* New Haven, Conn.: Yale University Press, 1961.

262. McKenna, Joseph C. *Diplomatic Protest in Foreign Policy.* Chicago: Loyola University Press, 1962.

263. MacKinder, Halford. *Democratic Ideals and Reality.* New York: W. W. Norton, 1962.

264. McNeil, Elton B. *The Nature of Human Conflict.* Englewood Cliffs, N.J.: Prentice-Hall, 1965.

265. McWhinney, E. "Changing International Law Method and Objectives in the Era of the Soviet-Western Detente." *American Journal of International Law* 59 (January 1965): 1–15.

266. Macridis, Roy C. "Interest Groups in Comparative Analysis." *Journal of Politics,* 1961.

267. ———. *Foreign Policy in World Politics.* Englewood Cliffs, N.J.: Prentice-Hall, 1967.

268. Mangone, Gerard J. *A Short History of International Organization.* New York: McGraw-Hill, 1954.

269. ———, ed. *UN Administration of Economic and Social Programs.* New York: Columbia University Press, 1966.

270. Marvick, Dwaine, ed. *Political Decision-Makers.* New York: Free Press, 1961.

271. Masters, R. D. "A Multi-Bloc Model of the International System," *American Political Science Review,* 55 (December 1961): 780–98.

272. ———. "World Politics as a Primitive Political System." *World Politics* 16 (July 1964): 595–619.

273. Mattingly, Garrett. *Renaissance Diplomacy.* London: Jonathon Cape, 1955.

274. Maurseth, Per. "Balance-of-Power Thinking from the Renaissance to the French Revolution." *Journal of Peace Research* 1 (1964): 120–36.

275. Meehan, E. J. *The British Left Wing and Foreign Policy: A Study of the Influence of Ideology.* New Brunswick, N.J.: Rutgers University Press, 1960.

276. Merritt, Richard L. *The Growth of American Community.* New Haven, Conn.: Yale University Press, 1966.

277. Merritt, Richard L.; and Rokkan, Stein, eds. *Comparing Nations: Use of Quantitative Data in Cross-National Research.* New Haven, Conn.: Yale University Press, 1966.

278. Milen, B. H. "International Trade and Political Independence." *American Behavioral Science* 6 (March 1963): 18–20.

279. Miller, Richard I. *Dag Hammarskjold and Crisis Diplomacy*. New York: Oceana, 1961.

280. Millikan, Max F.; and Blackmer, Donald L., eds. *The Emerging Nations: Their Growth and United States Policy*. Boston: Little, Brown, 1961.

281. Mitrany, David. *A Working Peace System: An Argument for the Functional Development of International Organization*. London: Royal Institute of International Affairs, 1943.

282. Modelski, George. "Agraria and Industria: Two Models of the International System." *World Politics* 14 (1961): 118–43.

283. ———. *A Theory of Foreign Policy*. New York: Praeger, 1962.

284. Morgenthau, Hans J. *In Defense of the National Interest*. New York: Knopf, 1951.

285. ———. "The Four Paradoxes of Nuclear Strategy." *American Political Science Review* 58 (1964): 123–35.

286. ———. *Politics Among Nations*. 4th ed. New York: Knopf, 1967.

287. Mueller, John E. *Approaches to Measurement in International Relations: A Non-Evangelical Survey*. New York: Appleton-Century-Crofts, 1969.

288. ———. "Presidential Popularity from Truman to Johnson." *American Political Science Review* 64 (1970): 18–35.

289. Murray, James N., Jr. *The United Nations Trusteeship System*. Urbana: University of Illinois Press, 1957.

290. Myrdal, Gunnar. *An International Economy*. New York: Harper, 1956.

291. Nagel, Ernest. *The Structure of Science*. New York: Harcourt, Brace & World, 1961.

292. Neumark, S. D. *Foreign Trade and Economic Development in Africa: A Historical Perspective*. Stanford, Calif.: Stanford University Press, 1963.

293. Nicholas, H. G. *The United Nations as a Political Institution*. New York: Oxford University Press, 1959.

294. Nicolson, Sir Harold George. *The Evolution of Diplomatic Method*. London: Constable, 1954.

295. ———. *The Congress of Vienna: A Study in Allied Unity, 1812–1822*. New York: Viking, 1961.

296. ———. *Diplomacy*. 3d ed. New York: Oxford University Press, 1963.

297. North, Robert C.; Holsti, Ole R.; Zaninovich, M. George; and Zinnes, Dina A. *Content Analysis; A Handbook with Application for the Study of International Crisis*. Evanston, Ill.: Northwestern University Press, 1963.

298. Numelin, R. *The Beginnings of Diplomacy: A Sociological Study of Intertribal and International Relations*. London: Oxford University Press, 1950.

299. Ogburn, William Fielding, ed. *Technology and International Relations*. Chicago: University of Chicago Press, 1949.

300. O'Leary, Michael K. *Politics of American Foreign Aid*. New York: Atherton, 1967.
301. Olson, Mancur, Jr. *The Logic of Collective Action*. Cambridge, Mass.: Harvard University Press, 1965.
302. Organski, A. F. K. *World Politics*. 2d ed. New York: Knopf, 1968.
303. Osgood, Robert E. *Ideals and Self-Interest in America's Foreign Relations*. Chicago: University of Chicago Press, 1953.
304. ———. *Limited War: The Challenge to American Strategy*. Chicago: University of Chicago Press, 1957.
305. ———. *NATO: The Entangling Alliance*. Chicago: University of Chicago Press, 1962.
306. Osgood, Robert E.; and Tucker, Robert. *Force, Order, and Justice*. Baltimore: Johns Hopkins Press, 1967.
307. Padelford, Norman J.; and Goodrich, Leland M., eds. *The United Nations in the Balance*. New York: Praeger, 1965.
308. Paige, Glenn D. *The Korean Decision: June 24–30, 1950*. New York: Free Press, 1968.
309. Peaslee, Amos J.; and Peaslee, Dorothy Xydis, eds. *International Governmental Organizations: Constitutional Documents*. The Hague: Martinus Nijhoff, 1961; 1962.
310. Pentony, DeVere E., ed. *The Underdeveloped Lands: A Dilemma of the International Economy*. San Francisco: Chandler Pub., 1960.
311. Petrie, Sir Charles, *Diplomatic History, 1713–1933,* London: Hollis & Carter, 1946.
312. Plano, Jack C.; and Riggs, Robert E. *Forging World Order: The Politics of International Organization*. New York: Macmillan, 1967.
313. Plischke, Elmer. *Conduct of American Diplomacy*. 3d ed. New York: Van Nostrand, 1968.
314. *Political Science Annual II*. Indianapolis; New York: Bobbs-Merrill, 1969.
315. Pool, Ithiel de Sola; Keller, Suzanne; and Bauer, Raymond A. "The Influence of Foreign Travel on Political Attitudes of American Businessmen." *Public Opinion Quarterly* (1956).
316. Poole, DeWitt C. *The Conduct of Foreign Relations Under Modern Democratic Conditions*. New Haven, Conn.: Yale University Press, 1924.
317. Potter, Pitman B. *An Introduction to the Study of International Organization*. New York: Century, 1922.
318. Price, Donald K., ed. *The Secretary of State*. Englewood Cliffs, N.J.: Prentice-Hall, 1960.
319. *Proceedings of the American Society of International Law* (1965).
320. Pruitt, Dean G. "An Analysis of Responsiveness between Nations." *Journal of Conflict Resolution* 6 (1962): 5–18.
321. Pruitt, Dean G.; and Snyder, Richard C. *Theory and Research on the Causes of War*. Englewood Cliffs, N.J.: Prentice-Hall, 1969.

322. Pryor, F. L. *The Communist Foreign Trade System*. London: Allen & Unwin, 1963.
323. Pye, Lucien W. *Politics, Personality, and Nation-Building*. New Haven, Conn.: Yale University Press, 1962.
324. Quester, George. "The Bargaining and Bombing During World War II in Europe." *World Politics* 15 (1963): 417–39.
325. Ranney, Austin, ed. *Essays in the Behavioral Study of Politics*. Urbana: University of Illinois Press, 1962.
326. Rapoport, Anatol. *Fights, Games and Debates*. Ann Arbor: University of Michigan Press, 1960.
327. ———. *Two-Person Game Theory: The Essential Ideas*. Ann Arbor: University of Michigan Press, 1966.
328. Rapoport, Anatol; and Guyer, Melvin. *Strategy and Conscience*. New York: Harper and Row, 1964.
329. ———. "A Taxonomy of 2X2 Games." *Peace Research Society (International) Papers* 6, Vienna Conference, 1966.
330. Raser, John R. "Personal Characteristics of Political Decision-Makers: A Literature Review." *Peace Research Society (International) Papers* 5 (1966): 616–82.
331. Reitzel, W.; Kaplan, Morton A.; and Coblenz, C. *United States Foreign Policy, 1945–55*. Washington, D.C.: Brookings Institution, 1956.
332. Reuter, Paul. *International Institutions*. New York: Praeger, 1961.
333. Richardson, Lewis F. "Generalized Foreign Politics." *British Journal of Psychology Monograph* 23 (1939).
334. ———. *Arms and Insecurity*. Chicago: Quadrangle Books, 1960.
335. ———. *Statistics of Deadly Quarrels*. Chicago: Quadrangle Books, 1960.
336. Rieselbach, Leroy N. *The Roots of Isolationism*. Indianapolis: Bobbs-Merrill, 1956.
337. Riggs, F. W. *Administration in Developing Countries*. Boston: Houghton Mifflin, 1964.
338. Riggs, Robert E. "The United Nations As An Influence on United States Policy." *The International Studies Quarterly. The International Studies Association* 11 (March 1967): 91–109.
339. Riker, William H., *The Theory of Political Coalitions*, New Haven, Conn.: Yale University Press, 1962.
340. Robertson, A. H. *The Law of International Institutions in Europe*. Manchester, England: Manchester University Press; New York: Oceana, 1961.
341. Robinson, James A. *Congress and Foreign Policy-Making*. Homewood, Ill.: Dorsey, 1967.
342. Robinson, Thomas W. "Systems Theory and the Communist System." *International Studies Quarterly* 13 (1969): 398–421.
343. Rosecrance, Richard N. *Action and Reaction in World Politics*. Boston: Little, Brown, 1963.
344. ———. *The Dispersion of Nuclear Weapons*. New York: Columbia University Press, 1964.

345. Rosenau, James N. *National Leadership and Foreign Policy: A Case Study in the Mobilization of Public Support*. Princeton, N.J.: Princeton University Press, 1963.

346. ———. *Public Opinion and Foreign Policy*. New York: Random House, 1965.

347. ———. ed. *Domestic Sources of Foreign Policy*. New York: Free Press, 1967.

348. ———. ed. *International Politics and Foreign Policy*. 2d ed. New York: Free Press, 1969.

349. Rossner, Gariella. *The United Nations Emergency Force*. New York: Columbia University Press, 1963.

350. Rostow, W. W. *The Stages of Economic Growth*. New York: Cambridge University Press, 1960.

351. Rummel, Rudolph J. "Dimensions of Conflict Behavior within and between Nations," *General Systems: Yearbook of the Society for General Systems Research*, Vol. 8, pp. 1–50, 1962.

352. ———. "A Field Theory of Social Action and Political Conflict Within Nations." *General Systems: Yearbook of the Society for General Systems Research*, Vol. 10, pp. 183–211, 1965.

353. ———. "A Foreign Conflict Code Sheet." *World Politics* 18 (1966): 283–97.

354. Russell, Frank M. *Theories of International Relations*. New York: Appleton-Century-Crofts, 1936.

355. Russett, Bruce M. "The Calculus of Deterrence." *Journal of Conflict Resolution* 7 (June 1963): 97–109.

356. ———. *Community and Contention: Britain and America in the Twentieth Century*. Cambridge, Mass.: MIT Press, 1963.

357. ———. *Trends in World Politics*. New York: Macmillan, 1965.

358. ———. *International Regions and the International System: A Study in Political Ecology*. Chicago: Rand McNally, 1967.

359. ———. "Pearl Harbor: Deterrence Theory and Decision Theory." *Journal of Peace Research* 4 (1967): 89–109.

360. ———, ed. *Economic Theories of International Politics*. Chicago: Markham, 1968.

361. Russett, Bruce M.; Alker, Hayward R., Jr.; Deutsch, Karl W.; and Lasswell, Harold D. *World Handbook of Political and Social Indicators*. New Haven, Conn.: Yale University Press, 1964.

362. Said, Abdul A., ed. *Theory of International Relations: The Crisis of Relevance*. Englewood Cliffs, N.J.: Prentice-Hall, 1968.

363. Sapin, Burton M. *The Making of United States Foreign Policy*. Washington D.C.: Brookings Institution, 1966.

364. Sarkissian, A. O., ed. *Studies in Diplomatic History and Historiography* (in honor of G. P. Gooch). London: Longmans, Green, 1961.

365. Satow, E. *Guide to Diplomatic Practice*. Edited by Nevile Bland. 4th ed. New York: McKay, 1957.

366. Sawyer, Jack. "Dimensions of Nations: Size, Wealth, and Politics," *American Journal of Sociology* 73 (1967): 145–72.

367. Schachter, Oscar. "The Enforcement of International Judicial and Arbitral Decisions." *American Journal of International Law* 54 (January 1960): 1–24.

368. Schelling, Thomas C. *The Strategy of Conflict*. New York: Oxford University Press, 1960.

369. ———. *Arms and Influence*. New Haven, Conn.: Yale University Press, 1966.

370. Schilling, Warner R.; Hammond, Paul Y.; and Snyder, Glenn H., eds. *Strategy, Politics and Defense Budgets*. New York: Columbia University Press, 1962.

371. Schwebel, Stephen M. *The Secretary-General of the United Nations*. Cambridge, Mass.: Harvard University Press, 1952.

372. Seabury, Paul, ed., *Balance of Power,* San Francisco: Chandler Pub., 1965.

373. Sewell, James P. *Functionalism and World Politics: A Study Based on United Nations Programs Financing Economic Development*. Princeton, N.J.: Princeton University Press, 1966.

374. Shubik, Martin, ed. *Game Theory and Related Approaches to Social Behavior*. New York: Wiley, 1964.

375. Sigler, John H. "News Flow in the North African International System." *International Studies Quarterly* 13 (1969): 381–98.

376. Simon, Herbert A. *Administrative Behavior*. 2d ed. New York: Free Press, 1957.

377. ———. "The Decision-Making Schema: A Reply." *Public Administration Review* (1958): 60–63.

378. Singer, J. David. *Financing International Organization: The United Nations Budget Process*. Geneva: Nijhoff, 1961.

379. ———. *Deterrence, Arms Control and Disarmament,* Columbus: Ohio State University Press, 1962.

380. ———. "Content Analysis of Elite Articulations." *Journal of Conflict Resolution* 8 (1964): 424–85.

381. ———, ed. *Human Behavior and International Politics*. Chicago: Rand McNally, 1965.

382. ———. "National Alliance Commitments and War Involvement, 1815–1945." *Peace Research Society (International) Papers* 5 (1967): 109–40.

383. ———, ed. *Quantitative International Politics: Insights and Evidence*. New York: Free Press, 1968.

384. Singer, J. David; and Small, Melvin, "Formal Alliances, 1815–1939: A Quantitative Description," *Journal of Peace Research* 3 (1966): 1–32.

385. ———. "The Composition and Status Ordering of the International System: 1815–1940." *World Politics* 18 (1966): 236–83.

386. Smoker, Paul. "Nation State Escalation and International Integration." *Journal of Peace Research* 4 (1962): 61–75.

387.   ———. "Sino-Indian Relations: A Study of Trade, Communication and Defense." *Journal of Peace Research* 2 (1964): 65–76.

388.   Snyder, Glenn H. *Stockpiling Strategic Materials, Politics and National Defense.* San Francisco: Chandler Pub., 1966.

389.   Snyder, Richard C.; Bruck, H. W.; and Sapin, Burton M., eds. *Foreign Policy Decision-Making: An Approach to the Study of International Politics.* New York: Free Press, 1962.

390.   Sorensen, T. C. *Decision-Making in the White House: The Olive Branch or the Arrows.* New York: Columbia University Press, 1963.

391.   Sprout, Harold H. and Sprout, Margaret E. "Geography and International Politics in an Era of Revolutionary Change." *Journal of Conflict Resolution* (1960): 145–61.

392.   ———. "Geographical Hypotheses in Technological Perspective." *World Politics* 15 (January 1962): 187–212.

393.   ———. *The Ecological Perspective on Human Affairs.* Princeton, N.J.: Princeton University Press, 1965.

394.   Stagner, Ross. *Dimensions of Human Conflict.* Detroit: Wayne State University Press, 1967.

395.   Steele, A. T. *The American People and China.* New York: McGraw-Hill, 1966.

396.   Stoessinger, John G. *The United Nations and the Superpowers: United States–Soviet Interaction at the United Nations.* New York: Random House, 1966.

397.   ———, et al. *Financing The United Nations System.* Washington, D.C.: Brookings Institution, 1964.

398.   Stuart, Graham. *American Diplomatic and Consular Practice,* 2d ed. New York: Appleton-Century-Crofts, 1952.

399.   Taylor, A. J. P. *The Struggle for Mastery in Europe, 1848–1941.* New York: Oxford University Press, 1954.

400.   ———. *The Origins of the Second World War.* Rev. ed. Greenwich, Conn.: Fawcett World. Revised, New York: Atheneum, 1962.

401.   Taylor, Maxwell D. *The Uncertain Trumpet.* New York: Harper & Brothers, 1960.

402.   Thayer, Charles W. *Diplomat.* New York: Harper & Row, 1959.

403.   Thomas, Ann Van Synen; and Thomas, A. J., Jr. *The Organization of American States.* Dallas: Southern Methodist University Press, 1963.

404.   Thompson, Kenneth W. *Political Realism and the Crisis of World Politics.* Princeton, N.J.: Princeton University Press, 1959.

405.   Thomson, David. *Europe Since Napoleon.* New York: Knopf, 1962.

406.   Triska, Jan F.; and Finley, David D. *Soviet Foreign Policy.* New York: Macmillan, 1968.

407.   Tucker, Robert W. "Professor Morgenthau's Theory of Political 'Realism'." *American Political Science Review* PS-287 (1952): 214–24.

408.   Wainhouse, David W., et al. *International Peace Observation.* Baltimore: Johns Hopkins Press, 1966.

409. Wallensteen, Peter. "Characteristics of Economic Sanctions." *Journal of Peace Research* 5 (1968): 248–67.

410. Walton, Richard E.; and McKensie, Robert B. *A Behavioral Theory of Labor Negotiations: An Analysis of a Social Interaction System.* New York: McGraw-Hill, 1965.

411. Waltz, Kenneth N. *Man, the State, and War.* New York: Columbia University Press, 1959.

412. ———. "The Stability of a Bipolar World." *Daedalus* 93 (Summer 1964): 881–909.

413. ———. *Foreign Policy and Democratic Politics.* Boston: Little, Brown, 1967.

414. ———. "International Structure, National Force, and the Balance of World Power." *Journal of International Affairs* (1967).

415. Ward, Barbara. *The Rich Nations and the Poor Nations.* New York: W. W. Norton, 1962.

416. Waters, Maurice. *The Ad Hoc Diplomat: A Study of Municipal and International Law.* The Hague: Nijhoff, 1963.

417. Waters, Maurice, ed. *The United Nations.* New York: Macmillan, 1967.

418. Westerfield, H. Bradford. *Foreign Policy and Party Politics: Pearl Harbor to Korea.* New Haven, Conn.: Yale University Press, 1955.

419. ———. *The Instruments of America's Foreign Policy.* New York: T. Y. Crowell, 1963.

420. White, Lyman C. *International Non-Governmental Organizations.* New Brunswick, N.J.: Rutgers University Press, 1951.

421. Wight, Martin. *Power Politics.* London: Royal Institute of International Affairs, 1946.

422. Wilkenfeld, Jonathan. "Domestic and Foreign Conflict Behavior of Nations," *Journal of Peace Research* 5 (1968): 56–69.

423. Wilkinson, David O. *Comparative Foreign Relations: Framework and Methods.* Belmont, Calif.: Dickenson, 1969.

424. Wohlstetter, Albert; and Wohlstetter, Roberta. *Controlling the Risks in Cuba.* No. 17, Adelphi Papers. London: Institute for Strategic Studies, 1965.

425. Wohlstetter, Roberta. *Pearl Harbor: Warning and Decision.* Stanford, Calif.: Stanford University Press, 1962.

426. Wolf, Charles, Jr. *United States Policy and the Third World: Problems and Analysis.* Boston: Little, Brown, 1967.

427. Wright, Quincy. *The Study of International Relations.* New York: Appleton-Century-Crofts, 1955.

428. ———. *Study of War.* 2d ed. Chicago: University of Chicago Press, 1965.

429. Wright, Quincy; Evans, William M.; and Deutsch, Morton, eds. *Preventing World War Three: Some Proposals.* New York: Simon & Schuster, 1962.

430. Yalem, Ronald J. "The Study of International Organization, 1920–1965; A Survey of the Literature." *Background* 10 (1966): 1–57.

431.   Young, Oran R. *The Intermediaries: Third Parties in International Crises.* Princeton, N.J.: Princeton University Press, 1967.

432.   ———. *The Politics of Force: Bargaining During International Crises.* Princeton, N.J.: Princeton University Press, 1968.

433.   ———. "Political Discontinuities in the International State," *World Politics* 20 (1968): 369–92.

434.   Zartman, I. William. "Africa as a Subordinate State System in International Relations." *International Organization* 21 (1967): 545–64.

435.   Zawodny, J. K. *Guide to the Study of International Relations.* San Francisco: Chandler Pub., 1966.

Index